Praise for
RETIREMENT INCOME REDESIGNED
Master Plans for Distribution
EDITED BY Harold Evensky and Deena B. Katz

"Expert advice for retirement planning is essential but too often flaky. Nothing in this book is flaky. The expert authors are sophisticated and knowledgeable. Their presentations are rock-solid, comprehensive, and clear. They cover every important aspect of the retirement problem. Any adviser or client who reads this book will be deeply grateful to Harold Evensky and Deena Katz for putting it together."

PETER L. BERNSTEIN
Author, *Against the Gods: The Remarkable Story of Risk*

"Once again, Harold and Deena have succeeded in putting together an A-team of financial experts. The end goal for this team is to help other financial professionals do the best possible job that they can as they guide their clients in their retirement years. This book is a must-have for anyone advising clients through retirement."

J. THOMAS BRADLEY JR.
President, TD AMERITRADE Institutional

"Advisers have an unprecedented opportunity to work with a generation that has shaped history and will reshape the future of retirement planning. *Retirement Income Redesigned* provides advisers with a valuable tool for understanding and addressing the unique needs of retiring baby boomers."

JOHN IACHELLO
Chief Operating Officer, Pershing Advisor Solutions
A service of Pershing LLC, a member of BNY Securities Group
    and a subsidiary of The Bank of New York Company, Inc.

"With 80 million baby boomers entering retirement over the coming decades, *Retirement Income Redesigned* is a must-read for financial advisers who are determined to grow their business and add value for clients. The book provides a valuable mix of conceptual planning principles, product guidance, and tangible planning 'how to's' to help advisers meet the needs of their in-and-near-retirement clients. It's a wonderful tool for gaining insights and ideas to maximize your firm's potential in attracting this valuable segment."

DEBORAH McWHINNEY
Former President, Schwab Institutional

Retirement Income Redesigned

Retirement Income Redesigned

Master Plans for Distribution

An Adviser's Guide for
Funding Boomers' Best Years

EDITED BY

Harold Evensky *and* Deena B. Katz

FOREWORD BY

Walter Updegrave

BLOOMBERG PRESS
NEW YORK

This publication contains the authors' opinions and is designed to provide accurate and authoritative information. It is sold with the understanding that the authors, publisher, and Bloomberg L.P. are not engaged in rendering legal, accounting, investment-planning, or other professional advice. The reader should seek the services of a qualified professional for such advice; the authors, publisher, and Bloomberg L.P. cannot be held responsible for any loss incurred as a result of specific investments or planning decisions made by the reader.

First edition published 2006

5 7 9 10 8 6 4

ISBN-13: 978-1-57660-189-1

The Library of Congress has cataloged the earlier printing as follows:

Retirement income redesigned : master plans for distribution : an adviser's guide for funding boomers' best years / edited by Harold Evensky and Deena B. Katz; foreword by Walter Updegrave.

  p. cm.

  Includes bibliographical references and index.

  Summary: "A how-to for financial advisers, offering practical suggestions and insights from a range of financial professionals on key issues relating to retirement income distribution planning." --Provided by publisher.

  ISBN 1-57660-189-7 (alk. paper)

  1. Retirees--United States--Finance, Personal.   2. Baby-boom generation--Finance, Personal. 3. Retirement income--United States--Planning. 4. Retirement--United States--Planning. 5. Saving and investment--United States. I. Title: Adviser's guide for funding boomers' best years. II. Evensky, Harold. III. Katz, Deena B. IV. Walter Updegrave.

  HG179.R3949 2006
  332.024'0145--dc22   2006002227

Acquired by Jared Kieling
Edited by Mary Ann McGuigan

We dedicate this book to the two people who made it a reality—

Mary Ann McGuigan and Martina Schramm

CONTENTS

ACKNOWLEDGMENTS

To Our Contributors

It takes a lot of talent to develop a book such as this one, and we've been blessed by having the privilege of offering readers the contributions of such an extraordinary group of professionals and academics. We believe each chapter, in and of itself, is reason enough to spend the time reading.

To Our Associates

The pleasure of working with such a sterling group of people as our friends and associates at Evensky & Katz and the continual support we receive from them certainly contributed to our efforts in this venture.

To Our Publisher

For authors, Bloomberg Press is a dream come true. This is our fourth journey working with the Bloomberg team and our acquisitions editor, Jared Kieling. The experience gets better each time.

To Our Team

Last, but assuredly not least, we wish to thank (a woefully inadequate word), Mary Ann McGuigan and Martina Schramm. Mary Ann is our editor. Her skillful and professional editing magically transformed 20 thoughtful but disparate chapters into a cohesive book. Martina Schramm is our personal assistant. Without her persistence, patience, coordination and tact, our book would never have seen the light of day.

ABOUT THE CONTRIBUTORS

Anna Abaimova is a research associate at the IFID Centre in Toronto, where she is the project manager for the center's models and data on payout annuities, longevity insurance, and retirement-risk management. She coauthored the software manual for the Retirement Income Probability Analyzer, which was developed in conjunction with the U.S.-based Society of Actuaries and profiled in the *Wall Street Journal*. Abaimova has a BBA in business administration from the Schulich School of Business at York University.

Roxanne Alexander, CFP, joined Evensky & Katz while finishing her MBA. She is now senior vice president, developing financial plans and investment policies for new clients, and a member of the adviser teams, addressing client issues. Before joining Evensky & Katz, Alexander was the owner and director of a real estate company in Kingston, Jamaica, specializing in locating and evaluating commercial real estate investments for multinational corporations starting operations in Jamaica. She is a member of the Financial Planning Association and the CFA Institute. Alexander received her bachelor's degree in management and accounting from the University of the West Indies and her master's degree in business administration with emphasis in investments and financial planning from the University of Miami.

Michael J. Anderson, JD, is a vice president of planning with Evensky & Katz and an advisory team member. In 2003, Anderson's paper "Strategic Personal Career Planning: An Entry Point for Students of Financial Planning" was selected as the student winner of the Financial Planning Association's Annual Call for Papers competition and was subsequently published in the FPA's *Solutions* magazine. A member of the Financial Planning Association, Anderson has been quoted and published opinions in the *Journal of Financial Planning,* financial-planning.com, *Investment News* magazine, currentofferings.com, TheStreet.com, the *New York Daily News,* and *Dermatology Business Management* magazine. He received his doctor of jurisprudence and master of science in personal financial planning from Texas Tech University and his bachelor's degree from Seattle University. Anderson served as an officer on active duty in the U.S. Army, where he held leadership positions in the 82nd Airborne Division at Fort Bragg, North Carolina. He was also an officer in the Texas National Guard.

Mitch Anthony is recognized in the financial-services industry for his work in the field of building client relationships. *Financial Planning* magazine named Anthony one of the "Top Movers and Shakers" in the industry in 2006. He is president of Advisor Insights and of the Financial Life Planning Institute, which are training companies serving advisers and financial-services corporations. He is the best-selling author of several books for financial professionals, including *Storyselling for Financial Advisors* (Dearborn, 2000), *The New Retirementality* (Dearborn, 2001), *Your Clients for Life* (Dearborn, 2002), *The Financial Professional's StoryBook* (Advisor Insights Press, 2003), and *Your Client's Story* (Dearborn, 2005). Anthony's column "Financial Life Planning" appears bimonthly in *Financial Advisor* magazine, and he is a contributing editor for *Research* magazine, where his feature "Your Clients for Life" appears. His work has been featured on *ABC Evening News with Peter Jennings,* CNN, Bloomberg TV, CBS MarketWatch, *Kiplinger's, Ticker, Registered Rep.,* and *Investment Advisor.* Anthony's radio feature, *The Daily Dose,* airs daily on 160 radio stations nationwide.

William P. Bengen, CFP, is a sole practitioner in El Cajon, California. He is a fee-only personal financial adviser, specializing in helping clients grow their wealth and enjoy that wealth. Bengen's independent research into sustainable withdrawals was published in the *Journal of Financial Planning* in a series of four articles beginning in 1994, and he has since been widely quoted in the media on the topic. He received a BS from the Massachusetts Institute of Technology in aeronautics and astronautics and a master's degree from the College for Financial Planning (now NEFE). Before beginning his career as a financial adviser, Bengen served as CEO of his family's soft-drink bottling firm in the New York area.

Laurence Booth, DBA, MBA, holds the CIT Chair in Structured Finance at the Rotman School, University of Toronto, and is the finance area coordinator there. His major research interests are domestic and international corporate finance and the behavior of regulated industries. A member of the faculty at the University of Toronto since 1978, Booth has taught graduate courses in business finance, international financial management, corporate financing, mergers and acquisitions, financial management, and financial theory, as well as short executive programs on the money and foreign exchange markets, business valuation, mergers and acquisitions, and financial strategy. He has published more than 40 articles in academic journals, as well as the widely used textbook *International Business,* with Alan Rugman and Don Lecraw (McGraw-Hill, 1985), and is on the editorial board of four academic journals. Booth's advice is frequently sought by the media, and he has appeared as an expert witness before the Ontario Securities Commission, the CRTC, and the National Energy Board, as well as most of the major provincial regulatory tribunals in Canada.

Joel P. Bruckenstein, CFP, CFS, CMFC, is the country's leading authority on applied technology and related practice-management techniques for financial advisers. He is a virtual-office consultant, freelance journalist, and book author. Bruckenstein has lectured at FPA retreats, NAPFA national conferences, NAPFA Advanced Planner Conferences, the AICPA Personal Financial Planning Conference, and other industry events. He is senior technology editor at MorningstarAdvisor.com and publisher of *Virtual Office News* (www.virtualofficenews.com). Bruckenstein writes for other publications, including *Financial Advisor* magazine and *Financial Planning* magazine. His practice-management and technology book, *Virtual-Office Tools for a High-Margin Practice* (Bloomberg Press, 2003), coauthored by David Drucker, has garnered universal praise from industry experts. The duo's second book, *Tools and Techniques of Practice Management* (National Underwriter, 2004), has received excellent reviews in the financial press.

R. H. "Rick" Carey is recognized as one of the nation's leading authorities on the variable annuity industry. He is the founder of the Variable Annuity Research & Data Service, or VARDS, where he designed and developed many of the industry's analytical standards and benchmarks in use today. VARDS, founded in 1988, provides research and data on variable-annuity products. Carey sold VARDS in July 2000 to Info-One and left the firm in July 2005 to explore projects that address pressing needs in the industry. At VARDS, he introduced the VARDS Greenwald Strategy Service, a joint venture with Mathew Greenwald & Associates, which provided research and consulting services to companies in the annuity business. Working with distributors and manufacturers, VARDS Greenwald focused its efforts on targeted issues related to annuity product design and distribution in the retirement-income marketplace. Carey has also developed the Retirement Income Solutions Enterprise. Still in its nascent phase, the organization seeks to fill the recognized educational gaps that hamper the maturation of the retirement-income market. In 1991, he pioneered the movement to create an industry association to foster VA consumer education. This effort was instrumental in the founding of the National Association for Variable Annuities, where Carey served as a founding board member for nine years and chairman in 1998. NAVA inducted him into its hall of fame in 2001. Today, Carey is a member of NAVA's *Outlook* editorial board and retirement-income education committee. He is a regular columnist for *National Underwriter, Annuity Market News,* and *Advising Boomers* and an information source for many financial-services publications. Before launching VARDS, Carey was a practicing registered investment adviser and president/principal of First Financial Investment Services, an NASD member firm. He holds degrees from the University of Miami and Florida State University, where he served for four years on the board of directors of the alumni association.

April K. Caudill, JD, CLU, ChFC, is the managing editor of *Tax Facts* and the *Advanced Sales Reference Service* at the National Underwriter Company, headquartered outside Cincinnati, Ohio. Her areas of specialty include qualified plans, ERISA, distribution planning, and the taxation of investments. Caudill is an associate editor and pension-planning columnist for the *Journal of Financial Service Professionals* and a member of the board of directors for the Society of Financial Service Professionals. She is the lead editor of *Tools and Techniques of Employee Benefit and Retirement Planning,* 9th ed. (Leimberg, 2005), and the coauthor of *The Mutual Fund Handbook* (National Underwriter Co., 2001). A frequent writer and speaker on retirement and distribution planning topics, Caudill writes regularly for *TaxFacts News, National Underwriter Life and Health Edition,* and Leimberg Information Service. She is a member of the American Bar Association, Taxation Section, as well as the Cincinnati Bar Association, and serves on its employee benefits committee. She is a graduate of the University of Cincinnati and the Salmon P. Chase College of Law of Northern Kentucky University.

Peng Chen, PhD, CFA, is managing director and chief investment officer at Ibbotson Associates in Chicago. Ibbotson Associates is an independent asset-allocation consulting firm that provides data, software, consulting, research, training, and presentation materials to investment professionals, and Chen is responsible for the firm's overall research activities. His research projects focus on asset allocation, portfolio-risk measurement, nontraditional assets, and global financial markets, and he has contributed to the development of various Ibbotson products and services, including software, consulting services, educational services, and presentation materials.

A recipient of the Articles of Excellence award from the Certified Financial Planner Board in 1996 and the 2003 Graham and Dodd Scroll Award from *Financial Analysts Journal*, Chen has written for numerous publications, including *Financial Analysts Journal, Journal of Portfolio Management, Journal of Investing, Journal of Financial Planning, Bank Securities Journal, Journal of Association of American Individual Investors, Consumer Interest Annual*, and *Journal of Financial Counseling and Planning*. Chen received his bachelor's degree in industrial management engineering from Harbin Institute of Technology and his master's and doctorate in consumer economics from Ohio State University.

Robert D. Curtis is the principal designer of MoneyGuidePro and the founder, president, and chief executive officer of PIE Technologies, which develops software for financial advisers. MoneyGuidePro was one of the first financial-planning programs created for the Internet; in May 2005, it was selected as one of the top three planning programs by Forrester Research. Curtis has more than 25 years' experience as an innovator in the software industry, and for the past 16 years he has taken a leadership role in developing easy-to-use, interactive software for use by financial advisers with their clients. Before forming PIE Technologies in 1997, Curtis was founder and CEO of Compulife, an investment and insurance marketing firm, and Compulife Investor Services, a registered broker-dealer. By working with bank brokerage firms, Compulife became one of the top 10 industry marketing companies and was consistently the leader in the use of sales technology. At Compulife and Compulife Investor Services, Curtis and his development team created the first three generations of MoneyGuide financial-planning software. Curtis sold his interest in Compulife and founded PIE Technologies, so that he could focus exclusively on developing the next generation of financial-planning software for the Internet. Before joining Compulife, Curtis owned and managed a software-development company that focused on accounting software for small businesses. He has a bachelor's degree in finance from Lehigh University.

Jeffrey K. Dellinger is president of Longevity Management Corporation, a consulting firm that advises institutions on retirement-income optimization, products, and markets. With more than 25 years in the financial-services industry, Dellinger is a fellow of the Society of Actuaries and a member of the American Academy of Actuaries, and has two variable-annuity patents pending. He provided successful leadership as Individual Annuity Profit Center Head for the Lincoln National Life Insurance Company, the third-largest U.S. annuity company, with $60 billion in assets. His responsibilities ranged from profitability and product development to marketing and distributor-relationship management. Dellinger's extensive experience and strong analytic skills provide a unique vantage point for sharing insights about annuities and retirement income. He is a frequent speaker at national annuities conferences. His articles have appeared in such publications as *Best's Review, Life Insurance Selling, The VARDS Report,* and *Reinsurance Reporter,* and he is the author of *The Handbook of Variable Income Annuities* (John Wiley & Sons, 2006), the most comprehensive volume on using variable annuities to generate retirement income. Dellinger's advice on annuities is solicited for articles appearing in publications such as the *Wall Street Journal, Fortune,* and *National Underwriter.* He is a Phi Beta Kappa graduate of Indiana University, holding bachelor's and master's degrees in mathematics.

Harold Evensky, CFP, is chairman of Evensky & Katz, a wealth-management firm in Coral Gables, Florida. He has chaired the TIAA-CREF Institute Advisory Board, the International CFP Council, the CFP Board of Governors, the Board of Examiners, and the Board of Appeals. He's also served as a member of the National Board of the International Association of Financial Planning and of the Charles Schwab Institutional Advisory Board and Council. He is a member of the Financial Planning Association, the Academy of Financial Services, and the CFA Institute, and an associate member of the American Bar Association. Evensky is an internationally recognized speaker on investment and financial-planning issues and has been honored by *Worth* as one of the Top 100 Wealth Managers, by *Investment Advisor* as one of the 25 most influential people in the financial-planning industry, and by *Financial Planning Magazine* as one of five Movers, Shakers and Decision Makers: The Most Influential People in the Financial Planning Profession. *Investment News* named him one of the 25 Power Elite in the financial-services industry, and *Accounting Today* has regularly listed him as one of the profession's most influential people. In 1999, he was awarded the Dow Jones Investment Advisor Portfolio Management Award for Lifetime Achievement, and in 2002, his paper "Changing Equity Premium Implications for Wealth Management Portfolio Design" won the *Journal of Financial Planning's* Call for Papers competition. Evensky is a contributing writer for *Financial Advisor* magazine and the *Asian Financial Planning Journal,* and a member of the editorial review board of the *Journal of Financial Planning.* He writes for and is quoted frequently in the national press, and is the author of *Wealth Management* (McGraw-Hill, 1997) and the coeditor with Deena Katz of *The Investment Think Tank: Theory, Strategy, and Practice for Advisers* (Bloomberg, 2005). Evensky received his bachelor's and master's degrees from Cornell University.

Mathew Greenwald, PhD, established his research and consulting company, Mathew Greenwald & Associates, in 1985. Since then, he has done strategic planning and marketing research for more than 100 of the most prominent financial-services companies and numerous other organizations. His firm has served Merrill Lynch, Fidelity Investments, Bank of America, MetLife, and Mass Mutual. Non-financial-services clients include AARP, Hershey Food Corporation, Sears, and the National Geographic Society. Before starting his business, Greenwald spent 12 years at the American Council of Life Insurance. From 1977 to 1985, he was ACLI's director of social research and was responsible for programs monitoring public attitudes toward financial-services issues, demographic research, and futures research. Greenwald served as a Congress-appointed delegate to the 1998 and 2002 White House–Congressional National Summits on Retirement Savings and has testified before the U.S. Senate Committee on Aging and the Securities Exchange Commission on retirement and retirement-oriented products. He has published numerous articles in academic journals and trade periodicals and is frequently quoted by national print, radio, and television outlets, including national publications like the *New York Times,* the *Wall Street Journal,* and *Time.* He has spoken at numerous press conferences and professional meetings and is currently an elected member of the Market Research Council, a group of the country's leading market researchers. Greenwald has a PhD in sociology from Rutgers University.

Douglas Head has been active in the viatical and life-settlement industry since 1992, having served as chair of the legislative committee, secretary, and president of the Life Insurance Settlement Association, based in Orlando, Florida. He has been the organization's executive director since 2001. Head has lived around the world—as a student in Singapore, a Peace Corps volunteer in Paraguay, an executive with Hilton Hotels Corporation and Hilton International in Europe. He later established his own firm, providing hotel and restaurant management services, and served as a political consultant. Head is a graduate of Lawrence University in Appleton, Wisconsin.

Michael C. Henkel, president of Ibbotson Associates since 1997, joined the firm in 1993 as vice president in charge of its institutional software group. Before joining Ibbotson, Henkel worked for a variety of companies—including Knight Ridder, Lotus Development Corporation, NewsEdge Corporation, and Data Resources—integrating technology, data, and investments. Henkel has been widely quoted in publications, including *Pensions & Investments, Plan Sponsor, Global Finance, Journal of Financial Planning,* the *Wall Street Journal, Worth,* and *Financial Planning.* Henkel, who was selected as a delegate to the National Summit on Retirement Savings in 2002, frequently speaks at investment conferences in the United States and in Europe on topics including disbursement planning and the role of technology in investment advice. He received his bachelor's degree in mathematics and economics from Rhodes College and his master's in finance and quantitative methods from Vanderbilt University.

Roger G. Ibbotson is a professor in the practice of finance at Yale School of Management. He is also the chairman of Ibbotson Associates, with locations in Chicago, New York, and Tokyo, providing investment consulting, software, data, and financial publishing to financial institutions. Ibbotson conducts research on a broad range of financial topics, including investment returns, mutual funds, international markets, portfolio management, and valuation. He serves on numerous boards, including Dimensional Fund Advisors' Funds and is a partner at Zebra Capital Management, a manager of equity hedge funds. Ibbotson's book *Stocks, Bonds, Bills, and Inflation* (Ibbotson Associates, 1983), coauthored with Rex Sinquefield, is updated in the annual yearbooks published by Ibbotson Associates and serves as the standard reference for information on investment market returns. Ibbotson also coauthored *Investment Markets* (McGraw-Hill, 1987) and *Global Investing* (McGraw-Hill, 1993) with Gary Brinson. He is currently working on *The Equity Risk Premium* and is a regular contributor and editorial board member on both trade and academic journals. A recipient of many awards—including the Graham and Dodd Scroll Award in 1979, 1982, 1984, 2001, and 2003 and AIMR's James R. Vertin award in 2001—Ibbotson frequently speaks at universities, conferences, and other professional forums. He received his bachelor's degree in mathematics from Purdue University, his MBA from Indiana University, and his PhD from the University of Chicago, where he taught for more than 10 years and served as executive director of the Center for Research in Security Prices.

Deena B. Katz, CFP, is an internationally recognized financial adviser and practice-management expert. She is the author of six books on financial planning. *Deena Katz on Practice Management* (Bloomberg Press, 1999) and her newest best-selling book, *Deena Katz's Tools and Templates for Your Practice* (Bloomberg Press, 2001), have become the leading texts on managing an independent financial-services business. More than 125,000 copies of her book *Long-Term Care* (Lee Simmons Assoc., 1993–1997) have been distributed to clients by major insurance firms. Katz served as editor-in-chief of the *Journal of Retirement Planning* and has been a contributing writer for *Investment Advisor, Financial Planning Magazine,* and *National Underwriter.* She was named one of *Financial Planning Magazine's* five most influential people for 2001, as well as one of *Accounting Today's* Top Ten Names to Know in Financial Planning in 2001 and 2002. *Worth* magazine has also included her on its list of top financial advisers numerous times. Katz is frequently quoted by major national news media and has made various television appearances on local and national network programs for CBS, ABC, and PBS. Her speaking engagements span the country, and global financial services organizations call on her to address international financial forums worldwide. Katz has served as a consultant to many companies within the financial-services industry, including institutional brokers, money managers, and insurance companies. She received her bachelor's degree from Adrian College and is a trustee of the college. She received a doctorate of humane letters from Adrian in 2001.

Robert P. Kreitler, CFP, is president of Kreitler Associates and a registered representative with Raymond James Financial Services. He specializes in financial planning, retirement planning, and investment management for professionals, including university professors. He writes frequently on retirement planning issues, is the author of *Getting Started in Global Investing* (John Wiley & Sons, 2000), and is a frequent guest on radio and television shows. Many of the ideas Kreitler writes about come from his firm's work in helping to solve client problems. He has been involved in investments and financial planning for 20 years. Before that he worked in private industry and the federal government at the Office of Management and Budget. He attended Carleton College and Yale University.

Donald G. MacGregor, PhD, is president of MacGregor-Bates, in Eugene, Oregon. MacGregor has been an active researcher and consultant in the field of human judgment, decision making, and the psychology of risk for more than 25 years. His work is directed toward advancing the scientific understanding of risk and its role in decision making and improving the management of risk through better risk assessment and communication practices. Under the sponsorship of the National Science Foundation as well as other federal research agencies, MacGregor has conducted and managed research on risk assessment and decision analysis and their application to management decision making. He has served as a consultant on risk assessment and decision analysis to numerous public organizations, including the U.S. Department of Energy, the National Aeronautics and Space Administration, and the U.S. Nuclear Regulatory Commission. He has also been a consultant to industry, including General Motors Corporation, ARCO, Suzuki America, and Volvo. MacGregor is a member of the American Psychological Association, the Society for Risk Analysis, the Judgment and Decision Making Society, and the International Traffic Medicine Association. He is an associate editor of the *Journal of Behavioral Finance*, and his work has been published in peer-reviewed and professional journals; his research has been cited in numerous media sources, including the *Wall Street Journal, Chicago Tribune, New York Times, Boston Globe, Kiplinger's Personal Finance*, National Public Radio, CNBC, and CBS MarketWatch. MacGregor received his bachelor's and master's degrees in psychology from California State University and his PhD in cognitive psychology from the University of Oregon.

Moshe A. Milevsky, PhD, is an associate professor of finance at the Schulich School of Business at York University and the executive director of the IFID Centre in Toronto. He is the co–founding editor of the *Journal of Pension Economics and Finance* and has published more than 30 scholarly articles and four books. Milevsky's most recent book, *The Calculus of Retirement Income* (Cambridge University Press, 2006), expands on the ideas he developed for Chapter 10. One of his popular articles for media received a National Magazine Award (Canada, 2004). Milevsky has lectured widely on the topic of retirement-income planning, insurance, and investments in North America, South America, and Europe and is a frequent guest on national television and radio. He has a PhD (1996) in finance and an MA (1992) in mathematics, and was elected as a fellow of the Fields Institute (2002).

Jim C. Otar, CFP, CMT, started his financial-planning career in 1995 after spending several years in engineering and investing. Otar's unique approach to wealth management comes from applying his engineering and technical analysis background to retirement planning. He is the author of two books, including *High Expectations and False Dreams: One Hundred Years of Stock Market History Applied to Retirement Planning* (2001). His first book was about Canadian dividend-reinvestment plans. Otar is working on a new book called *The Mathematics of Retirement*. He has written numerous articles and portfolio reviews for various magazines internationally and is quoted in the news media on retirement and financial-planning issues. His article series in *Retirement Planning* won him the prestigious CFP Board Award for 2001 and 2002. Otar's website tracks the best-performing mutual funds in Canada, using a unique technique called FingerPrinting, which he developed. He is the founding member of the Canadian Retirement Advocacy Association as well as an active member of the Canadian Association of Pre-Retirement Planners. He is a past director of the Canadian Society of Technical Analysts. Otar completed his bachelor of applied sciences degree in mechanical engineering at the University of Toronto in 1975 and received his master's in engineering there.

Cynthia Saltzman, PhD, CFP, is a professor of economics at Widener University, where she has been teaching since 1980. Her areas of specialization include monetary theory and financial institutions, productivity analysis, and topics in personal financial planning. Saltzman played a major role in the development of the financial-services undergraduate curriculum at Widener, and she teaches the capstone course in the program. Her work has been published in both academic economic journals and journals directed toward professionals in the financial-services industry. Saltzman is an associate editor for the *Journal of Financial Service Professionals*, where she writes the "Economics and Investment Trends" column three times a year. She received her bachelor's degree in political science from Pennsylvania State University and her PhD in economics from the University of Maryland.

Louis P. Stanasolovich, CFP, is the founder, CEO, and president of Legend Financial Advisors, a fee-only investment-advisory firm headquartered in Pittsburgh. Legend provides wealth-advisory services, including comprehensive financial planning and investment management, to wealthy individuals as well as business entities. Stanasolovich is a member of the Financial Planning Association and is a registered financial adviser with the National Association of Personal Financial Advisors, the nation's largest fee-only professional organization. He has appeared on national television on such programs as *CBS This Morning*, Wall Street Journal Television, CNBC's *Mutual Fund Investor* and *The Money Gang*, and Fox News Channel's *Fox on Money* and on various radio news broadcasts, including *The Bloomberg Money Show* and *The Bloomberg Countdown*. He has been quoted in a wide range of publications, including *Barron's, Business Week, Journal of Financial Planning, Money, Kiplinger's Personal Finance*, the *New York Times, USA Today*, and the *Wall Street Journal*. Stanasolovich's articles have appeared on websites and in many publications such as *Financial Planning Magazine, Financial Planning on Wall Street, Smart Business, Investment News*, and TheStreet.com. He was selected twice by *Robb Report Worth* magazine as one of the Nation's 100 Most Exclusive Wealth Advisors, six times by *Worth* magazine as one of the 250 Best Financial Advisors in America, five times by *Medical Economics* magazine as one of the 150 Best Financial Advisors for Doctors in America, and twice as one of the 100 Great Financial Planners in America by *Mutual Funds* magazine. *Investment Advisor* magazine named him to its 2004 IA 25 list, ranking the 25 most influential people in the financial-planning profession. *J.K. Lasser's New Rules for Estate and Tax Planning* (John Wiley & Sons) named Stanasolovich one of the top advisers in the United States in 2002 and 2005. He was also one of the contributing financial advisers to *Wall Street's Picks* by Kirk Kazanjian (Dearborn, 1998, 2000, 2001) and *Tips From the Top: Targeted Advice From America's Top Money Minds* edited by Edie Milligan (Alpha, 2002). Stanasolovich graduated from Pennsylvania State University with a bachelor of science degree in accounting.

Lewis J. Walker, CFP, CIMC, CRC, has been in independent practice as a financial planner and registered investment adviser since 1976. He is the president of Walker Capital Management Corporation, a financial-planning and investment-advisory firm in Norcross, Georgia. Walker appears on local and national news shows and financial-management programs and has conducted seminars and workshops on a range of financial and investment topics across the country and abroad. He writes a column on future trends for the *Journal of Financial Planning* as well as a monthly column on economic history for *On Wall Street* magazine. His weekly column "The Investment Coach" appears in the *Dunwoody Crier* newspaper. Walker's columns are also featured in the newspaper *Inside Gwinnett* and on the Web at www.moneybulletin.com. He was honored among the best financial planners by *Worth* magazine six years in a row and was cited as one of the leading financial advisers in the United States in *New Rules for Estate and Tax Planning* by Harold Apolinsky and Stewart H. Welch (J.K. Lasser, 2005). Walker has served as national president of the Institute for Certified Investment Management Consultants. As chairman of that organization, he helped to facilitate its merger into the Investment Management Consultants Association. He has served as national president and chairman of the Institute of Certified Financial Planners. In 1999, Walker received the John B. Keeble Award for Integrity and Excellence, presented by the Investors Financial Group. In 2004, the Money Management Institute recognized Walker with its prestigious Pioneer Award, citing his work in the blending of holistic financial-planning precepts with fee-based separate-account management. Walker received his undergraduate degree from the Georgetown University School of Foreign Service in 1960 and an MBA from Northwestern University in 1971. He achieved his Certified Financial Planner designation from the College for Financial Planning in 1975 and earned his Certified Investment Management Consultant designation in 1996. In 1999, the International Foundation for Retirement Education awarded him the designation of Certified Retirement Counselor.

The Challenge of Retirement-Income Planning

THE 76-MILLION-STRONG baby-boom generation is slouching toward retirement. Indeed, the oldest boomers, the flower children of the '60s, are now entering their 60s. Couple this transition from the work-a-day world to retirement with the demise of traditional defined-benefit pensions and concerns about the viability of Social Security, and you would think that almost all who are retired or nearing retirement would be making earnest preparations to turn savings in 401(k)s and other accounts into an income that can support them the rest of their lives.

But they're not.

For example, when Fidelity Investments polled just over 1,500 recent retirees and workers within a year of retiring for its Retirement Transition Study two years ago, it found that 68 percent of the preretirees hadn't done a budget of their anticipated income and expenses in retirement, 74 percent hadn't set an asset allocation strategy for managing their retirement income, and 72 percent had not decided which sources to tap first for income once they retire. How many claimed they had done *all* these things? Just 12 percent.

I'd like to report that things have dramatically improved since then. Alas, the feedback I get from my *Long View* column in *Money* magazine, as well as the *Ask the Expert* column I write for AOL and the CNNMoney website, tells me that's not the case. The process of generating a steady income from savings remains a hazy notion at best to most people.

And that, it seems to me, is what makes retirement-income planning such a formidable challenge. Not only must advisers grapple with the many technical investment and planning issues involved in turning 401(k) balances and other assets into an income that can last the 30 or more years many people will spend in retirement. They must also convince investors to think about this topic in a serious and realistic way, as opposed to falling back on some half-baked notions like living off dividend stocks or moving their entire retirement nest egg into bonds.

I have no doubt that financial-services firms will continue to develop software and tools that can help individuals—alone or with the aid of an adviser—perform key planning tasks such as estimating the amount of retirement income they'll need and settling on a withdrawal rate that can provide that income without depleting their assets too quickly. I'm also confident that advisers will continue to find innovative ways of boosting retirees' income, whether it's arranging a reverse mortgage, selling a life insurance policy to an investor, or trying something more exotic, like using call options on stock indexes to set a minimum income floor while providing potential for bigger gains. If nothing else, I think the range of strategies and ideas offered throughout this book justifies my optimism.

But tools and sophisticated financial strategies won't be enough to motivate people to create a retirement-income plan. Just as consumers had to become more attuned to the need to save and invest for retirement before IRAs and 401(k)s could become staples of backyard barbeque conversation, so too must we make people more aware that their retirement security truly depends on their ability to turn their IRA and 401(k) balances into lifetime income. In short, we've got to show them that creating a retirement-income plan is essential to achieving a happy and comfortable retirement.

Clearly, advisers can play a key role in this education process, as can employers through 401(k) and other company retirement savings plans. After all, work is where most people already do the bulk of their thinking and planning about retirement, or at least get their start. I believe we're beginning to see progress on this front, with more employer plans either offering retirement-income options or at least talking about them. But a lot more must be done.

So, that's the challenge. Daunting, yes, but one that I think the financial-services community can meet. And, for better or worse, journalists like myself are also eager to explain these issues and help people sort through the pros and cons of different options.

—Walter Updegrave
Senior editor, *Money* magazine
Author of *We're Not in Kansas Anymore:
Strategies for Retiring Rich
in a Totally Changed World*

PART ONE

FACING THE NEW REALITIES

The concept of retirement has changed over the past decade. Expectations for retirement have changed, as well. To better understand the challenges ahead, we've asked some practitioners and visionaries to paint their version of the coming landscape. Their perspectives demonstrate how advisers can become instrumental in putting this new age of retirement in context, not only for clients but for the positioning of their practices as well. Our opening chapters lay the foundation for the subsequent discussions addressing the problems of retirement-income planning.

Deena B. Katz

Boomers are the big kahuna in today's demographics, and by the time you read this, the first wave will be entering retirement (the vanguard reached age 65 January 2006). No wonder we call our book to the attention of advisers of boomer clients. Recognizing the importance of this group, Deena shines some much-needed light on the attributes of this influential cohort. However, she doesn't stop there. As a long-time practitioner (longer than she cares to admit), Deena knows that an adviser's time is valuable. You want both knowledge *and* actionable information. Boomers' needs and demands will dramatically change products and services as they evolve into commodities. Advisers will be valued for how they solve client problems and facilitate financial security rather than how they increase wealth. Consequently, Deena includes a section called the "Opportunities for Advisers, Transitioning From Trusted Adviser to Advocate for Boomers" and offers specific ideas and suggestions for suitable advice, products, and services.

Mitch Anthony and Lewis J. Walker

Mitch and Lew need no introduction for practitioners who have been in business for more than a week. For those of you who have not yet had the pleasure of reading their thought-provoking work, you're in for a treat. Advising is inherently psychological, and Mitch and Lew expand that concept by reminding us, "You cannot number crunch your way to emotional well-being and quality of life." Drawing an analogy between Maslow's hierarchy of needs and our clients' hierarchy of financial needs in retirement, Mitch and Don introduce the concepts of "survival," "what if," "freedom" and "gift" income. The result is a practical and powerful process for a financial-life planning process that amalgamates financial needs and quality-of-life issues into one conversation.

Donald G. MacGregor

As long-term practitioners, we know that advising is inherently about psychological issues; hence, we turned to one of the foremost authorities on human judgment and decision making to jump-start our book. Don begins his chapter with the warning: "Technical tools take you only so far; ultimately, effectiveness is a matter of good advice coupled with shaping the kind of judgment and decision-making skills in your clients that can lead them to achieve their objectives." To frame the discussion, he then introduces the reader to the two general streams of research in judgment—descriptive and prescriptive. Most important for the reader, Don follows through with specific concepts (for example, endowment and framing effects) and strategies (for example, sensitivity analysis) that enable us to better guide our clients' decision-making processes.

Mitch Anthony

Mitch makes a second appearance with this chapter on the changing nature of retirement. Anyone who knows Mitch will not be surprised that this discussion is full of pithy concepts: "refiring" not retiring; removing the "tired" from "retired"; financing the rewired life. Most important, he brings us all back to what a retirement plan should really be—based on individual needs not on theory. Toward that goal, Mitch pops the myth of the "golden years" and other "great retire-myths" (for example, that 65 is old), discusses old and new planning models, and encourages us to see and help our clients plan for the future instead of the past. As he so aptly concludes, "We're facing a radically different world in which being retired means anything but being 'out of it.' The time has come for financial professionals to begin a new retirement dialogue—one that doesn't begin and end with the kind of assets a client needs for retirement but instead focuses on the kind of life the client wants."

CHAPTER 1

Boomers

A Force for Change

DEENA B. KATZ

When *Time* magazine offered to extend my subscription for a discounted rate it was making available only to "senior citizens," I was truly puzzled. Don't get me wrong, I was pleased to receive 85 percent off the cover price, but there had to be some mistake. This offer certainly couldn't be for me. A "senior citizen" is a blue-haired grandma who reads *Reader's Digest* in the morning and eats the local Denny's early-bird special every night. That's not my routine. It's true I'm midway through my fifth decade, but I'm hardly a senior citizen. In fact, applied to me, I find the term offensive. And so would other baby boomers.

I'm a full-fledged boomer, having made my initial appearance in 1950. There are 77 million of us born between 1946 and 1964. Boomers are the products of a postwar global phenomenon that started abruptly and ended the same way. For most people the term "boomer" conjures up rebellious, protesting hippies of the 1960s, who became the materialistic *über*-consumers of the 1990s.

A 19-year span separates the vanguard boomers of the late 1940s and the later boomers of the early 1960s. When the early boomers were staging protests, the late boomers were barely into grade school; nevertheless, society tends to view us as a monstrous homogenous cohort. We're not. Yes, we're big, but we're diverse—in lifestyle, experiences, and values.

Our connection is not a shared lifestyle but rather a shared legacy: we inherited, encountered, and redirected social change. We were born into a postwar society in transition, requiring us to make choices about education, work, and family, the consequences of which set whopping trends in motion and profoundly affected succeeding generations.

Now those choices are about to shake up our industry, as the needs of baby boomers begin to redefine what's required of financial advisers. Planners who aren't prepared will find themselves tossed by some rapidly changing winds; those who are can navigate their way to some lucrative shores.

Boomer Retirement: The Times Are Changin'

To gauge boomers' powerful sociological—and economic—dominance, we need only look at how advertisers have pandered to us over the years. When I was fifteen, "cute young things" sold me soap, cosmetics, and clothing. Today, well-seasoned yet well-preserved celebrities show me how to grow older with grace and charm and nary a wrinkle. Boomer marketing wizards know just how to appeal to us. A recent ad in *AARP* magazine depicted a leather-clad fifty-something couple leaning on a Harley. The tagline read, "What are you waiting for?" And what were they selling? Motorcycle insurance, of course.

According to the U.S. Census Bureau, 10,000 boomers turn 50 every day. That's one every seven seconds! By 2020 more than 115 million people will be over age 50 (see **FIGURE 1.1**). That's an astounding 50 percent increase from 2005. But despite our getting older, we don't feel older.

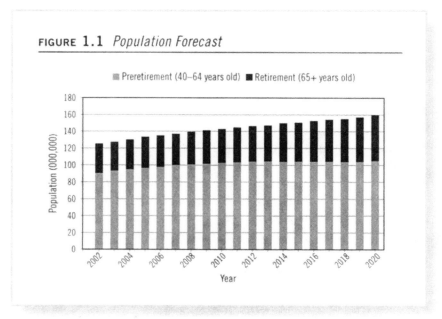

FIGURE 1.1 *Population Forecast*

Preretirement (40–64 years old) ■ Retirement (65+ years old)

Source: U.S. Census Bureau

That's why I was so surprised that *Time* elected to encourage me to "re-up" by rewarding my status as a senior citizen. One would think that *Time's* marketers would have done a bit more homework. I, for one, would have been far more inclined to take the offer if they had given me a "boomer" discount.

The cover of *AARP* magazine (which, by the way, doesn't mention the word "senior" anywhere) always features a boomer celebrity looking fantastic and claiming to have found the secret to longevity by keeping active, eating healthy, or exercising regularly. An article about sex after 60 is almost always included, as well as one on dating at older ages and another on jobs, new careers, or starting your own business after 50.

And for good reason. Life expectancy has changed dramatically. In 1935 the *average* mortality age was 61.4; by 2025 it will be 78.4. And that's just the average age; many will live longer. More important, we are living longer *and* healthier lives. Historically, as people aged, their health status decreased dramatically over a short period (see **FIGURE 1.2**). Today we're squaring that curve and living longer and remaining healthier during old age. Boomers intend to be older and healthier than their parents and are reacquainting themselves with exercise and healthy diets.

Early boomers continue to effect major changes in American life, including the rejection of stereotypes about aging and traditional retirement scenarios. We have been named "the sandwich generation," with parents and children simultaneously requiring our financial and emotional sup-

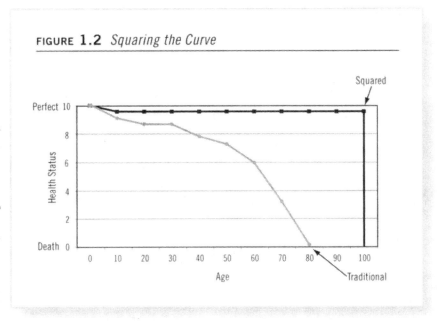

FIGURE **1.2** *Squaring the Curve*

Source: Neal Cutler, *Advising Mature Clients* (Wiley, 2002)

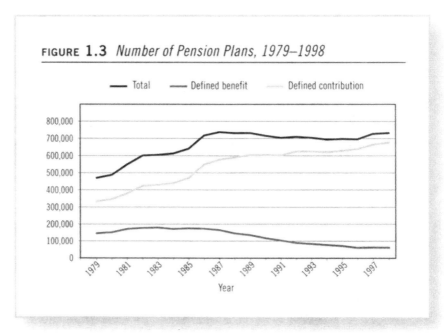

FIGURE **1.3** *Number of Pension Plans, 1979–1998*

—— Total   —— Defined benefit   Defined contribution

Source: Form 5500 series reports filed with the IRS, U.S. Department of Labor

port. Having started families later in life, we discovered that we needed to pay for higher education for our children at the same time we were trying to fund our retirement accounts. And because of advances in the medical field, our parents are living longer, often requiring us to support and care for them. The National Alliance for Caregiving and AARP Study 2004 found that 35 percent of boomers were responsible for the care of at least one elderly parent.[1]

What's more, adult children are returning home from bad marriages, failed financial forays, and postgraduate "lackamoney" disease. Plans to rediscover our spouses, take fabulous trips, and enjoy a debt-free life have been squashed by the burdens of parental caregiving and emotional and financial handouts to children and grandchildren.

As the responsibilities grow, financial help is dwindling. We're becoming increasingly responsible for managing our own savings and investing within our pension plans. Conventional retirement programs have shifted from defined-benefit plans with predictable income streams to defined-contribution plans with varied returns and outcomes (see **FIGURE 1.3**). Social Security is in a precarious condition, and our own savings are piteously poor compared to what they should be given our ages and circumstances.

All of this makes for a pretty sobering introduction to the financial dilemma boomers face. Given such obstacles, how can they meet the challenge of providing themselves "income for life"? Not easily. And probably not without considerable help from a financial adviser.

New Realities: Retirement Is Bad for You

As boomers rapidly approach the traditional age for retirement, we realize that after years of uncontrolled consumption and extravagant lifestyles, coupled with the new demands of family circumstances, we simply have not saved enough to retire. So in inimitable boomer style, we find an alternative: we won't retire. But we're not likely to admit that the decision to reject traditional retirement is forced on us by lack of resources. Boomers have never seen themselves as limited by a lack of resources. No. Boomers will undoubtedly retire "conventional retirement" by redefining it.

Boomers with creativity and opportunity will reframe the meaning of retirement and eventually assign negative connotations to the word, as if it meant dropping out and becoming physically and intellectually idle. We'll describe those who attempt full retirement as "slackers." Instead of retirement being a threat because we failed to save adequately, it will be a hazard because, like smoking, it's bad for us.

Already, researchers are producing studies suggesting that retirement speeds up emotional and mental deterioration. The emerging views support the conclusion that work is empowering and retirement is demoralizing. Merrill Lynch conducted a survey in 2005 of boomers ages 40 to 58 and found that 67 percent of them will continue to work after retirement age so that they can keep mentally active.[2] Ken Dychtwald, author of *Age Power: How the 21st Century Will Be Ruled by the New Old* (Tarcher/Putnam, 1999), refers to traditional retirement as an "intellectual wasteland." We're convincing ourselves that leading a productive, useful life by working as long as possible is the key to longevity.

According to the 2004 Spectrum Group report called *Serving Baby Boomer Retirees,* 74 percent of affluent boomers who are still at work do not plan to fully retire when they reach their chosen retirement age.[3] This supports findings of an AARP study in 1999, indicating eight out of 10 boomers expect to work at least part-time in retirement.[4] The AARP study was updated in May 2004 and confirmed the original results.[5]

In 2005, Northern Trust surveyed 1,312 millionaire clients of baby boomer age.[6] Asked to name their principal financial planner, 45 percent answered "myself." This is a significant finding because in some way, boomer clients are tuning out professional wisdom in favor of their own advice when told they simply do not have enough assets to retire. Many would call this a state of denial; I call it shifting the perspective to make the outcome positive.

Our positive attitudes about restructuring and reinventing the next phase of our lives will find us moving to new areas and starting new careers with energy and enthusiasm. Many boomers will move into roles in which they can be advisers, consultants, part-time teachers, and students. Those who retain their positions will take on the responsibility of training and mentoring the next generation of workers. About one in six boomers will start a business in lieu of traditional retirement.

Coincidently, this new trend toward continued full- or part-time work among boomers may go a long way toward solving the labor crisis in the workplace that's expected to result when boomers retire in seismic numbers at the traditional retirement age. By 2050, there will be only 2½ workers per retiree, compared with 1950, when there were 50 workers for every retiree.[7] Anticipating this demographic shift, proposed Internal Revenue Service regulations would allow phased-in retirement so that boomers can work part-time and collect partial pension benefits as well. The regulations, which apply to nonkey employees who have reached age 59½, would allow employees to choose to receive reduced working hours and a pro rata portion of their pension.

A Value Shift

Times will be a-changin'. After years of ultraconspicuous consumption, boomers will finally say, "Enough is enough." We'll embrace a simpler lifestyle, replacing visits to the Sharper Image with visits to Target. Many boomers will trade in their four-bedroom, three-car-garage houses for smaller and more manageable homes in smaller towns. Those who opt for larger cities will move to the urban downtown areas and live in smaller, newly refurbished condos with centralized community rooms to facilitate their new emphasis on relationships and spirituality. These housing trends will undoubtedly have a negative long-term effect on the real estate market, but that's a story for another book. The fact is boomers' goals will be more modest than they've ever been. Boomers want simplicity in their lives, and they're willing to downsize to get it.

Investing will once again become a means to an end, instead of a game of bragging rights and a contest to maximize returns. Boomers will focus on stable and predictable income over the long term. We'll learn to adjust our expectations for maximizing returns and be satisfied with realistically modest ones that will meet goals and objectives. We'll begin a period of introspection, focusing on spiritual and emotional growth, rediscovering our religious roots. We'll fully recognize the value of family and work to make a significant difference on future generations. The 2005 Merrill Lynch study found that boomers are exhibiting a new interest in becoming the "we" generation rather than the "me" generation.[8]

Boomers will redefine benefits and work-style flexibility for a progressively older workforce. We'll help society develop a new respect for the experience, expertise, and work ethic of the mature worker. We're likely to see more legislation along the lines of the Older Workers Benefit Protection Act of 1990, which will serve boomers as they continue in the workplace beyond the age of retirement.

Baby boomers will shed their disposable "paper-plate" mentality and adopt a respect for preservation, longevity, and usefulness. Our orientation toward materialism will change and more closely reflect attitudes of earlier generations. When my parents needed a refrigerator, for example, they saved until they could afford one. (Notice the word "needed.") During the boomer accumulation-and-consumption phase of life, when we wanted a new refrigerator, we bought it right away and paid for it on credit over time. (Notice the word "wanted.") But the boomers reinventing retirement won't want new refrigerators. In fact, it will be quite fashionable to see how long the old one can hold out. We won't want to take on additional debt to buy a new one in any case. The panache and status of having the newest gadgets and appliances will be replaced with the cachet of having the ones that are oldest and best preserved. We'll finally remember what we were screaming about in the '60s: we don't own things; they own us. Being debt-free and dependent-free will become the hallmark of boomer retirement.

The Decumulation Phase in Retirement Planning

Today's advisers have spent most of their careers helping clients accumulate assets for retirement. It's now time to change the focus and assist in the "decumulation" phase of retirement. Decumulation is an all-encompassing strategy, as opposed to the narrowly focused distribution strategies used in drawing down assets in the past. In planning, advisers will have to bring a new awareness to the management of assets as well as to all other aspects of boomer lifestyles. A focus on accumulating assets—the goal so vital to earlier phases—no longer fits the bill.

This new awareness isn't merely a matter of the skillful distribution of assets. Effective strategies at this stage require significantly more than just withdrawing funds periodically or employing reverse dollar-cost averaging. Advisers will have to address wealth preservation and the creation of income streams from illiquid assets. What's more, the risk of increased longevity will be of utmost concern as advisers try to figure out how to make the peanut butter and jelly run out at the same time.

A 2002 retirement income report by Cerulli Associates, the Boston-based research and consulting firm, indicates that the conventional retirement-income portfolio will need to be revised to accommodate three basic

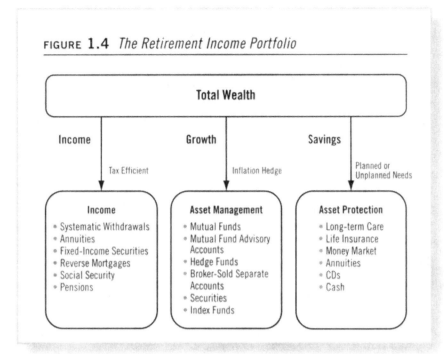

FIGURE **1.4** *The Retirement Income Portfolio*

Total Wealth

Income — Tax Efficient

Growth — Inflation Hedge

Savings — Planned or Unplanned Needs

Income
- Systematic Withdrawals
- Annuities
- Fixed-Income Securities
- Reverse Mortgages
- Social Security
- Pensions

Asset Management
- Mutual Funds
- Mutual Fund Advisory Accounts
- Hedge Funds
- Broker-Sold Separate Accounts
- Securities
- Index Funds

Asset Protection
- Long-term Care
- Life Insurance
- Money Market
- Annuities
- CDs
- Cash

Source: *Funding Retirement Income: Impact on Managers and Distributors* (Cerulli Associates, 2002)

financial needs: income, growth, and savings.[9] The portfolio should also be tax-efficient, provide a hedge against inflation, and have the flexibility to provide for planned and unplanned needs in the future (see **FIGURE 1.4**).

Holistic financial planning and investing for total return will be at the core of the most effective advice to clients. Advisers will need to use good capital-needs analyses and stochastic modeling to help clients plan realistically for the future. Boomers—a group more comfortable with paying for advice and services than for access to products—will be the first generation to truly embrace the concept of "fee for advice." Boomer demand will accelerate the current trend toward fee-based advice in financial services.

Financial products and services will change too. They will continue to become commodities—that is, valued for how they solve client problems and facilitate financial security rather than how they increase wealth. The possible privatization of Social Security and new distribution rules to accommodate the new "phased-in retirement" will generate opportunities for advisers to develop and implement creative distribution strategies for boomers. Successful product manufacturers will consult with experienced advisers to create products and services specifically to address the need for consistent, dependable, lifetime income streams with inflation protection. Examples of this trend include the growing popularity of low-cost, tax-efficient investments such as ETFs (exchange-traded funds), TIPS

(Treasury inflation-protected securities), and target-return and lifestyle mutual funds.

We already see a growing interest in the use of an immediate-income annuity. In the future, this product will be redesigned, incorporating lower expenses and more flexible strategies. Even newer strategies and alternative investment vehicles will give planners more flexibility in designing investment solutions for boomers.

Retooling Your Practice

Advisers who hope to transition from trusted adviser to advocate for boomers will need to develop a successful business model that suits the varied needs of this cohort. What follows are examples of the issues a practitioner will need to be informed about. They're based on my experience in consulting with a wide variety of practices.

Understand What Boomers Want

To become an advocate, you must understand what to advocate for. Studies have highlighted some basic trends regarding boomer "wants."

Simplicity: Simpler lifestyle, fewer material possessions. As an advocate, you'll want to provide both moral support and practical solutions—for example, seminars, consultation with lifestyle specialists, relocation resources.

Accessibility: Access to information and knowledge. By narrowing your boomer market (see "Narrow Your Market" below), you'll be able to develop specialized and targeted information and resources (for example, special Web postings, customized newsletters, white papers, and seminars).

Dignity: The ability to design their own "endgame." By leveraging the firm's resources with technology and reframing your business offering, you can move beyond advising your boomer clients to empowering them to take active control of their future.

Achievability: Manageable goals at work and at home. Again, as a process-oriented rather than a product-oriented practitioner, you can incorporate non-product-dependent strategies into your business offering. For example, the creative integration of part-time work/consulting, home-based office technology, and supplemental income strategies (for example, immediate annuities) may creatively and successfully transition your client from a traditional job to a happy nontraditional "retirement."

Responsibility: Increased interest in family. You can develop a program to encourage family communication and discussions. This is particularly useful in the areas of estate planning and other delicate family issues.

Narrow Your Market

The gap between early and late boomers is wide, with a big difference between their opportunities for future financial security. Early boomers will have more flexibility and choice for the next phase of their lives; however, they also have fewer financial resources. To customize your business offering (product and pricing) effectively, it's imperative that you first carefully define the subset of the market you wish to serve.

Emphasize the Investment Process, Not Products

Because your boomer clients' financial success and that of your business are long-term—and interdependent—goals, it's critical to position the relationship in terms of financial planning, not asset management. The success of process-oriented practices in maintaining and, in fact, growing their client base during the 2000–2002 bear market clearly demonstrated the worth of this positioning. During peak working years, many boomers were competitively focused on "beating the Joneses or beating the market." As boomers become more financially dependent on the income from their own investments, their focus will shift from competitive success to the achievement of personal goals. As a consequence, positioning your firm properly will become even more critical.

Consider total real rate of return. Total rate of return means return net of expenses, fees, taxes, and inflation. As Harold Evensky explains in *The Investment Think Tank: Theory, Strategy, and Practice for Advisers* (Bloomberg Press, 2004), it may be time to reconsider the design of investment portfolios, shifting from "efficient portfolios" to "optimal strategies" (for example, core and satellite versus conventional asset allocation). Such a shift will not only better serve the needs of boomers; it also adds another distinguishing advantage to the boomer practice.

Use alternative investments. Although the popularity of alternative investments is certainly not new, these investment strategies are likely to become a necessary element in most portfolios in what many experts expect to be a low-return market environment. The challenge for the boomer adviser will be to select and integrate these products intelligently in typical retail taxable accounts so that they serve as an element of the total solution, not just as a "story" sale or bandwagon investment.

Move beyond investment management. Again, success in this market will depend on a shift from portfolio management to holistic management—that is, true financial planning. Thus, the successful practice will incorporate the skill and talent to provide at least a basic evaluation of property and casualty, medical, and life insurance as well as other risk-management strategies.

Offer More Than Traditional Services

Become a career adviser. Advisers serving the boomer niches will become strategic lifestyle and employment coaches, providing career advice along with holistic financial planning. Subspecialties will include small-business consulting, guiding boomers who elect to make the leap from employee to employer as part of their lifestyle restructuring plans.

Serve as mentor and sounding board. Develop a program that positions you as your client's main support and chief strategist for financial- and life-planning issues.

Acquire expertise in financial gerontology. Practitioners will need to become much more knowledgeable about the ramifications of living longer and the kinds of help the elderly may require, especially if they're disabled or ill. This would include having the knowledge, resources, and professional relationships to assist clients with issues such as long-term care strategies (funding, services, and facilities), family dynamics and counseling, living wills, and health care surrogate documents. In the years ahead, reverse mortgages and life-income settlements are likely to become as much a part of our planning discussions with clients as disability coverage and long-term care insurance are today.

Become Part of the Solution

Boomers will make decisions about selecting and continuing to use a financial planner or adviser on the basis of relationships and shared values. They will look to advisers for perspective and advice on many aspects of their daily lives—not just the financial ones. Consequently, if you've been cultivating boomers as client prospects and raising your adviser role beyond asset management to becoming the trusted family advocate, you'll be well poised to ride the new wave that's about to hit the financial-advisory business.

Financial advisers like me, who are themselves boomers, will look for clients they can shepherd and mentor through their next phase of life. We'll focus our practices on retention as well as growth. Essentially, we'll follow the patterns our generation has followed all along. We'll look for simplicity, quality life experiences, and a flexible work style. We'll learn when to shut off our phones and ignore our e-mail. We'll learn that the most authentic financial advice and wealth management involve managing our own lives and priorities first.

These changes will happen fast as the early boomers (born 1947–1954) reach age 60 in the years just ahead. The opportunities for advisers with a boomer clientele are endless. You can begin now to adjust your practice to meet the challenges of this new and exciting era. If you're a boomer, it won't take much for you to shift your perspective, because you've probably been addressing some of these issues personally already. If you're not a boomer, talk to some of your clients who are. As the industry moves into this next phase, you'll need to rethink how you and your practice will serve this major market, providing advice, judgment, and solutions to its unique situations and opportunities.

Chapter Notes

1. The National Alliance for Caregiving and AARP Study 2004 (AARP, 2004).

2. *The New Retirement Survey* (Merrill Lynch, 2005).

3. *Serving Baby Boomer Retirees* (Spectrum Group, 2004), www.spectrum.com.

4. *Baby Boomers Envision Retirement* (AARP 1999), www.aarp.com.

5. *Baby Boomers Envision Retirement II* (AARP, 2004), www.aarp.com.

6. Northern Trust Retirement Survey (February 2005), www.northerntrust.com.

7. Jeremy Siegel, *The Future for Investors* (Crown Business, 2005).

8. Ibid.

9. *Funding Retirement Income: Impact on Managers and Distributors* (Cerulli Associates, 2002).

CHAPTER 2

Maslow Meets Retirement

MITCH ANTHONY AND LEWIS J. WALKER

Self-Actualization," wrote Abraham Maslow, "is the desire to become more and more what one is, to become everything that one is capable of becoming." If we're fortunate, that desire can be rekindled even when we thought it was lost.

At age 52, Briggs Matsko was about to retire from his financial-planning business. A friend heard about Matsko's plans and sent him *The New Retirementality: Planning Your Life and Living Your Dreams at Any Age You Want* (Dearborn Trade, 2001) by Mitch Anthony. Matsko said the book not only changed his life but also gave him a new passion and mission for the work he thought he was going to leave. "I had an epiphany when I read *The New Retirementality* and realized that the most foolish thing I could do is retire early and go into a life of wondering how to make a difference," said Matsko. "The opportunity for making a difference was right there in front of me in every client conversation. I just needed to change the focus from strictly numbers to a conversation about life followed by a numbers inquiry."

Matsko began telling clients about his awakening and giving them a copy of *The New Retirementality* to read before they came in for their appointment. He told them to come prepared first to discuss the sort of life they desired to live before they began a conversation about what to do with their money. When they came for their appointments, they were already primed to talk about the life they wanted.

The response from clients was very positive. One client told Matsko, "I need your help to start living the life I want to live and not wait any longer." This woman realized that she needed a relationship with a financial planner who would focus on her life goals and help her arrange her finances in a way that would lead to true self-actualization.

Matsko quickly realized how hungry people are to enter a dialogue about how to bring their life into balance and stop delaying their dreams. Once this dialogue regarding lifestyle takes place, it's time to move to the conversation about *how to pay for the lifestyle they desire.* But they're not ready for the money conversation until they've engaged in a dialogue about what they really want out of life. Money can either serve or impede a life worth living.

After the publication of *The New Retirementality,* a companion tool was created: a financial dialogue called "Income for Life," which overlays Abraham Maslow's hierarchy of needs onto a financial inquiry. Coincidentally, after reading the book, Matsko had created much the same thing to use in his practice. "One of the first things I did when coming back to work with my new vision," Matsko said, "was to create an income dialogue with clients in which we look at people's emotional needs before making financial decisions." Matsko had intuitively settled on the same solution—namely, that we need to design an income plan that simultaneously settles both the emotional and financial ledgers.

Too often, numbers are gathered and strategies are formed outside of the very context they are intended to address: our quality of life and our sense of emotional well-being. You cannot number crunch your way to emotional well-being and quality of life; nor can you achieve these ends without crunching the numbers and making the necessary adjustments. There is a need for a financial-life planning approach that integrates both realms into one conversation.

Income for Life

Seven years ago, the greatest fear Americans had was "dying," according to studies by Cerulli Associates, the Boston-based research and consulting firm. Today, Americans' greatest fear is *living.* People are fearful of living to be 100 and being poor. With the confluence of an aging revolution, rising health care costs, and the erosive power of inflation on our money—what will a gallon of milk cost in 2040?—it's easy to understand how people might not be optimistic about their welfare in their later years.

A Hierarchy of Financial Needs

We will all eventually need to engage clients in a conversation about developing an income stream that lasts as long as we do and outpaces the inflation that threatens to slowly but surely rot our nest egg. The best way

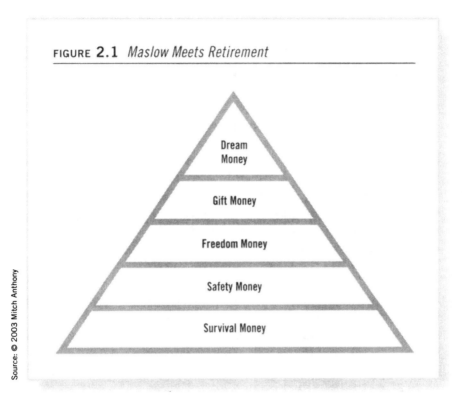

FIGURE **2.1** *Maslow Meets Retirement*

Dream
Money

Gift Money

Freedom Money

Safety Money

Survival Money

to accomplish this task is to work with Maslow's hierarchy of needs (with money in mind) and walk through the process of designing an income for life. (See **FIGURE 2.1.**)

Maslow taught that human beings are motivated by unmet needs and that lower needs must be satisfied before the higher needs can be addressed. People must have their most basic needs (like physical survival) met before they will be able to address other needs (like love or actualization). Rather than study rats (as did Skinner) or the mentally ill and the neurotic (as did Freud), Maslow developed his theory by studying people such as Albert Einstein, Eleanor Roosevelt, and Frederick Douglass. The hierarchy Maslow offered was physical survival, safety, love, esteem, and self-actualization.

For the purposes of discussing financial-life planning, we can tweak a couple of Maslow's categories. For a financial discussion, "gifting" is substituted for "love," since gifts are most often the material expression of love; "freedom" replaces "esteem"; and "dreams" replaces "self-actualization."

Following are the phases of financial preparation we need to attend to in planning "income for life."

Survival income: Money needed to make ends meet. How much do you need simply to survive each month? $3,000? $7,000? If you stripped away all the frills and thrills and paid only the bills of survival, what would that cost? Most people have never taken the time to answer this most basic financial question of all: what is the cost of survival? The money needed to pay for basic necessities is your survival income.

What-if income: Money needed to meet life's unexpected turns. What if everything doesn't work out as you hope and imagine it will? In life, the one thing we can predict with great assurance is that things rarely go exactly as planned. We're surrounded by risks—physical, financial, circumstantial, and relational. Financial risks exist in every category of our lives. Look at the financial risk associated with a divorce—a path that hastens financial ruin and is guaranteed to cut your assets in half and diminish your saving capacity.

A leading risk in the minds of individuals approaching retirement is the risk of outliving their money. Other key risks are health and paying for health care, investment risk, loss of income, and financial needs within the family. As much as possible, we want to protect ourselves against catastrophes related to our bodies, our money, and our stuff. The money needed to guard against these risks is your safety income.

Freedom income: Money needed to do the things that bring enjoyment and fulfillment to life. What is the cost of the activities and indulgences that bring pleasure and relaxation into your life? Some people engage in low-cost relaxation activities like walking; others prefer high-priced activities like walking after a golf ball. Travel, adventure, personal growth, and education should also be considered when calculating the amount needed to fund your freedom.

Gift income: Money for the people and causes that deserve our help. As we move up Maslow's pyramid of needs—securing our survival, safety, and freedom—our money is used for the higher calling of bringing blessings to people and causes we care deeply about. If you're a part of what has been characterized as "the sandwich generation," you're likely experiencing financial concerns on both ends of the generational spectrum. Many of us would love to do something for our parents and our children. Many of us also have aspirations to support causes and charities that connect with our heart and purpose. The money needed to pay for these gifts and benevolent annuities is gift income.

Dream income: Money for the things we dream of being, doing, or having. What do you want to be? What do you want to do? What do you want to have? These questions are all part of the financial conversation necessary for paying the bills of self-actualization. For some people, only a career change will bring them to this place. For others, it may require part-time involvement in activities more closely aligned with their sense of passion and purpose.

The cost of self-actualization is the time it takes to do the things that bring meaning into our lives. If we do not own enough of our own time to engage in these activities, then we must negotiate with our work schedule and personal finances to make the time available. There is often a cost associated with being what we want to be.

There are also costs associated with doing what we want to do and having what we want to have. Some people dream of owning a sailboat

FIGURE 2.2 *Income/Outcome Worksheet*

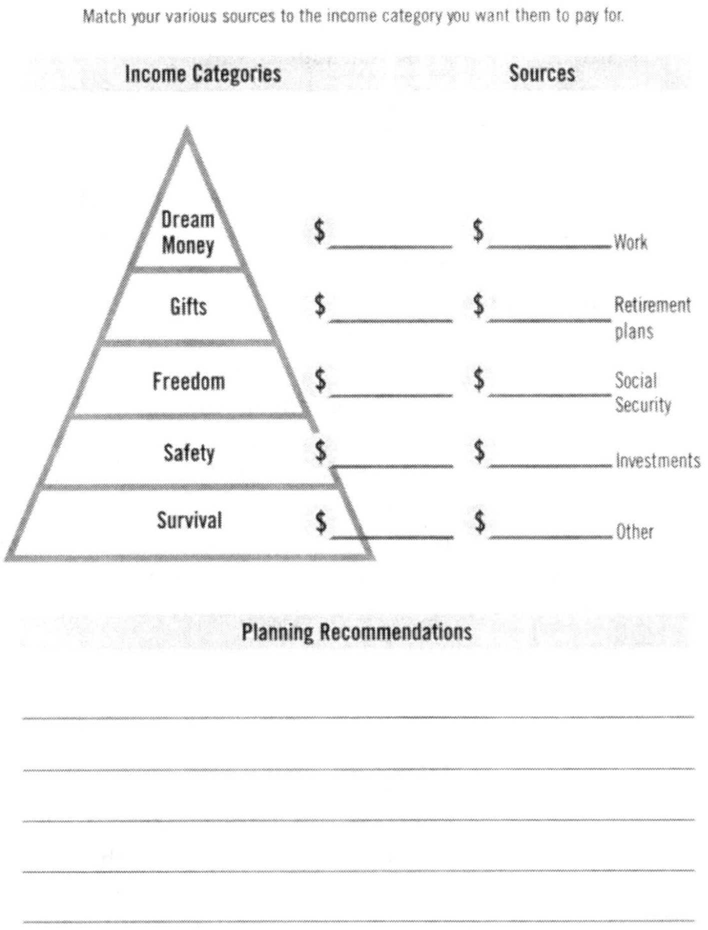

Match your various sources to the income category you want them to pay for.

Income Categories   **Sources**

Income Categories		Sources
Dream Money	$_____	$_____ Work
Gifts	$_____	$_____ Retirement plans
Freedom	$_____	$_____ Social Security
Safety	$_____	$_____ Investments
Survival	$_____	$_____ Other

Planning Recommendations

_____

_____

_____

_____

and spending a year sailing from port to port. Others dream of owning a recreational vehicle and seeing more of America. Whatever dreams and adventures your own musings on self-actualization bring to the surface, there will be bills to pay in the process. The money needed to pay these bills is your dream income.

Once clients have sorted out all their income needs, to complete this life-planning process, you'll need to help them examine their income sources to see how far they can rise on Maslow's hierarchy of needs and guide them in determining the preparations and self-negotiations necessary to cover every level. Potential income sources include income from work, retirement funds, income-earning investments, Social Security, rentals, and other sources of income. (See **FIGURE 2.2.**)

Paying the Bills

The final phase of the "Income for Life" discussion is to match income sources against income needs. Which sources will pay for which needs? If it's a case of having only enough to pay for survival and safety, then the client will at least have the comfort of knowing those two critical bases are covered.

Clients will also have a clearer picture of how much money they'll require to meet their "higher" needs. You can then set goals for saving and budgeting to expedite achieving the income necessary for funding these important needs of freedom, gifting, and dreams. As one financial planner puts it, "If your outgo exceeds your income, you may need to downsize to realize your upside." In other words, if your income isn't enough to meet your needs, you may have to negotiate with your needs.

By working through this sort of exercise, you can bring both clarity and hope into your clients' financial lives. Help your clients get a handle on what they need and what they have—without scaring them witless. This exercise produces clarity. Help them understand what they need to do to get what they want and how long it will take to get there. This exercise brings hope. Clients begin to view income not as just a way to pay the bills but as a means to funding a life—the life *they* want.

Organizing the Maslow Conversation

The Maslow Meets Retirement™ conversation has been organized around a series of data-gathering issues, as reflected in the *Income for Life Workbook I: My Life Index.*[1] Your conversation with clients should be exactly that—a conversation. You're demonstrating a "logic train" (a process), but at the same time, you're learning their story, about their family and the direction of their life. You want to understand their ambitions, cares, likes, dislikes, fears, and constraints (such as illness or obligations), and their view of life overall. You want to glimpse the "heart and soul" behind the money.

Your client should complete the *Income for Life Workbook I: My Life Index* as a supplement to other financial-planning data that you've gathered. As with any workbook, if you're dealing with a couple, have each partner fill out the worksheet individually. Do not assume that they think alike. Quite often, they do not.

The data from the workbook will define a client's survival, what-if, freedom, gift, and dream goals. A second workbook, *Maslow Meets Retirement™ Income for Life Workbook II: My Life Index,* is designed to help you, the adviser, guide the client conversation. The key prompts and examples described in this section are designed to illustrate the logic track to be followed.

Individualized Planning

The workbook's illustrations for each task are simple—and you can draw your own versions by hand on a piece of notepaper. You may be wondering why you would want to draw pictures during the conversation. Aside from the old bromide that "a picture is worth a thousand words," the drawings can help *personalize* the process for the client and demonstrate your *expertise* as a planner.

The presentation and drawings are just for you and your client. This professorial technique leads to an *interactive* discussion. Envision the impact as you sit with the client and have a meaningful dialogue highlighted by appreciative questioning, planning scenarios, having discussions, and making notes—focusing on each step in the Maslow process by drawing and filling in their goals and numbers.

The process is deliberately low-tech; it is not an impersonal, canned PowerPoint presentation. The conversation is "just for them" and shows that you know your stuff. Often, clients will ask for copies of the drawings and notes to take home. That request means you've hit a home run. (If they don't ask, make copies, and give them to the clients anyway. The reaction is always positive.)

Funding a Life

Task one. Task one, illustrated in **FIGURE 2.3**, involves sketching out a simple illustration of "financial horsepower" (that is, liquid assets capable of producing cash flow on a total return basis).

On the left side of the page are taxable personal assets—a bucket containing checking accounts, certificates of deposit (CDs), bonds, stocks, mutual funds, etc. You're not concerned at this stage about the specific

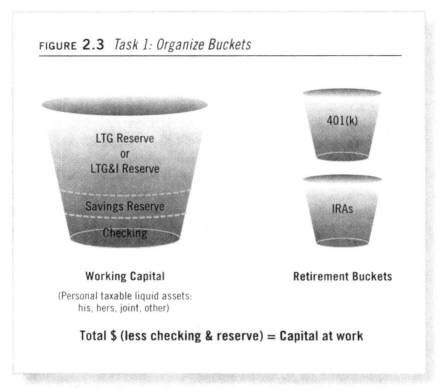

FIGURE **2.3** *Task 1: Organize Buckets*

LTG Reserve
or
LTG&I Reserve

Savings Reserve

Checking

401(k)

IRAs

Working Capital

(Personal taxable liquid assets:
his, hers, joint, other)

Retirement Buckets

Total $ (less checking & reserve) = Capital at work

assets owned. You will deal with deeper investment management and estate-planning issues later as part of a comprehensive analysis.

The personal bucket has three elements. The first two elements are checking account balances to handle ordinary monthly expenses and an emergency savings reserve. The savings reserve will be part of the client's what-if money. It may be described as a "financial teddy bear"—liquid funds that provide comfort. The reserve is for unforeseen expenditures (medical expenses, auto or home repairs, family needs, etc.), an escrow account for upcoming expenditures (tax bills, vacations, a new car, or appliance, lifestyle enhancements); it provides assured cash flow over two to three years without dipping into investment reserves. There are no hard-and-fast rules for what expenses or cash flow needs to include. Your job is to engage your clients, do some forecasting, and find out what makes them comfortable.

Explain that the money in the savings reserve is not an investment per se. Any interest earned is likely to be offset by taxes and inflation, and no meaningful real growth, net of inflation and taxes, is likely. Any growth of capital will have to come from assets at the top of the bucket—money designated as a long-term growth (LTG) reserve or a long-term growth and income (LTG&I) reserve.

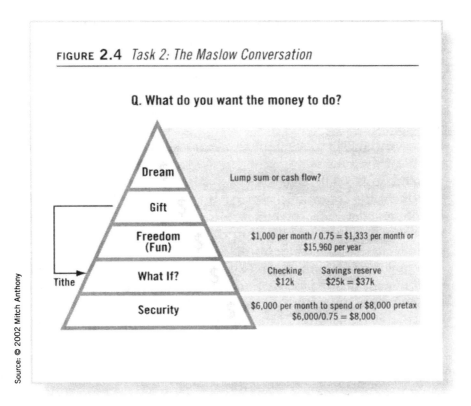

FIGURE **2.4** *Task 2: The Maslow Conversation*

Q. What do you want the money to do?

Dream — Lump sum or cash flow?

Gift

Freedom (Fun) — $1,000 per month / 0.75 = $1,333 per month or $15,960 per year

What If? — Checking $12k   Savings reserve $25k = $37k

Tithe

Security — $6,000 per month to spend or $8,000 pretax $6,000/0.75 = $8,000

The growth reserve is for clients not yet in retirement—those who do not plan to take distributions for a defined number of years. The growth and income reserve is for clients who want cash flow. They want money to spend, but they also want a return in excess of the withdrawal rate so as to retain integrity of principal adjusted for inflation and taxation.

Retirement buckets include any type of retirement plan, including nonqualified tax-deferred annuities, where pre- or post-age 59½ requirements and other tax considerations are a factor.

Since checking, money market, or savings deposits have little or no real return, we do not include them in the total dollars designed to produce growth and/or growth and income. Once you identify capital at work, you have some idea of the size of the engine block powering financial objectives, that is, "financial horsepower."

Task Two. This task, illustrated in **FIGURE 2.4**, is the basic Maslow security conversation. Ask the clients, "How much money do you spend each month for basic living—a lifestyle that's nothing fancy, but comfortable? How much does that cost in after-tax dollars?"

Suppose the client responds, "$6,000 per month." You've looked at his federal and state tax returns and have determined that on average he retains 75 cents, or 75 percent of every dollar earned. On that basis, he needs to earn $8,000 pretax per month, or $96,000 per year. The what-if conversation reveals that the client is comfortable with an average balance of $12,000 in checking and $25,000 in liquid savings as a "financial teddy bear."

Freedom money, or "fun money," provides the edge that brings enjoyment and flexibility to retirement. Using the same logic as applied to security money, $1,000 per month after-tax to spend on "fun stuff" translates into $1,334 per month pretax, or a cash flow need of $16,008 per year (rounded to $16,000).

The Maslow conversation also reveals how the client feels about gift and dream money. Do they tithe as part of their religious practice? For those who do, tithing is a committed obligation and may be included in security money as a monthly expense.

Is funding for gifts or dreams to be set aside in the savings reserve? If so, that money may not be part of the growth or income engine.

Task three. This task, illustrated in **FIGURE 2.5**, is an example of the buckets with the numbers filled in. In our example, the client had $2.2 million that could go to work.

Task four. In this example, as seen in **FIGURE 2.6**, the client did not

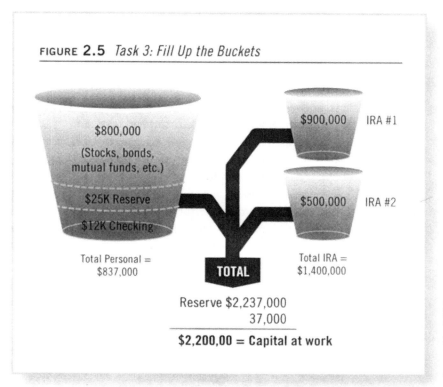

FIGURE **2.5** *Task 3: Fill Up the Buckets*

$800,000
(Stocks, bonds, mutual funds, etc.)

$25K Reserve

$12K Checking

$900,000   IRA #1

$500,000   IRA #2

Total Personal = $837,000

TOTAL

Total IRA = $1,400,000

Reserve $2,237,000
37,000
$2,200,00 = Capital at work

Source: © Lewis Walker

FIGURE **2.6** *Task 4: Establish Cash Flow Target*

Security Goal: $8,000 per month
Freedom Goal: $1,334 per month
Goal Total = $9,334 per month pretax

(Less) Pensions: – $0
(Less) Social Security: – $2,400

$6,934 per month × 12 = $83,208
needed per year from investments

Source: © Lewis Walker

FIGURE **2.7** *Task 5: Calculating My Life Index*

$2,200,000 Capital at Work
$83,208 Need

Formula —— Need/Capital at Work =
Annual Total Return to Meet Goal

e.g., $83,208/$2,200,000 = **3.8%**
Annual Total
Return Required

The Longevity Question!

She is age 59 and healthy
He is age 66 and still plays tennis and golf
How long does the money last?
Inflation @ 3% adjusted for taxes = (3/0.75=) 4%
4% + 3.8% = 7.8% Total   **7.8%** is **MLI** (My Life Index)

Source: © Lewis Walker

define specific gift or dream goals, preferring to leave those for later, if cash flow or growth of capital is sufficient.

To meet overall defined cash flow goals, our client needs $9,334 per month pretax. From that number, deduct pensions, annuitizations, Social Security, trust fund payments, and cash flows from a charitable trust or any other source of dependable cash flow not generated by capital at work. In our example, the gross need is $83,208 per year. How is that to be generated, at what risk level, and measured against what benchmark?

Task five. This task, shown in **FIGURE 2.7**, suggests that you forget about index benchmarks like the Standard & Poor's 500 index as your "measuring stick." How much money does the client need to fund his life goals? This is defined in the client's terms as My Life Index (MLI).

In our example, the clients need a 3.8 percent annual total return. Sound like a piece of cake? Au contraire. Ask the health questions and the longevity-expectation questions. Look at life-expectancy tables. Welcome to the 25- to 30-year retirement.

How long will their money last? Our couple wants to preserve capital adjusted for inflation and taxes. In the example, another 4 percent annualized is required over and above what they're spending to offset inflation and taxation (current or deferred). On that basis, 7.8 percent as an annualized average becomes the MLI target. That number is key to the development of the investment policy statement.

Getting Real

Task six. This task, seen in **FIGURE 2.8**, is a lesson in economic reality. In 1980, at the end of the massive inflationary and stagnating economic cycle of the 1960s and 1970s, the prime lending rate peaked at an eye-popping 21.5 percent. Following the Reagan-Volcker revolution, interest rates and inflation rates fell over time, fueling a long secular bull market in paper assets that we're unlikely to see again any time soon. At the same time, the World War II "greatest generation" and the post-1945 baby boomer wave were moving toward retirement. The emphasis was on growth and accumulation—the building of the nest egg.

A three-year bear market increased awareness of—and sensitivity to—risk and volatility. Meanwhile, the Federal Reserve pushed interest rates to their lowest point in more than 40 years to stimulate the economy. Now we have a thundering herd of retirees and soon-to-be retirees concerned about cash flow, distribution of money from their nest egg, and conservation of principal net of inflation. Interest rates have risen, and before long the prime rate may be higher than the number in the example. How high will interest rates go in the future? How will rising rates affect bond values, fixed-income alternatives, stock values, or other asset classes? These ques-

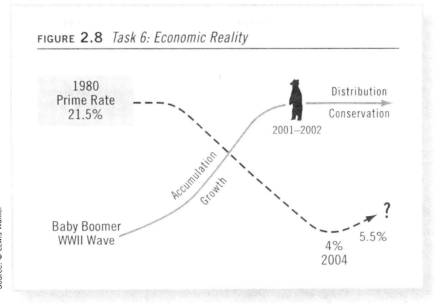

FIGURE **2.8** *Task 6: Economic Reality*

Source: © Lewis Walker

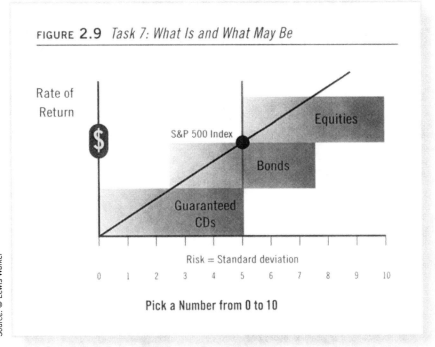

FIGURE **2.9** *Task 7: What Is and What May Be*

Source: © Lewis Walker

tions must be discussed with your clients in depth. Use current CD rates and 10-year Treasury note rates as a safety benchmark. How much risk must be assumed to achieve the client's MLI?

Task seven. This task, illustrated in **FIGURE 2.9**, provides a simple diagram of risk and reward, based on three major traditional asset classes—stable cash equivalents (money market, CDs), bonds, and equities. On the vertical axis, write in the MLI number at the top. Using current data, write in what may be available in liquid savings alternatives and CDs. Next, write in what may be available from short-maturity, short-duration, and high-quality bonds (or Treasury bills, notes, or bonds). How do these no-risk alternatives match up with the MLI target? For most clients, unless they are unusually frugal and rolling in money, it becomes obvious that some allocations to equities will be required to meet total return targets.

Explain that the risk-reward curve moves north by northeast. You may also wish to explain what standard deviation is, because most clients do not understand the statistic. Standard deviation can be your friend during the accumulation phase if you stay disciplined, you dollar-cost average, or you take advantage of buying opportunities. High levels of standard deviation are deadly during the withdrawal phase of retirement.

Explain risk of volatility on a scale from zero (no conventional risk, as with a CD) to 10 (high risk). Peg the market risk as level five using an index such as the S&P 500. Ask the clients to pick a number from 0 to 10. As their adviser, you can judge the feasibility of the number they pick. Can they achieve their goal with their current asset mix? Do they understand reality? What has to change? Do they need to take more risk? Lower their

FIGURE **2.10** *Task 8: Make Believe It Is All Cash!*

* Reexamine Maslow: fund gifts and dreams?

* How does that change money at work?
  Fund sub-buckets?

* How does that change targeted return?

* Evaluate current allocation versus ideal allocation.
  What fits? What does not?

expectations? Increase savings rates (if they are some years away from retirement)? Postpone retirement? Continue to work in some fashion?

Task eight. In task eight (**FIGURE 2.10**), ask the client to make believe their assets are all cash. That helps to keep them (and you) from getting tangled up in "what is" versus "what should be" based on their objectives.

Reexamine the Maslow targets. What may change? Is more funding needed in the sub-buckets? Do spending, saving, or return targets change?

Now you can benchmark the current holdings and allocations against the ideas and desired allocation. You are now in a better position to make tactical decisions—what assets to keep or sell and how to allocate cash in concert with a defined investment policy and asset allocation plan.

The beauty of the Maslow conversation—highlighted by diagrams on notepaper as you strategize—is simplicity. Clients get it. You have demonstrated your value as an educator and facilitator in a personal, friendly, and powerful way. You are seen as an adviser and coach who truly adds value.

Chapter Notes

1. The Maslow workbooks and other discovery tools for financial advisers, such as *The New Retirementality Discussion Guide,* are available at www.mitchanthony.com.

CHAPTER 3

Decision Making at Retirement

High Stakes for the Long Haul

DONALD G. MacGREGOR

When I speak to financial professionals about retirement income distribution, I often start my talk by asking, "How many of you are psychologists?" Usually, there is no response. My second question is, "Is there anybody here who isn't a psychologist?" Again, no one in the room raises a hand. This may seem like a contradiction, but it isn't. Of course, a financial adviser is not trained as a psychologist, per se, but invariably becomes one as part of the process of developing sound adviser-client relationships. Advising is inherently about psychological issues. Technical tools take you only so far; ultimately, effectiveness is a matter of good advice coupled with shaping the kind of judgment and decision-making skills in your clients that can lead them to achieve their objectives.

If you've done your job during the wealth-accumulation years, you've probably given your clients a reasonable education in personal finance. The more seasoned clients become, the more they learn to understand the world of financial planning and investment in the way that you do. Your mental model of finance has become theirs, and as a result of your guidance, they communicate more efficiently and likely have better weathered the ups and downs of market cycles, with a growing confidence that their wealth-accumulation plans are not forced askew by every market turn.

Few things in life are as challenging and engaging as decision making, particularly when the stakes are high and the resources are scarce. Judgment and decision making tap into all aspects of the intellect—memory, perception, reasoning, and emotion—along with whatever capacity we have to analyze and synthesize. Although we exercise judgment and make decisions every day, for the most part these choices are routine and our mental and emotional abilities are not much taxed. Indeed, many of the problems people face in decision making arise from the habits they develop over a lifetime of making small and incremental decisions that seem relatively inconsequential at the time. The problems occur most often when out-of-the-ordinary decisions arise—such as career changes, financial issues, real estate, and bequests. As a matter of routine, people seldom reflect on the choices they've made, and even less frequently do they consider the processes they used to make them. As people become financially successful, they may tend to attribute that success to the quality of their decision making—notwithstanding your good advice and the beneficence of financial markets.

As a financial adviser, you've probably been faced with a number of clients for whom decision making was difficult. In a survey study of 256 financial advisers, among the questions my colleagues and I asked were, "Do you have clients who may not be competent to make financial decisions in their own best interests?" (54.3 percent responded "yes") and "If 'yes,' about what percentage of your clients fall into this category?" (median response: 10 percent of clients).[1] Financial advisers are not strangers to the problems their clients experience in judgment and decision making.

Research in judgment and decision making tends to divide itself into two general streams: *descriptive research*, which reveals the processes people use in judgment and decision making, and *prescriptive research*, which identifies what people *should* do. Prescriptive methods are the basis for much of the advice and guidance that decision analysts give. However, that advice relies on understanding the psychological processes that are involved in judgment and choice and that point to the mental strategies and heuristics people use to work through complex problems. This chapter explores both of these streams.

The Cycle of Decision Making

Over a career of working with various groups of professionals seeking to improve their own decision-making skills as well as those of the clients they serve, I've found a useful framework for organizing the research and for communicating the basic concepts involved. It's called the *cycle of decision making* (see **FIGURE 3.1**). Essentially, most decisions in life (particularly financial decisions) occur in cycles. Some cycles are short, such as monthly decisions about expenditures; others are long, such as cycles relating to real estate purchases and sales. Decisions about spending occur in cycles as

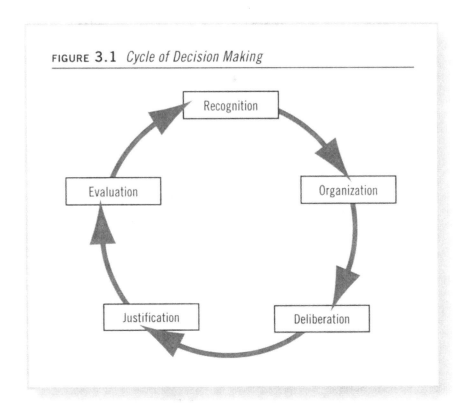

FIGURE **3.1** *Cycle of Decision Making*

well: cycles of one year, or perhaps two to three years, depending on how often an individual reviews his wealth-distribution plan.

Recognition

The first stage of the decision-making cycle is recognition. At this stage, people often do not recognize that a decision needs to be made. Rather than approach a situation as a sequence of decisions, they tend to accept the outcomes as an inevitable result of their entry into it. Essentially, they exhibit fatalism. For example, researchers have found that many of the problems young people experience in social situations that involve substance abuse or risky sexual behavior come about because they (particularly young women) fail to recognize the opportunities they have to decide *not* to participate in the risky activities of others. As a consequence, they tend to acquiesce to the situation rather than take charge of their own behavior (and outcomes) through effective decision making. The demonstrated solution is to provide an explicit model of the situation as a sequence of decisions, showing individuals where and under what conditions they have the opportunity to exercise choice. The operative concept here is *explicitness*—decision pathways to the most desired outcomes need to be made clear.

Organization

The stage of organization has received a great of deal of research attention, largely because this stage structures the decision problem, framing the way key problem dimensions are perceived and guiding how the problem is resolved. When it comes to difficult or unusual decisions, people are not inherently good at problem structuring and organization. A common tendency is to consider too few options or alternatives, often because alternatives are evaluated as favorable or unfavorable while they're being produced; in the process, good options are sometimes cast aside and not fully considered and poor options may be included because they exhibit sterling qualities, at least in a single dimension (for example, short-term monetary gain). A more prescriptive approach—and more appropriate—is to get all the alternatives out in front of the decision maker and then evaluate them against a set of objectives. For example, in the case of wealth-distribution planning, a number of different plans for wealth distribution over time could be prepared and then evaluated against a set of objectives relating to the use of wealth. If none of the plans fares well, then the goals and objectives should be used to create an alternative that does better than those already on the table. As in the stage of recognition, it's important to make decision alternatives explicit. At the root of good decision making lies self-awareness, the lack of which leads to unmet client expectations and, ultimately, to dissatisfaction.

Deliberation

Deliberation is not really a stage; rather it occurs all along the way as a problem is structured and restructured to accommodate new information and insights. The essence of good deliberation is time—time for intuition, experience, and emotion to do their work and for the best alternative to reveal itself. A delicate balance is required between deliberation and indecision. Taken to the extreme, too much deliberation can result in the euphemistic "analysis paralysis." A stalemate usually means that an underlying aspect of the problem has not been revealed. Perhaps not all the preferences or objectives are on the table. An individual may withhold—even from himself—important facets of the problem that are of deep personal concern. Lack of confidence is sometimes an issue: for individuals unaccustomed to taking charge of their lives, decision making can be a challenge to their self-esteem, leaving them without the emotional resources to shoulder the burden of difficult choices.[2] Deliberation can create emotional conflict, but the opportunity to talk through a decision with a confidential adviser can be most helpful. The assistance an adviser gives in structuring a client's problem affords the client some leverage over managing it in terms of his own strengths and weaknesses, thereby making the process of deliberation more tractable.

Justification

Justification involves explaining to oneself as well as to others how the decision was made. In our most private lives, we have only to account to ourselves for how we go about making the decisions we made. In our relationships with others, particularly marital relationships, justification and accountability are more explicit. The challenge of justifying a decision is that we don't often have to do so when things turn out well, but we're much more likely to be called on to do it when things go badly. The best framework for justifying the outcome of a decision is a clear picture of how the problem looked going into it. In hindsight, the outcome tends to appear inevitable and the link between decision and outcome is seen as deterministic when in reality the connection is a matter of probability.

Indeed, chance is a major determinant of outcomes, and the sources of uncertainty in a decision should be identified and acknowledged in advance as a buffer against assigning too much weight to some fault of the decision maker to explain a bad outcome. In the case of good outcomes, the result may be due as much to the "luck of the draw" as to a decision maker's skill. Consider the equity bubble of the 1990s, when investors' portfolios grew at double-digit rates almost regardless of what they bought. Many investors inaccurately attributed their success to their own good investment decisions when in reality they were virtually guaranteed good outcomes simply because the odds were with them. Again, people are not well attuned to the role that environment plays in their successes and failures; in exploring both, the tendency is to attribute outcomes to personal abilities or shortcomings.

Evaluation

The final stage in making a decision is evaluation: is the choice you made getting you what you wanted when you undertook the decision in the first place? No one should abandon a decision lightly. But a choice must continue to serve one's best interests. One way to test that is by continually returning to the objectives set out when the problem presented itself. Are these objectives still valid? Do the financial needs that were being addressed one or two years ago still exist? Perhaps they've changed. Emotional discomfort is one of the first indicators that the relationships between a decision, its outcomes, and its longer-term effects are no longer harmonious and that it may be time to revisit the decision.

Decision Making and Context

For years, all of your hard work acculturating your clients to the financial world has been focused on wealth accumulation. But as their retirement nears, you must shift to the concept of distribution. We can think of accumulation and distribution as two different contexts, or frames, that influence how judgments and decisions are approached. Several problems may arise as the shift is negotiated.

Endowment Effects in Distribution Planning

Advisers need to be cautious of an endowment effect in their clients—that is, a tendency noted by psychologists and behavioral economists for people to value something more highly when they own it than when they do not.[3] In short, it's difficult for people to let go of something they have, simply because they already have it. Add to this the psychological value of retaining wealth that they've spent a great deal of time and energy acquiring. The endowment effect can cause clients to overvalue their assets with respect to the goods and services those assets might buy, leading to monetary conservatism. Although this conservatism may be prudent and advisable from the perspective of asset conservation, it may conflict with other financial-planning guidelines (for example, minimum distributions) that dictate higher levels of distribution than a client may find comfortable.

Framing Effects of Gains Versus Losses

A second important framing effect induced by a shift from accumulation to distribution is that of gains versus losses. Despite the uneven road to wealth accumulation, the frame is generally one of gains that result from a long-term perspective, consistency of approach, and an appreciation for the value of diversification. The focus is on the portfolio and its expanding monetary worth. Although hardly a one-size-fits-all matter, the general strategies for wealth accumulation are well known and, given a few technical parameters, optimization is straightforward. From a psychological perspective, clients become accustomed to an ever-upward trend of wealth accumulation that leads to an optimistic frame filled with hope and positive expectation of gains. Although market perturbations along the way may produce temporary downturns, those dips tend to be perceived as transient conditions, especially when the expectation of growth triumphs and is met over time.

Distribution, however, may be perceived in terms of a loss frame, to which people tend to have a more extreme response than they do to a monetary gain.[4] Thus, an equivalent market downturn may draw a more negative reaction from a client in distribution years than it would during accumulation years. Loss frames can induce a tendency to pay an excessively high premium to avoid additional losses—that is, a larger premium than is warranted given the expected value of the loss. Thus, loss frames can lead to risk seeking—a tendency to accept relatively large risks to avoid additional losses once an initial loss has been incurred. This tendency can be seen when clients favor high-risk (but potentially high-return) investments for their portfolios after there has been a market downturn. In a loss frame, the psychological impact of an initial loss (such as a portfolio devaluation due to a market downturn) has already been borne; the potential loss associated with a risky investment is psychologically discounted, thereby making it more attractive than it would be otherwise.

The Problem of Evaluation

At least some of the work done with clients to foster good habits for accumulating wealth may need to be undone to encourage the right approach to the distribution of wealth. Several challenges arise. Years of wealth accumulation focused clients' attention on the dollar value of their portfolio. Although retirement and the (anticipated) life experiences that await them in retirement are occasionally part of clients' thinking about wealth accumulation, these thoughts are generally imprecise and do not have the clarity and exactitude of a quarterly report showing their accumulated wealth in monetary terms. As an adviser, you may need to help your clients translate their thoughts about life in retirement into structured objectives that can be directly linked to a distribution plan. It is, if you will, a matter of building a crosswalk from financial objectives that have been central to accumulation to life objectives that are central to distribution.

Clients can appreciate how effective a plan is only if they're prepared to understand the model by which the plan is evaluated. From a professional practice standpoint, the more complete (and, therefore, complex) the evaluation, the more precision is attained.[5] Communicating complex evaluations, however, can be difficult if a client is unprepared or unable to comprehend multifaceted models that involve positive and negative correlations. Recent research in judgment and decision making has emphasized that problems are often simplified through affective evaluation, by which complex problems are translated into a singular impression of "good versus bad." This strategy minimizes cognitive effort but may oversimplify the evaluation and place excessive weight on some factors (for example, short-term immediate, emotionally salient losses) at the expense of others (for example, long-term, emotionally bland deferred gains).[6]

FIGURE 3.2

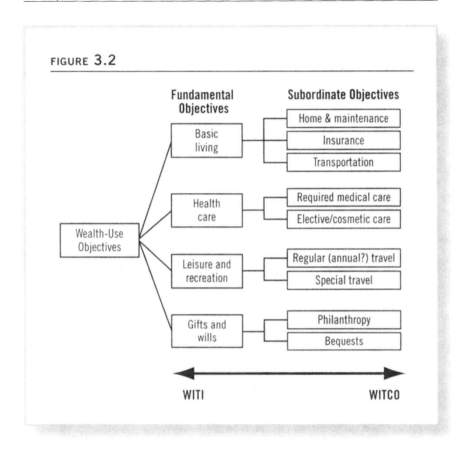

The Challenges of Decomposition

Not everyone is especially good at breaking down large, complex problems into smaller, more manageable ones.[7] The task of decomposition—the essence of analysis—is where the adviser comes in. Your analytical skills are needed to help your clients develop a portfolio of life objectives, in much the same way that you helped them develop a portfolio of investments. And the same general strategies of personalization and education apply here as well. Given the importance of client objectives in distribution planning, it's worthwhile to consider eliciting and constructing hierarchies of objectives, especially from clients who have some difficulty articulating the financial objectives they hope to achieve through plan distribution. One simple visual mechanism that can prove useful is the value tree (**FIGURE 3.2**). The process is relatively straightforward and involves the following basic steps:

- ❑ Elicit (verbally or in writing) or present (from a given framework such as the one shown in Figure 3.2) a set of initial objectives.
- ❑ Organize the objectives into a tree structure, beginning with fundamental objectives.

❑ For each fundamental objective, elicit subordinate objectives by asking, "What is this composed of (WITCO)?" WITCO takes clients further into their values and objectives and down the value tree to greater refinement.

❑ For each fundamental objective, ask, "Why is this important (WITI)?" WITI takes the client up the value tree to broader, more fundamental objectives and helps reveal subordinate objectives that have commonalities.

❑ Continue moving up and down the value tree using the questions WITI and WITCO, respectively. After a few iterations, many clients will be able to continue the exercise on their own.

Biases in Setting Priorities and Objectives

How are retirees likely to think about retirement distribution once they shift their thoughts away from wealth accumulation? A hint of their priorities can be gleaned from **FIGURE 3.3**, which shows partial results from a survey of leading-edge baby boomers—those in the age range of 45–55 years and for whom the beginning of wealth distribution is only seven to 10 years away. These data are from a national telephone survey of 400 households conducted in the spring of 2000.[8] Individuals surveyed were asked about their plans for retirement, including how they planned to

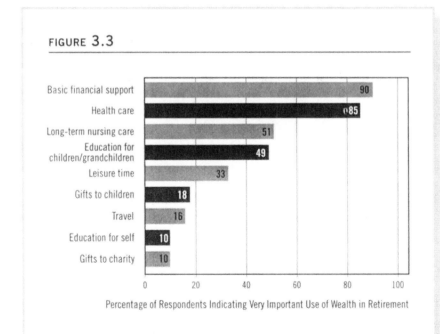

FIGURE 3.3

Percentage of Respondents Indicating Very Important Use of Wealth in Retirement use their wealth, concerns they have about retirement, and details of their financial planning.

Not only are these respondents at the front edge of the boomer generation, they are also at the front edge of those thinking about wealth distribution. The anticipated importance they assign to uses of wealth provides a hint of how many retirees may reorient their thinking about wealth once they enter their distribution years.

Several conclusions can be drawn from the data, most (if not all) of them based on what the data say about the values, goals, and objectives that people expect to have in retirement and that will drive decisions about wealth distribution. On average, people are often abysmally poor at setting priorities and maintaining them over a long period and in the face of a changing environment. There are several reasons for this: without the help of professional practitioners, few people make the effort to establish clear and *explicit* priorities, ones that are developed in the context of realistic trade-offs. In distribution planning, prioritizing objectives is key to consistent and effective decision making. Without explicit priorities, decisions may be made on the basis of whatever momentary needs speak the loudest, often in response to emotions triggered by a perceived urgency to act.

The use of what-if scenarios is a standard method in the decision analyst's tool kit to help individuals walk through possible futures and to develop a bit of cold cognition regarding how they would react and maintain their priorities. I've asked many people to share their visions of retirement, and most of them are idealistic and tend to emphasize pursuits or leisure activities that they've been unable to participate in during their accumulation years. Very few are aware of the impact that increasing longevity will have on their lives or have considered the possibility that their distribution years may outnumber their accumulation years.[9] A common bias in expressing priorities is to consider too restrictive a range of outcomes. People tend to lock onto a future and give relatively little consideration to how variable that future could be. They require a practitioner to help them conduct a sensitivity analysis—identifying fundamental assumptions, testing a scenario through a range of possibilities that go beyond what the individual might have considered, and identifying the implications of a number of different possibilities for their wealth-distribution plans.

Accounting for Client Change

All people everywhere change over the course of their life. The clients who sat before you at your first planning meeting are not the same individuals you face today. In addition to the personal experiences that have shaped their values and objectives are the factors that influence what becomes important to people as they grow older. Retirement distribution is a knotty problem not only because the framing of the financial-planning issues changes (from accumulation to distribution) but because the clients have changed as well—they've aged.

Estimating Health Care Expenditures

Aging brings with it all of the problems of physical change and, very often, infirmity of one sort or another. Health care costs are an important consideration in retirement and in retirees' use of wealth. Although most individuals have some form of health insurance, it rarely covers all of the costs of an individual's health care needs. Moreover, health insurance may not cover the costs of cosmetic procedures, such as facial change or cosmetic dental work. Such procedures, which earlier in life may have seemed of little value, can become important to the psychological and social functioning of the individual who seeks to preserve the appearance and functioning of youth. Most individuals in their preretirement (accumulation) years tend to underestimate what they will spend on health care in retirement (distribution). **FIGURE 3.4** summarizes income in retirement by quartile and shows the average income within each quartile, the average percentage of income expected for health care, as well as both yearly and monthly calculated expenditures on health.[10] Even at the highest income levels, monthly health care expense expectations barely reach $750. For some, this may be sufficient in light of Medicare and private insurance supplements, but for others the uncovered costs of prescription drugs and other health care needs, which increase as one ages (for example, optical care, dental care, prosthetic devices), may prove excessive.

FIGURE 3.4 *Preretirees Health Care Cost Expectations in Retirement*

QUARTILE	MEAN INCOME IN RETIREMENT	ESTIMATED INCOME ON HEALTH CARE	YEARLY HEALTH CARE EXPENSES	MONTHLY HEALTH CARE EXPENSES
Q1	$16,710	17.3%	$2,890	$240
Q2	33,872	13.2	4,471	372
Q3	51,827	13.7	7,100	591
Q4	77,890	11.5	8,957	746

What we see in these health care cost expectations demonstrates a tendency toward faulty judgment that has manifold implications for distribution planning: People are inherently poor at quantitative estimation. They don't decompose estimation problems sufficiently; they consider too few factors, anchor too strongly on those that they do consider, and tend to use one or two memorable examples or cases (for example, last year's health care costs) as a basis for making estimates. To estimate health care costs in distribution years, they need a model or a guide that will keep them from overlooking important elements. We see in these preretiree projections of health care needs a limited grasp of the effects of health care on retirement distribution. Part of this problem is a tendency toward optimism and a limited ability to project future needs. A potential role for financial advisers exists in aiding clients in making more accurate (or at least more reasonable) projections of health care costs and in linking the implications of health care cost projections to distribution plans.

Changes in Cognitions and Emotions

As your clients age, in addition to physical changes, they will undergo a number of psychological changes that affect both their cognitive abilities—thinking, reasoning, and memory—and their emotional life. The shortcomings of life in the advancing years are many and well documented in the research literature.[11] Memory span decreases, information retrieval becomes less reliable, and new information is less readily assimilated. As people get older, they appear to rely more and more on automatic processing of information, quick associations and the like, rather than deliberative and conscious reasoning. For the older mind, intuition is at least moderately preferred over analysis. For example, younger people tend to interpret stories analytically, focusing on details; older people tend to focus less on a story's details and more on its gist and its underlying significance to what's important to them, and they tend to do better at grasping and dealing with information in terms of its holistic meaning. The effects of these differences in information processing between young and old are evident in practical matters of everyday life, such as decision making and judgment. For example, older adults tend to simplify decision strategies more often than do younger adults. These simplifications, such as noncompensatory rules that consider only the positive or the negative aspects of a decision option but not both, relieve some of the psychological burden of making complex and effortful trade-offs, at the possible expense of efficiency and accuracy. Research also finds that as people age, they become less consistent in their use of information in making judgments and predictions; even reducing the overall information load and demands on memory does little to improve the reliability of their judgments.

These changes may occur very slowly and evenly over a decade or two, or they may occur in sudden steps. You may be faced with clients you haven't seen for a year and who now seem inattentive or unable to grasp the implications of their financial situation. That's a good time to consider applying some of the explicit problem-structuring techniques outlined in Figure 3.2 as part of the cycle of decision making and to consider as well some of the advisory practices shown in **FIGURE 3.5**.

FIGURE **3.5** *Deficits of Aging and Implications for Advising Practice*

Cognitive complexity more difficult to manage	• Simplify presentations and reports. • Emphasize only the most important information. • Repeat key, central ideas several times in conversations and reports.
Decrease in working memory capacity	• Reduce client memory load. • Provide memory aids, such as checklists. • Don't assume client will remember past conversation—summarize and repeat.
Difficulty filtering out irrelevant information and ideas	• Identify clearly the central ideas you want to communicate. • Avoid overuse of tables and complex graphics. • Personalize reports and presentations. • Avoid extraneous detail that is not relevant to a particular client's situation.
Reduced information-processing speed	• Allow more time for client interaction • Increase frequency of client interactions. • Ask follow-up questions during discussions.
Difficulty managing new information	• Carefully show direct relationships between new information and old information that the client already understands. • Focus on "distributed information management"—smaller amounts of new information presented and reinforced over a larger number of interactions. • Ask follow-up questions during discussions.

Current research on aging places increasing importance on the fit between the individual and his social context and takes greater account of how cognition is dependent on the features of one's environment. Some of the more relevant research for the advisory profession is that which considers how people's basic motivations may change across their life span. For example, researchers have found that people's motivations in later life are directed toward achieving emotional goals and objectives more often than toward cognitive ones.[12] Thus, the sensory experiences so attractive and sought after in youth are exchanged for a desire for emotional completeness and fulfillment. We would expect, then, that as people enter the last years of life, their sense of fulfillment would come from things that bring them closer to others rather than material rewards.

Indeed, we find in people's adaptive responses to the cognitive difficulties of aging a tendency to rely on social relationships to accomplish difficult tasks that they would otherwise have done on their own in their youth. They improve the fit between themselves and their environment by relying on their social milieu, with its accompanying emotional experience of belonging and caring. Thus, the cognitive declines that people experience as they advance in years may be compensated for by an increasing attraction to an emotionally fulfilling life through relationships with others. As a consequence, for distribution planning, priorities may shift toward using wealth in ways that offer emotional fulfillment and an improvement in their sense of social well-being. Essentially, as people age, their emotional life tends to assume a heightened importance, and they may choose to forgo financial opportunities in favor of peace of mind, even if it means they may fall short of the financial goals they once told their adviser they needed to achieve.

Coda

The notable psychologist B. F. Skinner, perhaps best known for his work on the laws that govern behavioral conditioning and his related studies using animals (having taught pigeons to play table tennis), was an intellectually vibrant individual, thoughtful and productive until his passing at age 86 in 1990. In a 1983 paper, Skinner reviewed the last stage of his life and considered his own aging process and the psychological challenges to be met in maintaining one's intellectual capacity.[13] In keeping with his theory of conditioning, he noted that as people age, their behaviors are less and less reinforced—things become less worth doing because intrinsic and extrinsic rewards for them diminish. One of his prescriptions for aging is the development of a *prosthetic environment,* one that is rich in both physically and psychologically supportive elements to help attenuate the effects of growing older. Much of the advice and guidance that can be drawn from the research on judgment and decision making points in the same direction. Financial advisers are encouraged to adopt a prosthetic view toward their interactions with older clients, for whom the intellectual demands of financial planning may be much more challenging in their distribution years than they were during wealth accumulation.

Chapter Notes

1. Details of the study methodology are in D. G. MacGregor, P. Slovic, M. Berry, and H. Evensky, "Perception of Financial Risk: A Survey Study of Advisers and Planners," *Journal of Financial Planning* (September 1999): 68–86.

2. Self-efficacy can be a problem when the dominant decision maker in a partnership or marriage is incapacitated or absent. Attention to this issue early in distribution planning can help mitigate problems downstream. Advisers should take special care, for example, to involve both partners in a financial relationship early on in distribution planning. The subordinate partner potentially loses efficacy in the decision-making process, with implications for the client-adviser relationship should the dominant partner become absent.

3. D. Kahneman, J. L. Knetsch, and R. H. Thaler, "The Endowment Effect, Loss Aversion, and Status Quo Bias: Anomalies," *Journal of Economic Perspectives* 5 (1991): 193–206.

4. For original formulation, see D. Kahneman and A. Tversky, "Prospect Theory: An Analysis of Decisions Under Risk," *Econometrica* 47 (1979): 263–291. See also D. Kahneman and A. Tversky, *Choices, Values, and Frames* (Cambridge: Cambridge University Press, 2000).

5. For example, see R. Levin, *The Wealth Management Index* (Chicago: Irwin, 1997).

6. P. Slovic, M. Finucane, M. Peters, and D. G. MacGregor, "Rational Actors or Rational Fools? Implications of the Affect Heuristic for Behavioral Economics," *Journal of Socio-Economics* 31 (2002): 329–342.

7. D. G. MacGregor, "Decomposition for Judgmental Forecasting and Estimation," in *Principles of Forecasting,* ed. J. S. Armstrong (Boston: Kluwer Academic Publishers, 2001).

8. Support for this research was provided in part by the AARP, Public Policy Institute, Washington, DC. Details of the study appear in D. G. MacGregor and P. Slovic, "Retirement Plans and Financial Expectations: A Survey of Leading-Edge "Baby Boomers" (Eugene, OR: Decision Research, 2000).

9. D. G. MacGregor, "Psychology, Meaning and the Challenges of Longevity," *Futures* 35 (2003): 575–588.

10. D. G. MacGregor, "Retirement Plans and Health Care Expectations: A

Survey of Preretirement Adults," *Journal of Retirement Planning*, (March-April 2001): 24–31.

11. A comprehensive review of the current research on the deficits of aging is available in P. C. Stern and L. L. Carstensen, *The Aging Mind: Opportunities in Cognitive Research* (Washington, DC: National Research Council, 2000).

12. L. L. Carstensen, D. M. Isaacowitz, and S. Turk-Charles, "Taking Time Seriously: A Theory of Socioemotional Selectivity," *American Psychologist* 54 (1999): 165–181.

13. B. F. Skinner, "Intellectual Self-Management in Old Age," *American Psychologist* (March 1983): 239–244.

CHAPTER 4

Reinventing Retirement

MITCH ANTHONY

I magine you're a blacksmith a century ago. You've prospered in your business for many years because you've provided an indispensable service to your community's chief transportation system. One day you look up and coming down the main street you see a loud contraption that people are calling the horseless carriage. "Huh?" you say. "That will be the day!" And back to your work you go. Ten years later your business is half of what it was before; 20 years later it no longer exists. You failed to recognize one key psychological axiom in succeeding with consumers: if there is a more efficient way to live, we will choose it even if it presents a whole new set of challenges. Many a regretful blacksmith probably discounted the motorized contraption as too complicated, problematic, and unproven for the majority of consumers to adopt.

Markets for popular products don't dry up overnight. The shift starts as a slow trickle, increases in current slowly, and years later, reaches a rushing torrent. Successful merchants keep fluid mind-sets as they watch trends develop and adapt their goods and services to them. The wise blacksmith a century ago would have expanded his business to include repairing horseless carriages as well as shoeing horses. This expansion would have been accompanied by a new learning curve on the workings of gasoline engines. Those who simply kept their nose to the grindstone with the same offering of goods and services were eventually replaced by a new breed of mechanic.

A similar fate may await advisers whose retirement-planning advice is based on assumptions that are no longer true.

Whatever Happened to the Golden Years?

Consider the following observations about retirement as we no longer know it. The mosaic these stories form reveals a radical shift in the "third age" of life—formerly known as the retirement years—and, for you wiser merchants, an opportunity to position your practice for the boom ahead.

❑ I went out for dinner with Dick and Gail, a writer and an architect, respectively, in their 50s. Gail shared the story of how she transitioned away from a top firm to work for herself from her home. Her reason for doing so? "I can't see myself working 50 to 60 hours a week anymore. By doing less of it I enjoy it more. As a matter of fact, after two months it dawned on me that I love my work so much that I can see doing this when I'm 80." Dick is a writer full of ideas and the idea of retiring sounds about as inviting to him as carbon monoxide poisoning. These two are into "refiring"—not retiring. Work, as they understand it, is not the problem. It's the hours and the company demands they want to prune.

❑ A local merchant who ran a successful tire shop for three decades and retired at age 65 opened a new store a year later. His back-in-business advertising campaign read, "I'm back in business because 'retirement sucks.'"

❑ Home Depot announced a national hiring campaign aimed at retirees (coordinated with the American Association of Retired Persons (AARP)). The rationale for the campaign? "They know more and they sell more." Welcome to the dawning of the Experience Age, in which gray hair indicates gray matter and the capitalist marketplace realizes the errors of its youth-seeking ways. Home Depot's move is an initial flare in what will become a firestorm of capitalizing on the commercial value of experience and wisdom—the kind of value that doesn't come in 25-year-old containers.

And What Will Happen to Retirement Planning?

How are these changes affecting your business? Are you a retirement blacksmith pounding out the same projections, or are you beginning to learn the modern mechanics of rewiring? Are the goods and services you sell today as progressive as they were 10 or 15 years ago? Do they resonate with the way people want to order and live their lives?

Years ago people bought into the idea of a compartmentalized life course:

❑ The first part of your life you spend learning.
❑ The second part of your life you spend working and earning.
❑ The last part (retirement) you spend in leisure or journeying.

That model for living is being rejected and rearranged for a tailor-made design for life. Consider current trends that are evidence of this paradigm shift in life-course navigation:

❑ Senior citizens are going back to college in record numbers. Thousands are "retiring" to university towns, instead of the traditional snowbird destinations.

❑ Many retirees are becoming entrepreneurs and reviving shelved dreams and passions.

❑ Many people in their prime earning years are cutting back on work hours to be present in their children's formative years. They believe they can make up for lost earnings when their children are grown, and they are no longer willing to sacrifice parental influence for immediate material advancement.

❑ Many people are rearranging their living circumstances in order to shift into more meaningful and fulfilling forms of work and less hectic lifestyles.

❑ More than 50 percent of retirees are going back to work after becoming bored with the prospects of full-time leisure.

❑ The idea of periodic sabbaticals from work is gaining popularity with high achievers and high earners. They view these breaks as necessary to reflect on their life direction.

❑ Adventure travel and learning vacations are popular with all age groups, especially the 50-plus crowd.

❑ Migration to the Sun Belt is declining, and more people are retiring and becoming more involved in their own communities.

Now, consider the following demographic and societal changes and ask yourself what they mean to your business going forward:

❑ The median age in the United States is 35 and is getting older every year.

❑ The workplace is facing a looming brain drain of managers and executives, and is beginning to offer phased retirement packages.

❑ Reversing a 50-year trend, the number of Americans working past age 65 is now rising (*New York Times,* February 26, 2001).

❑ With companies cutting pensions and health benefits, many aging workers will not be able to afford to fully retire.

❑ With the repeal of the Social Security earnings restrictions, a major economic disincentive to working past age 65 has been removed.

❑ Many baby boomers continue their expensive indulgences, not wanting to wait until they're older to enjoy them.

❑ Eighty percent of baby boomers say they intend to continue work in some form in their retirement.

❑ Two-thirds of Americans say they feel stressed from working too much ("Hilton Generational Time Survey," January 2001, reported in *USA Today*).

What conclusions can you draw from these patterns? What impact do you foresee in relation to the products and services you're selling and the manner in which you sell them? One question that begs asking is, "Is the traditional retirement planning process on the road to extinction?"

Removing "Tired" from Retired

Many people believe the concept of traditional retirement is hopelessly outdated and no longer applies to their lives. They find the times have changed so radically that even the term "retirement" is no longer appropriate. If people do not connect with the concept or even the word "retirement," how long will it be before they reject the process that leads to a concept they no longer embrace?

Rather than retire, the 77 million baby boomers (who began turning 59½ in 2005) are looking to "refire." Are you prepared for the great renaissance—formerly known as retirement—that is ahead for your clients? One baby boomer will turn 59½ every seven seconds between 2005 and 2025. Are you still starting your retirement-planning conversations with "How old are you, and how much money do you have?" If you are, you're missing the opportunity of a lifetime.

Graying boomers aren't interested in retiring their gray matter, or their endorphins, or their sense of curiosity. Rather than reclining, they're re-defining—looking for new mountains to climb; a new rhythm for their life; time to work, play, think, and explore. Do your conversations about retirement embrace this seismic cultural shift and help your clients explore the potential and possibilities of the next 30 years of their lives?

Living Well

What does the new retirement conversation look like? What does living well mean today? I offer the following acronym as a guide:

❑ **W** = *Work*, what I enjoy most and want to continue with. Things I do well bring value and meaning to my life.

❑ **E** = *Equilibrium*, the need to keep a sane pace, create space for breathing and thinking, and design a life in balance.

❑ **L** = *Leisure*, not full-time but enough to keep fun and adventure in my life.

❑ **L** = *Learning*, the desire to keep my mind sharp and challenged. Not only does mental acuity make today more interesting, but it also offers hope for my aging years since learning leads to greater acuity later in life.

To quote a friend, the adviser of the future is the person who can fulfill the role of "WELL-th" adviser. To fulfill that role in your clients' lives, you'll need to abandon the hackneyed retirement worksheets and become conversant in the issues that define the experience of living well.

Changing Times; Changing Plans

The extended working life is the result of a confluence of factors that are physical, psychological, and intellectual:

1 People live longer today, and many feel younger at older ages as a result.

2 People are beginning to view early retirement years as a "middle ascent" stage in which they can chase dreams in a childhood without supervision. Many retirees desire "re-creation" as much as recreation in their retirement years.

3 "Knowledge capital" and experience, rather than physical labor, are the modern bargaining chips in the marketplace.

4 Studies report on the importance of intellectual stimulation and purposeful pursuits for successful aging.

None of these factors has escaped the attention of the baby boom constituency. This group has often frustrated the financial-services industry with its free-spending, "live now" mentality. But this group, by and large, has looked traditional retirement in the eye and seen it for what it is: an outdated concept that no longer fits.

My book *The New Retirementality: The Definitive Guide to Becoming a Successful Financial Planner* (Dearborn Trade, 2002), offers a succinct history of how the idea of retirement got its start and how it established a foothold in American culture. The idea was invented in the late 1880s by German Chancellor Otto von Bismarck. At that time, the average male lived to age 46 and the retirement age was set at 70. Bismarck's social insurance program was intended to serve as disability insurance. The idea was imported to the United States by Franklin Roosevelt's administration in 1935 as a way to put young men to work during the Depression. It was an appropriate idea in an industrial society where age had a significant bearing on output. Also motivating FDR was the rise in power of both Mussolini and Hitler, which had been buoyed by similar employment struggles in Italy and Germany. In 1935, when the average male lived to the age of 63, the retirement age was set at 65; in 1937, it was lowered to 62.

The genesis of the traditional retirement model makes it clear that the retirement journey was designed to last for two to three years, not for 20 to 30 years. If a person expected to live only to the age of 63 and retire at age 62, it might make sense to fully indulge in a life of leisure and rest. But such full-time pursuits make no sense at all when one is faced with 20 to 30 years of retirement living. Society is struggling for a new term to describe this period of life because it senses that the traditional concept is no longer relevant or valid.

How much longer, then, can the retirement-savings industry continue to approach clients with the same plans and approaches? "Because it is inevitable that the vision of retirement will continue to undergo a metamorphosis, some would argue that it behooves today's planners to adopt an entirely fresh approach to retirement planning, to reinvent retirement planning itself," wrote Jacqueline Quinn in her article "The Metamorphosis of Retirement" (*Journal of Financial Planning*, April 2001). "Out are the old parameters of solely planning for a client's retirement, bearing in mind life-expectancy increases. It is a much broader picture of retirement planning, the dimensions of which not only encompass the finances of retirement but also the dimensions of the client's lifestyle (with its myriad nonfinancial issues). Planners are now helping clients plan not only for retirement but for how they are going to live in retirement."

Financing the Rewired Life

If your retirement planning process is simply about ensuring your client "has X dollars at X age," you're still hammering horseshoes on the anvil. That conversation does nothing more than prepare clients for the artificial finish line. Life does not end or begin at age 62. Many clients are working in second-choice careers with the hope that they can put away enough money to do the work they really want to do at age 62. These people apparently believe that life begins at age 62. Others are preparing only in fiscal terms for retirement from work at age 62 and making no preparations for their time, knowledge, and energies beyond that point. These people are grossly underprepared for life beyond age 62. The retirement-planning process can and must adapt to this new reality: *today's retiree has a lot of life left to be lived.* Let us begin using processes and services that better attend to this reality.

Michael Stein, author of *The Prosperous Retirement: Guide to the New Reality* (Emstco, 1998), suggests that "retirement is a time in life when an individual shifts from earning a living for the sake of economics to contributing to society with the goal of self-realization in mind." Retirement for baby boomers will become a classic animation of psychologist and educator Abraham Maslow's hierarchy of needs as people move their minds and money up the pyramid toward self-actualization. Tomorrow's planners will find themselves engaging in conversation with two types of self-aware clients:

1 Those who want meaning and balance in their life and can afford to retire
2 Those who want meaning and balance in their life but cannot afford to retire

Just because those in the first category can afford to fully retire does not mean that they should do so if they're interested in pursuing meaning and achieving balance in their lives. For many people who have the means to retire, part-time engagement in work that challenges and energizes them is the key to a happy retirement. Those who cannot afford retirement will need help exploring a work-life combination that will allow them to find the meaning and balance they desire, while providing the necessary income for the lifestyle they want.

The conversation clearly needs to move from calculating how much money our clients will need to reach the artificial finish line to defining the kind of life they hope to live once they reach that line. Even better is the conversation that helps clients remove the artificial finish line altogether and starts the work of transitioning to a life that will enable them to pursue interests they love—at a pace they can live with. Tomorrow's retiree will have little interest in being "finished."

For the conversation to move past the pot-of-gold mentality, clients must be made aware of the differences between yesterday's retirement model and today's. The conversation between the adviser and client needs to explore the realm of self-actualization, which is how the majority of prospective retirees are beginning to view the retirement—a time to rediscover themselves. This redefinition of retirement is not restricted to the 60-plus crowd. Self-actualization seems to be the driving force behind the baby boomers—and the hub for the career choices of the Generation Xers.

The redefinition of retirement raises a number of issues for advisers to discuss with clients. Consider the following:

❑ A trend has been established for retirees to live long and active lives. How long should we plan on your living? How active do you want to be, and what costs are attached to those activities?
❑ Many people are separating their retirements into many phases—reeducation, entrepreneurial pursuits, charitable giving, adventure trips, etc. What phases do you foresee for yourself, and what financial arrangements will be necessary to make these phases possible?

❑ Do you see the cost of your retirement lifestyle being the same as, less than, or more than what it is today? What adjustments need to be made?

❑ Will part-time work be one of your income sources in your retirement years?

❑ To accomplish your goals in your retirement years, you will need tax and estate planning and insurance to protect your plans. Are you aware of how to attain these various services?

Ross Levin, CFP, of Accredited Investors in Edina, Minn., tells a retirement transition story that fits quite well with the model of self-actualization as the target, rather than merely accumulating a set amount of money by a certain age. He tells of a 53-year-old client who sold his business but had concerns about his investment assets being enough to support his lifestyle. A dialogue with Levin led this client to take a position in the public service sector, which was something he had always wanted to do, rather than go back to work in the same industry. Despite the cut in salary, he is in the black—in terms of both income and self-actualization. How many advisers faced with this challenge would have done little more than tell the man how many years he would have to work to reach his retirement-income goal?

This client is entering phase one of what may be a 40-year retirement journey. It is vital that he work with an adviser who understands that model of retirement living and offers as many options for self-actualization as possible. The goal is more than monetary. Tomorrow's clients will measure their progress as much by what they contribute as by what they keep.

Advisers who want to stay in step with the times must allow clients to come to their own definition of retirement. In the late 1960s, labor economist Seymour Wolfbein wrote that people of the baby boom generation would have at least five distinct careers—not jobs, but careers. Wolfbein prognosticated a time of retraining and reinvention and placed no upper limit on when or where that training would end.[1] Wolfbein's crystal ball was crystal clear regarding the rewiring boom. The years previously set aside for reclining will now be used for redefining.

Consider the popular Silicon Valley myth that all the Internet start-ups were the inventions of 22-year-old Stanford Business School students. "The pervasive image is of a startup founder straight out of business school or still living in a college dorm," wrote Ian Greenberg in the June 12, 2000, issue of *Industry Standard*. "Only nine percent of those who have founded Internet firms are 29 or younger. People in their 40s and 50s make up nearly half of all startup founders." Add to this the founders who were older than 60 and the percentage of founders ages 40 to 60-plus goes to 58 percent. Gray hair equals greater gray matter. Make no mistake about it.

As much as this generation of baby boomers demands challenges, they crave balance between work and relationships. It is the convergence of self-actualization and the realization of what truly makes for happiness that has forced the razing of traditional retirement models and redefined this phase of life in more personal terms. Advisers who understand this and begin the redefinition dialogue with their clients will find themselves connecting with clients in a new and dynamic way. Looks as if it's time to leave the anvil behind and begin studying the quantum mechanics of the refiring or rewiring engine that will drive this society for the next 30 years.

The New Retirementality

"How dull it is to pause, to make an end, to rust unburnished, not to shine in use, as though to breathe were life," wrote the English poet Alfred, Lord Tennyson. It's a sentiment that many nearing retirement now espouse. On a recent plane ride, a businessman in his late 70s told me why he doesn't buy into the American dream of leisure-class retirement living. Every year he goes to Florida to visit his affluent peers who have long been retired. Here's the drill they go through every day: They get together and have breakfast and converse through the morning. At about 11:00, they start checking their watches because at 11:30 they can have their first cocktail. After a couple of drinks, it's on to lunch. After lunch it's on to someone's boat and more cocktails. Then it's home for a nap, a new round of cock-tails, and dinner. When he brings up the subject of productive work, they all talk about how great it is not to have to go to work anymore. After each visit he is reminded of how grateful he is to have meaningful work at this stage in life. He is so happy that his phone is still ringing. With each phone call, he is energized and feels like he still has something of value to offer.

Who has the vision of retirement that's most indicative of what the future holds? The affluent leisure class? Or the businessman in his late 70s whose phone is still ringing? My guess is that the vision of retirement with the phone ringing will replace the vision of a 20-year cocktail party. Granted, not all retirements are soaking in libation and boredom, but the retirement focused on nothing but leisure pursuits is losing its allure with a new generation approaching retirement.

Retirement was invented in an age in which physical labor was the norm and when a 62-year-old felt old because of prolonged physical strain. This image contrasts sharply with today's retirees, who primarily trade in intellectual capital and experience and are quite likely feeling in their prime at the age of 62.

Yet the traditional model of retirement is still touted in our society as if nothing has changed. Closer inspection of the thinking that undergirds the perpetuation of traditional retirement reveals what a cultural anachronism this thinking really is and exposes the myths that perpetuate it.

Although quickly eroding and no longer relevant to modern retirement, some of what I call "the great retire-myths" continue to influence our culture:

1 The age of 65 is old.
2 Being retired means you no longer work.
3 You have to be 62 to do what you really want to do.
4 Retirement is exclusively an economic event.
5 A life of ease is the ultimate retirement goal.
6 I can do my own retirement planning.

Myth No. 1: Age 65 Is Old

"How old would you be if you didn't know how old you were?" asked Satchel Paige, the oldest man to play major league baseball. Old isn't what it used to be. When the age for retirement was originally set, most people didn't even make it to that age. Now, they are living 20 to 30 years past the retirement age. The age of 65 in the 21st century has little resemblance to the age of 65 in, say, 1970. Most people today are not "old" at 65. They may or may not have slowed down. A renowned expert in gerontological studies informed me that the physical composition and health at the cellular level of today's 65-year-old is almost identical to a 45-year-old's in 1975.

Thirty years ago you didn't see many men in their 70s jumping out of airplanes or flying into outer space. The behavior of such super-septuagenarians may well serve as portents of the active lifestyles of seniors in the future. After a talk I gave on this topic, a 66-year-old man recently lamented to me, "I can't even get a senior discount at my favorite ski resort anymore because there are so many people my age filling the lifts. You now have to be 80 to get the senior discount!" Look for this trend to continue.

So how old is old? The answer to that question is as individual as the person answering it. We know that the marker for old is no longer 65. A 2003 survey by AARP revealed that most seniors now feel that the marker for old is at 78 years.

Myth No. 2: Being Retired Means You No Longer Work

The disconnect between retirement and work is disappearing. The retirement of the future will no longer call for a cold-turkey abstinence from work. In a study of baby boomers and retirement by the market research and consulting company Roper Starch, 85 percent of baby boomers stated that they wanted to "die with their boots on." They want to wear out—not rust out. No, they may not want the same hours or a megalomaniac boss, but they like and want work to some degree. They want to do what they want to do, as much or as little as they choose. Work makes them feel relevant, needed, and connected. They have observed the retirement of a generation earlier and know what they want and don't want. They've met the retired lawyer who now heads condo-association warfare meetings who says, "I went from being in *Who's Who* to 'Who's he?'" This generation is not interested in entering a race toward irrelevance. The majority of this crowd has no desire for a retirement in the sunset or a rocking chair.

The new retirement will be defined by degrees and phases instead of a work/retirement divide. Retirees will decide how much, where, and when they want to work. Some will work because they want to and others because they need to. Those who work because they need to may find it's a blessing in disguise that helps to ward off boredom, loss of mental acuity, aimlessness, and endless reruns of *Wheel of Fortune* on television.

Many corporations are looking at adopting phased retirement programs, by which they can stem the brain drain when valuable and experienced employees exit while negotiating lower-cost consulting arrangements that do not include benefits. For some retirees, this will mean working part-time; for others, it will mean entering and exiting the job market as they wish. The two extremes of the old retirement model—all work or no work—are simply relics of the past. We need to explore the manifold possibilities for work at any age.

Myth No. 3: You Have to Be 62 to Do What You Really Want to Do

"Most men have jobs that are too small for their spirits," wrote Studs Terkel, an author and radio broadcast personality. Indeed, millions of people are sacrificing the present in the hopes of following their heart at 62. Too many Americans go to work each day and leave their hearts in the glove box as they park their cars and head to their cubicles. Many who want to pursue a passion or dust off an old dream see retirement at 62 as their only hope. Many desire freedom from the drudgery of draining and stressful toils and long to move to the avocational pursuits they had previously entertained only as daydreams. Today, for the sake of burned-out clients, the financial-services industry urgently needs to explore approaches that help clients integrate their assets and income with their passions and life—without having to wait until they're 62.

Is life about making money, or is money about making a life? A tacit but pervasive theme in our society is that we should always choose the path with the biggest bucks and squelch all internal objections to this approach. Consequently, many people put their soul's work on the back burner while they travel a career path with the most money. Why? So they can someday have enough money (hopefully at retirement) to do what they really wanted to do in the first place.

This flawed philosophy of putting first things second in our career and life is the reason why so many people today are motivated to retire. They have chosen to mortgage their time in order to make enough money to someday make a life. By using the innovative approaches of financial life planning, you can help clients make the transition—at any age—to what they want to do with their life. All your clients have to decide is what they want to be when they grow up.

Myth No. 4: Retirement Is Exclusively an Economic Event

When we use the term "retirement preparation," we think of financial preparation, of course. We have been conditioned to think of retirement planning myopically and through a material lens, one that ignores all the other aspects of necessary preparation such as domestic, social, intellectual challenge, and the optimal use of time. As one retired executive put it, "What do you want me to do now? Sit around and hug my bank account all day?"

Ask the spouses of recent retirees whether they wish they had paid a little more attention to more holistic retirement preparation. It brings to mind the woman who said to her recently retired and restless husband, "I married you for better or for worse, but not for lunch. Now, get out of the house!" My mother-in-law made her retiring husband sign a "preretirement agreement"—sort of a "prenuptial meets retirement." What was her take on the situation? "I've been the CEO of this home for more than 35 years. I don't need any help now organizing the closets."

I've created an exercise called "the ideal week in retirement," designed to help financial advisers assist retirees in figuring out what they will do with their time—a reliable indicator of what they will do with their money. It's common for the client to say, "I'm going to play golf every day." OK, then tell the client to fill in his tee times. Now, what is he going to do the rest of the time? *That* is retirement planning.

The idea that retirement is simply an economic cliff for which we must have a parachute ready at age 62 has been the primary motivational message the financial-planning industry has offered for the last 40 years. The problem is that *many people are preparing a golden nest egg that will be placed in a dying tree.* The nest egg is their retirement savings and the dying tree is their retirement life. Retirement is a life event, not an economic event. The time has come to cease treating retirement exclusively as an

FIGURE **4.1** *The Ideal Week in Retirement*

Spending Your Time

	Morning	Afternoon	Evening
Sunday			
Monday			
Tuesday			
Wednesday			
Thursday			
Friday			
Saturday			

"Your most valuable asset is time, not money. A rich life is about spending that time well."
—**Mitch Anthony**

Source: © 2001 Mitch Anthony

economic event. We need to develop a more holistic approach that integrates an individual's aspirations, life stage, familial responsibilities, health issues, and concerns about money.

In the wheel of life, money is but one spoke. It's not the wheel and it's not the hub. People today want to talk to advisers who can engage in dialogues beyond, "How much do you have, and how much will you need?"

Myth No. 5: A Life of Ease Is the Ultimate Retirement Goal

William Shakespeare once said, *"If all I have is holiday and sport, then soon my holiday and sport become toil."* Once again, the bard's wisdom stands the test of time. According to modern research, a life of total ease is one step from a life of *dis*ease. The reason so many retirees are ill at ease is because without the contrast and paradox of meaningful labor and pursuits, leisure loses its meaning. As one recent retiree at the golf course informed me, "Without work, golf has become my work. I get a triple bogey on the first hole and it ruins my day." First you become bored and then you become boring. Fishing and golfing may be great fun, but recreation makes a poor full-time occupation for 25 years.

The New Retirementality debunks the myth of fulfilling full-time leisure as pictured in the retirement brochures. Many of us find meaning and purpose in our work and a needed catharsis in our leisure. It's difficult to enjoy the one without the other. The combination is a necessary paradox in our lives. Not surprising, then, that more than one-third of male retirees go back to some form of work within one year of retirement, and more than two-thirds take full-time jobs.

The age-worn and outdated model of life is based on bingeing. We binge on education in the first phase of life until many of us are so tired of learning that we replace it with entertainment. We binge on work in the second phase of life until we never want to work again and then try to fill the void that's left in the final phase of life by bingeing on leisure in retirement. Then we find that the leisure binge leaves us unsatisfied and unsettled.

A more enlightened approach to life seeks to integrate a balance of learning, work, and leisure into our everyday living instead of forsaking one binge for another. Isn't it time to start designing our lives along these lines? Many retirees are doing just that as university towns become popular destinations for the 60-plus crowd. The majority of retirees are discovering the ameliorating aspects of work (paid and unpaid), such as adding social value and challenging their intellectual faculties.

Myth No. 6: I Can Do My Own Retirement Planning

The proliferation of the self-directed 401(k) and the advent of online trading have led many people to believe that they don't need any help in planning their financial future. The market correction did much to dispel this myth, but there is still work to be done. Going this alone is akin to saying, "Because I can buy my own vitamins and pills, I don't need a doctor." Would-be financial healers must ask themselves some tough questions: Am I buying the right vitamins and pills for my particular situation? When is the last time I had a checkup? Or would I rather not have one and pretend instead I'm not at risk?

When it comes to dealing with the health of our wealth, many people fall into easy denial. The self-care phenomenon in health care is a good thing—as long as we do not begin believing that we know all there is to know about doctoring. Just as there is a time and a place for a health expert, there is also a time and a place in our lives for a wealth expert, adviser, or money coach. The time has come for financial professionals to feel the pulse of this generation and radically overhaul their retirement discussions with clients.

THE FINANCIAL PLANNER who is in touch with changing ideas about retirement can begin to take a new tack by initiating a discussion that's no longer based on rusted-out, industrial-age ideals. The most important facet in the retirement discussion today is what it will take to make each individual feel fulfilled and useful.

We're facing a radically different world in which being retired means anything but being "out of it." The time has come for financial professionals to begin a new retirement dialogue—one that doesn't begin and end with the kind of assets a client needs for retirement but instead focuses on the kind of life the client wants. The old discussion around retirement was about dying rich—the new discussion is about living rich. For some 70-something clients, living rich means that the telephone is still ringing.

Chapter Notes

1. Stephen Kindel and Raymond Goydon, *The Reggies Are Coming* (Fourth Wall, 2000).

PART TWO

ASSESSING THE RISKS

The changing retirement perspective requires us to address the inherent risks, reevaluating our current skills and tools, as well as client needs, circumstances, and psychology, so that we can be more effective in our planning. These chapters review the approaches to retirement-income analysis, including Monte Carlo, stochastic modeling and discuss the psychological barriers to facing the issues that must be addressed in the planning process. Creative challenges to old and new ways of analyzing client risks abound here.

Mathew Greenwald

Matt integrates his academic background, extensive involvement in research, and practical experience to bring to the reader clear, concise concepts on difficult psychological issues immediately applicable to daily practice. Drawing from Peter Bernstein's *Against the Gods: The Remarkable Story of Risk,* Pascal's wager, and "central tendency" theory, for example, Matt relates the lessons to retirement planning and the necessity to consider not only the likelihood of living well past normal life expectancy or experiencing high inflation or a market downturn but also the consequences of each. As with many of the chapters in this volume, his advice confirms the guidance of other contributors—for example, MacGregor and Curtis on stress testing, Milevsky and Saltzman on the misperception of mortality, and Chen on longevity risk.

Jim C. Otar

Today, our professional literature focuses on what is generally considered the two anchors to good planning—technical (for example, MPT, Monte Carlo analysis) and psychological (for example, behavioral, life planning). Unfortunately, as Jim points out, although we know the important role luck plays in retirement planning, we avoid talking about it because we don't know how to deal with it. In this thought-provoking chapter, Jim fills our educational void. Presenting a form of attribution analysis, he demonstrates that the influence of asset allocation, asset selection, and management costs often pales in comparison to the influence of luck. He expands this insight by bifurcating the impact of luck across portfolios subject to varying withdrawal rates. Jim is an active practitioner, and he does not simply leave us with food for thought. He continues with a discussion of distribution strategies and the relationship between individual and pooled distribution strategies, concluding—as do several other contributors—that immediate annuities will play an important role in managing retirement portfolios. Jim concludes with a simple but elegant analytical process for calculating the minimum amount of annuity required to eliminate the probability of premature portfolio depletion.

Cynthia Saltzman

True to her academic roots—she is a professor of economics at Widener University—Cynthia has, not surprisingly, packed her chapter full of formulae and tables, but don't let the academic rigor deter you. There is a plethora of items immediately applicable to a practitioner's daily job. For example, theory may suggest that someone with his head in the fridge and his rear in the oven may, on average, be comfortable, but Cynthia reminds us that although life expectancy for a 65-year-old man is about 16½ years, as planners, we need to consider that approximately 15 percent of this group will reach age 90. Recognizing that when evaluating longevity risk, the number of years in retirement cannot be known with certainty, she guides the reader in a discussion of how to model mortality probabilities into the analysis. In this manner, the financial planner can present an assessment of the risk associated with a particular distribution plan, at a defined point in time, for a specific individual with a given degree of risk aversion.

Robert D. Curtis

Full disclosure: Not only have we served as consultants for Bob's company, PIE Technologies, for almost a decade, but he and his partner, Karla Curtis, have become close friends. We know him well and, as a result, have had ample opportunity to conclude that he's one of the most thoughtful, knowledgeable, and creative professionals in the financial-planning software industry. Bob's chapter takes on the almost mystically revered tool, "Monte Carlo." It's not that he doesn't believe in the technology (he does; it's incorporated in his software, MoneyGuidePro). He simply cautions that the situation is never as simple as the software might make it look or as the software designer would like it to be. Good software can make it easier to do complex things, but it can't magically transform the complex into the simple. Within these limitations, Bob discusses both the pros and cons of Monte Carlo analysis and helps advisers properly frame its use in practice. In what is good news to those of us who believe our personal value transcends technology, he concludes that "financial-planning programs, with tools like stress testing and Monte Carlo, can help you accomplish this task, but none can replace your own informed judgment. And when it comes to illustrating important concepts to clients, understandable trumps sophisticated every time."

April K. Caudill

When April agreed to participate in this project, she asked to take on the subject of required minimum distributions. Given that the Internal Revenue Service can generally determine—as a result of today's reporting requirements—whether a taxpayer should be reporting a minimum distribution and that the penalty for noncompliance is 50 percent of the amount that should have been taken, the importance of the subject needs no emphasis. Still, we know it's a difficult topic. Many practitioners consider the subject unrelievably boring, some too complex, and others too obvious (they already know all that stuff). Undaunted, April has delivered a chapter that will be invaluable to anyone providing advice for clients facing RMDs. Chockful of practical and pertinent advice including issues related to qualified domestic relations orders (QDROs) and multiple and inherited IRAs, it's a chapter that can teach you a great deal—and your clients will be better served as a result.

CHAPTER 5

Psychological Impediments to Retirement-Income Planning

MATHEW GREENWALD

Many people, especially the affluent, start to look forward to the rewards of retirement as they reach their 50s and 60s. A relatively small proportion of affluent people want to work as long as possible. Those who plan to work well into old age do not have to save as much for retirement because the number of years they'll rely solely on their savings and investments for support will be relatively few, even if they live to a very old age. But the overwhelming majority of affluent people who want to retire by their mid-60s, with generally plenty of life expectancy left, will, in most cases, place quite a strain on their retirement savings. Their accumulations will often have to last—and be subject to inflation—for a long time.

I've conducted a great number of extensive interviews with affluent retirees and preretirees. The retirement most of them seek is very expensive. They want to maintain or even enhance the comfortable lifestyle they enjoyed before retirement. Enhancements include extensive travel, second homes, gifts to children, and expensive interests and hobbies. One retired person put it this way, "When I was working, I could not spend that much money; I was trapped in my office all day. Now that I'm retired, I have plenty of time to spend money." Of course, most affluent people want to take no risk of ending their lives in deprivation. And they want to avoid going into a nursing home if they need assistance, preferring to get personal care at home, which can be very expensive.

The affluent tend to live longer than average and will therefore have a longer retirement period. Given the high hopes and dreams this group has for its retirement, it's interesting that so many of its members have not thought through how much money they need to accumulate for retirement, or what their asset allocation should be after they retire. There's little danger that the affluent will not have enough assets for basic survival during the retirement period, because almost by definition they will. Even so, many have not accumulated enough to meet the lifestyle objectives they consider important.

The experience a wealthy banker shared with me illustrates this well. In 2001, I met with a senior officer of a major bank, who was obviously well compensated. He told me about a conversation he had with his wife the night before. She told him she was tired of losing money in the stock market and had decided to stop contributing to her 403(b) plan. (This was during a long bear market.) The banker noted that they had retirement savings of $1 million, and the wife told him that $1 million seemed enough to her. The banker suggested that once they retired, they could live on 6 percent of their assets the first year and maintain that level of purchasing power throughout their retirement. (Many financial planners believe that a 6 percent withdrawal rate, adjusted for inflation, is overly risky.) One million dollars of accumulation, the banker said, would allow them to live on $60,000 dollars a year of purchasing power, plus Social Security benefits. The wife expressed grave disappointment with that amount, so the banker suggested an accumulation target of $2 million. Again, the wife expressed displeasure with a lifestyle of $120,000 a year plus Social Security. The banker and his wife decided that evening to set a new accumulation target of $3 million by retirement. But, remember, the wife was initially satisfied with $1 million. Both the banker and his wife are very healthy and, if each retains that level of health to age 65, there is a 25 percent chance that one of them will live to age 97. The banker is planning on a lifestyle that costs $180,000 a year in current dollars and that will go up with inflation. His accumulation plan bears a significant risk of not being able to maintain the lifestyle that he and his wife want.

Of course, the banker and his wife are not alone in not thinking through issues of retirement financing and in not establishing a goal for accumulation that fits the lifestyle they want. Nor are they alone in their failure to understand the realities of managing money over the course of a retirement likely to last 25 to 40 years. A number of surveys that Mathew Greenwald & Associates has worked on—including the *Retirement Confidence Survey* done with the Employee Benefit Research Institute, the OppenheimerFunds' *Investing for Retirement Survey*, and MetLife's *Retirement Income Decision Survey*—reveal that strong majorities of the affluent do not (1) formulate goals for the level of assets they need by the time they retire, (2) change their asset allocation when they retire to meet their new needs and situation, (3) understand how much income can safely be derived from specific levels of assets, (4) spend a sufficient amount of time planning so they can make their assets last to the end of their lives.

Considering the goals people have for retirement, the extent to which they look forward to it, the relative ease of setting up reasonable accumulation goals and reasonable distribution strategies, why do so many people do such a poor job of planning? This is an important question because financial advisers require an understanding of the obstacles to proper retirement-income planning if they wish to help their clients establish effective accumulation goals and retirement-management plans. My firm's research has uncovered psychological impediments to proper planning for the management of assets and spending in retirement, fallacious thinking about financial management in retirement, and misperceptions about the realities of retirement living. To the extent that financial advisers can anticipate and address these problems, they will be more effective in helping their clients design financial plans with the greatest likelihood of meeting their financial goals.

The Risks of Retirement

Although the affluent most often state that they want to take zero risk of ending their lives in deprivation, most retirees expose themselves to very high levels of risk. Indeed, it's interesting to compare the degree to which people protect themselves against risk while they're working and then self-insure against risk when they're retired and much less able to cope with an adverse event.

During their working years, most affluent people

❑ buy life insurance to protect themselves financially against the uncertain timing of death

❑ acquire disability insurance to protect themselves financially against the risk of becoming disabled

❑ have the option to stay invested and wait out a bear market and protect themselves against market volatility

❑ are protected against inflation by the tendency of employers to grant larger raises during times of inflation to protect their employees' purchasing power

❑ have employer-provided health insurance to protect against major health care costs

After retiring, most affluent people

❑ do not protect themselves financially against the uncertain timing of death by buying a life annuity (for retirees, the key financial risk is not premature death but living beyond normal life expectancy)

❑ do not protect themselves financially against the risk of disability by buying long-term care insurance

❑ cannot wait out a bear market and do not protect themselves against market volatility by buying principal-protected products

❑ are not protected against inflation

❑ are more exposed to health care costs than those covered by employer-based plans

Thus, many affluent retired people are highly exposed to finance-related risks that can cause them major financial loss and lifestyle declines. But why do so many affluent people subject themselves at retirement to risks that they can clearly protect themselves against, and why do they self-insure at a point—retirement—at which they are least able to withstand an adverse situation? The main reason appears to be a willingness to risk falling into financial insecurity in old age (age 85 and over) and a related view that financial resources are less important at that time. Another factor is loss aversion. Behavioral economists have found that people fear losing more than they enjoy winning. Protecting against the risks inherent in old age leads to the risk of losing. One could buy long-term care insurance and not need nursing care, therefore losing the "bet" with the insurance company. One could buy a life annuity and not outlive life expectancy.

But the reality is that having financial resources in advanced old age can be of critical importance. Financial advisers seeking to help their clients develop effective plans should understand why many people cannot and do not prepare properly for financial security for their later years, because this understanding is a useful first step to helping these clients devise effective strategies to maintain the financial security they really do need.

Failing to Plan Effectively for Old Age

Extensive research conducted by Mathew Greenwald & Associates has found a number of reasons why so many people do not plan effectively to maintain their financial security for old age. Perhaps the most difficult to address are the psychological impediments to thinking clearly about financial security in old age. About half of the population lives past life expectancy, by definition, because life expectancy is an average. People retiring at age 65 can expect to live into their early 80s. If a man is healthy at age 65, he has a 25 percent chance of living past age 92; a healthy 65-year-old woman has a 25 percent chance of living past 94. Is it reasonable for people to plan for the possibility to live into the 75th percentile? It may seem so. But a 65-year-old man looking 27 years into the future knows there is a good possibility he will be dead in 27 years, or he may be infirm and unable to enjoy any lifestyle. It's unclear what the dollar will be worth in 27 years, and this uncertainty causes anxiety in many—and denial. These uncertainties prevent many from thinking clearly about their financial needs in old age.

The Central Tendency

Related to this problem is the difficulty people have in computing the mathematics of deferring immediate gratification for a possible benefit a quarter century or more from now. How much should one receive in 27 years for investing $1,000 now? It's hard for most to know what is a good deal and what is a poor deal.

Because of the uncertainties of reaching and being able to enjoy old age, many put a premium on the early years of retirement. They prefer to spend at a stage when they're more likely to be alive and able to enjoy their assets. Many are able to defer gratification enough while working to accumulate a large amount of money for retirement. But when they reach retirement age, they begin to place a strong premium on the here and now. This does not mean that retired people are unconcerned about their future; nor does it mean they're not concerned about running out of money. There is certainly a fear about outliving financial resources. The degree of concern, however, is insufficient to allow retirees to focus on the issue and come up with the most effective financial plan for guaranteeing a sufficient flow of income no matter how long they live.

Related to this problem is a tendency for people to plan for the average, also referred to as the "central tendency." For example, people will expect their investments to return 6 percent or 7 percent each year, if that is the average return for that type of investment. Although 6–7 percent may be the average, returns that similar never occur year after year. And sequence matters. If the market goes down by 25 percent in the first year of retirement, it can make a tremendous difference, even in a portfolio whose returns wind up averaging 6–7 percent. The average life expectancy for a 65-year-old man may be age 83, but only about 4 percent of 65-year-old men actually die at age 83.

Peter Bernstein, whose book *Against the Gods: The Remarkable Story of Risk* (Wiley, 1996) addresses how people learn to deal with risk, relates the 16th-century French mathematician Pascal's analysis of dealing with risk. Pascal wrote about how a man might live his life if he imagined that a coin would be flipped at the end of life to determine whether or not God existed: in other words, a 50-50 chance of Judgment Day. A man could live his life as if there is a God and choose not to sin if given the opportunity. If at death the coin is flipped and it turns out there is no God, one might say that the man who forswore the pleasures of sin made a mistake. He would have passed up an opportunity that would have had no negative repercussions. However, the mistake would not be a major one because a life without sin can be good and meaningful.

One could also choose to live life as if there is no God, in which case a person presented with an opportunity to sin might do so. But at the end of life, Pascal wrote, if there is a God, the sinner would spend eternity in damnation: the price was high.

Pascal's point was that the consequences of a choice are as important, or even more important, as the odds of something happening. If the odds of the existence of God are 50 percent, or even 10 percent, one must still weigh the consequences of not following God's law.

Applying this logic to retirement, it may be useful for people to consider not only the chances—however slim—of reaching age 92 or 95, but also the consequences of reaching that age without sufficient financial resources. If the consequences of needing to ask children for money, for example, are considered severe, then these consequences must be considered as well as the likelihood of reaching age 92. It's worthwhile, therefore, for retirees to consider not only the likelihood of living well past normal life expectancy or experiencing high inflation or a market downturn but also the consequences of each.

Misperceptions

Research by Mathew Greenwald & Associates has revealed three common misperceptions pertaining to retirement. First, people tend to underestimate their life expectancy. The reason for this is systematic. Although many people base their assumptions about life expectancy on family history, which is an effective method, they tend to overlook continued advances in medical treatment. For example, a woman may say that she expects to live to age 80 because her grandmother lived to age 80. This is reasonable, except to the degree that the woman, who may have been born in 1955, can expect to live longer than the grandmother who may have been born in 1905.

A second common misperception is the belief that people can maintain their lifestyles by spending roughly the same amount of money each year. My company recently conducted some research for MetLife that asked retirees if they thought they could maintain their lifestyles for the rest of their lives; most said yes. Then we asked what would happen if the cost of living went up by 30 percent in the next nine years. Most respondents said that if that happened, they would have to cut back significantly on their lifestyles. However, if inflation averages just 3 percent per year, the cost of living will go up by 30 percent in nine years. Therefore, most of these people should expect some likelihood of having to cut back on their lifestyle. Most people underestimate the corrosive long-term impact of inflation. But most will be exposed to inflation for a long time while they're retired. What's more, the cost of health care, one of the key expenses for retirees, has been going up considerably faster than other costs. The extra years of life that people are enjoying are very expensive because they occur long after the point of retirement, at a time when inflation has often injured the value of the original accumulation for retirement.

The third misperception about retirement is that the need for money declines with age. Our research has found that many people say they will not mind diminished assets in older age because they will be too old to travel and will need less money. However, many people need more money when they get older for health care or because they cannot care for themselves and need assistance—whether it be an assisted living facility or other special housing or an aide to help them with some of the activities of daily living. Nursing homes, hardly inexpensive options, are an option that can be much less expensive than round-the-clock aides. But many affluent people are strongly opposed to going into a nursing home. They highly value being able to stay in their own home and community and being able to maintain the privacy and quality of care that are difficult to achieve in many nursing homes. For those in old age who need assistance—and it is likely that almost half of the population who reach age 65 will need some kind of long-term care before they die—the cost of living is very high, and having adequate financial resources to pay for quality care is extremely important for those who were affluent during most of their adulthood and accustomed to good service and care.

Helping the Next Generation to Retire

The current generation of Americans age 85 and older is in very poor financial shape. Two-thirds have nonhousing assets worth less than $100,000, not much to live on when there are often a considerable number of years to live. Clearly, the members of this generation who lived into old age were very often unable to preserve their financial assets. The next generation to retire is much more likely to reach age 85. They have much higher lifestyle needs and much higher expectations about retirement. People who've been affluent during their working years most often wish to retain their expensive lifestyles after they retire. Of the next generation to retire, those who live longer than average face real risks of having their assets fall to a level that will not support the lifestyles they desire. This includes the affluent as well as the nonaffluent. Only through careful planning can the members of the next generation to retire develop the discipline to maintain an investment portfolio that can ensure they have the assets to support their desired lifestyle through their entire lives.

Financial planners who seek to help this next generation of affluent people to retire must learn how to help them overcome the psychological impediments to planning for old age. Our research suggests that one way to accomplish this is to help people who are just beginning their retirement understand the value of having financial independence later in life. To many, old age is an undesirable time, a time of pain and decline, with little need for financial resources. It's important, from a financial-planning perspective, for people to realize the importance of having the choices, independence, and feeling of security that sufficient assets bring.

Part of developing a financial plan is to have an accurate understanding of real life expectancy and the long-term corrosive impact of inflation. Financial advisers need to communicate this information to their clients. Finally, financial advisers must teach their clients about the most effective ways to deal with risk. The tendency to plan for the average result is dangerous, and retirees need to evaluate the consequences of some outliers and protect themselves against events that are unlikely but all too possible.

CHAPTER 6

Lifelong Retirement Income
How to Quantify and Eliminate Luck

JIM C. OTAR

L uck in investing is one of the most elusive factors to quantify. On the one hand, we strive to portray our fledgling financial-planning profession as a science. We talk about "scientific" studies[1] and research that conclude that "asset allocation accounts for more than 90 percent of the variation in a portfolio's investment return." On the other hand, when I open new accounts for clients, their parting words at the end of the meeting are invariably, "I hope we get lucky and our retirement savings last for as long as we both live!"

Most of us know the important role luck plays in retirement planning. We avoid talking about it because we don't know how to deal with it. After all, how can we gain the respect of our clients if we use terms like "luck" or "kismet" to describe their financial future?

In this chapter, we'll look at luck and all its aspects and how it plays havoc with retirement plans. We'll expose some of the misconceptions in retirement planning and present crystal-clear solutions for planning lifetime income. But first we must define and quantify luck's contribution to planning.

A Balancing Act: Assets and Cash Flow

The mathematics of retirement is simply a matter of balancing retirement assets and retirement cash flow. Think of it as Hoover Dam, holding huge quantities of water (retirement assets) and releasing some of it as needed (cash flow). First, we need to figure out what affects the water level behind the dam. Next, we need to consider what affects the water flow through the dam. Although the two issues are distinct, they are correlated: an unusually hot summer reduces the water level and concurrently increases the demand for water flow. Similar correlations exist in the dynamics of retirement portfolios.

Assets

Several factors influence the future value of a retirement portfolio. Markets are made up of waves of four sizes. They are

- ❑ secular trends
- ❑ cyclical trends
- ❑ seasonality
- ❑ random fluctuations

Secular trends. Secular trends are long-term market trends that can last as long as 20 years. They exert the greatest influence on market behavior. **FIGURE 6.1** depicts the secular equity market trends since 1900. Historically, secular sideways trends lasted between 12 and 20 years. Secular bull trends lasted between 8 and 18 years. Except for the 1929–1933 secular bear market, each secular bull trend was followed by a secular sideways trend.

Cyclical trends. These trends are the determinants of the secular trends (see **FIGURE 6.2**). They reflect economic activities that move in

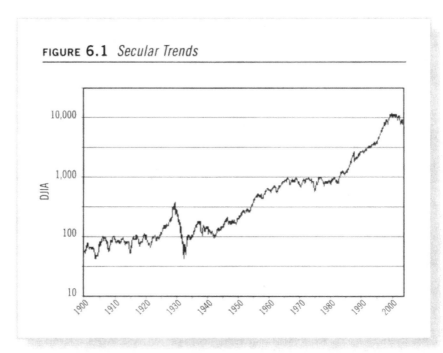

FIGURE **6.1** *Secular Trends*

Source: Dow Jones & Company

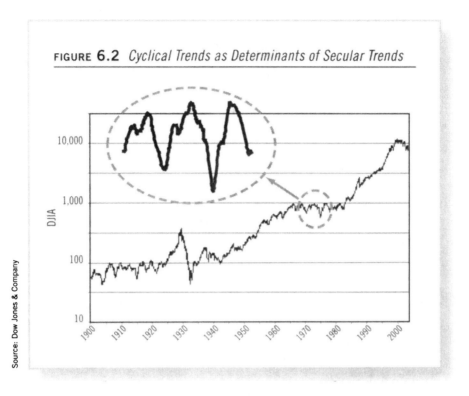

FIGURE **6.2** *Cyclical Trends as Determinants of Secular Trends*

Source: Dow Jones & Company

cycles.[2] The expectation of the onset of a new phase in an economic cycle triggers trends in bond markets, equity markets, inflation, interest rates, and commodity prices.

If peaks of the current cycles are higher than the peaks of the previous cycles, they form a secular bull trend (1921–1929, 1949–1965, 1982–1999). If they are about the same as the previous cycle, they form a secular sideways trend (1900–1921, 1936–1948, 1966–1982). If the troughs of the current cycles are lower than the troughs of the previous cycle, they create a secular bear trend (1929–1932). One of the most commonly known cyclical trends is the presidential election cycle.

Seasonal cycles. These recurring market movements, having a duration of one year, have no long-term influence on portfolio longevity. However, the strongest three months of the year for stocks are November, December, and January.[3] Accordingly, if you're withdrawing income annually, the best time to do so might be at the end of January, after the seasonal rise. Also, if you're withdrawing income monthly and you want to take advantage of the day-of-the-month effect[4] you might want to do so early in the month when, statistically, markets are slightly higher.

Random fluctuations. In addition to their secular, cyclical, and seasonal trends, markets fluctuate randomly. My analysis based on market history indicates that portfolio longevity varies no more than 9 percent as a result of random fluctuations. The advisory business pays excessive attention to the randomness of markets. Secular or cyclical trends, investment strategies, portfolio- and risk-management strategies, and management costs each have far more influence on the longevity of a retirement portfolio than do random fluctuations.

Cash Flow

Inflation compels a retiree to withdraw higher and higher amounts from his portfolio.[5] Over time, inflation reduces a portfolio's lifespan in two ways. Initially, it necessitates that more and more be withdrawn from investments to meet increasing expenses. To fight inflation, central banks occasionally increase short-term interest rates. The increase ultimately pushes down the share prices, which in turn reduces the value of your equity investments, at least temporarily. The net effect is that the investor ends up withdrawing increasingly larger amounts from his investments and must do so from a shrinking asset base.

The common wisdom is that stocks provide an inflation hedge. That is correct for long-term accumulation portfolios, but it's not true for distribution portfolios. **FIGURE 6.3** depicts the average market growth and inflation in each type of secular trend during the last century.[6]

In secular bull trends, the average annual inflation rate was 1.8 percent. The average annual growth rate of equities was 14.3 percent, which handily beats the inflation. In secular sideways trends, the average annual inflation rate was 5.2 percent, much higher than in secular bull trends. The average annual growth in equities was only 3.2 percent, which was far short of inflation.

FIGURE **6.3** *Inflation in Secular Trends —1900 to 2000*

TREND	AVERAGE ANNUAL DJIA GROWTH RATE (%)	AVERAGE ANNUAL INFLATION RATE (%)	AVERAGE LENGTH (YEARS)
Secular sideways	3.2	5.2	16
Secular bull	14.3	1.8	14
Secular bear	−31.7	−6.3	3
All markets since 1900	7.2	3.3	

Consider a retiree with an asset mix of 60 percent fixed income/40 percent equity, a 6 percent initial withdrawal rate, and a 2 percent dividend yield, retiring at the beginning of the market crash of 1929. His portfolio would have lasted 19.7 years. If he had retired in 1966, the beginning of a secular sideways market, his portfolio would have lasted only 16.7 years. Surprised? Here's the reason for the difference: the high inflation rate (6.9 percent) between 1966 and 1982 would have forced the retiree to withdraw more and more income, eventually depleting his portfolio. Its effect was worse than the 1929–1932 market crash. Do not fall for the common wisdom's faulty logic; equities *do not* necessarily provide an inflation hedge in a *distribution* portfolio.

Secular Trends and the Luck Factor

The secular trends create the "luck factor," which is a consequence of the time of entry into the retirement portfolio: if you're lucky, the start of your retirement coincides with the start of a secular bull market. Here is an example that shows why: Sam, 65, is retiring this year. His retirement savings are $500,000. He needs to withdraw $30,000 annually until age 90, indexed to inflation. He holds in his portfolio 60 percent fixed-income securities and 40 percent equities. His equities perform the same as the Dow Jones Industrial Average (DJIA). His fixed-income investment is a bond

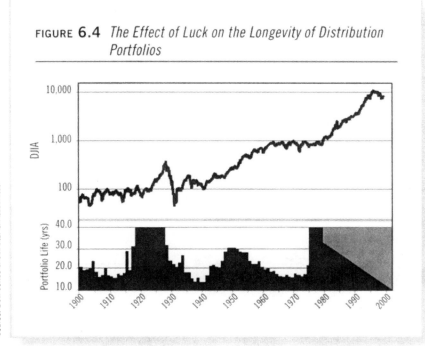

FIGURE **6.4** *The Effect of Luck on the Longevity of Distribution Portfolios*

Source: Dow Jones & Co./Otar & Associates

ladder with an average maturity of five to seven years.[7] Using the historical data, I can calculate his portfolio's life span based on Sam's having retired in any of the years since 1900. **FIGURE 6.4** depicts the outcomes.

The upper part of the graph shows the value of the DJIA over time. The lower part of the chart shows the portfolio's longevity, depending on the year Sam retired. If Sam draws down his portfolio as in the example above—withdrawing $30,000 indexed to actual inflation until age 90—in 66 percent of the cases, he will have run out of money by age 90.

Each of the starting portfolios had the same asset allocation, the same asset selection, and the same management costs. The only variable was the timing of Sam's retirement: if Sam was lucky enough to retire during the early years of any secular bull market, his portfolio would likely have been successful. If he retired at any other time, he would likely run out of money no matter what he did with his asset allocation. This is the luck factor.

Asset Allocation

Asset allocation has much less influence on distribution portfolios than on accumulation portfolios. **FIGURE 6.5** depicts the probability of depletion (the vertical scale) by the 25th year for different asset mixes (the horizontal scale). At lower initial withdrawal rates,[8] typically 4 percent or less, the right asset allocation significantly reduces the probability of depletion from near 50 percent to near 0 percent. But once the initial withdrawal rate reaches 6 percent, asset allocation has hardly any effect in reducing the probability of depletion.

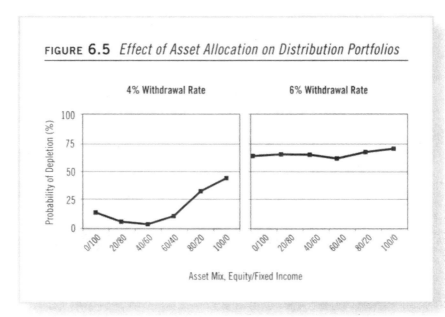

FIGURE **6.5** *Effect of Asset Allocation on Distribution Portfolios*

4% Withdrawal Rate

6% Withdrawal Rate

Probability of Depletion (%)

100

75

50

25

0

0/100 20/80 40/60 60/40 80/20 100/0   0/100 20/80 40/60 60/40 80/20 100/0

Asset Mix, Equity/Fixed Income

Source: Otar & Associates

Client risk-assessment questionnaires do fulfill regulatory require-ments and are used to establish asset allocations by formula. In reality, however, these asset-allocation decisions have negligible benefit, especially if the client's withdrawal rate is more than 4 percent.

Let's return to Sam as an example. Suppose Sam makes the wrong asset-allocation decision. Instead of the optimum asset mix, he invests all his money in equities. Using the same 6 percent withdrawal rate as before, what is the probability that he will run out of money by age 90? My calculation shows that the likelihood increases from 66 percent to 72 percent. This bad decision costs Sam an additional 6 percent in the probability of depletion. This illustrates that the contribution of luck (66 percent) is 11 times that of asset allocation (6 percent).

Asset Selection

Suppose that instead of a "buy-and-forget" strategy, Sam follows his in-vestments closely, with a disciplined system. He keeps only the best-per-forming equity funds in his portfolio. As a result, the equity side of his portfolio outperforms the DJIA by 4 percent each year.

The probability that Sam will run out of money by age 90 is reduced to 35 percent. His disciplined asset-selection system creates a 31 percent dif-ference in the probability of his portfolio's failure, calculated as 66 percent minus 35 percent. At 31 percent, asset selection as a contributing factor is about five times that of asset allocation (6 percent).

I'm not suggesting that one can necessarily outperform the index by 4 percent merely by paying more attention through skillful asset selection. I used 4 percent only as a possible upper limit for calculation purposes.

Management Cost

Over the long term, the cost of portfolio management erodes some of the portfolio growth. Let's assume that Sam's equity mutual funds underperform the index by 2 percent because of management expenses. In that case, the probability of running out of money by age 90 is 77 percent. The con-tribution of the cost factor is 11 percent, calculated as 77 percent minus 66 percent. That's about twice that of the asset-allocation factor.

The Successful Distribution Portfolio

How do we define success for a distribution portfolio? That depends on the withdrawal rate. If the actual withdrawal rate is larger than the sus-tainable withdrawal rate, the portfolio may run out of money during the investor's lifetime. In such cases, the prime objective of retirement plan-ning is to minimize the probability of depletion. Therefore, we define ccess as maximizing the portfolio's *probability of survival* when withdrawals are larger than the sustainable withdrawal rate.

On the other hand, when the actual withdrawal rate is less than the sustainable withdrawal rate, then, by definition, all portfolios will survive. In such cases, maximizing portfolio growth becomes the prime objective, and success is defined as achieving the maximum *growth rate.* **FIGURE 6.6** shows the contribution of each factor to the success of a distribution portfolio for different withdrawal rates during a 25-year time horizon.

The data in Figure 6.6 lead to some interesting observations.

Luck. The contribution of luck is lowest near the sustainable withdrawal rate. Once the withdrawal rate is greater than the sustainable withdrawal rate (near 4 percent for a 25-year time horizon), the luck factor increases substantially until it reaches 100 percent at the 12 percent withdrawal rate.

Asset selection. The contribution of asset selection is steady up to 6 percent withdrawal rate. After that, the higher the withdrawal rate, the less significant is the asset-selection factor.

Asset allocation. The contribution of asset allocation to the success of a portfolio peaks near the sustainable withdrawal rate. After that, the difference it makes declines sharply.

Management costs. The longer the portfolio survives, the larger the cumulative management costs over the life of the portfolio will be. Therefore, as the withdrawal rate exceeds the sustainable withdrawal rate, its contribution to the portfolio's success declines.

FIGURE **6.6** *Determinants of Success for Distribution Portfolios at Year 25*

	WITHDRAWAL RATE						
	0%	2%	4%	6%	8%	10%	12%
Contribution of Each Factor to the Success of a Retirement Portfolio							
Luck	40%	31%	19%	58%	78%	96%	100%
Asset Selection	21	19	23	27	14	4	0
Asset Allocation	22	32	38	5	4	0	0
Management Costs	17	18	20	10	4	0	0

Source: Otar & Associates

Cyclical Trends

Reverse Dollar-Cost Averaging

The most significant damage cyclical trends do to portfolios is the reverse dollar-cost averaging (RDCA). Keep in mind that this happens if, and only if, regular periodic income is taken out of a portfolio, as is the case in a distribution portfolio. During a bear market, more shares must be sold to maintain the same income stream. Once they're sold, even though markets may recover, the loss is permanent. In extreme cases, RDCA can cut the life of a portfolio in half.

Let's look at an extreme case: Say you retire at the beginning of 1929 and your initial withdrawal rate is 6 percent. You have a choice to allocate your money (a) 100 percent to equities or (b) to a balanced portfolio of 60 percent fixed-income investments and 40 percent equities. Figure 6.6 tells us that at a 6 percent withdrawal rate, asset allocation contributes only 5 percent to your portfolio's success. Because all other variables (luck, asset selection, management costs) are identical for this example, RDCA is the only remaining contributor to the portfolio's success or failure.

If you choose to invest all your money in equities, your portfolio runs out of money in about nine years. If you choose the balanced portfolio, your portfolio lasts about 18 years, or twice as long. Although this 1929 example is the most extreme one since 1900, it highlights the potential impact of RDCA. Asset allocation may have a small impact on portfolio longevity when viewed from the perspective of *secular* markets, but it has a greater influence in *cyclical* trends.

The following steps will minimize the adverse effect of RDCA:

❑ Use a balanced portfolio. Avoid periodic withdrawals from the fluctuating part of your investments. Withdraw only from the cash balance or money market funds.

❑ Avoid frequent rebalancing, which can cause significant damage to your portfolio. For withdrawal rates less than 6 percent, it's generally better to rebalance every four years at the end of the presidential election year. Furthermore, rebalance only if the equity percentage deviates by more than 2 percent.

Optimum Asset Allocation

The diagram in **FIGURE 6.7** identifies the optimum asset mix of equity and fixed-income investments for distribution portfolios. I developed it by maximizing the success of the distribution portfolio for each withdrawal rate at different relative equity returns, that is, maximizing the probability of survival if withdrawals are larger than the sustainable withdrawal rate or

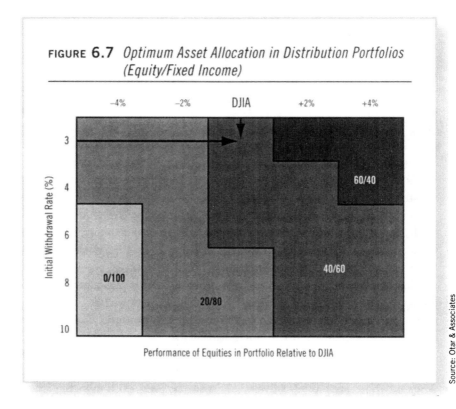

FIGURE **6.7** *Optimum Asset Allocation in Distribution Portfolios (Equity/Fixed Income)*

Source: Otar & Associates

maximizing portfolio growth if withdrawals are less than the sustainable withdrawal rate. If you use this methodology as a guide in asset allocation, you'll minimize the effects of RDCA.

The vertical scale in Figure 6.7 indicates the initial withdrawal rate. The horizontal scale indicates the performance of equities in the portfolio relative to the DJIA. The box in which the two values intersect identifies the correct asset mix. For example, if the initial withdrawal rate is 3 percent and the equities in your portfolio perform the same as the DJIA, then the optimum asset mix is 40 percent equity and 60 percent fixed income as indicated by the arrows.

Sustainable Withdrawal Rates

The sustainable withdrawal rate (SWR) is the maximum amount of money you can periodically withdraw from a distribution portfolio with no probability of depletion during your lifetime. The rate is expressed as a percentage of the total initial savings available at the start of retirement. For example, if you have $1 million at the beginning of your retirement and your SWR is 4 percent, then the most you can withdraw from your portfolio is $40,000 (4 percent of $1 million) during the first year of your retirement and indexed to inflation each subsequent year. Based on historical data, if you keep your withdrawals at or below the SWR, your portfolio will likely outlast you.

One of the pitfalls in current practice is overemphasizing the dividends on total return. Statements such as "Over the long term, half of total return is from dividends" have no place in distribution portfolios. There are three reasons for this:

❑ The compounding of total return takes time. If a distribution portfolio depletes in 15 years, there is no compounding because you would not only be drawing down the capital but also cashing out all the dividends. In other words, the total return becomes significant only if you are lucky and catch a secular bull market, in which case your withdrawals are likely to be less than the portfolio's growth.

❑ Dividends compound only if they are present. In many academic studies, *historical* dividends are added to index returns for estimating a *future* SWR. During the first 90 years of the past century, the average dividend yield was 4.5 percent. Since 1990, dividends have been decreasing, and they are now around 2 percent. They can go back to their historical levels only if markets lose more than half of their value while earnings remain the same, or if companies can double their dividends rapidly (or a combination of both). Until that happens, be conservative and use the prevailing dividend rates, not historical ones.

❑ If you invest in mutual funds, it's likely that the management costs will eat away most—if not all—of the dividends.

Another misconception is that it's feasible to withdraw the SWR amount *plus* the dividend. That may be the case for the average portfolios in average times. But when we talk about the SWR, we anticipate worst-case situations. At these times, the added benefit of the dividend does not stay constant. For example, if you had retired in the beginning of 1929 and received $100 per month in income from dividends, by 1932 you would have received only $30 per month because by that time stocks had lost 85 percent of their value and the dividend yield of surviving stocks had only doubled from 3.5 percent to 7 percent. The shortfall of $70 per month (subject to indexation) must come from the capital, but most of that was lost too.

FIGURES 6.8 and **6.9** show the sustainable withdrawal rates for various retirement time horizons. Use the first table (Figure 6.8) if your equities perform the same as the DJIA. If the total return of your equities outperforms the index by 2 percent, use the second table[9] (Figure 6.9).

These tables also include the optimum asset mix and the optimum rebalancing frequency information. The asset classes include Treasury

FIGURE **6.8** *Sustainable Withdrawal Rate: Equities Perform Same as DJIA*

TIME HORIZON (YEARS)	SWR (%)	OPTIMUM ASSET MIX (%)			REBALANCE
		EQUITY	BOND	TIPS	
10	9.7	15	0	85	Annually
15	6.7	15	0	85	Annually
20	5.3	20	20	60	Annually
25	4.2	30	30	40	Presidential election year
30	3.7	30	30	40	Presidential election year
35	3.4	30	25	45	Presidential election year
40	3.1	30	25	45	Presidential election year

Source: Otar & Associates

inflation-protected securities (TIPS) because they provide an excellent inflation hedge for distribution portfolios. TIPS should be considered an integral part of distribution portfolios.

Asset-Allocation Strategies

All examples given in Figures 6.8 and 6.9 are based on strategic asset allocation. Followers of this strategy decide on a suitable asset mix of different asset classes (typically equity, bonds, and cash) and maintain that asset mix over time. Strategic asset allocation is the most popular investment strategy. However, there are other strategies, including age based, tactical, and trend following.

Age-based asset allocation. In this strategy, the amount allocated to equities is based on the client's age. The model is based on the premise that as the retiree gets older, his or her portfolio should be more conservative. For example, the client might say, "In my portfolio, 105 minus my age is the percentage of equities." A client at age 85 would allocate 20 percent of the portfolio to equities (105 minus 85). The problem with this strategy

FIGURE **6.9** *Sustainable Withdrawal Rate: Equities Outperform DJIA by 2%*

TIME HORIZON (YEARS)	SWR (%)	OPTIMUM ASSET MIX (%)			REBALANCE
		EQUITY	BOND	TIPS	
10	9.8	18	0	82	Annually
15	6.8	25	20	55	Annually
20	5.5	25	30	45	Annually
25	4.6	30	30	40	Presidential election year
30	4.0	35	30	35	Presidential election year
35	3.8	35	30	35	Presidential election year
40	3.5	35	25	40	Presidential election year

is that as clients get older, more of their assets are placed in fixed income. Thus, the portfolio's ability to participate in a secular bull trend diminishes when it's needed most, in later years. In the long term, it's not a better technique than strategic asset allocation.

Tactical asset allocation. Based on the premise that the growth rate of equities eventually reverts to its historic mean, this strategy assumes that markets move at random, piggybacked onto the average historical growth rate. The portfolio starts with a base asset allocation, such as 60 percent fixed-income and 40 percent equity. At the end of the year, the portfolio is reviewed: if equity markets did well in the preceding year, fixed income is increased to, say, 75 percent to make the portfolio more defensive in the current year. If the equities lost money in the preceding year, the equity allocation is increased from 40 percent to, say, 60 percent to make the portfolio more aggressive this year. The problem with this strategy is that it ignores the existence of secular trends. In a secular bull trend, you may be sitting in a defensive position for several years and miss all that growth. This is definitely not good for client retention.

Trend-following asset allocation. Proponents of this strategy—the exact opposite of tactical asset allocation—believe that once a trend is set in motion, it will continue until it changes direction. If markets are trending up, an aggressive posture is taken, such as 70 percent equity and 30 percent fixed income. If the trend is down, a defensive posture is taken, such as 40 percent equity and 60 percent fixed income. The motto is, "The trend is your friend." The theory sounds fine, but there's a problem: an annual review of your clients' portfolios is not good enough. Trend analysis works only if you watch markets continually (weekly, for example) and with great discipline. When reviews take place annually, this strategy produces the worst results. In secular sideways trends, you lose money most of the time.

The problem with these strategies is that they're suited to smaller cycles, but they ignore the existence of secular trends. I've found that strategic asset allocation combined with optimum rebalancing is the least complicated yet the most effective technique of the four. I follow a variation of strategic asset allocation: In secular bull trends, my equity portion includes more of the passive index funds and my fixed-income portion holds more nominal bonds. In secular sideways trends, my equity portion includes actively managed funds and my fixed-income portion holds more TIPS. In either case, the equity portion of my portfolio is never more than 50 percent.

Cash Flow Strategies

The following cash flow strategies can be used in conjunction with any of the asset-allocation strategies:
- Reduce withdrawals when a portfolio does not grow.
- Link withdrawals to portfolio growth; for example, withdraw the lesser of the initial withdrawal rate (IWR) or the portfolio growth.
- Link withdrawals to portfolio value; for example, withdraw the lesser of the IWR or 5 percent of the portfolio value.
- Buy a term annuity and invest the rest.

Every so often, I come across a study that describes a novel strategy that claims, "If you do this and that, the portfolio should last you a lifetime." These strategies generally involve one or more of the asset-allocation and/ or cash flow strategies. The research underlying some of these studies uses insufficient market data covering only one secular cycle.[10] Others are too complicated to apply to client portfolios under current regulatory rules.

As intriguing as these tactics may sound, they cannot solve portfolio longevity problems without severe reduction or interruption of withdrawals. This brings us to a short explanation of pooled versus individual distribution portfolios.

Pooled Versus Individual Distribution Portfolios

The dynamics of money flow in an individual distribution portfolio are entirely different from those of a pooled portfolio. Results of studies based on pooled portfolios have little relevance to individual portfolios. Over the long term, the sustainable withdrawal rate from an individual distribution portfolio is significantly lower than the payout rate from a pooled source such as a life annuity or a sufficiently funded pension plan. There are several reasons for this:

❑ Individual distribution portfolios must include greater assets to overcome the luck factor. It's not enough to finance retirement cash flow alone; such portfolios must include additional assets to offset the luck factor. In a pooled portfolio, the luck factor is kept to a minimum.

❑ Individual distribution portfolios must be designed to last as long as the life expectancy of that individual retiree. Pooled distribution portfolios are designed for the average life expectancy of the members. A retiree

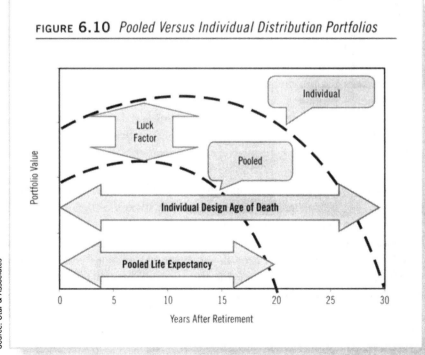

FIGURE **6.10** *Pooled Versus Individual Distribution Portfolios*

in an individual retirement plan may live 10 to 15 years longer than the average life expectancy of a pooled group. (See **FIGURE 6.10.**)

When these two factors—total assets needed and the difference in the design age of pooled and individual portfolios—are included, the asset premium required for an individual distribution portfolio compared with a pooled portfolio is 40 percent to 80 percent greater, depending on retirement age and time horizon. That's the price you pay to self-insure your portfolio. In other words, 40 percent to 80 percent more assets are needed to mitigate the effects of the luck factor and the difference in design age. Therefore, we must look for solutions not only in asset-allocation and cash flow strategies but also in transferring part of these retirement assets to pooled distribution portfolios to ensure increased payout *and* income security.

Average Growth Rate Versus Design Growth Rate

When I changed my career from engineering to financial planning, one common practice amazed me: advisers assume an average portfolio growth rate, plug that number into a retirement calculator, and call the process "designing a retirement plan." Imagine a civil engineer saying, "The average wind speed in Florida is 6 mph. Therefore, I will design this high-rise hotel for a wind load of 6 mph." That engineer would be fired on the spot for incompetence. What happens when a hurricane hits?

In the same way, we must avoid using the "average" growth rate in retirement planning. If we don't, the probability of depletion before death may exceed 50 percent.[11] This is obviously unacceptable because it jeopardizes clients' livelihoods at a time when they're most vulnerable. When I prepare a retirement plan, I consider all outcomes since 1900 and take the bottom decile for my models. I call this the *design growth rate*. The design growth rate is defined as the assumed portfolio growth rate one must use for projecting a retirement portfolio value for a 90 percent survival rate.

FIGURE 6.11 depicts the design growth rates for different asset-allocation and cash flow strategies based on market history[12] since 1900. The rates have been calculated using a 3 percent inflation rate. If you're using a standard retirement calculator, enter 3 percent for the assumed inflation rate. Then enter the design growth rate from the table as your assumed portfolio growth rate. The resulting asset projection will illustrate a 90 percent survival rate. These figures apply only to individual distribution portfolios and not to pooled portfolios. We use a different table for pooled portfolios.

FIGURE **6.11** *Design Growth Rate for Individual Distribution Portfolios*

	INITIAL WITHDRAWAL RATE			
	2%	4%	6%	8%
	DESIGN GROWTH RATE			
Strategic Asset Allocation	5.8%	5.2%	4.0%	2.4%
When combined with other cash flow strategies:				
A	5.9	5.4	4.1	3.0
B	5.9	5.6	4.3	3.4
C	7.5	8.0	8.7	10.3
D	5.9	6.1	8.1	10.6
Age-Based Asset Allocation	4.6	4.4	4.1	3.1
When combined with other cash flow strategies:				
A	4.6	4.5	4.1	3.1
B	4.7	4.6	4.3	3.8
Tactical Asset Allocation	5.5	4.9	4.2	3.5
When combined with other cash flow strategies:				
A	5.5	5.0	4.3	3.6
B	5.6	5.1	4.6	4.0
Trend Following Asset Allocation	4.8	3.1	0.9	(0.3)
When combined with other cash flow strategies:				
A	4.9	3.5	1.5	0.2
B	5.0	3.9	2.1	0.9

Cash Flow Strategies

A = 10 percent reduction in periodic withdrawals in years when the portfolio growth is negative

B = 20 percent reduction in periodic withdrawals in years when the portfolio growth is negative

C = the lesser of the initial withdrawal rate of the portfolio growth

D = the lesser of the initial withdrawal rate or 5 percent of the remaining portfolio value

Source: Otar & Associates

Ensuring Lifelong Income

Now, we can design strategies for lifelong income for *all* our clients. When we talk about managing luck, invariably we must look at insurance products. Pooling retirement capital is a very effective way of minimizing the luck factor. Life annuities[13] were originally created to meet this need. The key question is "How much life annuity is sufficient to eliminate the adverse effects of luck?" In other words, we're trying to find the perfect mix of annuities and investments to provide lifelong income. For an accurate answer, we need to ask three questions.

The first question is for the retiree: "How much money do I want each year from my portfolio?" We'll call this the required withdrawal rate (RWR). For example, if you need to withdraw $30,000 during the first year of your retirement, indexed to inflation each year thereafter, and you have $500,000 in retirement savings, your RWR is 6 percent, calculated as $30,000 divided by $500,000 expressed as a percentage.

The second question is for the market: "If I invest all this money in a properly balanced portfolio, how much can the market give me for as long as I live?" The answer, as we've already discussed, is the sustainable withdrawal rate (see page 86). Figures 6.8 and 6.9 show the sustainable withdrawal rate for various time horizons. For example, if you're retiring at age 65 and expect to live until 95, your time horizon is 30 years. If your equities perform the same as the Dow Jones, Figure 6.8 indicates the SWR as 3.7 percent. If you've saved $1 million for retirement, you can take out $37,000 at age 65 and index that amount until age 95 without running out of money, based on market history since 1900.

The third question is for the insurance company: "If I give you $100,000, how much are you willing to pay me for as long as I live?" We call this the annuity rate (AR). For example, if a $100,000 single premium buys a lifelong income of $500 each and every month (indexed to inflation annually), the AR is 6 percent, calculated as ($500 × 12) / $100,000. Look for an indexed life annuity to make sure the inflation risk is removed during retirement.

Now that we have all three numbers, we can calculate the minimum amount of annuity (MA) required to eliminate the probability of premature portfolio depletion. I developed the following formula to calculate it:

$$MA = 100 \times (RWR - SWR) / (AR - SWR)$$

Interpreting the Formula

The value of the minimum annuity can be less than zero, between 0 and 100, or larger than 100. Each of these outcomes points to a different strategy.

MA is less than zero. Congratulations! You have abundant savings. You have more than enough to finance your retirement *and* to neutralize the luck factor. With proper use, your balanced investment portfolio should give you lifelong income. If it makes you feel better, you can buy a life annuity for income security but you don't have to.

MA is between 0 and 100. Congratulations! You have sufficient savings for retirement. However, although your savings are enough to finance your retirement, they are not enough to offset the luck factor. To compensate, you need to buy some life annuity. How much? If the calculated value of MA is 35, take 35 percent of your retirement savings and use that money to purchase an indexed life annuity. Now you'll have lifelong income, some from the annuity and some from the investment portfolio.

MA is larger than 100. Regrettably, your savings are insufficient. They're not enough to finance your retirement, let alone to deflect the luck factor. Your options are working longer, spending less, or working part-time after your retirement. In any case, your only choice is to use all your savings to buy a life annuity. Regardless of how tempting it is, you have no place in the investment world, because it is highly likely that your portfolio will run out of money during your lifetime. A life annuity will provide you a lifelong income. It will likely be less than what you want, but you'll just have to make do.

By following these guidelines, you'll be bulletproofing your practice as an adviser, because your clients will have fewer reasons to complain or take legal action against you. More important, in all cases—whether your clients have abundant, sufficient, or insufficient savings—you'll be making it possible for them to achieve lifelong income.

Chapter Notes

1. Gary P. Brinson, Randolph L. Hood, and Gilbert L. Beebower, "Determinants of Portfolio Performance II," *Financial Analysts Journal* (January/February 1995).

2. National Bureau of Economic Research, "U.S. Business Cycle Expansions and Contractions," www.nber.org/cycles.html.

3. Yale Hirsch, *Stock Trader's Almanac* (Wiley, annual).

4. Research indicates that the last trading day and the first three trading days of the month have a higher return than any other days of the month. Bruce Jacobs and Kenneth Levy, "Calendar Anomalies," *MTA Journal* (Winter 1989–1990).

5. In this analysis, we exclude cash flows that are not related to inflation. These

should be considered in the cash flow analysis during the interview with the client on a case-by-case basis. See www.retirementoptimizer.com.

6. Because the start and the end of some secular trends are in the same year and the 1933–1936 time period does not count as a secular market (it was a cyclical bull market), the average secular market lengths will not add up to 100.

7. The bond portfolio is assumed to yield 2 percent plus the historical six-month certificate of deposit rate.

8. The initial withdrawal rate (IWR) is the periodic withdrawal amount as a percentage of the total retirement savings in the first year of retirement. Over time, the withdrawal amount will increase because of inflation. Also, the value of the retirement savings will fluctuate. However, the IWR calculated at the beginning of retirement will remain the same as long as the retiree's financial needs remain the same. When financial needs change—for reasons other than the effect of inflation—this number should be recalculated. Also, if there is a significant lump-sum deposit to or withdrawal from the portfolio, it should be recalculated.

9. You can generate your own sustainable withdrawal rate tables for different variables if you download my retirement calculator from www.retirementopti mizer.com.

10. This practice is called "data mining" in technical analysis.

11. That likelihood is because the distribution curve of the returns is skewed (lognormal). The median, where half of the portfolios deplete, is smaller than the average. This minor detail that many ignore causes most Monte Carlo simulations to yield outcomes that are too optimistic.

12. These figures are based on the optimum asset allocation of equities and fixed income. The total return of equities is assumed to be DJIA plus 2 percent.

13. Single premium immediate life annuity.

CHAPTER 7

Balancing Mortality and Modeling Risk

CYNTHIA SALTZMAN

In a 1997 paper called "Financial Planning in Fantasyland," William F. Sharpe neatly laid out the eventualities for retirement income. "Prior to retirement the account grows regularly due to new contributions and the unvarying rate of return on assets," wrote the Nobel laureate and professor of finance at Stanford University. "After retirement the account eventually begins to diminish as spending overtakes the rate of return, which remains resolutely constant. Eventually one of two things happens. Either you die (right on schedule) with money in the bank or you run out of money before you die."[1]

Sharpe was assessing the mechanics of retirement-planning software calculators. Basically, you chose an expected rate of return, an expected inflation rate, and the year you're expected to die. The calculations performed will tell you if the desired consumption stream from your nest egg can be attained. Choose the wrong numbers and you run the risk of either outliving your nest egg or leaving a large unintended bequest.

In fact, for many people, the costs of choosing wrong were relatively small before 1997. That's because the vast majority of wealth dedicated to retirement at that time was annuitized, in the form of either Social Security benefits or defined-benefit pension plans. Since distribution issues are primarily relevant to nonannuitized wealth, guessing wrong would not have had an enormous impact on the potential spending stream during retirement years for most people. For those yet to retire, however, the odds of coming up short are far greater for two reasons: (1) a trend away from defined-benefit to defined-contribution pension plans and (2) increases in longevity.

The increasing importance of nonannuitized assets in the retirement nest egg brings distribution issues to the forefront of retirement planning. This chapter reviews the degree of risk retirees with nonannuitized income now face and offers ways to calculate how long each client's retirement—and his assets—are likely to last.

Shifting the Risk

An analysis of waves 2 through 5 of the Health and Retirement Study (HRS), which examined the financial position of heads of households who had turned 65 by 2000, supports the contention that before 1997 the fraction of preannuitized wealth was small.[2] Based on the means of total wealth deciles, the study shows that annuitized wealth as a percentage of the financial and retirement wealth of married couples was more than 90 percent for the bottom four deciles, ranged from 86 percent to 75 percent for the fifth through eighth deciles, and fell to only 66 percent and 53 percent for the ninth and tenth deciles, respectively. The median 20 percent value was 86 percent for married couples and more than 90 percent for single men and women.

That said, various studies have documented a shift that began in the early 1980s from defined-benefit plans to defined-contribution plans. This is most easily seen in **FIGURE 7.1**, which looks at employees covered by pension plans and shows the proportion of them covered only by a

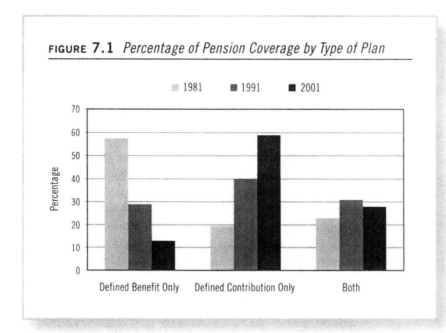

FIGURE **7.1** *Percentage of Pension Coverage by Type of Plan*

1981   1991   2001

Source: Center for Retirement Research

defined-benefit plan, only by a defined-contribution plan, or by both in the years 1981, 1991, and 2001.[3]

By the end of 2001, total assets in 401(k) and other defined-contribution plans exceeded $4 trillion. Analysts' estimates, based on contribution patterns during 2000 to 2005, project that 45-year-olds in 2005 will have an average household balance in defined-contribution plans of $103,000 (in 2000 dollars) upon reaching age 65.[4] Hence, the possibility of choosing the wrong numbers and the potential consequences of doing so can no longer be ignored in any serious discussion of the retirement-distribution process.

Mortality Trends

The period life tables constructed by the National Center for Health Statistics and the Social Security Administration indicate rising life expectancies for men and women who reach ages 65 and 75 in 2005.[5] More important, as can be seen in **FIGURE 7.2**, for men these increases appear to have accelerated at the end of the 1990s and the beginning of the 21st century. Female life expectancies, at each age, while somewhat higher, followed a similar pattern, although the gap between the sexes narrowed.

This rise in life expectancy correlates with an increase in the probability that a person who attains the age of 65 will live for another 10 years, 20 years, or more. This trend is illustrated in **FIGURE 7.3**, which plots the probability that a 65-year-old man will live for another 5 years, 10 years, 15 years, and so on. On the graph, T represents the number of years past age 65 and $_{(65+T)}P_{65}$ is the probability of a 65-year-old male reaching age 65+T. Hence, when T = 15, a male currently age 65 would then be age 80. According to Figure 7.3, the probability of a man age 65 reaching age 80 was roughly 54 percent in 2000 versus 49 percent in 1990.

Source: National Vital Statistics Reports

FIGURE **7.2** *Life Expectancy (in Years) at Ages 65 and 75: Calendar Years 1990, 1997, 2000, and 2002*

AGE	1990	1997	2000	2002	%Δ 1990–2000	%Δ 1997–2002
65	15.1	15.9	16.3	16.6	7.9	4.4
75	9.4	9.9	10.1	10.3	7.4	4.4

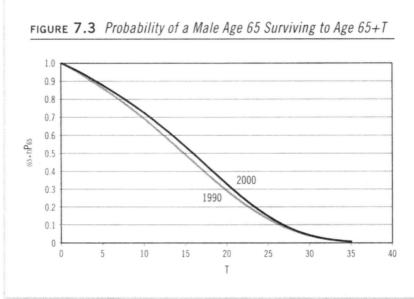

FIGURE **7.3** *Probability of a Male Age 65 Surviving to Age 65+T*

Source: Social Security Administration Actuarial Study No. 116

Based on the 2004 update to the Social Security 2000 period life tables, there was approximately a 15 percent probability that a 65-year-old man would live at least another 25 years to reach age 90, even though the life expectancy for this 65-year-old was only about 16½ years. There was also a good probability that he would die in less than 16½ years. For instance, the probability that he will die within 10 years is close to 28 percent. This randomness in the potential time span of retirement brings into focus the possibility of outliving one's nest egg. Coupling this with the increasing balances in defined-contribution plans that will be subject to longevity risk brings the issue to the forefront of the retirement-distribution process.

The Issue of Annuities

Obviously, if we can't pin down how many years retirement will continue, it's difficult to calculate a sustainable stream of withdrawals during the retirement-distribution phase. Moreover, the nest egg accumulated by the start of retirement needs to be placed in an investment portfolio, and a key variable determining the capacity of the retirement assets to support withdrawals throughout the retirement years is the return on the portfolio during those years. Of course, future investment returns are also unknown, both in nominal and real terms. Consequently, the financial planner, in developing a sustainable distribution plan, is left trying to juggle expected consumption flows and bequest desires without running out of money over the retiree's unknown remaining lifetime.

Clearly, one way to insure against longevity risk and also eliminate the need for active management of a nest egg portfolio is to take the lump sum and purchase an immediate life annuity. To date, however, the U.S. market for voluntary annuitization among retirees is relatively small. Economists have spent a lot of time trying to devise models that explain the apparent reluctance of retirees to take out longevity insurance through the purchase of annuities. One obvious answer is that annuitization limits the ability to bequeath wealth. Probably just as important is that annuitization of the retirement nest egg is irreversible. Consequently, the retiree loses liquidity and control over assets that might otherwise be available for emergencies.

Uncharted Territory: A Safe Withdrawal Rate

With so many unknown parameters attached to the potential sustainability of a withdrawal stream, there really are no rules of thumb. The best you can do is to introduce probabilities into the analysis and attempt to identify the relevant trade-offs under different scenarios. Not surprisingly, the probabilities obtained are very often affected by the way the scenarios are developed. This point was highlighted by a series of articles that began to appear in the mid-1990s.[6]

The early articles examined the appropriateness of using a constant expected rate of return applied to the nest egg portfolio to determine the sustainable withdrawal rate. The approach generally taken was to define the withdrawal rate as the percentage of the accumulated nest egg withdrawn at the beginning of the initial year of retirement; if the nest egg equaled $100,000 and the withdrawal rate was 5 percent, then $5,000 would be withdrawn initially. In subsequent years, the $5,000 would be adjusted each year for inflation. Given this value, using historical return data, calculations were performed over rolling time periods[7] to see how long the nest egg portfolio could fund the withdrawal stream. When the rolling time periods were annual and started in 1926, results indicated that a portfolio consisting of 50 percent bonds and 50 percent stocks would support a withdrawal rate of 3 percent for more than 50 years of retirement 100 percent of the time; a 4 percent withdrawal rate would support at least 35 years 100 percent of the time; and a 5 percent withdrawal rate would fail to fund at least 30 years of retirement 10 percent of the time. Altering the portfolio mix or looking at quarterly rolling time periods could lead to withdrawal rates of 5 percent funding at least 30 years of retirement up to 97 percent of the time. Discounting the years before World War II could achieve this 100 percent 30-year success period at withdrawal rates up to 7 percent.

The applicability of these findings, however, is predicated on the idea that particular sequences of historical returns will be replicated in the future without new extreme high or low values. Obviously, altering the sequence of yearly returns will change the probability of funding a desired stream of withdrawals over any given time period. To address this issue, Monte Carlo simulations, which use values for the mean and standard deviation of returns to generate tens of thousands of random sequences of returns, was introduced into the analysis.

Under the Monte Carlo approach, the sequences generated are applied to the nest egg portfolio to see how many years of retirement each sequence would support at different withdrawal rates. Generally, reported results indicate that for nest eggs dominated by stocks, withdrawal rates of approximately 4.5 percent are sustainable for up to 30 years of retirement at least 90 percent of the time. The exact sustainable withdrawal rate depends on the portfolio mix, mean value, and standard deviation used in the analysis.

Employing this analysis, someone planning a 30-year retirement would first determine the appropriate expected return and standard deviation of the proposed portfolio mix. Using these values to run simulations, the probabilities of sustaining the desired withdrawal stream over the retirement period can be calculated for different relevant withdrawal rates (see the appendix to this chapter). Choosing different values for the mean and standard deviation will change the probabilities of success for each time period; increasing the mean and lowering the standard deviation will increase the probabilities of sustaining withdrawals over all time periods.

These relationships can be seen in **FIGURE 7.4**, which starts with a mean value for the real return of a portfolio equal to 4.5 percent, standard deviation equal to 12 percent, and a 5 percent withdrawal rate.[8] The first half of the table in Figure 7.4 presents the impact of increasing the mean value by 10 percent while holding the standard deviation constant; the second half of the table holds the mean constant while increasing the standard deviation by 10 percent. One hundred thousand simulations were conducted for each pair of standard deviation and mean values. Some interesting insights can be gleaned from this table. For instance, the impact of increasing the real return is relatively constant in a given time period. During the 30-year period, increasing the mean real return by 10 percent consistently leads to a five-percentage-point increase in the probability of success. (That relationship continues to hold when the standard deviation is set at 13 percent and 14 percent.) There is also a higher probability of success at longer time periods. Conversely, when the mean is held constant and the standard deviation changed by 10 percent, the impact on the probability gets smaller at longer time periods. More important, during a given time period, a 10 percent change in the standard deviation has a smaller impact on the probability of success than a 10 percent change in the mean real return on the portfolio.

FIGURE **7.4** *Impact on Success Probabilities of Changing Mean (μ) and Standard Deviation (σ) Values*

μ	4.5	4.95	5.445	5.9895
σ	12.0	12.0	12.0	12.0
25 yrs	81%	85%	89%	92%
30 yrs	71	76	81	86
35 yrs	62	69	75	81
40 yrs	56	63	71	78
μ	4.5	4.5	4.5	4.5
σ	12.0	13.2	14.52	15.972
25 yrs	81%	78%	76%	73%
30 yrs	71	68	66	63
35 yrs	62	60	59	57
40 yrs	56	54	54	52

Once the probabilities have been calculated, exploring the individual's attitude toward risk will help determine the recommended withdrawal rate and identify the acceptable probabilities for given time periods of retirement. If someone is totally risk averse to any probability of outliving assets, the adviser must set the retirement time period to 40 years and find the withdrawal rate that leads to 100 percent probability that the withdrawals will be sustained throughout the retirement time period.

Although this approach sheds additional light on sustainability, it still tends to frame the distribution picture from the perspective of given retirement periods. The whole issue of mortality, and hence longevity risk, is that the number of years in retirement cannot be known with certainty. It's therefore important to identify ways to model mortality probabilities into the analysis.

Modeling Mortality Probabilities

There are several ways to incorporate mortality probabilities into the distribution analysis, some more complex than others. One method that's conceptually easy to grasp is to generate a random sequence of real returns and weight the withdrawal in each year by the probability that a person alive today will still be alive in the year the withdrawal is expected to take place. Essentially, you're calculating whether the retirement nest egg can support the expected present discounted value (EPV) of the anticipated withdrawal stream, using the randomly generated sequence of real returns as your discount rates:

$$\text{EPV} = \frac{{}_{n+1}\text{P}_n\text{C}}{(1+\text{R}_1)} + \frac{{}_{n+2}\text{P}_n\text{C}}{(1+\text{R}_1)(1+\text{R}_2)} + \ldots\ldots\ldots + \frac{{}_{n+T}\text{P}_n\text{C}}{\prod\limits_{i=1}^{T}(1+\text{R}_i)}, (1)$$

where

${}_{n+1}\text{P}_n$ = the probability that a person age n will be alive $n+1$ years from now

T = the number of years from age n to the maximum age on the period life table

C = the real value of the withdrawal amount

R_i = the real return in period i

This is an expected present value because probabilities are being used to weight the withdrawal stream.

For any given sequence of returns, if the expected present value is less than the retirement nest egg, that simulation is counted as a success. Running at least 10,000 simulations allows one to calculate the expected probability that the nest egg will sustain the withdrawal rate throughout the retirement years. This approach was used setting the value of the nest egg at $100,000, C at $5,000 (analogous to a 5 percent withdrawal rate), the mean value of real returns at 4.5 percent, and the standard deviation at 12.0 percent. Conditional survival probabilities were calculated from the November 2004 update to the Social Security Administration's 2000 period life tables; for males, these tables end at age 110. The Monte Carlo simulations conducted for a 65-year-old male result in an expected probability of 96.5 percent that a nest egg of $100,000 will fund a 5 percent withdrawal rate throughout the retirement years. This likelihood is substantially higher than the results reported in Figure 7.4.

The result seems almost too good to be true. Closer examination suggests that it is an overestimate of the true likelihood that any one person's nest egg will sustain a 5 percent withdrawal rate throughout their remaining years. Expression (1) is essentially the basic pricing equation for an immediate life annuity with a variable discount rate and no loading expenses. Its applicability as an expected probability is with reference to a large pool of individuals. Clearly, for any one person, it must be considered an over-estimate.

However, research using the HRS shows that retired individuals are fairly accurate in predicting their life expectancies.[9] Hence, one could modify the above analysis by setting all probabilities of survival—up to the predicted life expectancy—equal to one. For instance, if a 65-year-old male predicts he will live 20 more years, then the expression becomes:

$$\text{EPV} = \frac{1C}{(1+R_1)} + ... + \frac{1C}{\prod_{i=1}^{20}(1+R_i)} + ... + \frac{_{65+T}P_{65}C}{\prod_{i=1}^{65+T}(1+R_i)} \quad (2)$$

For this illustration, Monte Carlo simulations, using the same parameters as in the previous examples, result in an expected probability of 87 percent for sustaining a 5 percent withdrawal rate throughout the retirement years.

To this point, we've been discussing the withdrawal rate as the percentage of the nest egg withdrawn in the first year. That becomes the fixed amount withdrawn each year thereafter, adjusted for inflation. Given this fixed withdrawal amount, the Monte Carlo simulations are conducted to see if the balance hits zero in real value before the end of the potential lifespan. Alternatively, one could set up a distribution system whereby the withdrawal amount each year is a percentage of the nest egg balance. Mortality probabilities can be incorporated into the analysis by establishing a benchmark distribution amount, say $5,000, and calculating the probability that the actual distribution will be higher or lower, given that the retiree is still alive.

Under such a system the nest egg could not fall to zero; however, the actual withdrawal amount would vary each year. The distribution and nest egg in any given year would equal:

$$D_t = w_t{}^*N_t \quad (3)$$

and

$$N_t = (N_{t-1} - D_{t-1})(1 + R_t), \quad (4)$$

where

D_t = the distribution amount at the end of year t

w_t = the percentage of the nest egg balance withdrawn in year t

N_t = the nest egg balance at the end of year t

R_t = the rate of return during year t

Combining expressions (3) and (4) yields:

$$N_t = (1 - w_{t-1})N_{t-1}(1 + R_t) \tag{5}$$

If one makes the assumption that the investment returns, R_t, are lognormally distributed, then both N_t and D_t are lognormally distributed.[10] Consequently, we can use the cumulative distribution function to calculate both the probability that the actual distribution in any given year will be less than the benchmark value and the expected value of the distribution amount given that it's less than the benchmark.

Consider the following distribution rule:

$$w_t = \frac{1}{LE_t} \tag{6}$$

where LE_t is the life expectancy in year t. The November 2004 update to the 2000 Social Security period life tables shows the remaining life expectancy of a 65-year-old female to be 18.93 years. Hence

$$w_0 = \frac{1}{18.93} = .052826$$

If we assume a \$100,000 starting value for the nest egg, then the initial distribution would equal \$5,282.60. This amount can be made the benchmark value.

FIGURE 7.5 illustrates the calculations for the analysis; the mean value of real returns is set at 4.5 percent and the standard deviation at 12 percent. Using the cumulative distribution function, column (5) shows the probability in any given year that the distribution amount will be less than the benchmark value of \$5,282.60. Column (6) calculates the expected value of the distribution amount in any given year. Under the assumptions of the lognormal distribution, this expected value is calculated as:

$$w_t(\acute{w}_{t-1})N_0 e^{.045t + .5\sigma^2}, \tag{7}$$

where

$$\acute{w}_t = \prod_{i=0}^{t}(1 - w_i)$$

Column (7) is the expected value of the truncated cumulative distribution, given that the withdrawal amount is less than the benchmark value. Column (8) is the probability that a female, age 65 in the current period,

FIGURE 7.5

(1) T	(2) AGE₁	(3) LE₁	(4) W₁	(5) PROB D₁ <5282.6	(6) E(D₁)	(7) E(D₁) GIVEN <5282.6	(8) ₆₅₋ᴛP₆₅	(9) EXPECT LOSS	(10) PROB D₁ >5282.6	(11) E(D₁) GIVEN >5282.6	(12) EXPECT GAIN
0	65	18.93	.0528	—	—	—	1	—	—	—	—
1	66	18.18	.0550	.3976	5489	4861	.987	165	.6024	5903	369
2	67	17.44	.0573	.3593	5697	4725	.972	194	.6406	6241	597
3	68	16.71	.0598	.3328	5905	4632	.957	207	.6672	6540	803
4	69	16.00	.0625	.3136	6109	4558	.940	213	.6863	6817	991
5	70	15.29	.0654	.2978	6314	4498	.923	215	.7022	7084	1168
6	71	14.59	.0685	.2854	6515	4444	.904	216	.7146	7343	1332
7	72	13.91	.0718	.2765	6707	4395	.885	217	.7235	7590	1477
8	73	13.23	.0755	.2691	6895	4351	.863	216	.7308	7832	1610
9	74	12.57	.0795	.2646	7068	4308	.841	217	.7353	8062	1720
10	75	11.92	.0838	.2622	7229	4267	.818	218	.7379	8482	1809
11	76	11.29	.0885	.2622	7366	4226	.792	219	.7378	8669	1870
12	77	10.67	.0937	.2642	7484	4185	.765	222	.7358	8834	1907
13	78	10.07	.0993	.2689	7572	4143	.736	225	.7310	8973	1911
14	79	9.49	.1053	.2766	7625	4099	.705	231	.7234	9089	1883
15	80	8.92	.1121	.2866	7646	4054	.673	237	.7134	9174	1827
16	81	8.37	.1194	.3001	7623	4005	.639	245	.6999	9218	1740
17	82	7.85	.1273	.3184	7540	3950	.602	256	.6815	9232	1616
18	83	7.34	.1362	.3404	7414	3891	.564	267	.6596	9201	1470
19	84	6.86	.1457	.3685	7219	3824	.525	282	.6314	9138	1298
20	85	6.39	.1564	.4014	6975	3750	.484	297	.5986	9022	1117
21	86	5.96	.1677	.4432	6646	3662	.442	317	.5567	8878	920
22	87	5.54	.1805	.4909	6269	3563	.399	337	.5091	8694	730
23	88	5.15	.1941	.5471	5823	3446	.356	358	.4528	8485	550
24	89	4.78	.2092	.6102	5326	3308	.313	377	.3898	8250	391
25	90	4.44	.2252	.6799	4778	3142	.271	395	.3201	8003	258
26	91	4.12	.2427	.7516	4202	2946	.231	406	.2484	7749	156
27	92	3.83	.2611	.8221	3607	2711	.194	409	.1779	7500	85
28	93	3.56	.2801	.8844	3021	2435	.159	400	.1156	7262	41
29	94	3.31	.3021	.9338	2461	2121	.127	376	.0662	7037	17
30	95	3.09	.3236	.9681	1939	1771	.099	339	.0319	6833	6

(Continued)

FIGURE 7.5 *(continued)*

(1) T	(2) AGE$_t$	(3) LE$_t$	(4) W$_t$	(5) PROB D$_t$ <5282.6	(6) E(D$_t$)	(7) E(D$_t$) GIVEN <5282.6	(8) $_{65+t}P_{65}$	(9) EXPECT LOSS	(10) PROB D$_t$ >5282.6	(11) E(D$_t$) GIVEN >5282.6	(12) EXPECT GAIN
31	96	2.89	.3460	.9875	1477	1409	.076	291	.0125	6650	1.5
32	97	2.71	.3690	.9962	1085	1064	.057	238	.0379	6489	.29
33	98	2.55	.3921	.9992	767	762	.041	186	.0008	6349	.04
34	99	2.40	.4166	.9999	521	521	.029	139	.0001	6228	.004
35	100	2.26	.4424	.9999	340	340	.020	99	.00001	6123	.0002
36	101	2.12	.4717	.9999	213	213	.013	68	.0000007	6030	0
37	102	1.99	.5025	1	126	126	.009	45	0	5948	0
38	103	1.87	.5347	1	71	71	.005	29	0	5875	0
39	104	1.75	.5714	1	37	37	.003	18	0	5751	0
40	105	1.63	.6135	1	18	18	.002	10	0		0
41	106	1.52	.6578	1	8	8	.001	6	0		0
42	107	1.42	.7042	1	3	3	.0006	3	0		0
43	108	1.32	.7575	1	1	1	.0003	2	0		0
44	109	1.23	.8130	1	.28	.28	.0001	.7	0		0
45	110	1.14	.8771	1	.06	.06	.00006	.3	0		0
46	111	1.05	.9523	1	.008	.008	.00002	.1	0		0
47	112	.97	1	1	0	0	.00001	0	0		0
								EPV= 6659			EPV= 25189

is still alive in period 65+t. Columns (10) and (11) are, respectively, the probability that the withdrawal amount is greater than the benchmark and the expected value, given that the withdrawal amount is greater than the benchmark. Column (9) is the expected shortfall, given that the withdrawal amount is less than the benchmark and the retiree is still living during the time period. It is calculated as

(8)

probability that * {$5282.60 – [E(D$_t$) given D$_t$ < $5282.60]} * probability still
D$_t$ < $5282.60   alive in year t

Likewise, column (12) is the expected gain given that the withdrawal amount is greater than the benchmark and the retiree is still living during the time period. It is calculated as:

(9)

probability that * {[E(D$_t$) given D$_t$>\$5282.60] − \$5282.60} * probability still D$_t$ < \$5282.60   alive in year t

We can use the interest rate on the 20-year, inflation-indexed Treasury bond to calculate the expected present value (EPV) of the loss and gain. These values are shown at the bottom of columns (9) and (12). The EPV of the loss is a relatively small \$6,659 as compared to the EPV of the gain, at \$25,189.

Even though the yearly withdrawals do not hit zero during the potential life span, it's highly probable that they will get very small after 30 years. That's because the withdrawal percentage increases each year as the life expectancy decreases, causing expected withdrawals to be high and increase during the earlier years. We can reduce that effect by maintaining a constant withdrawal rate. **FIGURE 7.6** presents the calculations for a constant withdrawal rate equal to .052826 and a benchmark withdrawal value of \$5,282.60. Of interest is that the EPV of the loss, at \$12,203, is much closer to the EPV of the gain, at \$10,475. In fact, it's possible to find the constant withdrawal rate that will equate these two expected present values. These calculations are illustrated in **FIGURE 7.7**, which shows a constant withdrawal rate of .050861 and, hence, a benchmark withdrawal value of \$5,086.10.

RETIREMENT-DISTRIBUTION PLANNING can no longer be characterized as the plug-in-the-numbers activity critiqued by William Sharpe in 1997. Driven by the growing importance of nonannuitized wealth in the retirement nest egg, along with advances in life expectancies, the analysis of distribution planning has become increasingly sophisticated.

Today's financial planners need to have a solid understanding of how to incorporate probabilities associated with investment returns and mortality. Armed with that knowledge, the financial planner can present an assessment of the risk associated with a particular distribution plan, at a defined point in time, for a specific individual with a given degree of risk aversion. Because all of these variables are changeable over time, the prudent adviser will update the distribution-risk scenario and revisit the retirement-distribution plan at regular intervals.

FIGURE 7.6

(1) T	(2) AGE$_t$	(3) LE$_t$	(4) PROB D$_t$ W$_t$	(5) E(D$_t$)	(6) E(D$_t$) GIVEN <5282.6	(7) $_{65+t}P_{65}$	(8) EXPECT LOSS	(9) PROB D$_t$ >5282.6	(10) E(D$_t$) GIVEN >5282.6	(11) EXPECT GAIN
0	65	.0528				1				
1	66	.0528	.5308	5272	4797	.987	255	.4692	5809	244
2	67	.0528	.5436.	5261	4606	.972	357	.4565	6039	336
3	68	.0528	.5532	5250	4465	.957	432	.4468	6222	402
4	69	.0528	.5614	5239	4348	.940	493	.4386	6379	452
5	70	.0528	.5686	5228	4248	.923	543	.4314	6520	493
6	71	.0528	.5751	5217	4158	.904	585	.4249	6651	526
7	72	.0528	.5810	5207	4077	.885	620	.4190	6772	552
8	73	.0528	.5865	5196	4003	.863	648	.4135	6887	573
9	74	.0528	.5917	5185	3935	.841	671	.4083	6996	589
10	75	.0528	.5965	5174	3871	.818	689	.3987	7101	600
11	76	.0528	.6011	5164	3811	.792	701	.3945	7202	607
12	77	.0528	.6055	5153	3754	.765	708	.3903	7300	609
13	78	.0528	.6097	5142	3700	.736	710	.3862	7395	607
14	79	.0528	.6138	5132	3649	.705	707	.3824	7487	601
15	80	.0528	.6176	5121	3601	.673	699	.3786	7576	590
16	81	.0528	.6214	5110	3554	.639	686	.3750	7664	576
17	82	.0528	.6250	5100	3509	.602	668	.3715	7750	557
18	83	.0528	.6285	5089	3466	.564	644	.3681	7834	535
19	84	.0528	.6319	5079	3425	.525	616	.3648	7917	509
20	85	.0528	.6352	5068	3385	.484	583	.3616	7998	479
21	86	.0528	.6384	5058	3346	.442	546	.3585	8078	447
22	87	.0528	.6415	5047	3309	.399	505	.3555	8157	411
23	88	.0528	.6445	5037	3273	.356	461	.3525	8235	374
24	89	.0528	.6475	5026	3238	.313	415	.3496	8311	335

(Continued)

FIGURE **7.6** *(continued)*

(1) T	(2) AGE$_t$	(3) LE$_t$	(4) PROB D$_t$ W$_t$	(5) E(D$_t$)	(6) E(D$_t$) GIVEN <5282.6	(7) $_{65+t}P_{65}$	(8) EXPECT LOSS	(9) PROB D$_t$ >5282.6	(10) E(D$_t$) GIVEN >5282.6	(11) EXPECT GAIN
25	90	.0528	.6504	5016	3204	.271	367	.3468	8387	295
26	91	.0528	.6532	5005	3171	.231	319	.3440	8462	255
27	92	.0528	.6560	4995	3138	.194	273	.3413	8535	217
28	93	.0528	.6587	4985	3107	.159	228	.3387	8608	180
29	94	.0528	.6613	4974	3076	.127	186	.3361	8681	147
30	95	.0528	.6639	4964	3047	.099	148	.3335	8752	116
31	96	.0528	.6665	4954	3018	.076	115	.3310	8823	90
32	97	.0528	.6690	4944	2989	.057	87	.3286	8894	68
33	98	.0528	.6714	4933	2961	.041	64	.3262	8963	50
34	99	.0528	.6738	4923	2934	.029	46	.3238	9032	36
35	100	.0528	.6762	4913	2908	.020	32	.3262	9101	25
36	101	.0528	.6785	4903	2882	.013	22	.3238	9169	17
37	102	.0528	.6808	4893	2856	.009	14	.3215	9236	11
38	103	.0528	.6831	4883	2831	.005	9	.3192	9303	7
39	104	.0528	.6853	4872	2807	.003	6	.3147	9370	4
40	105	.0528	.6875	4862	2783	.002	3	.3125	9436	3
41	106	.0528	.6896	4852	2760	.001	2	.3104	9502	1
42	107	.0528	.6917	4842	2736	.0006	1	.3083	9567	1
43	108	.0528	.6938	4832	2714	.0003	0.54	.3062	9632	0.40
44	109	.0528	.6959	4822	2692	.0001	0.25	.3041	9697	0.19
45	110	.0528	.6979	4812	2670	.00006	0.11	.3021	9761	0.08
46	111	.0528	.6999	4802	2648	.00002	0.04	.3001	9825	0.03
47	112	.0528	.7019	4792	2648	.00001	0.02	.2981	9889	0.02
							EPV= 12203			EPV= 10475

FIGURE 7.7

(1) T	(2) AGE$_t$	(3) LE$_t$	(4) PROB D$_t$ W$_t$	(5) E(D$_t$)	(6) E(D$_t$) GIVEN <5282.6	(7) $_{65+t}P_{65}$	(8) EXPECT LOSS	(9) PROB D$_t$ >5282.6	(10) E(D$_t$) GIVEN >5282.6	(11) EXPECT GAIN
0	65	.050861	—	—	—	1	—	—	—	—
1	66	.050861	.5239	5086	4622	.987	240	.4761	5597	240
2	67	.050861	.5338	5086	4442	.972	334	.4662	5824	334
3	68	.050861	.5414	5086	4309	.957	403	.4586	6004	403
4	69	.050861	.5478	5086	4199	.940	457	.4522	6160	457
5	70	.050861	.5535	5086	4105	.923	501	.4466	6301	501
6	71	.050861	.5584	5086	4022	.904	537	.4416	6432	537
7	72	.050861	.5631	5086	3947	.885	568	.4369	6554	568
8	73	.050861	.5674	5086	3878	.863	592	.4326	6670	592
9	74	.050861	.5714	5086	3815	.841	611	.4286	6781	611
10	75	.050861	.5752	5086	3756	.818	626	.4248	6888	626
11	76	.050861	.5789	5086	3700	.792	636	.4211	6991	636
12	77	.050861	.5823	5086	3648	.765	641	.4177	7091	641
13	78	.050861	.5856	5086	3599	.736	641	.4143	7188	641
14	79	.050861	.5888	5086	3552	.705	637	.4112	7283	637
15	80	.050861	.5919	5086	3507	.673	629	.4081	7376	629
16	81	.050861	.5948	5086	3464	.639	616	.4051	7467	616
17	82	.050861	.5977	5086	3423	.602	599	.4023	7556	599
18	83	.050861	.6005	5086	3384	.564	577	.3995	7644	577
19	84	.050861	.6032	5086	3346	.525	551	.3968	7730	551
20	85	.050861	.6058	5086	3310	.484	521	.3942	7815	521
21	86	.050861	.6083	5086	3275	.442	487	.3917	7899	487
22	87	.050861	.6108	5086	3240	.399	450	.3892	7982	450
23	88	.050861	.6132	5086	3208	.356	410	.3868	8064	410
24	89	.050861	.6156	5086	3176	.313	368	.3844	8145	368

(Continued)

FIGURE 7.7 *(continued)*

(1) T	(2) AGE$_T$	(3) LE$_T$	(4) PROB D$_T$ W$_T$	(5) E(D$_T$)	(6) E(D$_T$) GIVEN <5282.6	(7) $_{65+T}P_{65}$	(8) EXPECT LOSS	(9) PROB D$_T$ >5282.6	(10) E(D$_T$) GIVEN >5282.6	(11) EXPECT GAIN
25	90	.050861	.6179	5086	3145	.271	326	.3821	8225	326
26	91	.050861	.6202	5086	3115	.231	283	.3798	8304	283
27	92	.050861	.6224	5086	3086	.194	241	.3776	8383	241
28	93	.050861	.6246	5086	3057	.159	201	.3754	8461	201
29	94	.050861	.6267	5086	3030	.127	164	.3733	8538	164
30	95	.050861	.6288	5086	3003	.099	131	.3712	8615	131
31	96	.050861	.6308	5086	2976	.076	101	.3691	8691	101
32	97	.050861	.6329	5086	2951	.057	77	.3672	8767	77
33	98	.050861	.6348	5086	2926	.041	56	.3652	8842	56
34	99	.050861	.6368	5086	2901	.029	40	.3632	8917	40
35	100	.050861	.6387	5086	2877	.020	28	.3613	8991	28
36	101	.050861	.6406	5086	2854	.013	19	.3594	9065	19
37	102	.050861	.6424	5086	2831	.009	13	.3576	9138	13
38	103	.050861	.6443	5086	2808	.005	8	.3557	9211	8
39	104	.050861	.6461	5086	2786	.003	5	.3539	9284	5
40	105	.050861	.6478	5086	2765	.002	3	.3522	9356	3
41	106	.050861	.6496	5086	2744	.001	2	.3504	9428	2
42	107	.050861	.6513	5086	2723	.0006	1	.3487	9500	1
43	108	.050861	.6530	5086	2703	.0003	0.47	.3470	9571	0.47
44	109	.050861	.6547	5086	2683	.0001	0.22	.3453	9643	0.22
45	110	.050861	.65634	5086	2663	.00006	0.09	.3437	9714	0.09
46	111	.050861	.6580	5086	2644	.00002	0.04	.3420	9784	0.04
47	112	.050861	.6595	5086	2625	.00001	0.02	.3404	9855	0.02
							sum= 14333			sum= 14333

APPENDIX

Monte Carlo Illustrations

Assumptions: Five percent withdrawal rate, $100,000 nest egg portfolio; mean value of real returns is 4.5 percent, with standard deviation of 12 percent; withdrawal taken at the beginning of the period; 30-year retirement period.

Simulation 1

TIME PERIOD	SEQUENCE OF REAL RETURNS	BEGINNING PERIOD BALANCE	BALANCE AFTER WITHDRAWAL	END PERIOD BALANCE
1	1.060645	100000.00	95000.00	100761.30
2	1.002492	100761.30	95761.31	95999.99
3	1.334429	95999.99	90999.99	121433.00
4	0.947566	121433.00	116433.00	110328.00
5	1.183682	110328.00	105328.00	124674.90
6	1.045693	124674.90	119674.90	125143.20
7	1.044188	125143.20	120143.20	125452.00
8	0.896337	125452.00	120452.00	107965.70
9	0.995936	107965.70	102965.70	102547.20
10	1.012329	102547.20	97547.24	98749.91
11	1.088467	98749.91	93749.91	102043.70
12	0.947298	102043.70	97043.68	91929.30
13	1.047548	91929.30	86828.30	91062.58
14	0.980687	91062.58	86062.58	84400.44
15	0.981216	84400.44	79400.44	77908.99
16	1.015027	77908.99	72908.99	74004.56
17	1.095334	74004.56	69004.56	75583.06
18	1.265428	75583.06	70583.06	89317.76
19	1.181206	89317.76	84317.76	99596.61
20	1.253307	99596.61	94596.61	118558.60
21	0.813326	118558.60	113558.60	92360.08
22	0.912455	92360.08	87360.08	79712.10
23	1.038824	79712.10	74712.10	77612.71
24	0.906729	77612.71	72612.71	65840.02
25	1.074046	65840.02	60840.02	65344.99
26	0.909283	65344.99	60344.99	54870.66
27	1.105457	54870.66	49870.66	55129.85
28	1.420160	55129.85	50129.85	71192.41
29	0.902970	71192.41	66192.41	59769.79
30	0.852283	59769.79	54769.79	46679.38

This simulation is counted as a success because the nest egg portfolio was able to sustain the withdrawal stream given the 5 percent withdrawal rate. There is even a $46,679.38 balance at the end of 30 years.

Simulation 2

TIME PERIOD	SEQUENCE OF REAL RETURNS	BEGINNING PERIOD BALANCE	BALANCE AFTER WITHDRAWAL	END PERIOD BALANCE
1	1.008972	100000.00	95000.00	95852.35
2	0.891678	95852.35	90852.35	81011.05
3	1.074311	81011.05	76011.50	81659.49
4	1.198177	81659.49	76659.49	91851.63
5	1.188802	91851.63	86851.63	103249.40
6	1.252976	103249.40	98249.39	123104.10
7	0.782969	123104.10	118104.10	92471.93
8	1.016898	92471.93	87471.93	88950.05
9	1.176403	88950.05	83950.05	98759.07
10	0.914596	98759.07	93759.07	85751.66
11	0.962176	85751.66	80751.66	77697.27
12	0.842148	77697.27	72697.27	61221.87
13	0.823371	61221.87	56221.87	46291.44
14	0.927684	46291.44	41291.44	38305.43
15	0.952179	38305.43	33305.43	31712.73
16	0.790848	31712.73	26712.73	21125.72
17	0.976849	21125.72	16125.72	15752.39
18	0.996514	15752.39	10752.39	10714.91
19	1.061182	10714.91	5714.91	6064.56
20	1.001141	6064.56	1064.56	1065.78
21	1.005761	1065.78	.00	.00
22	1.000571	.00	.00	.00
23	1.206117	.00	.00	.00
24	1.034766	.00	.00	.00
25	1.022661	.00	.00	.00
26	0.983415	.00	.00	.00
27	1.281665	.00	.00	.00
28	1.148881	.00	.00	.00
29	1.330079	.00	.00	.00
30	0.966411	.00	.00	.00

This simulation is counted as a failure because the nest egg portfolio ran out of funds before the end of the 30-year period. At this point, with only two simulations, there is a 50 percent probability of sustaining a 5 percent withdrawal rate for more than 30 years. We need to run about 98,000 additional simulations to get a more complete picture. One hundred thousand simulations results in a 71 percent probability of success; using a lognormal distribution to generate the real return sequences with a mean value of 4.5 percent, standard deviation of 12 percent, and a 5 percent withdrawal rate.

Note: Using real returns adjusts for changes in purchasing power and allows us to keep the withdrawal amount constant. For ease of exposition, the return sequences used in this illustration were generated from a normal distribution with a mean of 4.5 and standard deviation of 12.0.

Chapter Notes

1. For the full text of the paper, see http://www.stanford.edu/~wfsharpe/art/fantasy/fantasy.htm.

2. The Health and Retirement Study is a longitudinal study on health, retirement, and aging sponsored by the National Institute on Aging. The University of Michigan surveys 22,000 Americans every two years to obtain information on such topics as health, insurance coverage, financial status, retirement planning, and family support systems. For analysis, see Dushi and Webb, *Annuitization: Keeping Your Options Open*, CRR WP 2004-04 (Center for Retirement Research, March 2004).

3. Munnell, Triest, and Jivan, *How Do Pensions Affect Expected and Actual Retirement Ages?* CRR WP 2004-27 (Center for Retirement Research, November 2004).

4. Poterba, *Valuing Assets in Retirement Savings Accounts*, CRR WP 2004-11 (Center for Retirement Research, April 2004); Poterba, Venti, and Wise, "Saver Behavior and 401(k) Retirement Wealth," *American Economic Review* 90, no. 2 (2000): 297–302.

5. Period life tables represent the mortality experience of a given population based on death and population data available by time period. The Social Security tables examine the mortality changes in the Social Security population over time.

6. For example, see Ameriks, Veres, and Warshawsky, "Making Retirement Income Last a Lifetime," *Journal of Financial Planning* (December 2001): 60–76; Cooley, Hubbard, and Walz, "Choosing a Withdrawal Rate That Is Sustainable," *AAII Journal* (February 1998): 39–47; Gordon Pye, "Sustainable Investment Withdrawals," *Journal of Portfolio Management* (Summer 2000): 73–84; Larry Bierwirth, "Investment for Retirement: Using the Past to Model the Future," *Journal of Financial Planning* (January 1994): 14–25; William Bengen, "Determining Withdrawal Rates Using Historical Data," *Journal of Financial Planning* (October 1994; reprinted March 2004): 64–74.

7. "Rolling time periods" refers to the process of tracking an investment portfolio over a given time period, say 30 years, for someone who retired on January 1, 1926, then tracking the portfolio of someone who retired on January 1, 1927, etc.

8. This is roughly equivalent to the real return and standard deviation over the period 1926–1994 of a portfolio composed of 50 percent stocks and 50 percent bonds.

9. Smith, Taylor, and Sloan, "Longevity Expectations and Death: Can People Predict Their Own Demise?" *American Economic Review* (September 2001): 1126–1135; Hurd, Smith, and Zissimopoulos, "The Effects of Subjective Survival on Retirement and Social Security Claiming," *Journal of Applied Economics* (May 2004): 761–776.

10. A good reference on the mathematics is *Random Walks*, by John Norstad, which can be found at http://homepage.mac.com/j.norstad.

CHAPTER 8

Monte Carlo Mania

ROBERT D. CURTIS

Assuming the average [return] is achieved each year ... should not be a best practice; ... it should be called *malpractice*."[1] These are strong words from Dave Loeper, founder of Financeware and one of the evangelists of Monte Carlo. Since 2000, we've heard this message in one form or another many times from many experts. This standard practice of the profession went from being questioned to being criticized to being widely discredited. How could we have been so foolish as to think that we could predict a client's future results using average returns?

Obviously, no portfolio can be constructed to deliver average returns every year, and no client will ever receive them. Portfolio creation and investment decisions are always based on an expectation of volatility. Average returns reflect zero volatility. It takes very little analysis to demonstrate to anyone's satisfaction that the sequence of returns can make a great difference to the outcome of a plan. Hundreds of examples have been presented in various articles illustrating this point.

We certainly can't predict what the actual sequence of returns will be in the future, so if average returns aren't the correct assumption, how should projections be calculated? Fortunately, just as the use of average returns came under such great criticism, a replacement methodology was developed. And not only is the new method better than the old; it has been touted as "the answer" for financial planning. It would seem that the profession has been saved by the development of more powerful computers running more sophisticated software that can deliver a simple, precise answer for every client. Is the new approach really that good? It must be, if you judge by the activity it's generated. Indeed, it's promoted by many smart and influential people, including a Nobel laureate. Numerous new software companies have been created to exploit it. Older programs have been pressured to add it. Large employers have embraced it for their 401(k) participants. The financial press, both consumer and professional, write excitedly about it. The Securities and Exchange Commission and the National Association of Securities Dealers even created a new policy to allow its use by brokers.

The seductive solution, as readers of this book are likely aware, is Monte Carlo simulation, and it has quickly become the new "right way" to do financial planning. In 2002, Andrew Gluck, an editor at large at *Investment Advisor* magazine and the author of a monthly column called the Gluck Report, told us, "The future of financial planning is in Monte Carlo."[2] Monte Carlo replaces the misleading assumption of a single stream of average returns with the calculation of hundreds (or thousands) of possible sequences (called iterations) of returns. It then converts these many possible results into a single, seemingly more accurate answer—the probability that your client will meet all of her goals. But does the real-world application of Monte Carlo live up to its hype? In the same article in which he labeled Monte Carlo the future of financial planning, Gluck also said, "There are some serious misconceptions about how it works."

I believe that's an understatement.

Monte Carlo—Good? Bad? Good Enough?

"Have you heard of Monte Carlo? If so, what do you think of it? How do you use it with clients?" I have asked hundreds of advisers these questions during the past year, with interesting results. Almost everyone has heard of Monte Carlo. Those who seem to like it the most and question it the least tend to be the more traditional, transaction-oriented brokers, who use it more as a sales technique than as a planning process.

"Look. If you invest $300 a month in this variable annuity, you'll have _____" (fill in the blank from the list below).

- ❑ 88 percent instead of 62 percent
- ❑ sun instead of clouds
- ❑ go instead of stop
- ❑ success instead of failure
- ❑ comfort instead of uncertainty

For busy brokers, there is a great attraction to the idea that a really smart program can take the complexity (and judgment) out of financial planning and give them a simple answer that helps sell their client.

The response I get from more experienced financial planners, however, is much different. Surprisingly, many of them hesitate to state any opinion at all. Why would that be? These individuals are knowledgeable financial planners with successful practices. They usually have strong opinions about all aspects of financial planning and express them freely. What's so different about Monte Carlo?

First, most of what advisers have read and heard from the "experts" for several years tells them that Monte Carlo is the only valid way to project future results. It's been proved statistically. Can you debate math with the mathematicians? They can always prove their point of view with more numbers. And who's going to argue with a Nobel Prize winner? But even though many advisers feel compelled to accept the theory that Monte Carlo is better, their gut reaction tells them something different. The numbers *look* right and the expert arguments all *sound* right, but something just doesn't *feel* right. And while most advisers are reasonably good with numbers, they're even better with less tangible concepts like understanding client goals, hopes, and fears. When they look at the Monte Carlo results, they struggle with how to interpret them and how to explain them to their clients in a useful way.

"John and Ann, you have a 74 percent chance of reaching your goals, and you have 26 percent chance you won't." What does that really mean? Is it good or bad? What happens in the 26 percent of the time they fail? Where did these precise numbers come from?

Thoughtful advisers often feel uncertain about Monte Carlo even if they're not sure why and can't prove there's something wrong. So they're hesitant to embrace it but equally hesitant to criticize it. This chapter addresses some of the reasons why uncertainty and skepticism are perfectly appropriate reactions to Monte Carlo.

Friends of Monte Carlo

One group of people is never uncertain about Monte Carlo. The most vocal proponents of Monte Carlo—and, conversely, the most vociferous critics of average returns—are individuals who've developed financial-planning software that uses Monte Carlo analysis. A coincidence? Maybe. Or might there be a high correlation between the proponents' absolute belief in Monte Carlo and its potential for software sales? For full disclosure, I must report that I am personally the developer of financial-planning software (MoneyGuidePro)[3] that includes a Monte Carlo analysis, and that financial adviser Harold Evensky is our principal subject expert. I, too, have much to gain from the profession's acceptance of the planning methods embodied in our system. I am in no way suggesting that there is anything wrong with software developers' promoting concepts that benefit their products. On the contrary, the reason most of us develop such software is the strong belief that we can help you and your clients plan a better financial life.

But that confidence doesn't mean you should take our word that our methods and underlying assumptions are correct. You have a right—and an obligation to your clients—to be skeptical. As John D. Kingston, CFP, the principal of Custom Financial Planning, a registered investment advisory firm, said in 2001: "The profession may find this exercise [Monte Carlo analysis] is little more than hype developed by mathematicians and promoted by financial-planning software companies."[4]

I certainly believe that Monte Carlo has proved to be more than just hype, but it may well have been oversold. There are some important considerations every user of financial-planning software should keep in mind:

- ❑ The program must project results far into the future (20, 30, 40, even 50 years).
- ❑ The assumptions in every financial program reflect the opinions and biases of the designers.

This is true whether you're using your own homegrown spreadsheets or a commercially developed program. The designers make the core decisions—which factors to include or exclude, what assumptions are "reasonable," how calculations should be made and how accurate they need to be, and how to present results. They determine what is relevant and what is not. Their philosophy of planning affects the design of the planning software. The design of a Monte Carlo analysis, along with the assumptions within it, is just one highly publicized example.

Financial planning is not accounting or engineering. It is more art than science. That means that there are no truly right answers, no matter how many decimal places your software can calculate. There is, in fact, a conflict between a computer's inherent ability to provide endless columns of very precise, seemingly accurate values projected into the distant future and the great uncertainty that is the reality of financial planning. What this means for the practitioner is that the situation is never as simple as the software might make it look or as the software designer would like it to be. Good software can make it easier to do complex things, but it can't magically transform the complex into the simple. Most advisers inherently know that, and that is why they bring a healthy dose of skepticism to their judgment of Monte Carlo or any other new planning methodology.

So is Monte Carlo really "the answer"? If you can make the Monte Carlo analysis sophisticated enough, is that all your client needs? Fortunately, it isn't. I say "fortunately" because if all an investor required was a smart computer program to assure her financial success, she wouldn't need you. The opposite is true. Investors need advisers, and advisers need better tools (including software) to help them provide better advice. A Monte Carlo analysis is one such tool, but like every other, it has its strengths and weaknesses.

The Average-Return Problem

What problem is Monte Carlo intended to solve? We'll use a simple example to illustrate. John and Ann are 65 years old and have just retired. They've accumulated $1 million, which is invested in a 55 percent stock portfolio with a 7.56 percent expected average return. They want to withdraw $62,000 before taxes each year (inflating at 3 percent) from now until age 95. Will their money last? **FIGURE 8.1** shows three sets of results, each assuming an average return at 7.56 percent but with three different return sequences.

The results are startling. Although all three sequences realized the same average return for the entire 30-year period, the results for each sequence of returns differed substantially. Return sequence B shows that if we assume average returns every year, John and Ann can successfully

FIGURE **8.1** *Results for John and Ann Using Average Returns*

| | RETURN SEQUENCE | | |
	A	B	C
Withdrawal amount	$62,000	$62,000	$62,000
Return year 1	−10%	+7.56%	+29%
Return years 2–29	+7.56%	+7.56%	+7.56%
Return year 30	+29%	+7.56%	−10%
Average return for 30 years	+7.56%	+7.56%	+7.56%
Result: how long money lasted	22 years	30 years	30 years
Result: value at end	$0	$98,000	$1,543,000

withdraw $62,000 each year and still have a little money left at the end. In return sequence A, however, a loss in year one caused their plan to run out of money in just 22 years even though the early loss is offset by a big gain in year 30. In return sequence C, when the gain came in year one and the loss came in the last year, they were not only able to withdraw $62,000 each year, but had more than $1,500,000 left after 30 years.

The problem this simple example illustrates is that even though you may be comfortable with your long-term average return estimates, you can't predict the sequence in which returns will occur, and *return sequence does matter*. It creates a special kind of hidden risk that I'll call *return-sequence risk*. Even if your client obtains the long-term average return you projected over the entire planning period, certain sequences of returns will result in poorer-than-expected performance and can cause a wide fluctuation in results. Generally, the worst results are caused by losses in the early years of retirement. Return-sequence risk exists in every long-term financial plan and is the most obvious but not the only hidden risk. We'll examine others later.

The Monte Carlo Solution

Monte Carlo was developed to address the problem of return-sequence risk. Instead of guessing at any particular return sequence, Monte Carlo explores all possible sequences. Well, not quite all, because that would take forever. So it tests enough of the possible sequences to generate a statistically meaningful result (usually a few hundred to a few thousand; the statisticians argue about the minimum number required for a valid result). **FIGURE 8.2** illustrates one way a Monte Carlo analysis would show the results for John and Ann's retirement.

This example uses a simple method of Monte Carlo analysis, running 1,000 iterations and assuming a normal distribution. Many other assump-

FIGURE 8.2 *Monte Carlo Results for John and Ann: Value in 30 Years*

PROBABILITY	5%—WORST	50%—MEDIAN	5%—BEST
Withdrawal amount	$62,000	$62,000	$62,000
Result: how long money lasted	14 years	27 years	30 years
Result: value at end	$0	$0	$7,000,000

tions could be used instead, such as a different distribution (Latin hypercube, anyone?) and cross- or serial correlations among variables. Also note that in Figure 8.1, we varied the sequence of returns but kept the average return (7.56 percent) the same for all three calculations. In the Monte Carlo calculations, however, both the sequence of returns and the average return of each iteration vary widely.

The results in Figure 8.2 reflect a range of returns within two standard deviations, which means we would expect the result to fall within this range 95 percent of the time. The results clearly demonstrate that there can be a wide variance in possible outcomes because of the volatility of returns. It shows that there is an equal chance that John and Ann will run out of money in 14 years or will have more than $7 million left after 30 years. The range of results is so great that it's difficult to explain to John and Ann what they mean. Wouldn't it be better to have a single, simple answer? With Monte Carlo, you can have that too.

The most popular way to illustrate Monte Carlo results is to compare outcomes to the client's income goal and calculate a single answer, usually referred to as the *probability of success*. The probability of success is calculated by counting the number of Monte Carlo iterations that met the goal and dividing the sum by the total number of iterations. The result, shown in **FIGURE 8.3**, is that John and Ann have a 42 percent chance of meeting their withdrawal goal.

FIGURE **8.3** *Monte Carlo Results for John and Ann: Probability of Success*

GOAL	PROBABILITY OF SUCCESS
Withdraw $62,000 per year for 30 years without running out of money	42%

Without a doubt, return-sequence risk must be addressed for any financial plan to adequately serve the client, and using Monte Carlo to calculate a probability of success is one way to do so. But is it the most effective way?

The Problem With Monte Carlo

Problem 1: The Black Box

There is a fundamental contradiction in financial planning: No one can know what future returns will be, but you must predict them anyway. When you run a plan using average returns, you've made a single assumption—what you think is a reasonable average long-term return for the portfolio. Now, what happens when you introduce Monte Carlo? The Monte Carlo engine (the mathematical algorithm it uses for its calculations) also assumes an average return but adds at least two additional assumptions:

1 *Standard deviation for the portfolio.* This is calculated from the standard deviation of the classes within the portfolio, usually based on the assumption that historical volatility in the future will be similar to what it was in the past.

2 *Return distribution.* This is an assumption that annual returns always fall within some specific distribution pattern.

These two major, additional assumptions that Monte Carlo must make to better predict future returns aren't required when using average returns. The assumptions made in the Monte Carlo engine are critical to its results, and there are as many opinions about which assumptions are right as there are Monte Carlo programs. Mathematicians debate them endlessly. Change the assumptions a little, and the results will change a great deal.

In addition, as the mathematicians and software developers strive for more accurate projections to make their programs more valuable, they add greater sophistication (and complication). Here is how Bill Sharpe, a Nobel laureate and founder of Financial Engines, a provider of Monte Carlo–based financial-planning software, described his approach: "[I]t is true that a lot of people who use Monte Carlo continue to use simple assumptions, but they don't need to do so. If you know how to use the method, you have the luxury of representing the way in which returns can evolve more realistically. What do we do to achieve more realism? First, we have a layered approach where we start with a set of core macro variables—a term structure of interest rates, inflation, overall productivity of the economy and inflation. In our simulations, these evolve in ways that are realistic in two senses. First, they are correlated contemporaneously—for example, interest rates tend to be correlated contemporaneously with inflation. Second, they evolve so that they are correlated serially; for example, it's more likely to have high inflation following high inflation than it is to have high inflation following low inflation."[5]

This may sound impressive, but it seems to me that they're just adding a bunch of additional assumptions, based on someone else's judgment, about how to predict future returns. When working with something as unpredictable as future investment returns, I don't believe that more assumptions and more sophisticated analysis necessarily help the process. In fact, these layers can obscure the assumptions I'm comfortable with—like simple long-term returns. "Making five more unprovable assumptions and adding two decimal places," says Evensky, "is just pretending to a degree of accuracy that is nonexistent."[6]

Just how complicated is the Monte Carlo engine, that is, the mathematical algorithm it uses? Moshe Milevsky, a professor of finance at York University in Toronto who has written extensively on probabilistic analyses, thinks it's pretty complicated indeed. "These concepts [algorithms] need a Good Housekeeping seal of approval. They're not widgets," says Milevsky. "They're nuclear reactors. I would like to know that a competent nuclear engineer built my reactor."[7] Personally, I don't want to run someone else's nuclear reactor and then try to explain how it works to my client. I can use a financial plan effectively with a client only if I have confidence in its results and can readily explain them. That usually means I want to understand and be comfortable with the core assumptions and general calculation methods used to produce the results. A Monte Carlo black box, however, makes that difficult to do, and the more assumptions the black box makes, the worse it gets. So it would give us all some comfort if we could at least run several different Monte Carlo programs and get similar results.

Unfortunately, that's not possible either, as Ed McCarthy reported in two excellent articles in *Bloomberg Wealth Manager* magazine in 2002: "*Wealth Manager* looked at some of the Monte Carlo applications on the Internet available to advisers. We supplied each of the application providers with the same set of particulars about a couple in their 50s and asked them to run what we thought was a relatively straightforward sample retirement-planning scenario. As it turned out, the results varied startlingly. The likelihood that the couple's retirement assets would support their desired retirement income for their projected life spans ranged from less than 50 percent at one application provider to 95 percent at another." McCarthy explained how this might happen: "The variation is a testament to the complexity of Monte Carlo methodology. For example, the results can vary significantly depending on whether the model works with specific securities or with representative asset classes. The results also vary according to the inputs the model assumes, such as expected return and volatility. In fact, even as the idea of using Monte Carlo simulation continues to make inroads with financial advisers, the technology's critics are raising more and more caution flags. Some observers go so far as to challenge the validity of using Monte Carlo simulation at all for typical retirement forecasts; others question the assumptions and computational techniques behind the various softwares' results."[8] Monte Carlo is the perfect example of the infamous black box from which you always get answers but seldom understanding.

Problem 2: What Does the Projection Mean?

The most sophisticated analysis, the most elegant solution, or the most detailed report is useless if you cannot easily explain it to your client. And before you can do that, you must understand it yourself. Monte Carlo presents a few challenges when judged against this requirement. Assume you rerun the Monte Carlo for John and Ann with some changes that improve their probability of success to 70 percent. Is this new result good enough? Many programs decide for you. In some, good is more than 70 percent; bad is everything less. In others, 70 percent to 80 percent may be fair, and it takes 90 percent to reach excellent. One program defines 75 percent to 90 percent as the "comfort zone." Being in the comfort zone is good, lower means uncertainty, and higher means sacrifice. In another program, you get rained on at one probability and perpetual sunshine at another. Sun is always good, right?

On the surface, each of these may sound fine, but each defines good and bad differently. Which one is right? The problem is that none of them can possibly be right—at least not for every client and every situation. It's an example of using a computer program and cool graphics to make a subjective concept appear quantifiable. Such easy answers are what some salespeople find helpful. But these simplifications do not represent the real world and real clients. Everything truly important within financial planning is subjective. Investment decisions are primarily emotional, not logical. So when you say to your client: "You have a 70 percent chance of reaching your goals," she reacts emotionally, based on her unique situation. Who is the client and what are her goals? Is it Gail, a 75-year-old with one must-have goal, which is to pay for basic living expenses? She might not be comfortable with anything less than a 95 percent probability of success. Or is it Tom, a 35-year-old married man with two kids to put through college and at least 30 years until retirement? He may be very content now with a 50 percent to 60 percent result. In fact, it may be impossible for Tom to attain a higher probability without making unreasonable assumptions about what might happen in the distant future. Does it really help a client to categorize his or her situation as bad? As soon as you try to quantify the personal and subjective, you disconnect from the client's reality.

Another related problem is how this approach devalues the goal-setting process. The heart of financial planning is your ability to help clients identify, quantify, and prioritize goals. You want to give your client the freedom to share all their goals, including wants and wishes, not just needs. But if they do so and add more goals, their probability of success can quickly fall into the bad category. This is nonsense. A 60 percent chance of attaining all of her goals, including dreams and wishes, may be fine. You don't want your clients to limit their goals to only the most important ones just to get a higher score. That's why it's so important to prioritize goals and to be able to demonstrate not just that there may be some risk to attaining them, but which goals are most at risk. A Monte Carlo probability doesn't illustrate this well because its result is all-or-nothing. Your client succeeds at all goals or fails at all goals.

Now, let's look at the other side of probability. The probability of success for John and Ann is 70 percent, so, conversely, their probability of failure is 30 percent. What does that mean? More important, how does the client interpret the probability? When you say "failure" to a client who is retired, she's likely to say—or, more often, think to herself—"Oh no, I've got a 30 percent chance of running out of money! I'll be broke! I'll be living on the streets!" Is this what the numbers really mean? Obviously not. While the probability of failure does reflect the statistical projection that in 30 percent of the iterations there was not enough money to fund every dollar of every goal (so theoretically, the client would exhaust her portfolio), it misses several crucial points:

1 Monte Carlo assumes that no changes are made to the plan over its entire 30-year span, as if you and your client are on automatic pilot. Clearly, if your client gets unlucky and receives poor returns early, you'd suggest changes, like holding more stock through a down market or deferring some expenses.

2 Clients in retirement don't keep spending down to the last dollar. They adjust spending if necessary as they go along. As they get older, they even have a tendency to become too conservative in their spending, sometimes depriving themselves unnecessarily. A good adviser helps clients spend appropriately, which sometimes means giving them permission to spend more.

3 The projection doesn't say anything about how badly they failed. When failures are calculated, a shortfall of $1 is counted the same as a shortfall of $100,000. In addition, a Monte Carlo analysis can be very sensitive to small changes in assumptions. A small change in any one assumption can create a big change in results.

4 The projection can also be misleading. Even if the worst case happened and the client really exhausted her portfolio, is she broke? Most often, no. She often still has sources of income that will continue, such as Social Security benefits, a pension benefit, part-time employment, and rental or other income. Plus, many people have substantial value in their homes that could be tapped for cash if necessary. A discouraging Monte Carlo projection means only that there weren't sufficient assets *in her portfolio* to pay for everything the client wanted; it does not mean that she will go broke.

Problem 3: What Risk Does the Projection Hide?

Let's assume that you've made additional assumptions that improve John and Ann's plan and presented their new Monte Carlo results, including a colorful graph showing a 90 percent probability of success. After looking at the graph for a moment, they sit back in their chair with big smiles and Ann says, "Thanks, I feel so much better knowing that we won't run out of money during retirement." You're done, right? Well, not quite. While the Monte Carlo probability reflects the effect of return-sequence risk, which is a kind of systematic risk, there is another kind of risk that Monte Carlo cannot illustrate—unsystematic risk.

Unsystematic Risk. To illustrate unsystematic risk, let's start with a risk about which all of us are aware—the potential need for care in a nursing home. You've all seen the statistics:

- ❑ Forty percent of all people over the age of 65 will spend some time in a nursing home.[9]
- ❑ The average stay in a nursing home is 2.4 years.
- ❑ The average cost of a nursing home in the United States is about $70,000 per year.[10]

These findings indicate that although there is a fairly high chance that John will spend *some time* in a nursing home, there is a much lower chance that he will be there at least three years. And obviously, the length of time in a nursing home determines the total cost. The question you have to answer is, What does this mean for John and Ann's plan? Long-term care is a risk that is not and cannot be reflected in the Monte Carlo prediction of success. The possible need for long-term care, which includes not just nursing home but also assisted living and home health care, is a very different kind of risk than return-sequence risk. It cannot be adequately reflected in a probability analysis because it is not a probability problem. It's a *possibility* problem. The probability that John (or Ann) will have high long-term care expenses sometime in the future is relatively low but very hard to predict with any confidence. However, that's not what's important. The fact is, if John should be unfortunate enough to need even three years of care, the cost could be financially devastating. The probability of the event happening may be low, but the impact can be severe. The other big difference is that this is a risk John and Ann can eliminate by purchasing a long-term care insurance policy.

Concentrated stock is another unsystematic risk that is inadequately modeled with Monte Carlo (although some software developers certainly try). Predicting what any single stock will do in the future is much different from predicting the performance of a diversified portfolio. Although historical returns and standard deviation for an individual stock can certainly be calculated from historical data, using those assumptions in a long-term plan is dangerous. You cannot predict what a stock might do in the future. Not only can it sustain a major drop in value; it can go to zero, with little or no warning. Even some of the best and "safest" companies have suddenly failed. Enron and WorldCom are just two of the most recently publicized examples. How much did knowing their standard deviations help the stockholders? "If you tell me that the [Standard & Poor's 500 index] will grow by an average of 8 percent a year for the next 20 years, I can accept that," said Professor Milevsky, after reviewing a Monte Carlo program that included individual stocks. "But if you tell me that the stock of Merrill Lynch will grow 8 percent a year for the next 20 years, I'll feel queasy. I don't know if Merrill will exist in five years, let alone that if it does exist, its performance over the past five years will give us any indication of what its next five years will be like."[11]

Plugging some assumed standard deviation into your Monte Carlo does not properly reflect the risk of a single stock. And stock options can be even worse than a stock you hold, because they are highly leveraged. If the price of the stock drops a relatively small amount or simply fails to increase at the rate you expect, the gains you were counting on can be completely wiped out. Like long-term care, this is another case in which you must address the possibility, not just the probability, of an event occurring.

Life-Expectancy Risk. Another risk that some people, particularly actuaries, believe should be included within a Monte Carlo analysis is life-expectancy risk. Some proponents even argue that stochastic mortality is a requirement of a valid Monte Carlo analysis. It's obvious that no one can predict how long any client will live; yet, once again, you must make some assumption for life expectancy within the financial plan. Wouldn't it be wonderful if your program were smart enough to make this assumption unnecessary? That's what *stochastic mortality* is supposed to do. Actuarial predictions for life expectancy within large groups of people are very accurate. The same actuarial tables can easily be embedded within a Monte Carlo analysis so that the calculations reflect the exact probability of death occurring in any year of the plan, not just at the end of the life expectancy. In some of the iterations, because the clients are assumed to die early, they have money left and this counts as a success, which increases their overall probability of success.

This factor is statistically accurate but not very useful to real advisers and real clients. In his article "Puzzling Predictions," Ed McCarthy reported that "most of the experts we talked with say that modeling the client's life expectancy as a random variable can produce misleading results."[12] This is one question where I don't think you need to be an expert to see that it doesn't make sense. It certainly doesn't *feel* right. The purpose of financial planning is to make sure clients have enough money to last as long as they may need it, and you must assume they'll need it a long time. Your real worry isn't that they'll die early but that they will live too long. What possible sense does it make to tell your client that she can spend more money now because you're assuming in some of the Monte Carlo iterations that she'll die early? How does a person die "some of the time"? This is another example of sound mathematics conflicting with sound planning—not to mention with reality.

These three issues—long-term care, a concentrated stock position, and life expectancy—are important risk factors that must be addressed. And there are several other factors that may have a lesser but still significant impact, including future tax increases, Social Security changes, and the remote possibility your client might die tomorrow. None of these factors has anything to do with return projections and probability, and they cannot be accounted for using Monte Carlo analysis alone.

Stress Testing: More Effective Than Monte Carlo

Several significant problems affect the usefulness of any Monte Carlo analysis, but I am not suggesting that Monte Carlo is of no value. Used properly, it can provide additional information that can be helpful to client education. I am suggesting, however, that Monte Carlo doesn't do everything its promoters claim, and it is never sufficient by itself. Stress testing, an alternative to Monte Carlo, is both easier to use and more effective. Because the only way I can illustrate this alternative is with MoneyGuidePro, I want to acknowledge that this discussion is somewhat self-serving. However, as Harold Evensky would say, "I may be biased, but that doesn't mean I'm wrong."

The Process of Planning

Average returns are the only reasonable assumption you can make *as your starting point* for long-term financial planning. I believe, as do most advisers, that this statement is correct. Financial-planning professionals have had sound reasons for using average returns for all these years:

❑ It's a single, simple assumption based on historical results, adjusted according to your best judgment of the future. (Remember, historical results are the only true results we have.)

❑ Average returns are understandable and you can explain them to your clients.

Sound or not, using average returns doesn't make the problems of return-sequence risk or single-event risk go away. Those are real risks that must be addressed with every client. So what can the diligent adviser do, other than jump on the Monte Carlo bandwagon? There is, fortunately, another solution, that begins with average returns but doesn't end there.

Just as a Monte Carlo probability is not sufficient by itself, neither is an average-return result. As usual, there are no simple answers to long-term financial planning, and even the most sophisticated software cannot magically create one. But financial planning isn't an *answer* anyway; it's a *process*. Part of the process is the preparation of a financial plan that helps your client make better decisions over the long term. Before we discuss how we should analyze the results of a plan, we must first design a plan that is worth analyzing. Discussions with hundreds of financial planners suggested these three rules for effective financial planning:

Rule 1. Your client cares about only one thing—attaining his goals, even if doing so requires the acceptance of investment risk.

Rule 2. If a client actually loses money, risk becomes his foremost concern. (Rule 1 is lost to amnesia.)

Rule 3. Your advice is most effective when presented within the context of a financial plan consistent with rules 1 and 2.

To be most effective, a financial plan must focus on client goals and potential risks. It must include all goals—whether they be needs, wants, or wishes. But not all goals are equal, so they must have priorities, from the most important ("We must have X to just be OK") to the least ("Boy, wouldn't it be nice to have Y?").

Once the goals are specified, the plan must identify and illustrate the potential risks to the plan, including return-sequence risk and unsystematic risks. The plan must clearly demonstrate to the client her choices and how those choices will affect her ability to attain her goals and manage her risk. The best way to demonstrate the effectiveness of this approach is to create what I call a *retirement-lifestyle plan* for John and Ann.

The Retirement-Lifestyle Planning Process

The retirement-lifestyle planning process has five key steps.

1 Help the clients create a picture of their goals.

2 Create a base plan using average returns.

3 Stress test their plan for return-sequence risk and unsystematic risks.

4 Repeat steps 2 and 3 as required to create the plan that works for them.

5 Use Monte Carlo to compare relative results (if helpful for that client).

When the steps are completed, send them off to enjoy life and tell them to come back in a year to do it all again.

To see how this works, you'll need a little more information about John and Ann.

❑ Based on an in-depth discussion of their risk preferences, you determine that a 55 percent stock portfolio is appropriate (7.56 percent average return, 12.8 standard deviation).

❑ John and Ann will both receive Social Security benefits.

❑ Ann has a pension benefit.

❑ They own a home currently worth $665,000, appreciating at 5 percent per year.

Unlike in our earlier, simpler examples, all calculations will include taxes, and goal expense amounts are in current, after-tax dollars.

Step 1: Goals

A retirement-lifestyle plan is unique in its approach to identifying goals for retirement. Traditional retirement-distribution plans ask only one question: "How much income do you need?" Such plans assume that people have accomplished all their goals before they retire, and now all they have is a single expense need each year. In fact, the opposite is usually true. Once they retire, people often have more discretionary goals, which vary greatly by client, and even for each client will vary greatly over the course of retirement. The goals also vary greatly in relative importance.

A retirement-lifestyle plan asks a very different question: "John and Ann, what would you like to do during retirement? What are your goals?" The completed lifestyle goal summary is shown in **FIGURE 8.4**. This single page reflects all the goals John and Ann care about (rule 1) and indicates how important they consider each (the priority). That's why we call it a retirement-lifestyle plan; it's their personal picture of how they would like to live during retirement.

Source: MoneyGuidePro financial-planning software. © PIE Technologies, Inc.

FIGURE 8.4

My Financial Goals

Priority	Goal Description
1	Retirement - Minimum Living Expense $66,000 from 2005 thru 2030 (Both retired) $54,000 from 2031 thru 2033 (Ann alone)
2	Main Car - Lexus RX 330 $30,000 in 2008 Recurring every 3 years for a total of 7 times
3	Travel (until 80) $18,000 in 2006 Recurring every year for a total of 15 times
4	Fun Car -Mini Cooper $20,000 in 2010 Recurring every 4 years for a total of 4 times
5	Gifts to Susan $12,000 in 2010 Recurring every year for a total of 10 times
6	Extra Living Expense $10,000 in 2005 Recurring every year until end of Ann's plan

Step 2: Base Plan

FIGURE 8.5 shows the plan results for John and Ann, assuming their portfolio earns an average return of 7.56 percent every year. The percentage shown for each goal is *not a probability*. It is simply the percentage of the goal that was funded in the plan (using average returns) divided by the total amount needed for the goal over the entire plan period. One unique feature of this plan is that the goals are funded in priority order rather than in sequential order. In this example, because all goals are fully funded (100 percent), priority order doesn't make a difference. You'll see the usefulness of this approach when we look at stress testing in Step 3.

Step 3: Stress Testing

At the bottom of Figure 8.5 is an amount called the *safety margin*. This is the portfolio value at the end of the plan, after all goals have been funded. It's one of the most important numbers for the education of your client. Consider three possible results for the safety margin. If any goal is not funded to 100 percent, the safety margin must be zero. There can't be any

FIGURE 8.5

Current Plan

These Results are calculated using an average return for your pre-retirement and post-retirement periods. In the real world, returns are generally not received smoothly and, in fact, can vary greatly from the average return from year to year.

Goal	Estimated % of Goal Funded
1 Retirement - Minimum Living Expense $66,000 from 2005 thru 2030 (Both retired) $54,000 from 2031 thru 2033 (Ann alone)	100% ☆☆☆☆☆
2 Main Car - Lexus RX 330 $30,000 in 2008 Recurring every 3 years for a total of 7 times	100% ☆☆☆☆☆
3 Travel (until 80) $18,000 in 2006 Recurring every year for a total of 15 times	100% ☆☆☆☆☆
4 Fun Car -Mini Cooper $20,000 in 2010 Recurring every 4 years for a total of 4 times	100% ☆☆☆☆☆
5 Gifts to Susan $12,000 in 2010 Recurring every year for a total of 10 times	100% ☆☆☆☆☆
6 Extra Living Expense $10,000 in 2005 Recurring every year until end of Ann's plan	100% ☆☆☆☆☆

Safety Margin (Portfolio Value at End of Plan in 2033)

Current Dollars
$288,000

Source: MoneyGuidePro financial-planning software. © PIE Technologies, Inc.

money left if it was all used to fund goals. If all goals are funded to 100 percent and there is a small safety margin, it indicates that the goals will be fully funded only if everything works *exactly as predicted* in the plan. If anything goes even a little worse than expected (like lower returns), some goal(s) will not be met because there is no safety margin to make up the difference. If the safety margin is relatively large, however, you know there is some protection against things going wrong. The larger the safety margin, the greater the protection.

The safety margin is a simple concept that's easy to illustrate and explain to John and Ann. You show them the results in Figure 8.5. You're pleased to point out that they can attain all their goals and still have a safety margin of $288,000 (current dollars). But you know that the plan assumes they will earn an average return of precisely 7.56 percent each year; you also know that won't happen. The safety margin certainly gives them some protection against losses, but is it enough? How can you tell?

You could run a Monte Carlo analysis, which would show a probability of success of just 55 percent. Now the plan doesn't look very good. But

FIGURE 8.6

Stress Testing - Bad Timing
Target Port

Goal	Estimated % Funded	
	Average Returns Every Year	Bad Timing
Retirement - Minimum Living Expense	100%	100%
Main Car - Lexus RX 330	100%	100%
Travel (until 80)	100%	100%
Fun Car -Mini Cooper	100%	100%
Gifts to Susan	100%	100%
Extra Living Expense	100%	34%

Safety Margin
(Value at End of Plan)   Current Dollars: $288,000 $0

as we discussed before, additional analysis may create more questions than answers. How do you explain what it means to John and Ann that their plan will fail 45 percent of the time? Should they change their goals based on numbers generated from a black box?

The alternative to Monte Carlo is *stress testing*. We identified earlier that the biggest risk during retirement is often return-sequence risk. Even if your client obtains the average return you projected over the life of the plan, bad returns in the early years will cause disproportionately poor results, as was clearly demonstrated in our first example (Figure 8.1). We will now use that same approach with John and Ann. **FIGURE 8.6** shows the results of a stress test called *bad timing*, which compares the average-return result with the bad-timing result. Bad timing assumes that the plan gets two of the worst-performing years immediately: −18.04 (two standard deviations below average) in year one and −5.24 (one standard deviation below average) in year two. A slightly higher average return follows every year thereafter so that this result has the same total average return (7.56 percent) for the entire plan. Note that unlike a Monte Carlo analysis, both results are based on the same average return over the entire plan period.

The result for the "bad timing" column shows that if John and Ann were unlucky enough to get the worst two years of returns right away, they would be unable to fund all their goals. That's the bad news. The good news is that the only goal not fully funded is their lowest-priority goal—extra living expense—with 34 percent funding. All their higher priority goals are fully funded. This is the power of creating a retirement-lifestyle plan that funds goals in priority order. It changes the nature of your conversation with your client. You don't have to explain what it means to fail 45 percent of the time. Instead, you can confidently tell John and Ann that they are likely to attain their most important goals, and that they don't have to worry about running out of money. Then you can discuss the relative risk to their less important goals. Clients are generally comfortable with the idea that if returns don't go as well as expected, they might have to reduce spending on less important goals.

Step 4: Repeat Steps 2 and 3 to Create a Workable Plan

Of course, John and Ann could make changes to their plan that would increase their safety margin, but that might not be necessary. When an often-overlooked asset is included in the stress test, their plan may actually be more secure than it first appeared. Their home is worth $665,000 today and appreciating at 5 percent per year. Instead of making sacrifices now to create a greater safety margin, you can show John and Ann how they could use the value of their home to provide for extra cash in the future if it were ever needed to offset poor returns. **FIGURE 8.7** shows their plan results if they withdrew $600,000 cash (future dollars) from their home in 17 years, at which time it will be worth $1,750,000. Again, even with bad timing, they still maintain a safety margin of $273,285 (current dollars).

Earlier, I identified three types of risk that are not addressed within a Monte Carlo analysis—long-term care (LTC), concentrated stock, and longevity. These can also be handled more effectively with stress testing.

FIGURE **8.7**

Stress Testing - Bad Timing
Cash from House

Goal	Estimated % Funded	
	Average Returns Every Year	Bad Timing
Retirement - Minimum Living Expense	100%	100%
Main Car - Lexus RX 330	100%	100%
Travel (until 80)	100%	100%
Fun Car - Mini Cooper	100%	100%
Gifts to Susan	100%	100%
Extra Living Expense	100%	100%
Safety Margin (Value at End of Plan)	Current Dollars: $777,000	$273,285

Source: MoneyGuidePro financial-planning software. © PIE Technologies, Inc.

FIGURE **8.8**

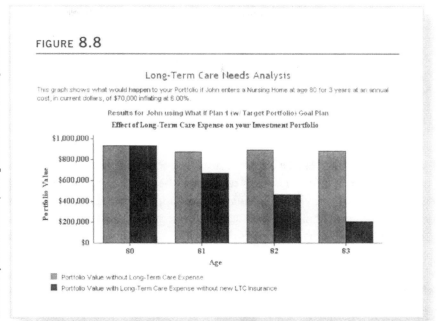

Long-Term Care Needs Analysis

This graph shows what would happen to your Portfolio if John enters a Nursing Home at age 80 for 3 years at an annual cost, in current dollars, of $70,000 inflating at 6.00%.

Results for John using What If Plan 1 (w/ Target Portfolio) Goal Plan

Effect of Long-Term Care Expense on your Investment Portfolio

- Portfolio Value without Long-Term Care Expense
- Portfolio Value with Long-Term Care Expense without new LTC Insurance

What would happen if John required nursing home care at age 80? As **FIGURE 8.8** shows, within just three years, the value of their investment portfolio is almost wiped out. That presents a significant risk that must be addressed. Fortunately, you can eliminate this risk by recommending the purchase of an LTC policy, which would cost them about $3,000 per year. You could also easily demonstrate how they could include that cost in their retirement lifestyle plan and still meet their goals.

The risk of a concentrated stock position can be demonstrated in a similar way. Assume John and Ann have $300,000 in company stock (30 percent of their portfolio). The risk isn't that their stock position will cause greater return volatility, as reflected in a higher standard deviation, but rather that the value of the stock could drop rapidly and unpredictably by 25 percent, 50 percent, or even 100 percent. The stress test can demonstrate to John and Ann the devastating impact this could have on their plan and the benefit that could be derived from diversifying as soon as possible.

Longevity risk is different from LTC expenses or a concentrated stock position in that it results from good fortune. Based on current life expectancy tables, John has a 30 percent chance of living to age 90, and Ann has a 30 percent chance of living to age 93. But what happens if they live longer? Will they still have enough money? To find out, we can stress test their plan by extending life expectancy by five years. In this case, with the future cash from the home included, the bad-timing result shows that John and

Ann still have a safety margin of $180,000, indicating that longevity is not a significant risk for them.

Stress testing is an effective way to educate your client about return-sequence risk and unsystematic risks. It leads to more realistic client expectations and demonstrates the benefits of sticking with a long-term plan. It's the best way to counter the client amnesia of rule 2, when potential risk becomes actual loss.

Step 5: Monte Carlo

Can stress testing replace Monte Carlo? For some advisers and for some clients, it can. For others, stress testing can be used in conjunction with Monte Carlo to provide additional information. Rather than focusing on the *absolute* probability of the success of one plan, Monte Carlo is most valuable when used to compare the *relative* probability of the success of two or more alternate plans. For John and Ann, it would show that if they include the potential cash from their home in their plan, their probability of success increases from 55 percent to 95 percent. This might make you and them more comfortable with the plan.

A financial plan is of lasting value only if your clients stick with it over the long term, even as losses occur (rule 3). To accomplish this, clients must take ownership of the plan. It must be *their* plan, not *your* plan for them, and this can only happen if they understand it, believe in it, and are prepared for its inherent risks. It must help them have realistic expectations. The retirement-lifestyle plan for John and Ann is an example of this kind of plan.

As I CONDUCTED the research for this chapter, I had a curious experience. Normally, I expect that by reading more articles, gathering more opinions, and analyzing more examples, I will quickly gain insight and understanding about my topic. This has not been true for my research into Monte Carlo. Rather than finding answers that make sense, what I found instead was a seemingly endless series of increasingly complex questions. There is always another math or statistics expert who can demonstrate the flaws in any Monte Carlo methodology you might select and then recommend necessary and more complex improvements.

If normal distributions aren't good enough, try lognormal ones. Still not good enough? Go to Latin hypercube or leptokurtic distributions. Are you assuming the random walk theory for returns? That's no good; you should use cross- and serial correlations with reversion to the mean. Your Monte Carlo runs only 1,000 iterations? You need at least 10,000 for results to be accurate. And if that isn't confusing enough, other experts can present compelling analyses that prove Monte Carlo shouldn't be used for financial planning at all. David Nawrocki, a professor of finance at Villanova University who has written extensively on the use of Monte Carlo, has been suggesting exactly that since at least 2001.[13]

If, amid all this uncertainty, the only result you present to your clients is their probability of success from the Monte Carlo analysis, it should include the following disclaimer:

Result: Your probability of success is 87 percent.

Disclaimer: Projections are based on many unprovable assumptions for future returns and do not reflect the risks of long-term care, premature death, tax increases, changes in Social Security, longevity, concentrated stock positions, or changes in your goals.

A financial adviser who repeatedly adds sophistication to the Monte Carlo algorithm in an effort to gain accuracy but ignores stress testing is like the captain of the Titanic who assigns a crew of experts to continually fine-tune the engine to gain a little more speed but has no one on deck looking out for icebergs. Because there are only a few icebergs in a very big ocean, the captain knows that his chances of hitting one are very low. Therefore, the *probability* of reaching New York safely is very high. What is ignored, however, is that as long as there is at least one iceberg in the ocean, there's a *possibility* the ship will hit it. And it takes only one iceberg to sink an "unsinkable" ship.

All advisers want to do the right thing for their clients. Unfortunately, in the uncertain world of financial planning, where almost every fact is an assumption and every result an estimate, it's difficult to know what is right. The greatest value you provide your clients is not just to analyze probabilities but to consider possibilities, whether they be dreams or disasters. Financial-planning programs, with tools like stress testing and Monte Carlo, can help you accomplish this task, but none can replace your own informed judgment. And when it comes to illustrating important concepts to clients, understandable trumps sophisticated every time.

Chapter Notes

1. David B. Loeper, "Do You Perceive a Contradiction? Examining the Premises of Financial Advisors" (posted August 6, 2003), http://www.financeware.com/.

2. Andrew Gluck, "The Nuts and Bolts of Monte Carlo," *Investment Advisor* (June 2002), http://www.investmentadvisor.com.

3. MoneyGuidePro is a financial-planning program developed by PIE Technologies, where I am CEO and principal stockholder.

4. John D. Kingston, "Monte Carlo Simulation: Challenging the Sacred Cow," *Journal of Financial Planning* (November 2001), http://www.fpanet.org/journal/index.cfm.

5. Evan Simonoff, "Sharpe Focus," *Financial Advisor* (February 2002), http://www.financialadvisormagazine.com.

6. Conversation with author, December 2004.

7. Gluck, "The Nuts and Bolts of Monte Carlo."

8. Ed McCarthy, "Puzzling Predictions," *Bloomberg Wealth Manager* (December 2002/January 2003): 40.

9. Agency for Healthcare Research and Quality, U.S. Department of Health and Human Services, "AHCPR Research on Long-Term Care," www.ahrq.gov/research/longtrm.1.htm.

10. MetLife Mature Market Institute, "MetLife Market Survey of Nursing Home and Home Care Costs," (September 2004), p. 2.

11. Gluck, "The Nuts and Bolts of Monte Carlo."

12. McCarthy, "Puzzling Predictions," p. 40.

13. David Nawrocki, "The Problems with Monte Carlo Simulation," *Journal of Financial Planning* (November 2001), http://www.fpanet.org/journal/index.cfm.

CHAPTER 9

Understanding Required Minimum Distributions

APRIL K. CAUDILL

N o discussion of distribution planning would be complete without an explanation of the rules that govern lifetime required minimum distributions (RMDs). These somewhat complex rules, set forth in the Internal Revenue Code and amplified by extensive regulations, affect every individual who lives much past age 70 while owning an individual retirement account (IRA),[1] qualified plan account, or tax-sheltered (Section 403(b)) annuity.[2]

The minimum-distribution requirements actually serve two useful functions. First, they implement the legislative intent of assuring that retirement accumulations are in fact used for funding retirement rather than as a tax shelter of indefinite duration or as a means of transferring wealth to the next generation. Second, they give taxpayers a ballpark idea of how much (or how little) they should be taking out of their retirement accounts to make the funds last for their average life expectancy.

The Rules and How They Apply

Essentially, the minimum-distribution rules require the IRA owner or plan participant to begin receiving distributions from the account by his *required beginning date* (which usually occurs shortly after age 70½) and to receive at least a certain amount each year to avoid a penalty. The penalty for noncompliance is substantial—50 percent of the amount that should have been taken—and it's built into Form 1040 among the tax payment provisions. Consequently, if the taxpayer files an accurate return, the penalty is imposed automatically rather than the error being revealed later by an audit.

Starting Distributions

The kickoff point for RMDs is known as the "required beginning date." For non-Roth IRA owners,[3] the individual's required beginning date is the April 1 that falls after the calendar year in which the individual reaches age 70½.[4] The required beginning date rule does not apply to Roth IRAs because they are not subject to the *lifetime* minimum-distribution requirements.[5] For a qualified plan participant who does not own 5 percent[6] or more of the company that is sponsoring the plan, the required beginning date is April 1 of the year after the individual *retires*, if that year is later than the year he or she turns 70½.[7]

Tax-sheltered annuities (TSAs) generally operate in the same manner as qualified plans, but because TSAs are operated by governmental or tax-exempt employers, the 5 percent owner rule does not apply. Thus, TSA participants generally may wait until April 1 of the year after *retirement* to begin distributions from the account.[8] An additional exception applies to TSA participants whose accounts contain funds accrued before 1987 (if the plan custodian has kept adequate records of pre-1987/post-1986 balances). Such a participant may wait until age 75 to take distributions from the pre-1987 balance. This exception is explained under "Tax-Sheltered Annuities" (see page 150).

An individual reaches age 70½ on the date that falls exactly six months after his 70th birthday.[9] Thus, an individual born on November 30, 1934, for example, would reach age 70½ on May 30, 2005. His required beginning date for minimum distributions would be April 1, 2006. Because of the way this rule is written, an individual born from July 1 through December 31 will start distributions a year later than individuals born from January 1 through June 30 of the same year.

How Much to Take

The amount that must be distributed each year is determined by dividing the individual's account balance as of December 31 (or the last valuation date) of the prior year by a life expectancy based on the individual's age for the year for which the distribution is being made.[10] This life expectancy is generally taken from the Uniform Lifetime Table (see **FIGURE 9.1**) published by the Treasury Department in final regulations in 2002.[11] The factors in the Uniform Lifetime Table are based on the joint and survivor life expectancy of the individual who owns the account and on a hypothetical beneficiary who is 10 years younger than the account owner.

FIGURE **9.1** *Uniform Lifetime Table*

AGE OF EMPLOYEE	DISTRIBUTION PERIOD	AGE OF EMPLOYEE	DISTRIBUTION PERIOD
70	27.4	93	9.6
71	26.5	94	9.1
72	25.6	95	8.6
73	24.7	96	8.1
74	23.8	97	7.6
75	22.9	98	7.1
76	22.0	99	6.7
77	21.2	100	6.3
78	20.3	101	5.9
79	19.5	102	5.5
80	18.7	103	5.2
81	17.9	104	4.9
82	17.1	105	4.5
83	16.3	106	4.2
84	15.5	107	3.9
85	14.8	108	3.7
86	14.1	109	3.4
87	13.4	110	3.1
88	12.7	111	2.9
89	12.0	112	2.6
90	11.4	113	2.4
91	10.8	114	2.1
92	10.2	115+	1.9

Source: Treas. Reg. §1.401(a)(9)-9, A-2

An individual's first distribution is due by April 1 of the year after he reaches age 70½. The second distribution is due December 31 of the same year (the year after he reaches 70½). Thereafter, all distributions are due December 31 of each subsequent year. Each distribution amount is calculated using (a) the account balance as of December 31 of the *prior* calendar year and (b) the applicable life-expectancy factor from the Uniform Lifetime Table for the age he reached in the year for which the distribution is being made.

For example, assume that Anthony turned 70½ in August 2004. His IRA balance was $500,000 on December 31, 2003, and he reached age 70 on his birthday in 2004. The Uniform Lifetime Table factor for age 70 is 27.4 years; thus, his first distribution, which was due by April 1, 2005, is $18,248 ($500,000 ÷ 27.4). Assume the account balance on December 31, 2004, was $530,000. At age 71 in 2005, Anthony's Uniform Lifetime Table factor would be 26.5 years, so his required distribution due by December 31, 2005, would be $20,000 ($530,000 ÷ 26.5). If Anthony did not wish to have more than $38,000 of taxable distributions in 2005, he could have taken the first distribution during 2004. However, if he did not do so, he would be required to receive both amounts in 2005.

The first year's required distribution does not have to be delayed until April 1 of the following year. Individuals who want to avoid having two taxable distributions in one year may take the first distribution in the year they reach age 70½, or they may purchase an annuity (see "Annuity Payments," below). The extension of the first RMD deadline to April 1 of the following year is simply a procedural "grace period" that allows taxpayers a little longer to determine the amount and timing of the distribution.

There is one additional exception to the use of the Uniform Lifetime Table. If the IRA owner or plan participant has a spouse beneficiary who is more than 10 years younger than the participant, a somewhat longer payout period is permitted under a joint and survivor life expectancy.[12] This longer payout period[13] takes into account the longer life expectancy of the younger spouse. Aside from this "younger spouse rule," the identity of the beneficiary has no effect on the amount or term of a lifetime RMD payout from an individual account.

Annuity Payments

The requirements for minimum distributions are slightly different when payouts are made from an annuity rather than from an individual account, because annuity payment amounts are predetermined (generally by an insurance company) based on the annuity funding level, design features, and age of the annuitant rather than being calculated each year. Most of the rules that apply to annuities apply whether the annuity distributions are provided under a qualified plan, an individual retirement annuity, or a Section 403(b) tax-sheltered annuity.[14]

Annuity payments must begin by the employee's required beginning date. A distribution of the annuity contract itself will *not* satisfy the minimum-distribution requirement.[15] If the plan is a defined-benefit plan and the employee retires later than the year he reaches age 70½, generally the plan must actuarially increase his accrued benefit to reflect the delay in the commencement of benefits.[16]

The general rule for annuity payments is that distributions must be made as periodic payments, at least annually, for one of the following periods: (a) the life of the employee, (b) the joint lives of the employee and beneficiary, or (c) a period certain that is no longer than one of these two periods.[17] Special limits may apply if the beneficiary is not the employee's spouse.[18] From the employee's standpoint, this means that as long as these rules are followed, individual annuitants do not need to perform calculations to make sure they're receiving enough to avoid the penalty for failure to take minimum distributions. Many retirees choose an annuity that includes a lifetime payout with a guarantee of payments for a specified number of years (that is, a "period-certain" guarantee).[19]

The amount of the first RMD payment must be the amount that is required for one payment interval (for example, monthly, bimonthly, semiannually, or annually). After the first payment, the second payment is not required until the end of the next interval, even if the interval ends in the following calendar year.[20] For example, let's suppose John was born in September 1933 and reached age 70½ in 2004. He was required to begin distributions from his IRA by April 1, 2005, but he chose to begin an annuity payout in 2004. The value of the IRA at the end of 2003 was $530,000. Assume John purchases an immediate annuity (age 71, single-life annuity with a 10-year guarantee) and that he receives $3,820 monthly, or an annual payout of $45,840. If he receives his first monthly payment of $3,820 in December 2004 and continues the monthly payout in January 2005 and thereafter, his distribution requirement for 2004 will be satisfied, even though he received only one monthly payment during the 2004 calendar year.

As a very general rule, annuity payments may not increase over the life of the annuity; however, there are a number of exceptions to this rule. Annuity payouts may increase (1) for cost-of-living adjustments,[21] (2) to provide "pop-up payments" following a divorce or the death of a survivor beneficiary, (3) for changes resulting from a plan amendment, and (4) to allow a beneficiary to convert the survivor portion of a joint and survivor payout to a lump-sum payout after an employee's death.[22] In the case of a noncommercial annuity (such as one paid directly by a large employer's defined-benefit plan), a limited group of additional increases are provided.[23] A few additional increases are permitted for commercial annuities purchased from an insurance company.[24] These exceptions are particularly important for owners of variable annuities, which increased sharply in popularity during the 1990s bull market.

Life changes may result in an annuitant or beneficiary wanting to change his or her payments (this is referred to in the regulations as a *reannuitization*). Annuitants who continue to work after starting a required payout may need a higher income when they actually retire. An individual may get married and want to change to a joint and survivor payout. In some cases, a plan termination may mandate a change to the payout, or the annuitant may want to switch from a period-certain payout to a life annuity. In each of these situations,[25] the RMD regulations allow the annuity payout to be modified, as long as the new payouts satisfy the minimum-distribution requirements and the modification is treated as a new annuity starting date.[26]

Surviving Spouses

The rules and choices available to a surviving spouse are an important consideration in retirement-income planning, even though they occur after the death of the participant or IRA owner. A surviving spouse has options that are not offered to any other beneficiary, and the choices he or she makes in the immediate aftermath of the participant's death can have lasting tax consequences. It should be noted that although the regulations define "spouse" as an individual who is treated as such under applicable state law, for federal tax law purposes, only a member of the opposite sex may be considered a spouse.[27]

Surviving spouse beneficiaries have three options with respect to a deceased spouse's qualified plan interest: (1) they can roll over the plan interest into an IRA of their own (or into a qualified plan that accepts such rollovers), (2) they can begin receiving distributions by the end of the year after the employee's death, or (3) they can begin receiving distributions by the end of the year the employee would have reached age 70½.[28] Of course, if the decedent and spouse were already receiving payments under a joint and survivor annuity, the spouse could continue to receive those payments.[29] Surviving spouses use the after-death single-life expectancy table (**FIGURE 9.2**) for options (2) or (3). Note that the rollover option is available for all or part of a qualified plan distribution, but for only 60 days following receipt of a payout.[30]

For a surviving spouse IRA beneficiary, one additional option applies: such a spouse generally may elect to treat a decedent's IRA as his or her own, which means that the RMDs are calculated as if the spouse were the

FIGURE **9.2** *Single-Life Table*

AGE	LIFE EXPECTANCY	AGE	LIFE EXPECTANCY
0	82.4	28	55.3
1	81.6	29	54.3
2	80.6	30	53.3
3	79.7	31	52.4
4	78.7	32	51.4
5	77.7	33	50.4
6	76.7	34	49.4
7	75.8	35	48.5
8	74.8	36	47.5
9	73.8	37	46.5
10	72.8	38	45.6
11	71.8	39	44.6
12	70.8	40	43.6
13	69.9	41	42.7
14	68.9	42	41.7
15	67.9	43	40.7
16	66.9	44	39.8
17	66.0	45	38.8
18	65.0	46	37.9
19	64.0	47	37.0
20	63.0	48	36.0
21	62.1	49	35.1
22	61.1	50	34.2
23	60.1	51	33.3
24	59.1	52	32.3
25	58.2	53	31.4
26	57.2	54	30.5
27	56.2	55	29.6

(Continued)

Source: Treas. Reg. §1.401(a)(9)-9, A-1

FIGURE **9.2** *Single-Life Table (continued)*

AGE	LIFE EXPECTANCY	AGE	LIFE EXPECTANCY
56	28.7	84	8.1
57	27.9	85	7.6
58	27.0	86	7.1
59	26.1	87	6.7
60	25.2	88	6.3
61	24.4	89	5.9
62	23.5	90	5.5
63	22.7	91	5.2
64	21.8	92	4.9
65	21.0	93	4.6
66	20.2	94	4.3
67	19.4	95	4.1
68	18.6	96	3.8
69	17.8	97	3.6
70	17.0	98	3.4
71	16.3	99	3.1
72	15.5	100	2.9
73	14.8	101	2.7
74	14.1	102	2.5
75	13.4	103	2.3
76	12.7	104	2.1
77	12.1	105	1.9
78	11.4	106	1.7
79	10.8	107	1.5
80	10.2	108	1.4
81	9.7	109	1.2
82	9.1	110	1.1
83	8.6	111+	1.0

Source: Treas. Reg. §1.401(a)(9)-9, A-1

original owner of the account. For a younger surviving spouse, this option will delay distributions the longest. No special procedures are provided for making this election, and there is no deadline for doing so. However, a surviving spouse will be deemed to have made the election if (a) no RMDs are made under the options described in the preceding paragraph or (b) the surviving spouse contributes any additional amounts to the IRA.[31]

Under some circumstances, the election by a surviving spouse to roll over an inherited account or treat it as his or her own IRA may be unwise. If the funds in the account are needed to provide for the surviving spouse's support and the spouse has not yet reached age 59½, a 10 percent premature distribution penalty may apply to withdrawals occurring after the election is made. Since the 10 percent penalty does not apply to *any* required minimum distributions made to a beneficiary, regardless of his or her age, careful consideration should be given to the younger surviving spouse's financial needs before retirement funds are moved to a qualified plan or IRA.

Qualified Domestic Relations Orders

With the divorce rate in the United States averaging an estimated 50 percent,[32] it's inevitable that some participants' retirement accounts will have been divided before the commencement of required minimum distributions or may even be divided after age 70½ as a result of a qualified domestic relations order (QDRO).[33] A QDRO can be enforced in two ways, each having a potentially different effect on the participant's compliance with the minimum-distribution requirements.

By definition, all QDROs provide for a portion of an employee's qualified plan account to be payable to a spouse, former spouse, child, or other dependent (alternate payee).[34] For RMD purposes, the alternate payee will be treated as the employee's spouse (or surviving spouse). QDROs for defined-contribution plans are typically drafted to require that the account be segregated and the alternate payee's interest in the account paid out, as most plan sponsors do not want the responsibility or cost of maintaining an investment account for an ex-spouse.

Assuming the QDRO provides that the employee's benefit will be divided and a portion allocated to the alternate payee, the alternate payee's account will be treated as a separate account (or segregated share) for RMD purposes. Distributions must begin by the *employee's* required beginning date, but they will be calculated separately on the segregated account.[35] Since the account must separately satisfy the RMD rules, the failure on the part of the alternate payee to take minimum distributions does not affect the employee's distribution requirements.

If the QDRO does not provide for a division of the plan benefit (as may occur in a defined-benefit plan) but instead merely states that a portion of the employee's benefit is to be paid to an alternate payee, the employee's required beginning date still governs, but the combined benefits are treated as one account.[36] In other words, all distributions to either spouse are aggregated for purposes of satisfying the RMD requirements. This means that if the alternate payee fails to take minimum distributions as required, the employee would be obliged to take a higher amount, or if the alternate payee takes more than the required amount, the employee may be able to take less.

Following a court's issuance of a domestic relations order, the plan administrator has up to 18 months to determine whether the order satisfies the requirements to qualify as a QDRO.[37] During that time, the plan must segregate the amounts that would be payable to the alternate payee if the order is approved as a QDRO. If the order is neither approved nor modified to comply with the QDRO rules within the 18-month period, the funds can be paid out as though the order had never existed. A special exception to the RMD requirement is provided for the segregated portion during this 18-month period, so that no compliance failure will occur if distributions are not made. Amounts in the segregated account will be treated in the same manner as nonvested funds (see "Vesting Restrictions," page 151).[38]

Tax-Sheltered Annuities

Tax-sheltered annuities (TSAs, also known as Section 403(b) contracts) are typically the retirement plan of teachers and other employees of public schools and tax-exempt organizations. Generally, minimum distributions for TSAs are calculated in the same manner as for qualified plan accounts; however, there is a significant difference that affects some older employees with plan accumulations dating before 1987. The reason for the special rule is that the minimum-distribution requirements of IRC Section 401(a)(9) technically apply only to tax-sheltered annuity amounts accruing on or after January 1, 1987, and to growth since that date on amounts accrued prior to 1986.[39] For those amounts, the rules are essentially the same as those described for qualified plans, except as noted.

The special rules for pre-1987 account balances are available only if the plan custodian has adequate records to distinguish between pre-1987 and post-1986 balances. If the custodian does not have such records, the entire balance is treated as accruing after 1986.[40] Distributions required under the RMD rules reduce the post-1986 balance, but to the extent the participant takes any additional distribution beyond the required amount, the excess reduces the pre-1987 balance.[41] The distribution requirement for pre-1987 balances in TSAs with sufficient records to distinguish between the two account balances does not begin until the later of retirement or age 75.[42] Generally, this rule requires that the present value of the aggregate payments made to the participant be more than 50 percent of the present value of the total payments to be made to the participant and his beneficiaries.[43]

Tax-sheltered annuity participants are free to choose to apply the minimum-distribution requirements (as described above for qualified plans) to the entire balance in their account, regardless of when the amounts were accrued.[44]

Vesting Restrictions

In unusual circumstances, an employee who is not yet 100 percent vested in his account may reach his required beginning date while remaining employed (for example, if he began the job at a late age and the plan document does not provide for delaying distributions until after retirement). In this situation, a required distribution would be calculated as if the account were fully vested, but the actual distribution would come only from the vested portion of the account. As the employee's vesting percentage increases, his distributions would have to be increased by the sum of any amounts that could not be distributed in prior years because his vested percentage was less than the RMD amount.[45]

Multiple IRAs

The lifetime RMD requirements for non-Roth IRAs are the same whether the account is a traditional IRA; a SEP IRA, formed as part of a simplified employee pension (SEP) or salary reduction SEP (SAR-SEP); or a SIMPLE IRA, formed as part of a savings incentive match plan for employees (SIMPLE plan).[46] Many individuals reach retirement having several IRAs either because they have participated in one of these employer plans or because they established different IRAs for different purposes or investments. In any event, an individual who has more than one IRA must calculate the required distribution for each IRA; however, he or she can then take the entire RMD amount from any one IRA.[47]

This rule does *not* apply if the taxpayer has IRAs acquired through inheritance, either as a surviving spouse or as a beneficiary of another IRA. Inherited IRAs are subject to different payout requirements than those applying to the individual's own IRA or one acquired as a surviving spouse; thus, RMDs from these different types of IRAs must generally be calculated separately and each taken from the appropriate account. For example, suppose Irene, age 72, was named as beneficiary of both her late husband's and her late father's IRAs. She also has two IRAs of her own. Despite the option to treat her husband's IRA as her own (see

"Surviving Spouses," page 146), she elects to leave the account in her husband's name and take distributions as beneficiary. She also receives a distribution from her father's IRA each year. Neither of these distributions (nor any additional amount taken from either of these accounts) affects the amounts she must receive from her own two IRAs. However, with respect *only* to her own IRAs, she may aggregate the RMD amounts and take them both from one account if she wishes.

Reporting Requirements

Under regulations that were finalized in 2002, IRA trustees and custodians are subject to two reporting requirements with respect to *lifetime* distributions—one for the IRS and one for the IRA owner.[48] Under the requirement for owners, the IRA provider servicing the account as of December 31 must provide one of two notices by January 31 of each year in which a distribution will be required. The notice can (1) merely inform the IRA owner that a minimum distribution is required and offer to calculate the amount at the owner's request or (2) inform the IRA owner of the amount of the required minimum distribution and the date by which it is required. IRA trustees are permitted to use either or both of these alternatives and may use one for some owners and the second for other owners.[49] IRA trustees are also required to report to the IRS whether a distribution is required from the IRA for the calendar year.[50]

Since an IRA trustee obviously knows the balance in the account it is servicing, it would essentially need to know only the owner's age in order to make the correct calculation using the Uniform Lifetime Table (see Figure 9.1, page 143). For purposes of the reporting requirements, an individual is presumed *not* to have a spouse more than 10 years younger, which would otherwise allow the couple to use a longer payout period.[51] The IRA trustee is not required to ascertain that the distribution amount is actually taken from that IRA, because as noted above, the owner may aggregate his IRA RMDs and take them all from one account if he or she wishes.

The 50 Percent Penalty

The penalty for noncompliance with the RMD rules is 50 percent of the amount that should have been taken but was not.[52] The 50 percent penalty is reported on Form 5329, and the penalty is carried over to Form 1040; thus, unless the taxpayer wants to take his chances with noncompliance, reporting and payment of the penalty are unavoidable. Furthermore, as a result of the reporting requirements for IRA custodians (see "Reporting Requirements," above), the IRS can generally determine—at least with respect to IRAs—whether a taxpayer should be reporting a minimum distribution. While this system is not perfect and will undoubtedly be subject to adjustments, it will make it more likely that the IRS will identify noncompliance.

THE MINIMUM-DISTRIBUTION requirements are not adjusted for income level, investment returns, or for the presence of sophisticated trusts or other estate-planning techniques. They apply across the board, whether the client needs the retirement income or dreads it. Planning techniques abound for the wealthiest taxpayers, who may seek to use charitable planning or some other tool to offset the unwanted increase in their taxable income. At the other end of the spectrum, those with lower account balances may be surprised to learn how small the annual required distribution amount is and wonder if it will make ends meet. Of course the *minimum* required distribution is just that, and taxpayers are never prohibited under these rules from withdrawing larger amounts. But the RMD amounts are designed to assure that the account funds will last throughout the account owner's life, and individuals who take larger amounts may risk depleting the retirement portfolio.

Ideally, the combined IRA, qualified plan, and other retirement account funds are just one part of the proverbial three-legged stool (together with Social Security and personal savings) that together meet the retiree's income needs. If, as many expect, the boomer generation retires later and is more likely to work part-time in early retirement, required minimum distributions could turn out to be among their first retirement payouts. Even given increased longevity predictions, this pattern could bode well for their late-life financial stability.

Chapter Notes

1. For Internal Revenue Code purposes, "IRA" refers to both individual retirement accounts and individual retirement annuities. See IRC Secs. 408(a), 408(b). The minimum-distribution requirements for payouts from an individual retirement annuity vary slightly from those of an individual retirement account, as explained in the section "Annuity Payments" (see page 144).

2. See IRC Sec. 401(a)(9); Treas. Regs. §§1.401(a)(9)-1 through 1.401(a)(9)-9, 1.403(b)-3, 1.408-8.

3. For purposes of this chapter, "non-Roth IRAs" refers to traditional IRAs, simplified employee pension IRAs, SIMPLE IRAs, and any other individual retirement accounts or annuities (as that term is defined in IRC Sec. 408) *other than* Roth IRAs.

4. Treas. Reg. §1.408-8, A-3.

5. Roth IRAs are subject to the *after-death* minimum-distribution requirements in the same manner as any other IRA. These requirements are beyond the scope of this chapter.

6. For this purpose, a 5 percent owner is determined one of two ways. In a corporation, a 5 percent owner is any person who owns or is deemed to own, under the constructive ownership rules, more than 5 percent of the outstanding stock of the corporation or stock possessing more than 5 percent of the total combined voting power of all the stock of the corporation. In any other entity (for example, a partnership), a 5 percent owner is any person who owns more than 5 percent of the capital or profits interest in the employer. IRC Sec. 416(i)(1)(B)(i).

7. IRC Sec. 401(a)(9)(C).

8. Under regulations proposed in 2004, if any part of the Section 403(b) contract is *not* part of a government or church plan, then the required beginning date as to that part of the contract would be the *earlier of* age 70½ or retirement. See Prop. Treas. Reg. §1.403(b)-6(e)(3).

9. Treas. Reg. §1.401(a)(9)-2, A-3.

10. Treas. Reg. §1.401(a)(9)-5, A-1.

11. See Treas. Reg. §1.401(a)(9)-9, A-2.

12. See Treas. Reg. §1.401(a)(9)-5, A-4.

13. See Treas. Reg. §1.401(a)(9)-9, A-3, for the joint and last survivor table.

14. See T.D. 9130, 2004-26 IRB 1082, which sets forth the final regulations for annuity distributions (Treas. Reg. §1.401(a)(9)-6).

15. Treas. Reg. §1.401(a)(9)-8, A-10.

16. See IRC Sec. 401(a)(9)(C)(ii); Treas. Reg. §1.401(a)(9)-6, A-7.

17. Treas. Reg. §1.401(a)(9)-6, A-1(a) and A-3; see IRC Sec. 401(a)(9)(A). Note that if a joint and survivor annuity has a period-certain guarantee, the survivor's payments may have to be reduced after the period-certain guarantee expires. See Treas. Reg. §1.401(a)(9)-6, A-2(d).

18. Two additional rules apply if the beneficiary is not the employee's spouse: (i) an adjustment of the payments may be required following the employee's death (see Treas. Reg. §1.401(a)(9)-6, A-2(c)), and (ii) a period-certain guarantee may not extend beyond the period set forth in the Uniform Lifetime Table for the employee (see Treas. Reg. §1.401(a)(9)-6, A-3(a)).

19. Period-certain guarantees of five to 20 years are common. However, the term of a period-certain guarantee that is combined with a life payout may not exceed the participant's life expectancy (as shown in Figure 9.1) as of his age in the year of his annuity starting date. But if the annuity is payable for a period certain only (with no lifetime guarantee), that period certain can be as long as the joint life expectancy of the participant and spouse, provided the spouse is the sole beneficiary.

Treas. Reg. §1.401(a)(9)-6, A-3(a).

20. Treas. Reg. §1.401(a)(9)-6, A-1(c).

21. The cost-of-living index used must be one of several listed in the regulations, such as the consumer price index issued by the Bureau of Labor Statistics. See Treas. Reg. §1.401(a)(9)-6, A-14(b). This exception also permits adjustments at set times (such as specified ages) that do not exceed the cumulative total of permissible cost of living adjustments. Treas. Reg. §1.401(a)(9)-6, A-14(a)(2).

22. See Treas. Reg. §1.401(a)(9)-6, A-14(a).

23. These permitted increases are (1) a constant percentage applied no less frequently than annually, at a rate that is less than 5 percent per year, (2) certain payments after the employee's death (essentially a payment that does not exceed the excess of the present value of the employee's accrued benefit, as defined in the regulations, over the total of payments before the death of the employee), and (3) as a result of dividend payments or other payments resulting from certain actuarial gains. See Treas. Regs. §§1.401(a)(9)-6, A-14(d) and A-14(e).

24. If the total future expected payments from a commercial annuity exceed the total value being annuitized, payments will, nonetheless, satisfy the "nonincreasing payment" requirement if the increases are calculated any of the following ways: (1) by a constant percentage no less frequently than annually (that is, *not* limited to 5 percent, as are noncommercial annuities), (2) for certain payments after the employee's death that are no more than the total value annuitized minus the total of payments before the death of the employee, (3) by dividends or similar payments resulting from actuarial gains, and (4) for certain accelerations of payments resulting from a full or partial commutation of the future annuity payments. See Treas. Regs. §§1.401(a)(9)-6, A-14(c) and A-14(e).

25. These specific circumstances in which modifications are permitted are set forth in Treas. Reg. §1.401(a)(9)-6, A-13(b).

26. See Treas. Reg. §1.401(a)(9)-6, A-13(c).

27. See Treas. Reg. §1.401(a)(9)-8, A-5; Defense of Marriage Act, P.L. 104-199 (signed September 21, 1996).

28. See IRC Sec. 401(a)(9)(B)(iv); Treas. Reg. §1.401(a)(9)-3, A-3(b).

29. Note that the minimum-distribution incidental benefit rule limits the amount (on a percentage basis) of survivor annuity that an annuity payout may provide. If the spouse is 10 or fewer years younger than the participant, the survivor annuity can be up to 100 percent of the life annuity amount. But if the spouse is more than 10 years younger, the survivor annuity is limited as provided in the table set forth at Treas. Reg. §1.401(a)(9)-6, A-2(c)(2). It should also be noted that this rule does not affect a period-certain guarantee, where the surviving spouse is guaranteed a certain number of years of payments regardless of when the participant dies. But after the period certain expires, the requirement kicks in. Treas. Reg. §1.401(a)(9)-6, A-2(d).

30. See IRC Sec. 402(c)(9). The IRS has become somewhat liberal about waiving the 60-day rule when the deadline is missed due to circumstances such as casualty, error by an adviser or institution, illness, or even mistake of fact.

31. See Treas. Reg. §1.408-8, A-5(c).

32. For specific marriage and divorce statistics for each state from 2001 to 2003, see http://www.cdc.gov/nchs/fastats/pdf/nvsr52_22_t3.pdf.

33. A QDRO is a domestic relations order that meets special criteria set forth in the Internal Revenue Code for being qualified. See. IRC Sec. 414(p).

34. The QDRO rules are not applicable to IRAs or tax-sheltered annuities.

35. Treas. Reg. §1.401(a)(9)-8, A-6(b)(1).

36. Treas. Reg. §1.401(a)(9)-8, A-6(c).

37. See ERISA Sec. 206(d)(3)(H); IRC Sec. 414(p)(7).

38. See Treas. Reg. §1.401(a)(9)-8, A-7.

39. Prop. Treas. Reg. §1.403(b)-6(e)(6)(i); Treas. Reg. §1.403(b)-3, A-2(a).

40. Prop. Treas. Reg. §1.403(b)-6(e)(6)(ii); Treas. Reg. §1.403(b)-3, A-2(b).

41. Prop. Treas. Reg. §1.403(b)-6(e)(3); Treas. Reg. §1.403(b)-3, A-2(b).

42. See Let. Ruls. 9345044, 7825010.

43. Rev. Rul. 72-241, 1972-1 CB 108; Rev. Rul. 73-239, 1973-1 CB 201; see also Let. Ruls. 8642072, 7843043, 7825010. The preamble to the 2004 proposed regulations (which may not be relied on until finalized) briefly addressed the application of this "old" rule to pre-1987 balances. See REG-155608-02, 69 Fed. Reg. 67075 (November 16, 2004). See also Let. Rul. 9345044.

44. Prop. Treas. Reg. §1.403(b)-6(e)(6)(vi); Treas. Reg. §1.403(b)-3, A-3.

45. See Treas. Reg. §1.401(a)(9)-5, A-8.

46. Treas. Reg. §1.408-8, A-2.

47. Treas. Reg. §1.408-8, A-9.

48. See T.D. 8987, 67 Fed. Reg. 18988 (April 17, 2002); Treas. Reg. §1.408-8, A-10; Notice 2002-27, 2002-1 CB 814. The requirement applying to IRA owners took effect in 2003.

49. See Notice 2003-3, 2003-1 CB 258, clarifying Notice 2002-27, above.

50. Notice 2002-27, 2002-1 CB 814. This requirement took effect in 2004.

51. See Treas. Reg. §1.401(a)(9)-9, A-3, for the joint and last survivor table.

52. See IRC Sec. 4974(a).

PART THREE

Shaping the Solutions

As advisers, it is essential that we master the effective use of various strategies to maximize the retirement resources of our clients in this revolutionary age of retirement. These chapters emphasize the challenges to advisers, who must synthesize vast quantities of information and creatively design solutions to meet the clients' current and future needs. The task is complex. But with these tools in your retirement toolbox, you'll be able to effectively guide clients through this important next stage of their lives.

Moshe A. Milevsky With Anna Abaimova

Moshe—a contributor to *The Investment Think Tank*—and his coauthor Anna remind the reader that planning for retirement is fraught with risk—portfolio risk, consumption and inflation risk, and mortality and longevity risk. Noting the oft-quoted statistic that life expectancy at birth is between 78 and 82, the authors remind us that although that's true, it's not particularly meaningful for planning purposes. For a married couple, each age 65, there is a better-than-even chance that at least one partner will live another 25 years. Add to this sobering fact the reality that inflation for the elderly exceeds the standard CPI measure by 0.5–1 percent, and it's obvious that retirement may be hazardous to financial health. Introducing the concept of a "retirement collar," Moshe and Anna provide a strategy for the evaluation and selection of immediate annuities as an essential element in managing the risk of providing lifetime income.

Harold Evensky

This chapter presents an implementation strategy to balance your client's cash flow requirements, longevity risk, behavioral factors, and portfolio volatility. As a retread engineer, Harold reiterates many of the concerns raised by Bob Curtis regarding the naive reliance on Monte Carlo analysis. He proposes instead a simple yet elegant distribution strategy. Supporting the credibility of his strategy with analytics, he demonstrates its viability during various difficult market periods. The goal of his chapter is pragmatic—to provide you with a practical and client-tested strategy for cash-flow distribution. Indeed, our firm has used this method, the Evensky & Katz Cash Flow Reserve Strategy, for almost 20 years—and it works.

Laurence Booth

Given that Professor Booth holds the CIT Chair in Structured Finance, you won't be surprised at the impressive formulae supporting his discussion; you may be surprised—and will certainly be rewarded—by his very practical ideas regarding the management of your clients' portfolios. Focusing on what he calls the three iron laws of finance—the laws of time, tax, and risk—he shows how an understanding of the primary issues (time value of money, tax value of money, and risk value of money) can help in structuring the solution to investment uncertainties and their impact on planning for retirement income. One particularly insightful framing strategy is to eliminate the commonplace aim of replacing 70 percent income at age 65 with a retirement target that incorporates uncertainty, such as "70 percent of 70@65," meaning a 70 percent probability of achieving 70 percent income replacement at age 65. As he concludes, implementing solutions to retirement-income problems by using objectives such as this will go a long way toward realistically addressing the uncertainty in investment returns.

William P. Bengen

If anyone can lay claim to "inventing" the subject of sustainable withdrawal, it's Bill Bengen. We couldn't have conceived of this book without a contribution from Bill. If you've not yet read his seminal piece, "Determining Withdrawal Rates Using Historical Data," you should now. First published in the October 1994 *Journal of Financial Planning*, it was reprinted in the March 2004 issue and can be found on the *Journal's* website. Bill's thesis in his original article, as well as in this chapter, is that market declines are powerful enough to overwhelm a portfolio already stressed by withdrawals. In short, secular bear markets cannot be ignored. In this work, Bill introduces the powerful planning and behavioral concept he calls "safemax"—that is, the maximum safe initial withdrawal rate, which historically has always resulted in a 30-year portfolio longevity, regardless of the year of retirement. Using his safemax concept, Bill evaluates alternative withdrawal schemes and the influence of varying equity allocations, providing practitioners with thoughtful and sound guidelines for designing and implementing their own distribution strategies.

Robert P. Kreitler

Harold thought that including a single strategy might be adequate (namely his); however, his coeditor reminded him that there were other practitioners with equally good (maybe even better) ideas. Consequently, we wanted to include a contributor who had a significantly different approach, whose strategy was practical, who had significant professional credibility, and who could effectively communicate ideas to the reader. We didn't have to look long; our obvious first choice was Robert Kreitler. Bob's chapter delivers on all points. His "tools and pools" strategy incorporates the behavioral "separate pocket" math discussed by Joel Bruckenstein, addresses the funding, investment, longevity risk, catastrophic risk, and "bad luck" risk noted by others, and provides for the flexibility necessary in an uncertain world.

Louis P. Stanasolovich

Lou is a good friend and an original member of the Alpha Group, a professional study group we've participated in for more than a decade. Our Alpha meetings and interim discussions with Lou have convinced us that he is one of the more creative thinkers in our field. During the last few years, he has been developing and improving his concept of a low-volatility portfolio, sharing with us his thought processes along the way. When we envisioned this book, we recognized that a key factor in extending the likelihood of distribution survival is the portfolio's volatility. So we asked Lou to share his insightful intellectual capital with our readers. Although Lou has devoted untold hours to the development of his strategy, it was no surprise to us that he readily agreed. Lou's premise is that strategic asset allocation in most portfolios is poorly devised at best, because the portfolios tend to be constructed solely from traditional capitalization-weighted asset classes that are highly correlated. In this chapter, he provides a detailed discussion on how to break out of the style-box paradigm and design a portfolio with significantly lower volatility.

Roxanne Alexander and Michael J. Anderson

We're especially proud of this chapter. As with life settlements, we've not yet recommended reverse mortgages to our clients; however, we believe that in the future they will play a significant role in distribution planning. We also had limited knowledge of the subject. So we searched for an authoritative expert. We never found one. During the process, we sought the assistance of our associates to help in the search and, having had no luck, two of those associates suggested we let them tackle the job. We did. In delivering their chapter, Roxanne and Mike did what we all hope to do for our clients—they exceeded expectations. Drawing on their educational backgrounds (business, planning, and law), their academic bent, and their practical experience in dealing with clients daily, they provide an unbiased and comprehensive introduction to the complex world of reverse mortgages.

Douglas Head

Although we have not yet used life settlements in our practice, we believe they will become a significant strategy in a practitioner's arsenal of distribution solutions. But we're embarrassed to admit we had little knowledge regarding the subject. In conversations with other advisers, we found we were not alone—all the more reason to include the subject in this book. And all the more reason to select an exceptionally knowledgeable contributor to address it. Consequently, we went to the source. We were delighted when Doug Head, former chair of the legislative committee, secretary, and president of the Life Insurance Settlement Association and now executive director of the association, agreed to participate. Doug's chapter frames the concept of life settlement by noting that although the idea behind life insurance for many generations has been to manage the risk of "premature" death by spreading the risk, the fact is that large numbers of insurance policies lapse with no claims ever being filed. The first recognition of this disconnect arose in the early '90s due to the tragedy faced by those with AIDS. That realization led to the emergence of the viatical industry. By 2005, the nascent viatical industry had morphed into a viable and growing life-settlement business. Doug introduces us to the concept and the industry, describes how they work, and explains the circumstances in which this evolving strategy may be appropriate.

Roger G. Ibbotson, Michael C. Henkel, and Peng Chen

A cadre of coauthors doesn't get much more blue blooded than this. Having had the honor of their contribution to our last book, *The Investment Think Tank* (Bloomberg Press, 2004), we couldn't resist inviting them to join us once again. In brilliant form, they extend their previous effort to focus on a key element in distribution planning—longevity risk. As many other contributors note, the Ibbotson team concludes that a significant strategy for managing this risk will be the inclusion of immediate (lifetime) annuities in the asset-allocation process. Based on their extensive personal knowledge and years of research on issues related to the integration of immediate annuities in the planning process, their chapter addresses the pros and cons of this vehicle and the significant factors a practitioner should consider in the implementation process.

R. H. "Rick" Carey and Jeffrey K. Dellinger

For variable annuities, we turn once again to the experts. If one were to compile a list of the people most knowledgeable about this subject, Rick and Jeffrey would rank at the top. Instrumental in the founding of the National Association for Variable Annuities (NAVA) and founder of Variable Annuity Research & Data Service (VARDS), Rick has been involved in the universe of VA for almost 20 years. Jeffrey is a fellow of the Society of Actuaries and a 30-year veteran of the financial-services world who is active at a senior level in all aspects of the annuity business. The two provide a definitive overview of a product we believe may be the single most important element in distribution planning—immediate annuities. As they note, "an immediate variable annuity is the optimal instrument for maximizing retirement income while minimizing—to zero—the probability of outliving that income." We agree and believe that all practitioners owe it to their current and future clients to carefully read the ideas presented in this chapter and learn from these experts.

Joel P. Bruckenstein

In the universe of financial-planning software, if Bob Curtis offers us the best-of-the-best in the developers' universe, Joel represents the best-of-the-best in the world of practitioners. He spends a good deal of his time thinking about software from the practitioner's view, so when he offers suggestions regarding how one might model retirement-planning analysis, as he does in this chapter, the reader is in for an informative treat. One of his most interesting insights, and an issue that we'll be considering further in our practice, is balancing the financial logic of holistic distribution planning (in which the total portfolio serves as the source for all income needs) and the behavioral reality of our clients' mental math that leads them to think in terms of separate portfolio buckets, each designed to provide income streams for different goals (for example, a college-funding portfolio or a retirement portfolio). On this and the many software issues he addresses, he is a model of wisdom.

CHAPTER 10

Risk Management During Retirement

MOSHE A. MILEVSKY WITH ANNA ABAIMOVA

Jorge Guinle—the famous Brazilian playboy—died on March 5, 2004, in Rio de Janeiro. According to the obituary that appeared in the *Financial Times*, Guinle had been born to one of the wealthiest families in Brazil and spent a large part of his life and disposable income dating famous Hollywood starlets such as Rita Hayworth, Lana Turner, and Marilyn Monroe. This hobby was obviously quite expensive, and he apparently squandered most of his family's fortune well before his death at the age of 88. His investment acumen did little to offset his spending. He is reported to have invested (and lost) millions in a variety of poorly executed business ventures. In fact, in an interview a few years before his death, Guinle said, "The secret of living well is to die without a cent in your pocket. But I miscalculated, and the money ran out too early."

Guinle was obviously a very colorful character and hardly the typical client for a financial adviser, but imagine for a moment that you had the opportunity to speak to Guinle on his deathbed and ask him: "Jorge, why did you run out of money? Is it because you spent too much, or because you did so poorly with your investments, or is it because you lived too long?" What do you think Guinle would have answered? Obviously, all three factors contributed to his estate's disarray, but which one was the most critical?

Threats to Retirement Income

These questions—though they might seem a tad crude to some—are the crux of the retirement-income dilemma. There are three basic financial

FIGURE 10.1 *Conditional Probability of Survival at Age 65*

TO AGE	FEMALE (%)	MALE (%)
70	93.9	92.2
75	85.0	81.3
80	72.3	65.9
85	55.8	45.5
90	34.8	23.7
95	15.6	7.7
100	5.0	1.4

Source: Society of Actuaries RP-2000 Table with full projection

risks outside of your clients' immediate control that they face during the retirement-spending phase of the life cycle. The first is investment and portfolio risk, the second is consumption and inflation risk, and the third is mortality and longevity risk. This chapter will discuss each of these risks in detail and link them all using some ideas from probability and statistics. Within a risk-management framework, we'll carefully examine the root causes of the unfortunate and undesirable experience of approaching old age "without a cent in your pocket."

Longevity Risk

Human beings have a random (and finite) life span, and any serious discussion concerning retirement planning must take this uncertainty into account. Figures 10.1 and 10.2 illustrate the probabilities of survival based on mortality tables from the U.S.-based Society of Actuaries.

According to the mortality table in **FIGURE 10.1** (and there are hundreds of them), a 65-year-old female has a 34.8 percent chance of living to age 90, whereas a 65-year-old male has a 23.7 percent chance of living that long. The probabilities of survival decline exponentially, and sometimes even faster, with age, as illustrated in **FIGURE 10.2**, reaching close to zero sometime between ages 105 and 115, depending on the mortality table, projection method, and gender. And although the often-quoted statistic for life expectancy is somewhere between 78 and 82 years in the United States, this projection is relevant only at birth. By the time pensioners reach their retirement years, they may be facing

Source: Society of Actuaries RP-2000 Table with full projection

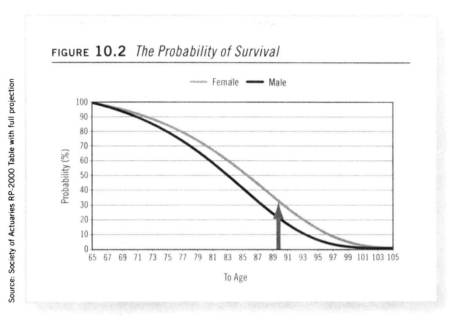

FIGURE **10.2** *The Probability of Survival*

25 to 30 more years with substantial probability, especially if they've been healthy all their lives. From a retirement-spending perspective, a 65-year-old might live 20 more years, 30 more years, or only 10 more years. That's the nature of longevity risk.

FIGURE 10.3 focuses on a couple rather than an individual and answers the following question: if a married couple is 65 years old, what is the probability that at least one of them will survive to age 90? In this case, there is a 50.3 percent chance that either one or even both could survive for the next 25 years.

Clearly, the prospect of living a longer-than-average life is not unimaginable. In fact, life spans have been steadily increasing in recent decades, confirming once again that longevity risk must be recognized, managed, and incorporated into all retirement plans. Obviously, we are not the first—and will certainly not be the last—to emphasize the critical role of longevity risk in retirement-income planning. For further discussion of longevity risk, see chapter 18, by Ibbotson, Henkel, and Chen, or the articles by Ameriks, Veres, and Warshawsky (2003) or Blake, Cairns, and Dowd (2000).

Inflation Risk

Another real risk that presents a challenge for retirement planning is inflation, or the rate of change in price levels as measured by the consumer price index (CPI).[1] One might think of this as consumption risk, or the risk that you will consume "too much" if prices increase by more than you

Source: Society of Actuaries RP-2000 Table with full projection

FIGURE 10.3 *Survival of a Couple Aged 65*

TO AGE	AT LEAST ONE (%)
70	99.5%
75	97.2%
80	90.6%
85	75.9%
90	**50.3%**
95	22.1%

expected. **FIGURE 10.4** illustrates that even under a fairly benign inflation rate of 2 percent—which some consider to be the Federal Reserve's ideal target—a $1,000 income flow in today's dollars would be worth only

FIGURE 10.4 *Inflation: What Does a $1,000 Payment Really Buy You?*

YEARS IN FUTURE	REALIZED INFLATION RATE DURING EACH YEAR						
	0%	1%	2%	4%	6%	8%	10%
1	$1,000	$990	$980	$962	$943	$926	$909
5	1,000	952	906	822	747	681	621
10	1,000	905	820	676	558	463	386
15	1,000	961	743	555	417	315	239
20	1,000	820	**673**	**456**	312	215	149
25	1,000	780	**610**	**375**	233	146	92
30	1,000	742	552	308	174	99	57
35	1,000	706	500	253	130	68	36

Source: U.S. Department of Labor, Bureau of Labor Statistics

FIGURE **10.5** *Inflation: Relative Weights*

CATEGORY	CPI-W	CPI-E
Food	17.9%	14.3%
Housing	37.6	**45.9**
Apparel	3.9	2.8
Transport	18.8	13.8
Medical Care	5.1	**10.2**
Recreation	5.3	4.4
Education	5.1	2.9
Other	6.1	5.6

$610 in 25 years, in real terms. That is, by the end of the 25-year period, the purchasing power of $1,000 would drop by nearly 40 percent.

Indeed, we believe that unanticipated inflation is a greater risk factor and concern for the retired elderly than it is for the rest of the population. We are not alone in this belief. For the last 20 years, the U.S. Bureau of Labor Statistics has compiled a unique inflation index called the CPI-E (for the elderly), which is distinct in composition from the more commonly used CPI-W (or CPI-U, where "U" is derived from all urban consumers) index. The retiree inflation index outpaced the regular broad-based CPI during the last 20 years by almost 0.5 percent to 1 percent per year. As **FIGURE 10.5** indicates, the difference in composition between the two indices arises because categories such as housing and medical care are assigned different weights within the broad-based CPI-W and the focused CPI-E. Retirees typically consume more health care services but less food—which should come as no surprise. The lesson is clear for financial advisers and their newly retired clients: think about your inflation rate.

Will the Money Run Out?

Monte Carlo simulations have become a widely used technique for quantifying the risks of retirement spending and asset-allocation strategies. (For some of the earlier work in this area, see the papers by Ho, Milevsky, and

Robinson [1994] or the one by Pye [2000].) Monte Carlo simulations enable financial advisers and their clients to answer questions such as: If a 65-year-old female allocates half of her $100 nest egg to stocks and half to bonds and withdraws $5 per year, what are the chances that she too will meet Guinle's fate of running out of money before running out of time? **FIGURE 10.6** shows one possible outcome based on a sequence of random returns. Under this particular sequence—and there are obviously millions of possibilities—if she insists on consuming $5 each year, she will run out of money in 20 years. There is a nearly 50 percent chance that she will still be alive at that point, so this is the probability of ruin for this scenario. If we run thousands of these scenarios—each with a unique return sequence—we can estimate the overall probability that she will run out of money before she dies.

Of course, we can vary a number of factors—such as the age, gender, asset allocation, and the fixed consumption rate—all of which will affect the probability of retirement ruin. As **FIGURE 10.7** shows, a 65-year-old male who invests half of his $100 nest egg in equity and withdraws a constant real $5 per annum has a 10.6 percent chance of running out of money within his lifetime. If she makes the same investment and consumption choices, a 65-year-old female has a 12.3 percent probability of retirement ruin—as shown in **FIGURE 10.8**. The higher ruin probability makes intuitive sense because on average females are expected to live longer than males. Notice

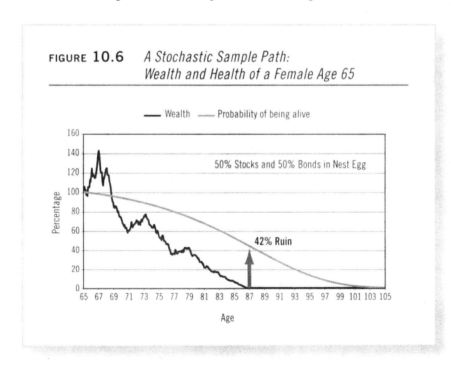

FIGURE 10.6 *A Stochastic Sample Path: Wealth and Health of a Female Age 65*

—— Wealth —— Probability of being alive

50% Stocks and 50% Bonds in Nest Egg

42% Ruin

Percentage

Age

FIGURE 10.7 *Probability of Retirement Ruin Assuming Fixed Real Consumption*

MALE 65	C = $4	C = $5	C = $6	C = $7	C = $8
0% Equity	8.3%	19.9%	33.3%	45.8%	56.0%
25% Equity	4.2	12.8	24.8	37.8	49.3
50% Equity	3.8	10.6	20.4	31.8	42.9
75% Equity	5.0	11.4	19.8	29.4	39.0
100% Equity	7.3	13.7	21.3	29.7	37.9

that if the female decides to lower her fixed real annual consumption by $1, her probability of retirement ruin drastically drops to 4.5 percent.

These numbers were generated using standard simulation techniques assuming a 7 percent expected return, 5 percent growth rate, and 20 percent volatility for equity investments and a 2.5 percent expected return, 2 percent growth rate, and 10 percent volatility for bond investments. Obviously, these numbers are all provided in inflation-adjusted terms and are consistent with (but slightly lower than) historical returns, as documented by Ibbotson Associates (2004). The mortality tables used are similar to the numbers provided in Figures 10.1 and 10.2.

FIGURE 10.8 *Probability of Retirement Ruin Assuming Fixed Real Consumption*

FEMALE 65	C = $4	C = $5	C = $6	C = $7	C = $8
0% Equity	9.9%	23.1%	37.4%	50.3%	63.3%
25% Equity	5.1	15.0	28.2	41.9	53.6
50% Equity	4.5	12.3	23.1	35.3	46.7
75% Equity	5.9	13.0	22.2	32.4	42.4
100% Equity	8.4	15.4	23.5	32.3	40.9

FIGURE 10.9 *Probability of Retirement Ruin Assuming Fixed Real Consumption*

MALE 75	C = $4	C = $5	C = $6	C = $7	C = $8
0% Equity	1.3%	4.5%	9.9%	17.0%	24.6%
25% Equity	0.5	2.6	6.7	12.8	20.0
50% Equity	0.6	2.4	5.8	11.1	16.7
75% Equity	1.1	3.1	6.5	11.2	16.7
100% Equity	2.0	4.5	8.0	12.5	17.6

Using the same inputs, if we age our retirees by 10 years so that the male and female begin withdrawing $5 per year from their initial $100 nest egg at age 75, the probabilities of retirement ruin drop, as seen in **FIGURES 10.9** and **10.10**. For example, the 75-year-old male faces a probability of ruin of 2.4 percent, and the 75-year-old female faces a probability of 4.5 percent under the same 50 percent equity allocation and $5 consumption rate. Again, the reduced probabilities of retirement ruin can be attributed to the reduction in the number of expected remaining years of life.

What's clear from Figures 10.7, 10.8, 10.9, and 10.10 is that regardless of age or desired consumption (spending) rates, a balanced portfolio pro-

FIGURE 10.10 *Probability of Retirement Ruin Assuming Fixed Real Consumption*

FEMALE 75	C = $4	C = $5	C = $6	C = $7	C = $8
0% Equity	2.9%	8.5%	16.6%	25.7%	34.6%
25% Equity	1.4	5.2	11.6	20.1	29.1
50% Equity	1.4	4.5	9.8	17.1	25.2
75% Equity	2.1	5.4	10.3	16.6	23.7
100% Equity	3.5	7.1	12.0	17.8	24.0

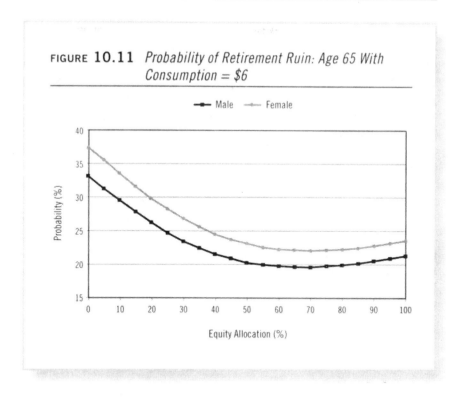

FIGURE **10.11** *Probability of Retirement Ruin: Age 65 With Consumption = $6*

vides the best odds for the plan to remain viable. Only at unrealistically high consumption rates do we see "corner" allocations providing the best odds, and that is more like a gambling scheme than a prudent investment strategy. Clearly, for most reasonable spending patterns, an overly conservative asset allocation as well as an overly aggressive asset allocation will only increase the risk of running out of money too soon. **FIGURE 10.11** illustrates the risk and return trade-off for a male and a female, both age 65, who consume $6 per annum.

The Retirement Ruin Formula

Although the widely used technique of Monte Carlo simulations can help shed light on sustainable withdrawal rates and optimal portfolios, the approach is not without problems. First, many thousands of simulations are needed to produce increasingly accurate and meaningful results, and results are difficult for others to replicate.

An alternative method is to use a simple analytic expression that captures the relationship between spending, aging, and a random portfolio return to estimate the probability that a given spending rate is sustainable. This formula brings together the longevity, spending, and investment risk factors under one unified umbrella. We call it the exponential reciprocal gamma (ERG) formula. Space does not allow us to describe the derivation of this formula here, so we refer interested readers to Milevsky and Robinson (2005). What follows are some examples of the formula, which can be implemented easily in Microsoft Excel or in any other spreadsheet program. We find that the formula reproduces results that are typically within 5 percent to 10 percent of the results generated by extensive Monte Carlo simulations.

The formula—which is the probability of retirement ruin—can be computed as follows:

$$\Pr[\text{Ruin}] = \text{GammaDist}\left(\frac{2\mu + 4\lambda}{\sigma^2 + \lambda} - 1, \frac{\sigma^2 + \lambda}{2} \mid \frac{1}{w}\right), \qquad (1)$$

where the expression GammaDist(. | .) denotes the cumulative distribution function (CDF) of the gamma distribution and the four parameters $\{\mu, \sigma, \lambda, w\}$ capture the portfolio's expected return, investment volatility, (inverse of) life expectancy, and initial nest egg per dollar of desired spending, respectively. In Excel, the approximation can be implemented

FIGURE 10.12 *How Good Is the Simple (ERG) Formula for Predicting Retirement Ruin?*

PROBABILITY YOUR RETIREMENT NEST EGG IS NOT
ENOUGH TO SUSTAIN YOUR RETIREMENT

Withdrawal ($ per initial $100)	RP 2000	Gompertz	Exponential	ERG Approx.
2	0.32%	0.30%	1.05%	2.76%
3	1.93	2.22	4.44	6.94
4	5.94	6.16	10.60	12.69
5	12.51	12.70	17.70	19.53
6	21.73	22.27	28.44	26.96
7	32.00	31.98	37.42	34.59
8	42.935	42.92	48.18	42.10

Note: Portfolio is assumed to earn 7 percent (inflation adjusted) in any given year, with a volatility (uncertainty, risk) of 20 percent. This leads to a (geometric mean) growth rate of 5 percent.

using the following syntax: GAMMADIST(spending rate as a fraction of initial wealth, $(2\mu + 4\lambda)/(\sigma^2 + \lambda) - 1, (\sigma^2 + \lambda)/2$,TRUE).

FIGURE 10.12 compares the results of this formula against more extensive simulations. For instance, if a 65-year-old male withdraws $6 per $100 adjusted for inflation for the rest of his life, the ERG formula indicates that there is a 26.96 percent chance that the money will run out before he dies. This result differs by roughly 5 percent from extensive Monte Carlo simulations, under which the probability of ruin is 21.73 percent (using RP 2000 mortality tables). Figure 10.12 also summarizes simulation results under two other mortality assumptions, known in the actuarial literature as Gompertz and exponential assumptions.

We believe the ERG formula is simple and easy to use and can play a substantial role in demonstrating the link between spending rates, uncertain longevity, and uncertain returns—all critical variables affecting retirement planning. A typical number for $\{\mu\}$ might be 7 percent, while $\{\sigma\}$ is 20 percent, and $\{\lambda\}$—a mortality rate—is 5 percent or 3.3 percent, depending on age. Finally, $\{w\}$ is the ratio of the initial nest egg to desired spending. For example, $\{w = 100/5 = 20\}$.

For example, start with an endowment or nest egg of $20 invested in an equity fund that's expected to earn a continuously compounded return of $\{\mu = 7 \text{ percent}\}$ per annum, with a volatility or standard deviation of $\{\sigma = 20 \text{ percent}\}$ per annum. Assume that a 50-year-old female early retiree with a median future life span of 27 years (according to actuarial mortality tables) intends on consuming $1 after inflation per annum for the rest of her life.

Note that if the median life span is assumed to be 27 years, then the probability of survival for 27 years is exactly 50 percent, which implies that the "mortality rate" parameter is $\{\lambda = \ln[2]/ = 0.0257\}$. According to equation 1 (and after entering GAMMADIST(1/20, 2.695, 0.0328, TRUE) into Excel), the probability of retirement ruin is approximately 26 percent.

A simple formula like this can be of great pedagogical use in the field of retirement-income planning. Essentially, here's what the formula reveals: withdrawing more than (an inflation-adjusted) 5 percent of initial capital annually appears excessively risky, even under an aggressive asset allocation, and could well prove to be the reason for a failed retirement plan.

The Critical Years

Clearly, earning a higher return across all retirement years—either because of good investment choices or plain old good luck—results in a decreased probability of ruin. But which years are the most critical? Monte Carlo simulations can again be of use in finding the answer. **FIGURE 10.13** provides some insight into this issue.

FIGURE 10.13   *Male Age 65 with Consumption = $7 and 100 Percent Equity: Ruin Probability Conditional on Returns*

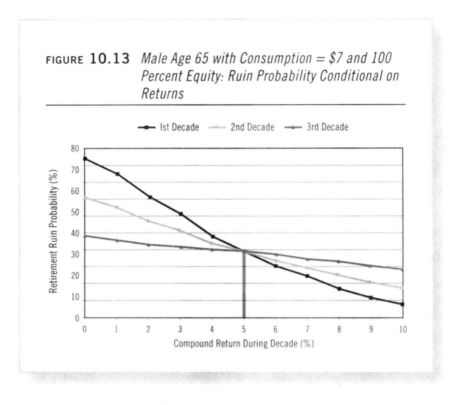

Recall from Figure 10.7 that if a 65-year-old male invests his entire nest egg in risky equities—which are expected to grow at 5 percent per annum—and he consumes an inflation-adjusted $7 each year, the probability of retirement ruin is approximately 30 percent. Our simulations, however, as displayed in Figure 10.13, indicate that earning a 10 percent compound annual return each year during his first decade of retirement—that is, between the ages of 65 and 75—and allowing for random returns during his remaining lifetime would reduce his probability of retirement ruin by roughly 23 percentage points, to 7 percent. Conversely, fixing the annual return at 0 percent for the first decade of retirement would increase the probability of ruin from 30 percent to 75 percent. This reduction should make sense intuitively: better-than-expected returns lead to better odds and vice versa.

What's interesting is that fixing the annual returns throughout the second and third decades of retirement—as opposed to the first—has a much smaller impact on the retirement ruin probability. Notice in Figure 10.13 that if the compound annual return during the second decade was fixed at 10 percent per annum, the retirement ruin probability would be reduced to 15 percent from 7 percent. And if the compound annual return during the third decade was fixed at 10 percent, the probability would drop only to 25 percent.

It's much more favorable to earn the abnormally high return in the first decade of retirement than it is in the second or third decade of retirement. Likewise, earning poor investment returns in the first decade, rather than in the second or third, exacerbates the retirement ruin probability. Whereas fixing a return of 1 percent for the first decade results in a ruin probability of nearly 70 percent, earning the same rate in the second decade results in lower ruin odds of about 50 percent. Fixing the rate in the third decade lowers the odds to about 35 percent. In the language of probability theory, the conditional probability of retirement ruin is most sensitive to the returns during the first few years of retirement.

Clearly, the first decade of retirement is the most crucial one in determining whether a retirement plan will be successful. Thus, attention must be focused on these years. This brings us to the role of product allocation for retirement-risk management, which is quite different from the role of asset allocation.

The Role of Downside Protection

Because the first decade of retirement is the most crucial for achieving a sustainable financial plan, it makes sense to seek out financial products that provide downside protection during this particular period. In effect, this protection allows your client to increase the sustainable spending rate without taking on additional risk.

A Place for Derivatives

If a retiree decides to invest too heavily in risky equity, he or she runs a higher risk of retirement ruin if markets perform poorly during the first decade of retirement (as Figures 10.11, 10.12, and 10.13 suggest). Conversely, investing too little in equity funds also heightens the risk of ruin because the funds cannot grow sufficiently to support the chosen spending rate. It appears you're "damned if you do and damned if you don't."

However, there is a third alternative, and that is to use derivatives— namely, put and call options—to concentrate investment returns around a central value that, in most cases, will improve the sustainability of the portfolio. The value of these derivative instruments is derived from the value of some underlying investment such as a stock or bond. Buying a call option (or call) grants an individual the right but not the obligation to purchase an investment at a predetermined price, whereas buying a put option (or put) guarantees the holder the right to sell the underlying investment at a predetermined price.

The strategy known as a *retirement collar* involves selling a call with a strike price K_c and then using the proceeds to purchase a put with a lower

FIGURE 10.14 *Probability of Retirement Ruin Under a Fixed Spending Rate*

MALE 65	$4	$5	$6
No Downside Protection	7.3%	13.7%	21.3%
−5% against +6.6%	1.5	6.0	16.8
−10% against +12.8%	4.1	9.7	18.3

strike price K_p. Thus, if the asset's market price falls below K_p, you're guaranteed a minimum return because you have the right to sell it at a price of K_p. If the asset's value increases above a value of K_c, however, you will have to sell the asset to the holder of the call at a price of K_c, thereby limiting the gains you could have earned on the portfolio.

FIGURE 10.14 provides an example of how this strategy would work for a retirement portfolio. Imagine that at retirement you decide to allocate your $100 nest egg (which can arbitrarily be scaled up or down) and consume $4 per year from this nest egg. If all of the money is invested in equity-based products, the simulation results suggest that the probability of retirement ruin is 7.3 percent for a male and 8.4 percent for a female (see FIGURE 10.15). But if your client purchases three-month put options that are 5 percent out of the money, which means that the strike price is initially at $95, and you fund this purchase by selling a call option that's 6.6 percent out of the money, the put-call combination will reduce the dis-

FIGURE 10.15 *Probability of Retirement Ruin Under a Fixed Spending Rate*

FEMALE 65	$4	$5	$6
No Downside Protection	8.4%	15.4%	23.5%
−5% against +6.6%	2.4	10.5	24.0
−10% against +12.8%	5.9	14.1	25.1

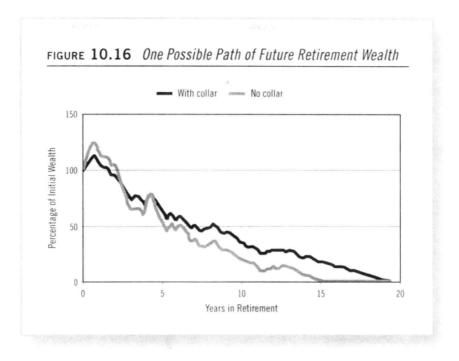

FIGURE **10.16** *One Possible Path of Future Retirement Wealth*

person of your portfolio and reduce the probability of ruin to 1.5 percent for a male and to 2.4 percent for a female.

Essentially, the improved probability results from removing the very large negative returns from all scenarios, thereby increasing the chances that the initial nest egg will be sufficient to maintain the desired standard of living. This collar strategy, however, is not a free lunch, because the large negative returns are reduced at the expense of reducing the upside potential of the portfolio. This wrinkle is yet another manifestation of the universal trade-off between financial risk and return. Thus, although the portfolio's income will last longer by "delaying its date" with zero, the portfolio will not grow or increase in value as rapidly as the uncollared, or unprotected, portfolio. Sample paths of the wealth in retirement with and without collar protection appear in **FIGURE 10.16**.

FIGURE 10.17 illustrates another possible result of this strategy. The upper line represents the expected value of wealth from 0 to 40 years in retirement, assuming a 100 percent allocation to risky equity expected to earn 7 percent per annum, with a standard deviation of 20 percent. The lower line represents the expected value of wealth, assuming the 100 percent equity allocation is protected with a collar whose three-month put option is 5 percent out of the money. Remember, this means that during any given quarter the most the portfolio can lose is 5 percent. This put option is funded by selling a three-month call option that is out of the

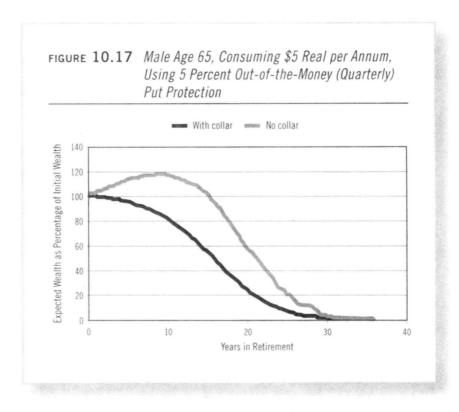

FIGURE 10.17 *Male Age 65, Consuming $5 Real per Annum, Using 5 Percent Out-of-the-Money (Quarterly) Put Protection*

money. Notice that although both curves start off at a value of 100, the expected level of wealth of the uncollared portfolio is uniformly higher throughout the 35- to 40-year horizon. Thus, the downside (variance or standard deviation) risk is reduced, but so is the upside potential.

The portfolio protection comes at a price, but the strategy has the potential to play a critical role in mitigating the risk of retirement ruin, especially when used in the early years of retirement. The underlying logic of "trading upside participation for downside protection" is at the heart of the innovative riders and guarantees that have recently been attached to variable annuity policies. Indeed, guaranteed minimum withdrawal benefits extend the natural life span of a portfolio by implementing a similar trade-off.

Why Longevity Insurance?

Maintaining a balanced asset allocation, purchasing downside protection in the form of option guarantees, and selecting a sensible consumption rate help to improve the odds that a given retirement plan will be financially sustainable. However, the probabilities of retirement ruin under many scenarios cannot be completely eliminated, and this risk can be managed using longevity insurance—namely, payout annuities.

Most retirees are hesitant to annuitize their variable annuity con-tracts—or, for that matter, to purchase immediate annuities with their IRAs, 401(k) plans, or other liquid wealth—because they fear losing con-trol or believe they can do better with other investment alternatives. Odd-ly enough, when people within a traditional defined-benefit pension plan are coaxed to switch into a money-purchase defined-contribution pension plan and give up the implicit life annuity, most turn the offer down, while others react negatively and litigiously. A fog of confusion surrounds the financial benefits of annuitization. In an effort to keep it simple, we'll share a simple story that illustrates the benefits of annuitization and longevity insurance and positions the product firmly within the realm of investment risk and return.

Imagine a 95-year-old retiree who loves playing bridge with her four best friends on Sunday every few months. Coincidentally, all five of them are exactly 95 years old, quite healthy, and have actually been retired—and playing bridge—for 30 years. But the game has become somewhat tire-some, and one of them has decided to juice up their gatherings. Last time they met, she proposed that they take $100 out of their wallets and place the money on the kitchen table. "Whoever survives to the end of the year gets to split the $500," she said. "If you don't make it, you forfeit the money." Yes, this is an odd gamble, but you'll see the point in a moment.

Let's assume that all five women thought it was an interesting idea and agreed to try it but felt it was risky to keep $500 on the kitchen table for a whole year. So they decided to put the money in a local bank's one-year certificate of deposit, paying 5 percent interest for the year.

What will happen next year? According to statistics compiled by actuar-ies at the U.S. Social Security Administration, there is a 20 percent chance that any given member of the bridge club will pass away during the next year. This, in turn, implies an 80 percent chance of survival. Virtually anything can happen during the next 12 months of waiting, but there are, in fact, six relevant combinations of how events may unfold, and the odds imply that *on average* four 96-year-olds will survive to split the $525 pot at year-end.

Note that each survivor will get $131.25 as her total return on the original investment of $100. The 31.25 percent investment return con-tains 5 percent of the bank's money and a healthy 26.25 percent of "mor-tality credits." These credits represent the capital and interest "lost" by the deceased and "gained" by the survivors.

The catch, of course, is that the deceased forfeited her claim to the funds. And although the beneficiaries of the deceased might be frustrated with the outcome, the survivors get a superior investment return. What's more important, they all get to manage their *lifetime income risk* in ad-vance, without having to worry about what the future will bring.

We think this story does a nice job of translating the benefits of longevity insurance into investment rates of return. Personally, we find no other financial product that guarantees such high rates of return, conditional on survival.

In fact, the analogy can be taken one step further. What if the club decided to invest the $500 in the stock market or in some risky Nasdaq high-tech fund for the year? Moreover, what happens if this fund or subaccount collapses in value during the year and falls 20 percent in value? How much will the surviving bridge players lose? Well, if your guess is "nothing," that is the correct answer. They divide the $400 among the surviving four and get their original $100 back.

Such is the power of mortality credits. They subsidize losses on the downside and enhance gains on the upside. In fact, once you wrap true longevity insurance around a diversified portfolio, the annuitant can actually afford and tolerate more financial risk.

Of course, real live annuity contracts do not work the same way the bridge club does. The tontine contract is renewable each year and the surviving 96-year-olds have the option to take their mortality credits and go home. In practice, annuity contracts are for life, and these credits are spread and amortized over many years of retirement. But the basic insurance economics underlying both contracts are exactly parallel.

A logical question to ponder is whether this life roulette game would yield such high returns for younger participants, and the answer is no. **FIGURE 10.18** provides a rough estimate of the relative magnitude from annuitizing—with true life annuities—at different ages. At age 55, the mortality credits are less than 1 percent, or a mere 35 basis points. At age 65, the number increases to 83 basis points, which is still nothing to get excited about. To put these numbers in context, unless a recent retiree thinks he can't earn 83 basis points more than the pricing rate used by the annuity vendor, he's better off not annuitizing today and instead managing the money with a systematic withdrawal plan. This benchmark, or hurdle, rate of return can be used to assess the relative benefits from annuitization at different ages. Note that by the mid-80s it becomes virtually impossible to beat what we like to call the *implied longevity yield*.[2] To put it crudely, too many people are dying. In fact, we find that the best deal can be obtained by acquiring longevity insurance at a relatively young age—the mid-40s, for example—but have it start paying income in the late 70s. For more information on the design of these contracts, see Milevsky (2005a).

Pension or life annuities provide a unique and peculiar kind of insurance. It's virtually the only insurance that people acquire during the course of their life and actually hope to use. Although we're all willing to pay for home insurance, disability insurance, and car insurance, we never want to

Source: The IFID Centre calculations, assuming 40m/60f (static) annuity 2002 table at 6 percent net interest

FIGURE 10.18 *Value of Unisex Mortality Credits: What You Must Earn Above the Pricing Rate to Justify Not Annuitizing*

AGE OF ANNUITANT	SPREAD ABOVE PRICING INTEREST RATE*	AGE OF ANNUITANT	SPREAD ABOVE PRICING INTEREST RATE*
55	35	80	414
60	52	85	725
65	83	90	1256
70	138	95	2004
75	237	100	2978

*In basis points = 0.01 percent.

actually exercise or use the policy. After all, who wants his house to burn down, his leg to break, or his car to crash? But the insurable event underlying pension annuities is living a long and prosperous life. Perhaps that's why the industry has yet to achieve the same level of success in marketing and selling these products—it's too accustomed to scaring consumers. We hope simple tales like the one about the bridge club can help retirees and their financial advisers understand the benefits, risks, and returns of buying longevity insurance.

The Essentials

As you address the many financial questions clients face in preparing for an upcoming retirement, keep these key points in mind.

1 25-year retirement is quite feasible and highly probable for today's generation of baby boomers. Indeed, at least one member of a couple aged 65 will likely reach age 90. This longevity risk cannot be ignored. It should be hedged and insured like all other risks we face during our human life cycle.

2 Retirees face a unique type of inflation risk, which has been confirmed by the design of the Bureau of Labor Statistics' CPI-Elderly index. What's more, after 25 years of retirement, a steady source of (nominal) income will likely be worth a third to a half less than it was at the start of retirement.

3 From a statistical perspective, there is very little justification for spending more than 5 percent of initial capital, adjusted for inflation, during retirement. The probability of ruin during retirement will exceed 15 percent if the planned consumption rate is higher than 5 percent.

4 The first seven to 10 years of retirement represent the most critical investment period in one's life, with returns that are highly correlated with the probability of a sustainable retirement.

5 A very strong case can be made for using nonlinear instruments, such as put options and other downside protection, to limit the impact of a catastrophic first decade of retirement. Insurance products that provide downside protection—even at the expense of upside participation—will reduce the probability of retirement ruin and hence increase the sustainability of the portfolio.

6 The implicit rate of return on longevity insurance—and, by extension, pension annuities—can reach 20 percent and even higher as people age. Thus, there are substantial benefits to annuitization, and it should be encouraged as a risk-management strategy.

References

Ameriks, J., R. Veres, and M.J. Warshawsky (2003), "Making Retirement Income Last a Lifetime," *Journal of Financial Planning* 14(2): 60–76.

Blake, D., A.J. Cairns, and K. Dowd (2000), "PensionMetrics: Stochastic Pension Plan Design During the Distribution Phase," Pensions Institute Working Paper.

Chen, P., and M.A. Milevsky (2003), "Merging Asset Allocation and Longevity Insurance: An Optimal Perspective on Payout Annuities," *Journal of Financial Planning* 16(6): 52–62.

Ho, K., M. Milevsky, and C. Robinson (1994), "How to Avoid Outliving Your Money," *Canadian Investment Review* 7(3): 35–38.

Ibbotson, R.G., M.C. Henkel, and P. Chen (2005), "Longevity Risk Insurance," chapter 18 in this book.

Ibbotson Associates (2004), *Stocks, Bonds, Bills and Inflation 2004 Yearbook*, Chicago: Ibbotson Associates.

Milevsky, M.A. (2005a), "Real Longevity Insurance With a Deductible: Introduction to Advanced Life-Delayed Annuities," *North American Actuarial Journal* 9(4): 109–122.

Milevsky, M.A. (2006), *The Calculus of Retirement Income: Financial Models for Pensions and Insurance*, Cambridge: Cambridge University Press.

Milevsky, M.A., and C. Robinson (2005), "A Sustainable Spending Rate Without Simulation," *Financial Analysts Journal* 61(6): 89–100.

Pye, G.B. (2000), "Sustainable Investment Withdrawals," *Journal of Portfolio Management* 26(4): 73–83.

Chapter Notes

1. CPI-W: More than one-half of the household's income must come from clerical or wage occupations and at least one of the household's earners must have been employed for at least 37 weeks during the previous 12 months. The CPI-W's population represents about 32 percent of the total U.S. population and is a subset, or part, of the CPI-U's population.

2. The Implied Longevity Yield and its acronym, ILY, are registered trademarks and are the property of CANNEX Financial Exchanges.

CHAPTER 11

Withdrawal Strategies
A Cash Flow Solution

HAROLD EVENSKY

Planning income for life involves a matrix of issues, many of which are unrelated to finance and investment strategies. Invariably, the crux of the problem hinges on how to get adequate cash flow out of an investment portfolio.[1] At a time when a significant portion of the population is rapidly aging and our clients are facing ever-increasing risks to their long-term financial well-being, this problem is becoming far more difficult to solve. This chapter introduces the Evensky & Katz Cash Flow Reserve Strategy (E&K-S), first implemented by our firm more than a decade ago. The years have proved it to be an extraordinarily effective strategy.

To make the case for the E&K-S and to provide a framework for evaluating alternatives, I'll first address issues that need to be considered in the development and selection of an effective sustainable cash flow strategy. I'll also discuss some of the market myths that hinder effective cash flow planning.

Cash Flow Strategy: Clearing the Hurdles

Any strategy for generating cash flow must take into consideration the primary risk factors that can hobble an otherwise thoughtfully crafted solution. Once the risk factors are enunciated, practitioners have a set of criteria against which they may test proposed product and strategy solutions. The factors I recommend for consideration include several key risks and the client's unique needs.

Longevity Risk

Our clients' biggest economic fear should be living too long. Many years ago, a client visited me to complain about the poor return he was getting as he rolled over his one-year certificates of deposit. Because rates had dropped so significantly, his renewal yield was less than half the return he had received in the prior year. Rather naively, I began discussing a balanced total return portfolio. I had barely spoken the word "stock" before he threw up his hands and said, "No stock! That's too risky." I then suggested a bond portfolio alternative, but he terminated that discussion too. It seems that bonds were way too long a commitment for him. Finally, in frustration, I said, "I give up; why not just roll your CDs over from one-year to five-year maturities?" He looked at me incredulously and said, "Harold, five years? Long term for me is a green banana!" After a few seconds of reflection, I responded, "Go ahead; make my day—die.[2] If you die, I'll be very upset 'cause you're a good friend, but if there's money in the bank, at least I'll have done my job. What keeps me awake at night and ought to keep you awake is the possibility that you'll never die—at least not for a long while yet."

Purchasing Power Risk (Inflation)

Occasionally, media articles may continue to extol the power of the Federal Reserve, but inflation is not "dead and gone forever." If not today then tomorrow, we're sure to be reading headlines announcing, "Inflation once again rears its ugly head." Any cash flow strategy that ignores inflation ignores reality.

Volatility

Although most investors have little or no understanding of the concept of volatility drain on portfolio returns, they're even more clueless about the impact of volatility drain on cash flow. Unfortunately, we do not live in an average world; hence, volatility drain is a critical factor to be addressed in any successful cash flow strategy.

Financial Flexibility

Planners plan; after all, that's what our clients pay us to do. Unfortunately, we can only plan, not guarantee. Clients' needs and markets change; hence, a successful strategy must be flexible.

Behavioral Risk

As behavioral finance research has so eloquently demonstrated, our clients are not rational investors. They are human and, as such, subject to numerous behavioral heuristics[3] and dubious mental math.[4] Recognizing and managing these behavioral issues is a necessity for a strategy to be effective.

Client Needs

Our clients have a variety of needs—financial and behavioral. An effective strategy must meet those needs.

Financial. There are three aspects to consider:

❑ *Real cash flow.* As we've noted, the erosion of purchasing power is a major risk. Unfortunately, the risk is so insidious that many investors either forget it exists or pay only lip service to its impact.

❑ *Income (as in dividends and interest) versus cash flow (as from total-return portfolios).* The confusion of these two concepts—a problem exacerbated by the marketing of "income" portfolios—is the root of many strategy failures.

❑ *Tax and expense efficiency.* Clients' cash flow needs translate into a need for net-net real cash flow—net of expenses and net of taxes. In a low-return environment (as expected in the years ahead by many professionals), the impact of expenses and taxes mushrooms.[5] Thus, the management of expenses and taxes is another significant attribute of an effective strategy.

Behavioral. Good theory and good practice are not necessarily equivalents. This is often evident when the good theory conflicts with what our clients consider good sense. In planning for our clients' lifetime income needs, a major behavioral stumbling block is what my partner, Deena Katz, refers to as the "paycheck syndrome." Until retirement, investors purchase their groceries, meals, mortgages, and vacations out of the proceeds from their paycheck. The excess (if any) is set aside for savings. As savings grow, it becomes corpus, or the "nest egg." One spends a paycheck, never corpus. This is a classic example of a mental math concept that behavioral economists refer to as "separate pockets." Although it may be intellectually obvious that spending 5 percent of a portfolio's assets derived from dividends and interest is economically equivalent to spending 5 percent of a fully reinvested, total-return portfolio, for most investors it will not feel the same. Dividends and interest feel like a paycheck. Selling assets to generate cash flow feels like invasion of corpus.

An effective cash flow strategy must incorporate the following primary elements of the paycheck syndrome:

❑ Paychecks are consistent; cash flow strategies need to provide consistent cash flows. Any strategy that results in significant variations in annual cash flow subjects the recipient to an unpleasant roller-coaster ride in their standard of living.

- ❑ Paychecks are independent of the market; cash flow strategies should be designed to insulate the client's cash flow from market volatility.
- ❑ The source of paychecks is visible and considered reliable; the source of cash flow should be visible and reliable.
- ❑ Clients understand paychecks; they need to be able to understand their cash flow strategy.
- ❑ An effective strategy should reframe the structure of the cash flow to actively incorporate a client's tendency to think in terms of separate pockets.

Myths and Nonsense

"I'm retired," the client insists, "I need an income portfolio." The myth of the income portfolio is among the most damaging myths foisted on the public. An income portfolio is designed to provide an investor with an income stream generated by interest and/or dividend payments. The flaws associated with this strategy are numerous—and fatal.

Portfolio Design

By constraining the portfolio design to generate cash flow solely from dividends and interest, an arbitrary limit is set on the allocation to equities. Consider a portfolio allocated between bonds and stocks with the bond investment in the Putnam Income Fund and the stock investment in the Fidelity Fund.[6]

Let's also assume that the cash flow design constraint is 5 percent. With those parameters, what would be the composition of the portfolio? Natu-

FIGURE 11.1 *Recommended Allocations*

BASED ON	MAXIMUM ALLOCATION TO STOCK (%)
2004	N/A[7]
Prior 5 years	0
Prior 10 years	18
Prior 15 years	33
Prior 20 years	50

rally, the design will depend on the expected interest return on the Putnam allocation and the dividend return of the Fidelity allocation. **FIGURE 11.1** illustrates a range of recommended allocations, depending on the historical time frame selected for projecting future expected returns.

These allocation constraints, having been set by market forces, obviously have no relationship to the client's unique needs and risk tolerance.

Inflation

As experienced practitioners will recognize, the severely constrained stock allocations in Figure 11.1 are unlikely to provide the necessary growth to insure against long-term purchasing power erosion. Using the same investment choices, consider an income-portfolio investor implementing a conservative all-bond portfolio 20 years ago (1985). Unfortunately, due to inflation erosion, this conservative portfolio would have collapsed by October 2001.[8]

Monte Carlo Saves the Day

Although Monte Carlo analysis is often presented as if it's a new discovery that will solve all the ills associated with old-fashioned point-estimate planning, it is in reality a long-established mathematical tool that's been used in its modern form since the 1930s, when Enrico Fermi used *Monte Carlo* analysis in the calculation of neutron diffusion. Although very effective as an educational tool, in retirement cash flow planning, it is too often abused.

Greater accuracy or more guesswork? In developing a point estimate (for example, to maintain an inflation-adjusted income of $84,000 per year for the client's lifetime), the practitioner has to estimate at least three items: the return on the portfolio, the inflation rate, and the client's longevity. Each factor is obviously uncertain. Now consider how a planner using Monte Carlo analysis might report to her client: "You can maintain

FIGURE **11.2** *Assumptions for Monte Carlo*

	EXPECTED	LOW	HIGH
Portfolio return (%)	8	6	9
Inflation (%)	3	2	4
Longevity (age)	87	82	92

a $72,250-per-year inflation-adjusted income for life, with a 70 percent probability of success, or a $67,530-per-year income, with an 85 percent probability." What did the practitioner have to do to provide this more sophisticated analysis? She had to make a number of additional assumptions (see **FIGURE 11.2**).

Although the effort made to develop a probabilistic recommendation may be impressive, the reality is that rather than reaching a conclusion based on three estimates, this sophisticated solution is, in fact, based on nine additional estimates (that is, the end points of the range and the distribution of the range for each item). Most Monte Carlo simulations used by practitioners simplify this estimation process by assuming that all ranges are normally distributed; however, in many cases, there is little justification for this assumption (for example, the inflation distribution may well be positively skewed—expected 3 percent, low 2 percent, high 5 percent[9]). The point is that powerful analytics do not ensure accurate or even credible results. As with a Markowitz mean-variance optimization, Monte Carlo analysis may simply be an effective way to maximize errors.

Costly comfort. The introduction of probability via Monte Carlo analysis has also resulted in unrealistic targets for a "comfort level" of success. For example, in professional publications, it's not uncommon to read such observations as "most clients are satisfied with a 90 percent to a 95 percent probability of success." Although that statement is undoubtedly true, I believe that targeting such a high level of statistical success is dangerous to our clients' well-being. Often, setting such a high threshold for success can be accomplished only by significantly reducing the recommendation for sustainable cash flow.[10] Advising clients to radically reduce their standard of living in order to protect against the unlikely probability of three standard deviation events is inappropriate.

What's more, the "chance of success" provides only a portion of the information necessary to make a knowledgeable decision. What's missing is some measure of the significance of failure. If a portfolio has a 65 percent chance of success and a 35 percent chance that the client's standard of living will fall to 50 percent or less than desired, the investment plan is unlikely to be a viable solution. However, if there is "only" a 65 percent chance of success but a 90 percent chance that the client can maintain 90 percent of the desired standard, then the portfolio may be quite appropriate.

Statistics may not lie; however, they may mislead. A clever educational tool called the Monte Carlo Card Game[11] developed by PIE Technologies puts this reality in perspective. **FIGURE 11.3** is a picture of table 50 (a portfolio composed of 50 percent bonds and 50 percent stock). The value $72,708 is the traditional "point estimate" solution. It is the average real dollar withdrawal rate that an investor could consistently withdraw annually without running out of funds (that is, a Monte Carlo simulation would conclude a 50 percent probability of success).

In this example, the client is uncomfortable with a 50 percent chance

FIGURE 11.3 *Scenario 1: Balancing Withdrawal Sustainability and Standard of Living*

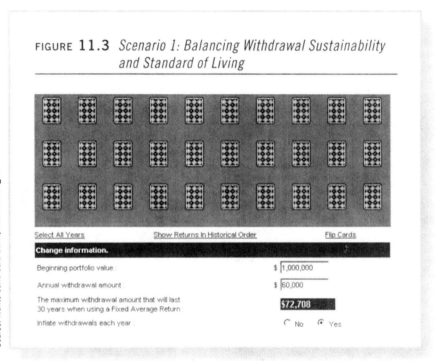

Source: Monte Carlo Card Game, PIE Technologies

FIGURE 11.4 *Scenario 1: 81 Percent Chance of Success*
Balancing Withdrawal Sustainability and
Standard of Living
Monte Carlo Simulation

Monte Carlo - Game 2 - Table 50

Your Goal is for your Portfolio last at least 30 years.
This assumes you started with $1,000,000, withdrew $60,000 per year (inflating each year) and earned the Historical Average Return each year, as shown in "Play Cards"

What are the chances you will run out of money sooner?
To find out, this Monte Carlo simulation will automatically "play" Game 2 a thousand times and calculate how many Games run out of money in less than 30 years.

How Many Games Ran Out of Money in Less Than 30 Years?

Number : 185

Percentage : 19%

Source: Monte Carlo Card Game, PIE Technologies

of failure, so Figure 11.3 reflects a reduced client goal of $60,000 (a 17 percent reduction in living standard).

FIGURE 11.4 is a Monte Carlo simulation based on the $60,000 withdrawal. Not surprisingly, the more modest withdrawal has an increased

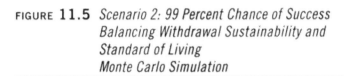

FIGURE **11.5** *Scenario 2: 99 Percent Chance of Success*
Balancing Withdrawal Sustainability and
Standard of Living
Monte Carlo Simulation

Monte Carlo - Game 2 - Table 50

Your Goal is for your Portfolio last at least 30 years.
This assumes you started with $1,000,000, withdrew $42,000 per year (inflating each year) and earned the Historical Average Return each year, as shown in "Play Cards".

What are the chances you will run out of money sooner?
To find out, this Monte Carlo simulation will automatically "play" Game 2 a thousand times and calculate how many Games run out of money in less than 30 years.

How Many Games Ran Out of Money in Less Than 30 Years?

Number : ▮6▮

Percentage : ▮1%▮

Source: Monte Carlo Card Game, PIE Technologies

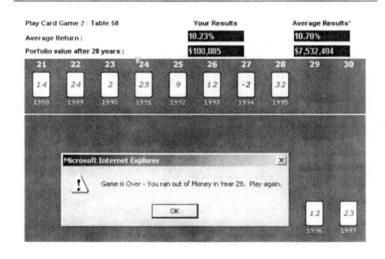

FIGURE **11.6** *Scenario 2: 99 Percent Chance of Success*
Balancing Withdrawal Sustainability and
Standard of Living
Historical Test

Play Card Game 2 - Table 50	Your Results	Average Results*
Average Return :	10.23%	10.70%
Porfolio value after 28 years :	$100,085	$7,532,404

21	22	23	24	25	26	27	28	29	30
14	24	2	25	9	12	-2	32		
1988	1989	1990	1991	1992	1993	1994	1995		

Microsoft Internet Explorer ✕

⚠ Game is Over - You ran out of Money in Year 28. Play again.

OK

12	23
1996	1997

Source: Monte Carlo Card Game, PIE Technologies

likelihood of success (81 percent probability). Unfortunately, 81 percent falls well below the often-recommended 90 percent to 95 percent standard, so the withdrawal is reduced to $42,000—a whopping 43 percent reduction in living standard. The client may not be able to spend much; however, as **FIGURE 11.5** illustrates, the likelihood of success is 99 percent. The client can now rest assured that his Alpo diet will remain fully funded, no matter what happens to the markets—or can he?

Monte Carlo is fun, but reality sometimes isn't. **FIGURE 11.6** is a test of how the $42,000 withdrawal (that is, the 99 percent success scenario) would have performed during the last 30 years. The result shows that it would have failed.

The assumptions underlying Monte Carlo results are numerous and subject to significant estimation error. It's a danger to our clients' well-being to place inappropriate reliance on this soft foundation. Monte Carlo is an excellent educational tool for clients; it is not an answer to their retirement-income planning needs.

Evensky & Katz Cash Flow Reserve Strategy

We developed the Evensky & Katz Cash Flow Reserve Strategy (E&K-S) in the mid-1980s. At that time, the traditional solution to providing cash flow from an investment portfolio was either a traditional income portfolio or a form of reverse dollar-cost averaging from market investments. We had already concluded that the constraints of the traditional income portfolio made no sense, and we were uncomfortable with the obvious disadvantages of reverse dollar-cost averaging (transaction costs, negative tax consequences, volatility drain, and the related conversion of the benefits of dollar-cost averaging into a negative[12]).

At the time, our firm had a long-established five-year philosophy. The mantra "five years, five years, five years" was frequently repeated to our clients to remind them that we believed the real risk faced by investors was having to sell at the wrong time. Consequently, we discouraged making any investment unless the client expected that the funds could remain invested for at least five years. For example, for a client with a $1 million portfolio, who indicated a need for $100,000 for a special purpose in three years, we would design a $900,000 total-return portfolio and a separate portfolio with $100,000 invested for a target maturity in three years. With a five-year window for the investment portfolio, we believed that it would be very unlikely that a client would have to sell a portion of his portfolio at a significant loss.

Although our mantra had been developed to protect a significant liquidation of corpus, we thought that the same concept might be applicable to our clients' regular, but more modest, cash flow needs. We first considered

FIGURE 11.7 *Portfolio Allocation*

POSITION	INVESTMENT ($)	%
Bonds		40
1–3 years (short term)	130,000	
3–5 Years (short–intermediate term)	135,000	
5–10 years (intermediate term)	135,000	
Stock	600,000	60

FIGURE 11.8 *Portfolio Allocation: 5 Percent Annual Cash Flow Need*

POSITION	INVESTMENT ($)	INVESTMENT PORTFOLIO (%)	TOTAL PORTFOLIO (%)
Reserve			
Money market	50,000		10
Short-term bonds	50,000		
Bonds		27	23
1–3 Years	80,000		
3–5 Years	80,000		
5–10 Years	80,000		
Stock	660,000	73	66

simply carving out five years' worth of our clients' cash flow needs, similar to the carve-out we would have proposed for a single goal. Unfortunately, our calculations indicated that the opportunity cost[13] would exceed the benefit. As we modeled various alternatives, we concluded that a two-year cash flow reserve's carve-out was both economically and behaviorally optimal.

The Strategy

Conceptually, E&K-S is very simple. **FIGURE 11.7** shows a proposed portfolio allocation for Mr. Kiran, with $1 million of investable assets and for whom the planning process has determined that a 40 percent bond/60 percent stock portfolio allocation will meet his long-term goals.

FIGURE 11.8 shows the modification to the allocation for a client with the same assets but with a 5 percent annual cash flow need.

In implementing this strategy, we establish three separate accounts. One is the cash flow reserve (CFR) portfolio, the second is the investment portfolio (IP), and the third (which generally already exists) is a local checking account. As an example, in Figure 11.8, we've funded Mr. Kiran's CFR portfolio with $100,000 and his IP with $900,000. The allocation to equities in the IP has been increased by $60,000 to offset the opportunity cost associated with placing the $100,000 reserves in lower-return, short-term liquid investments. Mr. Kiran understands that the IP is long term, that is, it's being managed as a total-return portfolio with all dividends, interest, and capital gains reinvested and that the CFR portfolio is going to be the source of his cash flow.

Presenting the strategy to the client goes something like this:

Mr. Kiran, based on our discussions, we've mutually concluded that you need about $4,200 per month (in real dollars) to supplement your other income [for example, Social Security benefits, pension, part-time work, rental income] to maintain your current lifestyle. Also, over time, you need to earn about 5 percent real return on your investments to maintain your lifestyle for the balance of your life. Here's how we're going to manage this.

We've opened three accounts for you: Kiran's cash flow reserve portfolio, Kiran's investment portfolio, and Kiran's local checking account. In the CFR account, we left $50,000 in money market funds and invested $50,000 in a very low-cost bond fund investing in high-quality short-term (duration about one year) municipal bonds. The CFR account is the one you can look to for your grocery money. Think of the CFR as your payroll account. Once a month, write yourself a paycheck for $4,200 and deposit it into your checking account (increasing the withdrawal over time to compensate for inflation). You won't have to worry about where your next meal's coming from if the market's way down; the cash will be sitting there waiting for you.[14] The balance of your investments is in the IP account, and we've invested that money in the bonds and stock funds we discussed earlier.

As we go forward, our job will be to monitor and manage your IP, and your job will be to go out and enjoy your life. However, just to be sure you remain on course, we'll regularly review your IP to ensure that it remains properly invested. At the same time, we'll also take a look at your CFR balance. If we conclude that we need to make some changes in your IP, we may take the opportunity to fill your CFR back up to the original $100,000. If we determine that the IP is fine and requires no attention and your CFR is funded with at least a year's worth of your cash flow needs, we won't do anything.

As time goes on, we may go for more than a year with no need to change your IP, but by then your withdrawals from your CFR portfolio may have reduced it to less than a year's reserve. If so, we'll review the positions in your IP, and if we can carve out funds without significant losses, we'll do so and bring the CFR balance back up to the two-year reserve of $100,000.

What could go wrong? Because markets are fickle and occasionally treacherous, it's possible that we may go for well over a year when both stocks and bonds have significant losses. Should that happen—which is unlikely—we would then look to the short-term and short–intermediate-term bond investments in your IP. We refer to these funds as your second-tier emergency reserves. No matter how bad the markets get, these bond investments are unlikely to sustain significant losses, so we would begin to fund your CFR account by liquidating a portion of the bond positions. In doing so, there is a risk that the equity allocation might exceed our target; however, we will be buying valuable time to defer the sale of stock in the midst of a bear market. Between the initial CFR allocation ($100,000) and the IP bond positions ($240,000) you're covered for approximately 5½ years. Once again, although there are no guarantees, this five-year window is likely to be long enough to ensure that your cash flow needs are never likely to require a sale of assets at a significant loss in a bear market.

Evaluation

Let's evaluate the E&K-S and see how well it protects against the risks we discussed earlier in this chapter.

Purchasing power risk. As the reserve requirement is reviewed regularly (in our practice, the review is quarterly), it's quite easy to increase the reserves to adjust for inflation. The strategy also provides the flexibility to increase the reserve by variable amounts to reflect an inflation factor unique to each client.[15]

Volatility. By providing significant control over the timing of investment liquidations, most volatility drain related to cash flow can be eliminated.

Financial flexibility. The strategy provides extraordinary flexibility in meeting the unique and changing needs of real clients. Experience has demonstrated that the most frequent adjustment required is to reduce the frequency and size of transfers to the CFR account. In the early stage of planning, in an effort to be conservative, many investors overestimate their needs. Many cash flow strategies generate cash flow whether needed or not. The reinvestment of this unneeded cash flow results in unnecessary transaction and tax costs and, occasionally, in opportunity costs.

Client needs—financial. By providing for total flexibility, the E&K-S enables the practitioner to carefully calibrate and adjust the client's need for real cash flow. It also minimizes the frequency of transactions (reducing transaction costs) and enables an adviser to manage more efficiently the tax consequences of funding the client's cash flow needs.

Client needs—behavioral. The strategy manages the paycheck syndrome. Cash flow to the client is consistent and independent of market volatility. The source of the cash flow is visible and reliable (money market and short-term high-quality municipal bonds). Clients understand the strategy, and it frames the accounts in a manner consistent with a client's separate-pocket mentality.[16]

Does It Work?

Indeed, the E&K-S works very well. We've used this strategy, with minimal modification, for more than a decade. It was seriously tested by two very different but equally trying market conditions—the panic after Black Monday in October 1987 and the bear market of 2000–2002. Our cash flow–dependent clients weathered these events without undue discomfort, and most attributed a significant degree of credit for that outcome to the E&K-S. They may not have understood what was going on in the market, but they did know that the funds for their next meal were safe, sound, and available in their money market accounts. Given that emotional anchor, our clients were able to appreciate our counsel: Although their IP was suffering along with the broad market, they owned small investments in thousands of companies around the world and the firms had not all gone bankrupt. Given time, the domestic and world economies would recover—and our clients had time to recover with them.[17]

I recognize that although the strategy was tested during the short but precipitous 1987 drop and the recent long and painful equity bear market of 2000–2002, we have not had occasion since the inception of the E&K-S to test it during a period similar to the early 1970s, when both bonds and stocks were devastated and inflation was rampant. So I prepared a hypothetical stress test for this period and compared the results of three strategies—income from an all-bond portfolio, regular equal withdrawals from a portfolio balanced 50 percent bonds/50 percent stock, and an E&K-S portfolio. The hypothetical investments were made in January 1968 and consisted of one or a combination of money market, Putnam Income Fund (for bond allocations), and Fidelity Fund (for stock alloca-

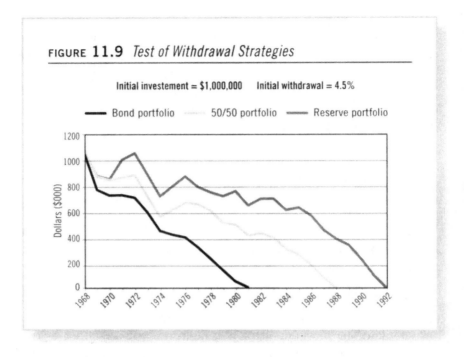

FIGURE **11.9** *Test of Withdrawal Strategies*

Initial investement = $1,000,000   Initial withdrawal = 4.5%

━━━ Bond portfolio   50/50 portfolio   ━━━ Reserve portfolio

tions). The cash flow withdrawal was set at a real annual after-tax rate of 4.5 percent, and withdrawals were monthly. Inflation was set at the rate for 1968 (slightly less than the subsequent 30-year average). The rebalance parameter for the two bond/stock portfolios was set at 10 percent, and the tax rate set at 30 percent for ordinary income and 20 percent for long-term capital gains. Commissions were eliminated. The results of this comparison are quite dramatic.

As shown in **FIGURE 11.9**, an attempt to provide real cash flow by withdrawals from a fixed-income portfolio ended with the complete erosion of the original investment by the close of 1980. The 50/50 balanced portfolio had a significantly longer survival rate; however, it met its demise by 1988. The good news is that the E&K-S portfolio was clearly a superior strategy during these trying times: it managed to sustain the real cash flow until 1992. The bad news is that it, too, could not overcome the early portfolio erosion and it ultimately failed in 1992.

No WITHDRAWAL STRATEGY can guarantee protection for investors requiring income for life.[18] Reducing the withdrawal rate is certainly the most effective technique; however, for most investors, that's not a viable option. I believe the next best strategy is some form of an E&K-S. It provides significant behavioral benefits resulting in greater client comfort during trying market conditions, minimizes the impact of taxes and transaction costs, maximizes the withdrawal period, and maximizes planning flexibility.

Chapter Notes

1. In this chapter, "income for life" and "cash flow" are used interchangeably to mean real (that is, inflation-adjusted) cash flow.

2. Although I was influenced by my appreciation of the finer points of quality films (that is, Clint Eastwood in *Dirty Harry*), my spontaneous response to my client was admittedly a bit brash. Because he was also a longtime friend, I was not surprised that he took my comment in the humorous manner it was intended. I was, however, surprised that my joking comment was so effective in getting his attention. I've subsequently used that story with new clients and found it an effective vignette for focusing their attention on longevity risk; I hope you too will find it of use.

3. We live in a complex and often confusing economic environment. To manage huge amounts of information and understand market complexity, investors use what behavioral finance calls judgmental heuristics (mental shortcuts).

4. The application of unsound but seemingly logical mathematical analysis.

5. In a study prepared for a presentation at the April 2002 Financial Planning Association retreat, I concluded that during the last 20 years, the net-net real return from a balanced portfolio was approximately 7.5 percent. Based on what I believe to be reasonable forward-looking projections, I concluded that the same portfolio, in today's markets, will return approximately 2.5 percent.

6. These two funds will be used as examples throughout the chapter. They were selected because they have attributes that make them ideal candidates for demonstration purposes:

- Both are publicly available to retail investors.

- Both have extensive, well-documented histories. Putnam Income was established in November 1954 and Fidelity in April 1930.

- Both are effective for general asset class investments. According to Morningstar Principia, Fidelity has a 36-month correlation with the Standard & Poor's 500 index of 99 and Putnam Income has a 36-month correlation with the Lehman Brothers Aggregate Bond Index of 99. A 20-year correlation analysis indicates a still high correlation of 95 for Fidelity and the S&P and 93 for Putnam and the Lehman.

- Fidelity has an R^2 of 98 with the S&P 500, and Putnam 98 with the Lehman.

- The analysis is based on purchase and sale at net asset value.

7. In 2004, the income return for Putnam was only 2.8 percent and 1.4 percent for Fidelity. There was no possibility of generating 5 percent from dividends and interest.

8. To avoid grossly exaggerating the impact of taxes, I used a 15 percent ordinary and capital gains tax to simulate a comparable tax-free portfolio return.

9. Reality is likely to be even more complex. For example, equity market returns are generally considered to be leptokurtic with a positive distribution skew.

10. Running a number of hypothetical portfolios, I estimate the reduction in sustainable cash flow to be approximately:

Increase Probability of Success		Reduction in Sustainable Cash Flow
From	To	
70%	90%	13%
60	90	25
60	95	44

11. The game allows a player to select one of 10 tables. Each table represents a portfolio, changing allocations between bonds and stocks in 10 percent increments, ranging from all bonds to all stock. For example, Table 60 represents a portfolio 40 percent bonds and 60 percent stock. Once a table is selected, 30 cards are displayed, face down. Each card's face value reflects the return on a 40/60 portfolio for one of the last 30 years.

12. Dollar-cost averaging is based on the purchase of larger quantities of a position when the price is low and smaller quantities when the price is high. The result, over a market cycle, is that the average price of the positions accumulated is lower than the average market price of that same position. Reverse dollar-cost averaging results in the average price of the positions sold being less that the average market price of the position over the cycle.

13. The opportunity cost is the difference between the expected total return on the investment portfolio and the expected (but lower) return on the funds invested in shorter-term, liquid investments times the value of the funds set aside for reserves.

14. Obviously, this example is greatly simplified. In practice, many clients fund their checking account only quarterly or intermittently. In some cases, we set up automatic monthly checks to transfer money from the CFR account to their checking account. In a surprising number of cases, the CFR funds last much longer than the anticipated two years, because clients often overestimate their cash flow needs.

15. Although the consumer price index is a handy measure for general planning, experienced practitioners recognize that the impact of inflation on an individual client depends largely on the nature of his personal expenses. For example, older retirees' effective inflation is often much higher than the reported CPI because so much of their expenses are related to health care costs.

16. One "pocket" is the source of the client's grocery money—the CFR account. The investments are simple, nonvolatile, and comfortable. The second pocket is the IP. Because it's clearly identified as a long-term portfolio (remember the five-year mantra) and the client is looking at his other pocket for spending money, the client tends to pay little attention to short-term market fluctuations in the IP.

17. On October 19, 1987, the morning of Black Monday, we called all of our clients. One of my first calls was to a retired widow. I was particularly concerned about her because she had been a 100 percent CD investor before working with us, and we had repositioned her investments to a 50 percent bond/50 percent stock portfolio. I began my call by saying she may have noticed a slight dip in the market. Before I could go on, she said, "So what? Remember five years, five years, five years. I have plenty of cash to last me for years in my other account. Don't bother with me. Why don't you call someone who's worried?" I was flabbergasted. Even more amazing, her response turned out to be typical of those we heard throughout the day.

18. Of course, immediate annuitization, a subject addressed by other contributors in this book, is a potentially complementary strategy.

CHAPTER 12

Asset Allocation

The Long View

LAURENCE BOOTH

R etirement problems are all about saving and spending. How much money must be saved each year so that in retirement the wealth can be drawn down and spent? Both sides of the issue—saving and distribution—involve the same challenges: how to deal with uncertainty in the personal circumstances of the individual, such as death and disability, and how to deal with uncertainty in investment returns. This chapter focuses on the investment uncertainties that must be addressed in planning retirement income and shows how the three iron laws of finance—the laws of time, tax, and risk—can help in structuring the solution.

The three iron laws tell us that there is a time value of money, a tax value of money, and a risk value of money. The first two concepts are relatively straightforward, but dealing with the risk value of money—that riskier securities, such as common equities, tend to generate higher rates of return—is tricky, to say the least. But probability targets can be introduced into retirement-income planning. It is commonly said that the target for income replacement in retirement should be something like "70@65," meaning retirees should aim for 70 percent income replacement at age 65. However, given the uncertainty of investment returns, a more reasonable retirement target would be something like "70 percent of 70@65," meaning a 70 percent probability of achieving 70 percent income replacement at age 65. Of course, some planners have clients whose wealth may be substantial enough to reach this target simply by investing in fixed-income government securities. This chapter will not be of interest to them. For most of us, however, aiming for 70 percent income replacement in the face

FIGURE **12.1** *Interest Rates on Government Debt*

TREASURY BILLS (%)	ONE-YEAR BILLS (%)	FIVE-YEAR NOTES (%)	LONG BOND (%)
2.63	3.32	3.93	4.64
N/A	0.50	1.14	1.84

of declining Social Security benefits, increasing dependency ratios, and lengthening life expectancies is a challenge that requires help. This chapter aims to provide it.

The Retirement-Income Problem

The Time Value of Money

The first iron law of finance—that of the time value of money—is fairly simple. **FIGURE 12.1** shows the interest rates on government debt issues of different maturities as of May 2005.

The rates in the first row of Figure 12.1 reflect the nominal interest rates current at that time. A very short-term investment in U.S. government 90-day Treasury bills yields 2.63 percent; for a one-year bill, the rate rises to 3.32 percent; for five years, it's 3.93 percent; and for the longest outstanding U.S. government bond it's 4.64 percent. In saving for retirement, we should use the 4.64 percent rate as indicative of a long-term default-free rate. But these rates are nominal because regular Treasury bonds have payments, both interest and return of principal, that are fixed in nominal terms—that is, they do not vary with future inflation rates. The problem, of course, is that the 4.64 percent yield on the long-term bond doesn't look very good when inflation is zipping along at almost 3 percent.

The second row in Figure 12.1 gives the yield on Treasury inflation-protected securities, or TIPS. The principal on these securities is indexed to the general inflation rate, so that the interest earned, as well as the amount paid back at maturity, goes up with the principal. But this inflation protection comes at a price: the yield on a TIPS with a maturity of about a year is only 0.5 percent, increasing marginally to 1.14 percent for a five-year bond and to 1.84 percent for a 30-year TIPS.

Compare the yield on the TIPS versus the nominal bonds and you'll see that they differ by about 2.8 percentage points, an indication of the long-run expected inflation rate. The difference underscores one implication of the time value of money: that what we are interested in is the *real* interest rate, that is, how much we can actually buy in the future by not buying things today.

The Tax Value of Money

A 1.84 percent real interest rate on a 30-year TIPS is enough to dampen anyone's motivation for saving, but it gets worse. Consider the second iron law of finance, that of the tax value of money. Interest is taxable and, unfortunately, so is the increase in the principal value of the inflation-indexed bond. So if the 30-year TIPS is held to maturity, some of that value will be lost each year in tax revenue to the different layers of government. Taxes are complex and are affected by the alternative minimum tax (AMT) as well as by a host of other factors, but a 35 percent tax rate will cut that 4.64 percent interest rate to 3 percent, or to a real rate of return close to zero.

And what does a zero real interest rate do to our retirement-income formula? The good news is that it makes the calculations extremely simple. Suppose we have a typical 35-year-old male—let's call him John—earning $65,000 a year and looking to retire at age 65. If his real income is expected to be constant, then with a zero real interest rate, we can simply sum the income over his lifetime and say that the real wealth is $1,950,000. If the individual is in good health, he can expect to live for 11 years in retirement, or until age 76, so this wealth has to last for 41 years. This means that John's real consumption is only $47,560 a year, which means the balance of $17,440 is the required level of savings. That calls for a whopping 27 percent savings rate.

For most people, a savings rate of 27 percent is simply out of the question, and luckily it is not needed, because the second iron law of finance, the tax value of money, comes into play. As long as the savings are made within an individual retirement account (IRA), their value can compound tax-free; this compounding gives us back our 1.8 percent real interest rate. What's more, most people do not need the same amount of money to live in retirement as they do while working. For example, in a Delphi study of financial planners, Greninger and others (2000)[1] indicated that the average ratio of replacement income was 74 percent of preretirement income at age 62.

Let's recalculate with tax-free compounding factored in. For the sake of convenience, we'll use a rate of 70 percent of preretirement after-savings income at age 65, so the retirement target is set at "70@65." In this case, the level of savings required drops to 15 percent. This is the result of the 1.84 percent real interest rate's reducing the savings rate to 20 percent and the 70 percent replacement rate's cutting it further to 15 percent.

The Risk Value of Money

Having applied the first two iron laws of finance, we generate numbers that start to look reasonable. Although a savings rate of 15 percent seems extremely high, once it's split 50-50 with the employer, a 7.5 percent personal savings rate for someone like John, starting quite late in life at age 35, isn't completely outrageous. But the third iron law of finance—the risk value of money—remains. By now everyone has heard the dictum "Stocks for the long run," so perhaps that paltry 1.84 percent real rate of return can be boosted by taking some risk and moving some of the portfolio assets into more risky equities and away from long-term TIPS.

FIGURE 12.2 shows the realized returns from holding a portfolio of equities versus investing in long-term Treasury bonds from 1926 until 2004.

The first column in Figure 12.2 gives the arithmetic return, which is simply the average of each year's rate of return. For equities, this average return is 12.39 percent, whereas for holding the long bond, it's 5.77 percent. On average, investing in equities earned 6.62 percent more than investing in long bonds.[2] If the past can be expected to repeat itself in some way, then this 6.62 percent earned risk premium goes a long way toward solving our problem. For example, combined with the 1.84 percent real return on TIPS, we get a real equity return of 8.46 percent, which is close to the average real equity return of 9.10 percent from 1926–2004. If we substitute 8.46 percent into our retirement-income formula, the required savings rate drops to 3.81 percent and our retirement-income problem seemingly disappears: a 3.81 percent split between an employer and employee isn't such a big deal. No wonder Einstein reportedly described compound interest as the greatest discovery of the 20th century.

FIGURE **12.2** *Realized Returns: Equities Versus Treasuries*

	ARITHMETIC RETURN (%)	GEOMETRIC RETURN (%)	VOLATILITY (%)
S&P 500 equities	12.39	10.43	20.31
Long Treasuries	5.77	5.39	9.29
Risk premium	6.62	5.04	—

Managing the Risk of Equities

Before we plunge in and put our wealth heavily into equities, we need to understand what these historical past returns really mean and in particular what the average rate of return means. To take an extreme example, suppose we invest a dollar and it earns a 100 percent rate of return the first year before losing 50 percent the next. In this case, the dollar goes to two dollars before dropping back to a dollar, so the geometric rate of return over these two periods is zero.[3] The arithmetic return, however, is simply the average of 100 percent and –50 percent, or 25 percent. In this case, assuming that the investor can earn 25 percent could be misleading, and some use the geometric rate of return as a better estimate of the long-term rate of return.[4]

In Figure 12.2, we can see that while the arithmetic return on equities averaged 6.62 percentage points greater than the return on long bonds, the geometric return averaged only 5.04 percentage points more. This difference, combined with the 1.84 percent real return, gives a forecasted real geometric equity return of 6.88 percent, slightly less than the actual real geometric equity return of 7.01 percent. If this geometric return is used as the forecasted real equity return, the required savings rate increases to 5.4 percent. Although the example shows how sensitive the results are to the real return assumptions, here it seems to imply that there is no problem: 5.4 percent split equally between employer and employee seems manageable.

Unfortunately, these results are deceptive and seriously misleading because in all cases the arithmetic return is the best estimate of the next period's rate of return, whereas the geometric return is only one estimate of what might have been earned over this very long investment horizon: neither one is appropriate for investment horizons in between these two extremes.[5] What's more, Figure 12.2 also shows the volatility, or the standard deviation, of the annual returns. In the case of equities, this volatility is 20.31 percent; for long Treasury bonds, it's 9.29 percent. On average, returns in the equity market have been twice as volatile as those in the bond market.[6] But note the difference in the arithmetic and geometric returns: in the case of equities, it's 1.96 percent; for bonds, 0.38 percent. Clearly, the equity returns are more volatile than bond returns, and the difference between the arithmetic and geometric returns is also greater.

The arithmetic return is approximately the geometric return plus half the variance in the arithmetic rate of return. In the case of equities, the volatility is 20.31 percent; for simplicity, call it 0.20, in which case the variance (square of the standard deviation) is 0.04 and half the variance is 0.02, or 2 percent. The approximation indicates a difference of 2 percent between the arithmetic and geometric returns, whereas the actual mates differ by 1.96 percent; similarly, for bonds, the approximation icates a 0.43 percent difference, whereas the estimates actually differ by 0.38 percent.

The closeness in these numbers is not an accident. It's well known that annual portfolio returns, such as the return on the Standard & Poor's 500 index, are approximately normally distributed. The return earned over many periods, however, is just the product of these uncertain future rates of return. For example, the wealth at the end of two periods is just the starting wealth (W_0) multiplied by one plus the returns earned in periods 1 and 2. The wealth at future time T (W_T) is then just

$$W_T = W_0 \, \Pi_{t=1}^{T}(1 + r_t) \tag{1}$$

It is not quite so well known that application of the central limit theorem to this future wealth shows us that it is lognormally distributed. We can see this by simply dividing through by starting wealth and taking natural logarithms, so that the logarithm of the increase in terminal wealth $Ln(W_T) - Ln(W_0)$ is simply the sum of the additive terms $Ln(1 + r)$, which by the central limit theorem means that $Ln(1 + r)$ is normally distributed. $Ln(1 + r)$ is then simply the continuously compounded annual rate of return.

Using the same data as were used in Figure 12.2, we can estimate the expected continuously compounded real equity rate of return at 6.12 percent.[7] In this case, we have an analytical formula for the distribution of terminal wealth because we know from the application of the central limit theorem that the logarithm of terminal wealth is normally distributed, or

$$Ln\,W_T \sim \phi[Ln\,W_0 + 0.0612T, \ .20\sqrt{T}] \tag{2}$$

For example, suppose we are completely invested in the stock market. What would the distribution of our wealth look like after one year versus 20 years? **FIGURE 12.3** gives us the answer based on both having standardized distributions around an expected value of 1.0.

Figure 12.3 illustrates the impact of compounding over time. After one year, the distribution is approximately normal, or bell shaped. But after 20 years, the distribution is decidedly nonnormal; it is most obviously not symmetric. That is what the lognormal distribution looks like; it's skewed with the median value to the left, or lower than the average or expected value. Further, the distribution becomes more skewed as the underlying annual rates of return become more volatile, so that a 100 percent equity portfolio, for example, generates more skewed terminal wealth than does a balanced portfolio of equities and bonds.

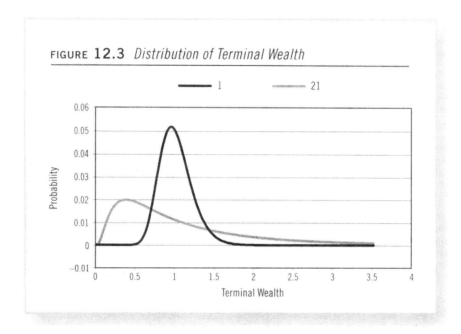

FIGURE **12.3** *Distribution of Terminal Wealth*

The Median and the Mean

The difference between the median and the mean is very important to understand. Both the median and mean are estimates of the "middle" value of the distribution. But the median simply gives the middle value when 50 percent of the values are above and 50 percent below—without taking into account how far above or below they are. In contrast, the mean takes into account not only whether a value is above or below the middle value but also by how much. As a result, the mean is affected by outliers.

The difference between the median and the mean is not merely a statistical distinction; it has profound implications for money invested over long periods of time and the likelihood of achieving a retirement target. Over a 20-year time horizon, the possibility exists for a sequence of tremendous equity returns, which would make the individual fabulously wealthy. The very low possibility of this "outlier" pulls up the mean and causes it to exceed the more likely outcomes. As the 20-year distribution of terminal wealth indicates, most of the "probability mass" is below or to the left of the mean. This tells us that the probability of actually earning the mean rate of return is not the 50-50 one might expect from a normal distribution.

FIGURE 12.4 plots the probability of failing to earn the mean return as well as the probability of earning less than the risk-free rate, assumed to be the 1.84 percent return from the TIPS. Note that after one year the

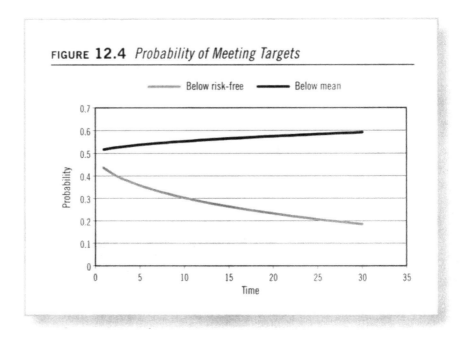

FIGURE **12.4** *Probability of Meeting Targets*

──── Below risk-free ━━━━ Below mean

probabilities are close to 50 percent. The probability of failing to earn the mean is actually 53 percent, because the distribution even after one year is not perfectly symmetrical. Obviously, the probability of failing to beat the lower real bond return of 1.84 percent is lower, but at 41 percent, it's still very high. This underscores the obvious fact that with a standard deviation of 20 percent, we can be 99 percent certain that the equity return will be between +/– three standard deviations of the mean. That's a range of +/– 60 percent and clearly represents a huge range of outcomes with a significant probability of being less than the risk-free rate. This, in turn, emphasizes that short-term investors should not be in the stock market: there is simply too much volatility.

However, note that during the 30-year horizon, both probabilities change dramatically. The good news is that the probability of beating the risk-free rate drops, so that by the end of 30 years, the probability of failing to earn the 1.84 percent a year is only 12 percent. The bad news is that the probability of earning the mean return increases, because there is now a 71 percent probability of falling below it.

Figure 12.4 offers two major insights. The first is well known: as the investment horizon increases, the riskiness of the stock market decreases. This is simply because a positive risk premium compounds over time.[8] In this case, the dictum "stocks for the long run" makes sense if we judge the risk to be the failure to beat the alternative investment, which is the return on bonds. There is, however, a second implication, which is lesser known: basing retirement-income planning on mean, or expected, returns is extremely dangerous.

Addressing Risk in Retirement-Income Planning

This cautionary note brings us back to our retirement-income problem, which we thought we'd solved: because equities are expected to earn more than bonds, simply invest in the stock market and earn the higher rate of return. Problem solved. Not quite, however—as Figure 12.4 indicates, the chance of earning less than the mean, or expected, return is 71 percent. How many people would accept a retirement-income solution with a 71 percent chance of failure? Our 100 percent equities solution to the retirement-income problem took the good side of the third iron law of finance, the risk value of money, to mean higher expected equity returns while ignoring the flip side, which is that this value also entails significant risk. We cannot plan merely on the basis of expected, or mean, values without taking into account the risk attached to earning them. If we could truly solve all our problems simply by investing in the stock market, then obviously we're missing something. Life is not that simple.

Financial planners are well aware that investing in equities is not a panacea and that there is risk involved in the equity market. They deal with this risk by using a diversified portfolio of both stocks and bonds and using the "your age in bonds" rule to adjust for the equity market risk—that is, as investors get older they should move more of their portfolio toward bonds to lower the risk. For example, Greninger and others (2000) found that financial planners generally recommend moving to a more conservative portfolio three to five years before retirement. In the case of John, our 35-year-old investor, this would mean a portfolio of 65 percent equities and 35 percent bonds, with a real expected annual rate of return of 6.143 percent. This combination would require an annual savings rate of 6.33 percent, real income after savings while employed of $60,844, and retirement income of $42,619. However, this still doesn't address the risk attached to meeting this 70@65 retirement-income target.

Incorporating risk into retirement-income planning is relatively easy. First, suppose John had portfolio wealth of $55,795.27. Investing in a portfolio of 65 percent equities and 35 percent bonds at the 6.143 percent expected rate of return compounds the starting wealth to the wealth target of $333,368, which is enough to satisfy the retirement objective. However, we can now use the wealth distribution as of the retirement date to estimate the probability of getting the targeted wealth of $333,368, and it is only 41 percent. That means there is a 59 percent chance of falling below the target of 70@65. This is certainly less than the 71 percent probability of earning the mean with a 100 percent equity portfolio, because the more balanced port-folio of 65 percent equities and 35 percent bonds is less risky.[9] Most people, however, would not consider a target of 41 percent of 70@65 reasonable.

To counter the probability of failing to earn the target rate of return, we can directly incorporate the probability constraint into the retirement objective function. For example suppose the objective is a 70 percent chance of getting 70@65. The probability target can be written as:

$$N(\frac{Tk - TE(r)}{\sigma\sqrt{T}}) < 30\% \qquad (3)$$

where $N(.)$ is the unit normal density function, k is the target rate of return and $E(r)$ the continuously compounded expected rate of return, T the time horizon and the volatility. With the 70 percent probability target, the constraint imposes a value of -0.5244. This states that 70 percent of the probability mass of a unit normal density function is between -0.5244 standard deviations to the left of the mean and infinity, or, conversely, that 30 percent is below -0.5244 standard deviations to the left of the mean.

The optimal equity (α) allocation given this probability target is

$$\alpha = \frac{(r - R) - 0.5244\sigma T^{-0.5}}{\sigma^2} \qquad (4)$$

The reasoning behind this solution is straightforward.[10] Without the probability target, the solution is the growth optimal portfolio, because the terminal wealth is assumed to be lognormally distributed. In this case, the optimal equity allocation is the expected risk premium ($r - R$) divided by the variance of the equity portfolio (σ^2). A mean-variance solution, in contrast, would have the variance multiplied by the investor's risk aversion: the bigger the risk aversion, the larger the denominator and the smaller the equity allocation. The argument for mean-variance analysis is that it is more general than the growth optimal portfolio in allowing for more general individual preferences.

In the solution with the probability target, the target plays the same role as risk aversion in the mean-variance model. As the investor wants more assurance of meeting his retirement target—for example, with an 80 percent rather than a 70 percent probability of meeting the target—more is subtracted from the risk premium. As a result, the equity alloca-tion is smaller. Also note that as T gets bigger, the effect of the probability constraint gets smaller and the equity allocation gets larger, so the time horizon in this model does affect the optimal equity allocation.

We can understand this point better by using our values for the continuously compounded market-risk premium of 6.3 percent and market volatility of 20 percent as follows:

$$\alpha = \frac{(0.06297) - 0.5244 * .2 * T^{-0.5}}{.04} \quad (5)$$

Optimal Equity Allocation

FIGURE 12.5 shows the optimal equity allocation depending on the investor's time horizon.

The optimal allocation obviously depends on the values used for the market-risk premium and the volatility,[11] but with these values the optimal decision for a one- or two-year investment horizon is zero equities. To see how this works, consider the one-year solution. Here, the probability constraint subtracts 10.48 percent from the market-risk premium (0.5244 * .2) so that the optimal equity allocation involves shorting the equity market and a negative expected rate of return. That's because a one-year horizon increases the risk of not meeting the target so much that satisfying the 70 percent constraint requires an investment that exceeds the target. In this case, of course, the target can be met with a 100 percent probability by investing in the risk-free asset. The same logic holds for a two-year horizon; and even for a three-year horizon, the equity allocation is very small. Gradually as the investment horizon is lengthened, the equity allocation increases until for a 20-year investment horizon the allocation is 100 percent. Thereafter, the optimal solution involves a leveraged portfolio.[12]

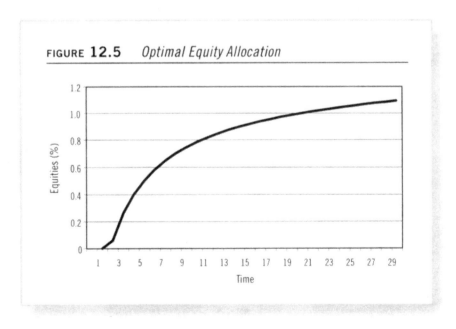

FIGURE **12.5** *Optimal Equity Allocation*

What is clear from adding the probability target model is that the equity allocation depends on the time horizon. Although the effect of the probability constraint is easily seen in the case of a single sum invested for multiple years, the solution for the standard retirement-income problem involving annual savings over many years is less obvious. That's simply because the savings in year 30 aren't at risk at all because they come from the final year's earnings, whereas in each prior year, the savings are invested for different lengths of time. As a result, the compounding effect of investing for multiple years is dampened because not all of the wealth is outstanding for the full 30 years. Just as the duration of a coupon bond is shorter than its maturity, so too the effective investment horizon for the savings problem is shorter than its maturity.

Although our retirement-income savings problem has a horizon of 30 years, no money is actually invested for the full 30 years. The savings invested at the end of the first year have the longest investment horizon, which is 29 years. If we define the effective maturity of the investment the same way as the duration of a bond, the horizon is only 18.7 years. The probability of meeting the target with an 18.7-year investment horizon is 43 percent. We can check this using Monte Carlo simulation in which each year the prior solution of $4,115 is invested, but the investment return—instead of being a constant 6.14 percent—is calculated from 1,000 random draws each period from a distribution with an expected return of 6.14 percent and standard deviation of 13 percent. At the end of 30 years,

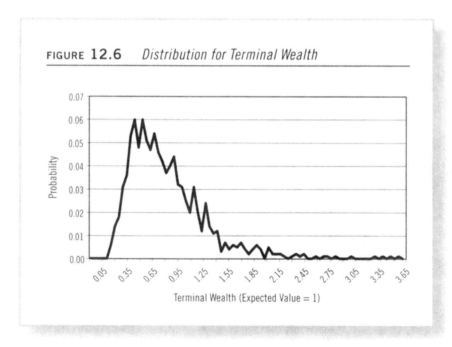

FIGURE **12.6** *Distribution for Terminal Wealth*

a little more than 40 percent of the 1,000 possible investment experiences resulted in the target wealth being met. The difference between this 40 percent and the analytical solution using the effective maturity of 18.7 years is mainly the result of the particular random numbers in the Monte Carlo simulation.

FIGURE 12.6 illustrates the distribution of the terminal wealth. It is not as smooth as the analytical distribution discussed in Figure 12.3 earlier simply because it reflects the particular random number used in the simulation. But it illustrates that the distribution of terminal wealth is still skewed, indicating that planning on the basis of the mean, or expected, portfolio return implicitly exposes the retiree to significant downside risk well above the 50 percent probability one might expect.

A key point to remember here is simply that the standard savings-annuity problem can always be converted into a simple single-sum problem. For our example, savings of $4,115 per year for 30 years are equivalent to the problem of investing $55,795 for an effective investment horizon of 18.7 years. We saw that the optimal equity allocation for a single-sum problem with an 18.7-year investment horizon is basically 100 percent.

A Word to the Wise Planner

Heuristics, such as the "your age in bonds rule" have validity. The closer clients are to retirement, the more they should invest in bonds and the less in equities. At the extreme of very short horizon problems—say, less than three years—100 percent should be invested in the short-term bond market. As the investment horizon lengthens, more should be invested in equities because the probability of beating the bond market return goes up. The distribution of terminal wealth, however, becomes more skewed, so that the probability of earning the mean or expected rate of return goes down. Consequently, planning on the basis of historical market performance is risky.

Instead, the risk of failing to meet the retirement target can be incorporated into the planning process by specifying retirement targets on the order of "70 percent of 70@65," meaning a 70 percent chance or probability of getting 70 percent income replacement at age 65. That target can be achieved quite easily in the case of single-sum problems, because the distribution of wealth through time is lognormal and exact analytical solutions are available. For the savings problem in which the amount saved each period varies, the general case can always be solved by Monte Carlo simulation, or a close approximation can be made by estimating the *effective* investment horizon, calculated in the same way as the duration of a bond, and then treating the retirement-income problem as single-sum problem.

Implementing solutions to retirement-income problems by using objectives like "70 percent of 70@65" goes a long way toward realistically addressing the uncertainty in investment returns.

Chapter Notes

1. S. Greninger, V. Hampton, K. Kitt, and S. Jacquet, "Retirement Planning Guidelines: A Delphi Study of Financial Planners and Educators," *Financial Services Review* 9(3) (2000): 231–245.

2. TIPS do not go back far enough to permit meaningful estimates of their annual rates of return.

3. This is the compound rate of return using an annual compounding frequency.

4. Note that the arithmetic return over the two periods is 0 percent, so the difference between the arithmetic and geometric returns is really a matter of the appropriate investment horizon.

5. For a full discussion of this, see Marshall Blume, "Unbiased Estimators of Long Run Expected Rates of Return," *Journal of the American Statistical Association* (September 1973): 634–638.

6. I have shown elsewhere that the relative risk of equities versus bonds has not been constant over the period since 1926; see Laurence Booth, "Estimating the Equity Risk Premium and Equity Costs: New Ways of Looking at Old Data," *Journal of Applied Corporate Finance* (Spring 1999): 100–112.

7. This is the expected annual arithmetic return of 8.46 percent; converting to continuous compounding gives 8.12 percent and subtracting half the variance to convert it to a compound rate of return gives 6.12 percent; see J. Hull, *Options, Futures, and Other Derivatives,* 4th ed. (Prentice Hall, 2001), for a more detailed discussion.

8. Obviously, those that believe in a skimpy risk premium should probably not be in the equity market, given that it is unambiguously risky.

9. For convenience, the 1.84 percent is assumed to be constant—that is, it is a zero-coupon stripped bond. It is easy to incorporate riskiness in the bond return as well.

10. Laurence Booth, "Meeting Retirement Targets," *Financial Services Review* (Spring 2004): 1–18.

11. Note that this historically based market-risk premium would be regarded as excessive by many people (including myself). It is used simply for illustrative purposes. Obviously, the analysis goes through with different parameter values.

12. Clearly, for these short horizon problems, the term of the risk-free investment should match the planning horizon, and funds should not be invested in 30-year TIPS: remember the time value of money.

CHAPTER 13

Sustainable Withdrawals

WILLIAM P. BENGEN

There's a certain reasoning about retirement income that can be very seductive for many clients. It goes like this: in retirement I need a blend of growth and income investments. Over long periods, common stocks have averaged approximately 10 percent returns annually, and bonds about 5 percent. A portfolio allocated to 60 percent stocks and 40 percent bonds will have an expected average annual return of 8 percent. Returns should be augmented by about 10 percent by annual rebalancing of the portfolio, providing a compound annual return of about 8.8 percent. I want to increase my withdrawals annually by inflation. Assuming that inflation averages about 3 percent, I should be able to withdraw 5.8 percent from my portfolio the first year, give myself a 3 percent cost-of-living adjustment each year after that, and my money will last forever.

Or maybe not.

Outliving a Portfolio

The flaw in this reasoning is revealed in the chart in **FIGURE 13.1**, which reconstructs the investment experience of two individuals, one retiring on January 1, 1963, and the other on January 1, 1961. Both retirees employed a portfolio allocation of 63 percent large-cap stocks, with the remainder in intermediate-term (five-year) government bonds. They both withdrew 6 percent of their initial portfolio value at the end of the first year of retirement, then gave themselves a cost-of-living adjustment (based on the consumer price index, or CPI) each subsequent year. They both rebalanced their portfolios to the original allocation at the end of each year.

As the figure shows, the 1961 retiree exhausted his portfolio in its 23rd

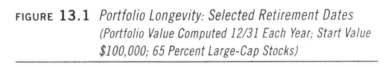

FIGURE **13.1** *Portfolio Longevity: Selected Retirement Dates (Portfolio Value Computed 12/31 Each Year; Start Value $100,000; 65 Percent Large-Cap Stocks)*

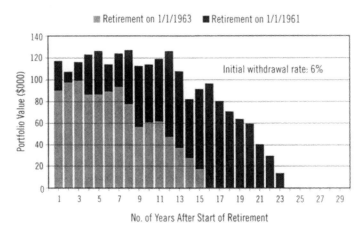

FIGURE **13.2** *Portfolio Longevity: All Retirement Dates (Fixed Asset Allocation; 63 Percent Large-Cap Stocks and 37 Percent Intermediate-Term Government Bonds)*

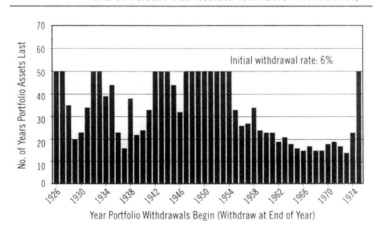

year. If he had retired at age 65, that would be age 88, an age many retirees attain today. The 1963 retiree fared even worse, exhausting his portfolio after only 15 years, at age 80—well shy of the life expectancy of most retirees today. What went wrong?

FIGURE 13.2 explores this phenomenon in greater detail. It re-creates the investment experience of 50 retirees who retired on January 1 of each year from 1926 through 1975. Included are the two retirees mentioned earlier. The portfolio asset allocation (63 percent equities, 37 percent government bonds) is the same, as is the annual rebalancing policy and the 6 percent initial withdrawal rate.

The salient observation is that although some portfolios sustained withdrawals for as long as 50 years (or longer), most portfolios expired much sooner. The sharp dips in the chart correspond to the three major bear stock markets of 1929–1932, 1937–1938, and 1973–1974. The latter appears to have been the most devastating of all, affecting even those who retired in the late 1950s.

The recurrence of major bear stock markets explains the failure of the "average rate of return" method of calculation. Such declines are powerful enough to overwhelm a portfolio already stressed by withdrawals. In short, secular bear markets cannot be ignored. This chapter explores what constitutes "safe" levels of sustained withdrawals, how they can be optimized, and how to counsel clients on the choices they face in these matters.

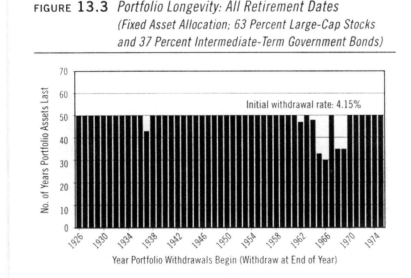

FIGURE **13.3** *Portfolio Longevity: All Retirement Dates*
(Fixed Asset Allocation; 63 Percent Large-Cap Stocks
and 37 Percent Intermediate-Term Government Bonds)

Initial withdrawal rate: 4.15%

No. of Years Portfolio Assets Last

Year Portfolio Withdrawals Begin (Withdraw at End of Year)

Methodology

My approach to exploring the issues of sustained withdrawals is deterministic; that is, it uses historical data on investment returns and inflation. This method contrasts with stochastic approaches, such as Monte Carlo simulation, which constructs mathematical models of the markets, then runs probability trials to simulate the behavior of portfolios.

My primary source of data on the markets and inflation is the *SBBI Yearbook* produced annually by Ibbotson Associates. This work is a treasure trove of information for investment returns from 1926 to date. Virtually all the conclusions of my research are grounded in the bedrock of that book's database.

Analysis in the early sections of the chapter is performed on a baseline portfolio for the sake of simplicity. The baseline portfolio consists of only two assets—large-cap stocks and intermediate-term government bonds. The portfolio is tax-deferred, making calculations simpler.

Retirement for the client occurs on January 1 in each case. Withdrawals are made at the end of each year. The first year of retirement, the dollar withdrawal is computed as a percentage of initial portfolio value. Each subsequent year, the dollar withdrawal is adjusted in accordance with the prior year's consumer price index, so as to give the client a cost-of-living adjustment. Portfolios are rebalanced to the desired allocation at the end of each year, after withdrawals are made. At the time of this writing, the last year of data available was for 2004. For a portfolio whose life is expected to extend beyond that year, the missing years of data are filled in with average return figures for inflation and the various asset classes involved. Because 1975 is the last year of retirement studied, no

The Maximum Safe Withdrawal Rate

In Figures 13.1 and 13.2, we saw that a 6 percent initial withdrawal rate often leads to premature portfolio exhaustion. What, then, is a safe initial withdrawal rate? And what is the maximum such rate, or "safemax"?

To answer those questions, we must agree on a time horizon for the retired client. For our first look at the problem, I've arbitrarily selected 30 years as the desired portfolio longevity, which means the portfolio must support 65-year-old clients through their 95th year. That longevity encompasses the

portfolio will begin with less than 30 years of actual market and inflation data, which appears adequate.

Limitations of the Deterministic Approach

I would be remiss in not pointing out some of the limitations of the deterministic approach. First and foremost, the Ibbotson database goes back only 80 years. That is a relatively limited pool of data with which to conduct studies for time horizons of 30 to 50 years, which are typical in retirement planning.

Conversely, even if data were available for much longer time periods, they might still be of limited use because markets change. For example, the high dividend yields on stocks prevalent in the 1930s no longer hold today. Furthermore, markets in today's postregulation, technology-driven world may perform much differently than earlier markets.

Of course, stochastic approaches such as Monte Carlo methods have their own difficulties, not the least of which is developing an appropriate mathematical model for the markets. But I will not debate the relative strengths of the two approaches: I believe they both have merit. I am convinced that deterministic methods, despite the above shortcomings, provide eminently useful guideposts for financial professionals.

We cannot be certain how closely future markets will resemble those of the past. But historical market data embody many of the human tendencies that lead to extreme market behavior. Awareness of those phenomena is critical to developing effective lifelong withdrawal strategies for our clients.

great majority of retirees and hence will serve as a good starting point. By reducing the initial withdrawal rate used in Figure 13.2, we can eventually make all bars reach at least the 30-year longevity level. As seen in **FIGURE 13.3**, for the baseline portfolio, this occurs at an initial withdrawal rate of 4.15 percent. *The withdrawal rate of 4.15 percent is thus the safemax, or maximum safe initial withdrawal rate, which historically has always resulted in a 30-year portfolio longevity, regardless of the year of retirement.* In dollar terms, this equates to a $41,500 first-year withdrawal from a $1 million portfolio.

Obviously, the 4.15 percent safemax is much lower than the 5.8 percent our hypothetical client computed using commonly accepted wisdom. One could think of the difference as an insurance premium that the retiree is paying into his portfolio each year to guard against the draconian consequences of a major bear market in stocks.

Remember that our analysis uses a retirement date of January 1 of each year. However, when retirement on June 30, 1929, or September 30, 1929, is considered, the computed safemax is much lower—less than 3 percent. That's because those retirement dates suffered from the immediate effects of the 90 percent decline in the stock market in the ensuing three years, without the benefit of the strong upward move in the stock market during the first six months of 1929. However, I've chosen to ignore these events as being anomalous and not likely to be repeated. The 1973–1974 bear market thus represents our worst-case scenario.

The safemax for taxable portfolios of various average tax rates is shown in **FIGURE 13.4**. In each case, we assume that the portfolio pays income taxes on all dividend and capital gains income generated by the portfolio at the average tax rate specified. As expected, the safemax is lower for taxable accounts. The sharpest decline is from tax-deferred portfolios to a 15 percent average tax rate. For higher tax rates, the rate of decline of safemax moderates. A simple, reasonably accurate rule of thumb for a taxable portfolio is that the percentage reduction in the safemax from

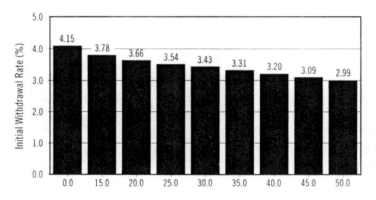

FIGURE **13.4** *Maximum "Safe" 1st Year Withdrawal Versus Portfolio Tax Rate*
(63 Percent Stocks, Fixed Allocation; Remainder Intermediate-Term Government Bonds, 30-Year Longevity)

the 4.15 percent rate brings it to roughly the average tax bracket. As an example, for a portfolio with a 30 percent average tax rate, the 3.43 percent safemax is 17 percent less than the 4.15 percent rate. Seventeen percent is approximately one-half of 30 percent. Note that withdrawals from taxable portfolios will be fully spendable, whereas withdrawals from tax-deferred portfolios will be subject to taxation.

Safemax for Other Portfolio Longevities

Not all clients expect to live 30 years in retirement. Some hope to live longer; others, for reasons of genetics or health, may expect shorter life spans. **FIGURE 13.5** expresses the relationship between safemax and required portfolio longevity for the baseline portfolio.

For time horizons greater than our initial 30-year assumption, the decline in the safemax, although expected, is quite modest. For extremely long-lived clients, whom I call "Methuselah clients," the safemax approaches an asymptotic value I estimate to be 3.5 percent. This is the initial withdrawal rate with which a client could be reasonably confident that his portfolio would, indeed, last forever.

For time horizons less than our initial 30-year assumption, the increase in the safemax is dramatic. Clients needing to increase their withdrawals late in life for health-related or other reasons can take comfort in these much higher withdrawal rates.

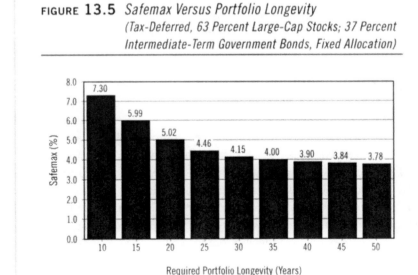

FIGURE **13.5** *Safemax Versus Portfolio Longevity*
(Tax-Deferred, 63 Percent Large-Cap Stocks; 37 Percent Intermediate-Term Government Bonds, Fixed Allocation)

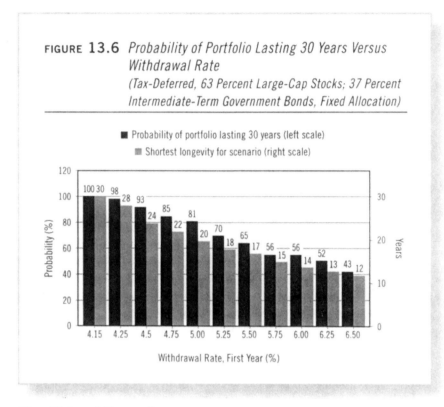

FIGURE **13.6** *Probability of Portfolio Lasting 30 Years Versus Withdrawal Rate*
(Tax-Deferred, 63 Percent Large-Cap Stocks; 37 Percent Intermediate-Term Government Bonds, Fixed Allocation)

■ Probability of portfolio lasting 30 years (left scale)
▩ Shortest longevity for scenario (right scale)

The Risks of Exceeding the Safemax

Not all clients will be satisfied with the withdrawals they can make as specified by the safemax. Some will want more; a few, considerably more. **FIGURE 13.6** quantifies the risks to clients of exceeding the safemax.

The chart in Figure 13.6 is for the baseline portfolio, with a required portfolio longevity of 30 years. Initial withdrawal rates begin with the safemax, 4.15 percent, at the far left and increase toward the right. There are two sets of bars for each withdrawal rate. The dark bar, the success bar, represents the probability of the portfolio lasting 30 years at the indicated initial withdrawal rate. The white bar represents the worst-case portfolio longevity recorded historically for the indicated withdrawal rate.

The safemax withdrawal rate of 4.15 percent is at the far left of the chart. Obviously, by definition, the probability bar is 100 percent, and the portfolio longevity bar is at the maximum of 30 years. As we move right on the chart, initial withdrawal rates increase, and success probabilities and worst-case portfolio longevity both decline. At an initial withdrawal rate of 5 percent, for example, the client's portfolio still has more than an 80 percent probability of lasting the required 30 years. However, in the worst case, the client might obtain only 20 years of withdrawals from his or her portfolio. At a 6 percent initial withdrawal rate, with which this chapter began, the client's chances of successfully negotiating 30 years is only a little better than the odds in a coin flip. The worst-case scenario would cause the portfolio to be exhausted in only 14 years.

Figure 13.6 is a powerful tool for helping clients understand the trade-offs between risk and reward when considering initial withdrawal rates higher than the safemax. I have not reproduced charts for taxable portfolios here, but those charts look much like those in Figure 13.5.

Raising Safemax Through Asset Selection

Can the safemax be increased without courting additional risk? We can explore that question by altering our assumptions about which asset classes we include in the portfolio, as well as their relative proportions.

Safemax Versus Equity Allocation

FIGURE 13.7 illustrates how the safemax varies with changes in equity (large-cap stocks) allocation for the baseline portfolio. A portfolio longevity of 30 years is assumed.

The chart in Figure 13.7 was one of the first to emerge from my research, and, to me, remains the most surprising. *Observe that for a wide range of stock allocations—between about 40 percent and 70 percent—the safemax is virtually constant.* That means an individual with 40 percent stocks in her

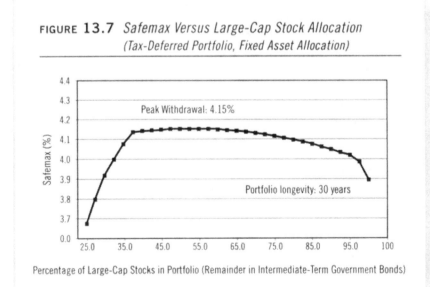

FIGURE **13.7** *Safemax Versus Large-Cap Stock Allocation (Tax-Deferred Portfolio, Fixed Asset Allocation)*

Percentage of Large-Cap Stocks in Portfolio (Remainder in Intermediate-Term Government Bonds)

portfolio cannot expect to safely withdraw more than an individual with 70 percent stocks in his portfolio. A counterintuitive finding, indeed.

Note also how steeply the chart drops off on both the left and the right. On the left side of the chart, bonds dominate the portfolio. Clearly, the low returns from bonds seriously reduce the safemax for bond allocations greater than about 60 percent.

On the right side, when stocks dominate the portfolio, the safemax also declines, although not so precipitously as when bonds do. Clearly, the higher returns of stocks are offset by their higher volatility when they're given allocations greater than about 70 percent. However, judging from the shape of the curve, it appears safer to err with an extremely high stock allocation, than with an extremely high bond allocation.

In earlier figures, I used a 63 percent large-cap stock allocation for our test portfolios without explaining why, but it's apparent from Figure 13.7 that this stock allocation falls on the magic plateau near the peak safemax, which is why I selected it.

Introducing Small-Company Stocks

According to the Ibbotson database, small-cap stocks have enjoyed higher returns than large-company stocks since 1926, albeit with much greater volatility. **FIGURE 13.8** illustrates how the safemax is affected when small-cap stocks are included in the asset allocation. Each line represents a portfolio with a fixed ratio between small-cap stocks (SCS) and large-cap stocks (LCS). For example, the second line from the bottom of the chart, labeled "10% SCS" represents a portfolio where small-cap stocks represent 10 percent of the equities in the portfolio (*not* 10 percent of the total portfolio).

The bottom line in the chart is for the baseline portfolio, whose entire equity allocation is dedicated to large-cap stocks. This line serves as a source of comparison with the lines above it, all of which include small-cap stocks to varying degrees. Notice that as the fraction of small-cap stocks increases from bottom to top on the chart, the safemax for the portfolio also increases. For a portfolio in which small-cap stocks represent 100 percent of all equities, the safemax attains a maximum value of about 4.6 percent. This is significantly higher than the peak 4.15 percent safemax for a portfolio with only large-cap stocks.

However, note also that the "100% SCS" line takes a sharp dip at higher equity allocations. This is not a desirable characteristic, in my opinion, and results from the considerably higher volatility of small-cap stocks. Portfolios composed of 10 percent to 50 percent small-cap stocks appear to have a safemax that is less sensitive to overall equity allocation. These portfolios provide a peak safemax of 4.4 percent to 4.5 percent, close to the 4.6 percent peak safemax of the "100% SCS" line, and still signifi-

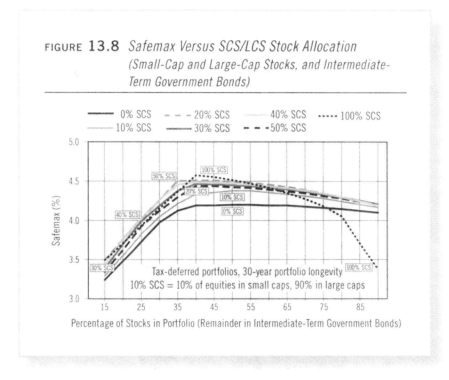

FIGURE **13.8** *Safemax Versus SCS/LCS Stock Allocation (Small-Cap and Large-Cap Stocks, and Intermediate-Term Government Bonds)*

cantly higher than the 4.15 percent peak safemax generated by large-cap stocks alone. That seems to make them more appropriate choices for the retiree. Clearly, including small-cap stocks in a retirement portfolio *can significantly increase the safemax.* Allocations to small-cap stocks of 10 percent to 50 percent of the total equity allocation appear to represent a good trade-off between lower volatility and a higher safemax.

Introducing Treasury Bills

It makes sense for portfolios that are supporting regular withdrawals to maintain a cash balance at all times. The returns on cash investments, however, are usually low.

How large a cash balance can be maintained in a retirement portfolio without compromising withdrawal rates? As a proxy for cash, I turned to the Treasury bill data series in the Ibbotson yearbook. Since 1926, Treasury bills have generated compound annual returns of 3.7 percent, with expected low volatility. In introducing cash into the portfolio, my plan is to replace intermediate-term government bonds with a like allocation in Treasury bills. The chart in **FIGURE 13.9** displays the effect on a portfolio's safemax of introducing Treasury bills in this manner. The portfolio used the baseline portfolio, with a required portfolio longevity of 30 years.

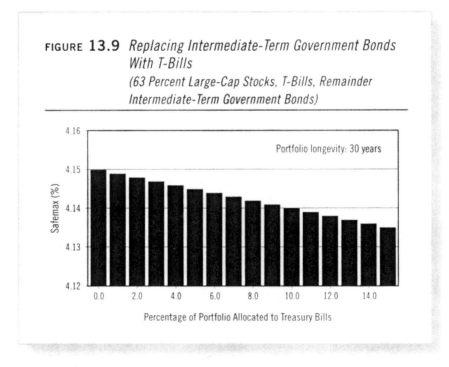

FIGURE **13.9** *Replacing Intermediate-Term Government Bonds With T-Bills*
(63 Percent Large-Cap Stocks, T-Bills, Remainder Intermediate-Term Government Bonds)

It's clear from Figure 13.9 that even cash balances as high as 15 percent of the portfolio value negligibly affect the safemax. In fact, looking deeper, one could make a case for replacing bonds completely with Treasury bills. My conclusion is that using cash in a retirement portfolio, in lieu of up to 15 percent intermediate-term government bonds, *has no significant effects on the safemax.*

Other Asset Classes

In addition to the asset classes discussed above, advisers use many others in managing client portfolios, such as real estate investment trusts, international stocks, international bonds, commodity futures, long-term bonds, and Treasury inflation-protected securities. For most of these asset classes, there is no long-term database comparable to Ibbotson's, so I have not included here an analysis of their effects on retirement portfolios. Their exclusion does not mean their use is inappropriate. In fact, it's likely that the safemax can be increased by adding some or all of these asset classes, although the effects of diminishing improvement with increasing numbers of asset classes probably applies.

When it comes to long-term bonds, however, my studies have indicated that they add no value to retirement portfolios, in that they do not improve the safemax.

Raising Safemax Through Alternative Withdrawal Schemes

Most clients want to maintain their lifestyle, and thus their real spending, throughout their lifetime. What if a client is willing to accept lower real spending later in retirement, so that he can withdraw more money earlier in retirement? Alternatively, what if a client is willing to roll the dice on her investment returns, hoping that she's not affected by a major bear market in stocks during retirement? Let's explore these possibilities.

Spending More Now, Less Later

In *The Prosperous Retirement: Guide to the New Reality* (Emstco, 1998), Michael K. Stein postulates a model of retirement spending with three phases: active retirement (higher spending because of travel and the like), passive retirement (lower spending, less activity), and a transitional phase between the two. For an individual retiring at age 65, the active and transitional phases each lasts 10 years, followed by the final, passive phase of the client's life, which could extend for many years.

It seems reasonable to assume that lower levels of withdrawals later

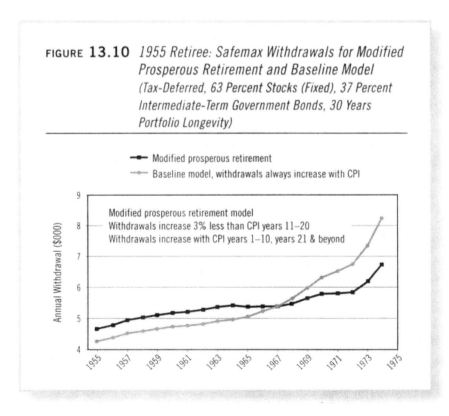

FIGURE **13.10** *1955 Retiree: Safemax Withdrawals for Modified Prosperous Retirement and Baseline Model (Tax-Deferred, 63 Percent Stocks (Fixed), 37 Percent Intermediate-Term Government Bonds, 30 Years Portfolio Longevity)*

- Modified prosperous retirement
- Baseline model, withdrawals always increase with CPI

Modified prosperous retirement model
Withdrawals increase 3% less than CPI years 11–20
Withdrawals increase with CPI years 1–10, years 21 & beyond

Annual Withdrawal ($000)

in retirement would permit higher levels of withdrawals earlier in retirement. I adapted Stein's model to my methodology to test that assumption. In creating the modified prosperous retirement (MPR) model, I used the assumptions of our baseline model, including 30 years' longevity. In addition, I allowed expenses to increase with the CPI in years 1 through 10 and years 21 and later, but in the transitional phase, expenses increased an arbitrary 3 percent less than the CPI each year. This resulted in a gradual ratcheting down of real withdrawals during the transitional phase.

FIGURE 13.10 shows the results of these computations for an individual retiring January 1, 1955. Annual withdrawals (based on an initial portfolio value of $100,000) are shown for both our baseline model and for the MPR model. For the sake of clearer comparisons, only the first 20 years of withdrawals are depicted. The safemax for the MPR model is 4.59 percent, higher than the 4.15 percent for the baseline model. This is an increase of approximately 10 percent, which many clients would consider significant.

Notice that MPR withdrawals remain higher than baseline withdrawals for the first 13 years (age 78 for the client), after which they cross over. In the 20th year (1974) MPR withdrawals are $6,667, about 17 percent less than the baseline withdrawal of $8,030 for the same year. This is the price paid for the higher withdrawals early in retirement. Only the client can determine if the price makes sense. Spending less later in retirement in order to spend more at the start can result in *a considerably higher safemax*, but the client must have the discipline to reduce spending later in life.

Performance-Based Withdrawals

Consider a scheme in which each year's withdrawals are based on a fixed percentage of the prior year's ending portfolio value. This would permit clients who had the good fortune of a long bull run during their retirement to enjoy escalating dollar withdrawals, as illustrated in FIGURE 13.11.

This chart displays the real (adjusted for inflation) value of withdrawals for a client who retires on January 1, 1955. Consider the line labeled "Fixed-percentage withdrawal." It represents the real value of withdrawals computed by applying an arbitrary 5 percent to the value of the portfolio on December 31 of the preceding year (starting portfolio value is $100,000). We see that through early retirement the client's withdrawals climb significantly, eventually peaking at about $6,500, or 30 percent higher than the first year's withdrawal. However, due to the far-reaching effects of the 1973–1974 bear market, those withdrawals drop precipitously in later years. At their low point, the real value of withdrawals is only about 50 percent of their initial value of $5,000—a very large and disconcerting change in lifestyle.

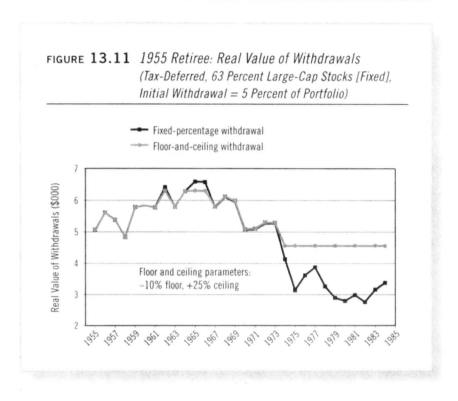

FIGURE **13.11** *1955 Retiree: Real Value of Withdrawals*
(Tax-Deferred, 63 Percent Large-Cap Stocks [Fixed],
Initial Withdrawal = 5 Percent of Portfolio)

Figure 13.11 also illustrates an alternative withdrawal scheme, which I consider less risky. This scheme imposes a floor and ceiling on the real values of the client's withdrawals. I have chosen to depict what I consider to be a near-optimum set of parameters: withdrawals are permitted to rise no higher than 25 percent above the initial value of $5,000 ($6,250) and fall to no more than 10 percent below the initial value ($4,500). As Figure 13.11 shows, a client employing this strategy would have enjoyed most of the rise in withdrawals experienced by a client using the unrestrained "fixed-percentage" approach, but would have been spared much of the subsequent severe decline.

The safemax associated with the −10 percent floor, +25 percent ceiling withdrawal model is 4.58 percent. This represents an improvement of almost 10 percent over the baseline safemax of 4.15 percent. I believe many clients would find "floor-and-ceiling" an attractive approach to withdrawals from their portfolios, although it does entail some record keeping on the part of the financial adviser to track the real value of withdrawals over time.

Raising Safemax Through Investment Returns

So far we have assumed returns that match the market returns for the various asset classes employed in the client's portfolio. Many advisers do, in fact, use index funds and other passive forms of management designed to yield average returns that match the market, so that assumption is broadly applicable. However, other advisers strive to outperform the market. What are the effects on a client's withdrawal rate of being successful in the latter endeavor, and what are the consequences of failure?

FIGURE 13.12 provides some answers to these questions, using our baseline portfolio. It was constructed by adding fixed percentages to the annual returns of large-cap stocks (that is, the Standard & Poor's 500 index) and computing the safemax for a 30-year portfolio longevity. Although no money manager would in fact experience such regular returns relative to the index, this approach provides a simple format to analyze the problem.

The baseline portfolio appears as the 0 percent bar, indicating that the equity returns in that portfolio matched those of the S&P 500 index. A "superinvestor" whose stock returns consistently exceeded those of the S&P 500 index by 2 percent annually (a compounded annual return of 12.2 percent annually) would permit his clients to safely withdraw 4.80

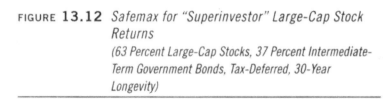

FIGURE **13.12** *Safemax for "Superinvestor" Large-Cap Stock Returns*
(63 Percent Large-Cap Stocks, 37 Percent Intermediate-Term Government Bonds, Tax-Deferred, 30-Year Longevity)

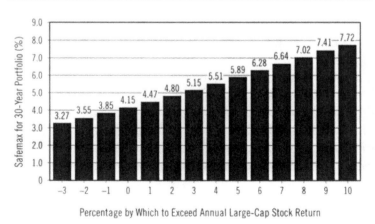

percent of their portfolio the first year. That represents withdrawals 15 percent greater than those afforded the client whose stocks earn average market returns. Obviously, the benefits to the client of superior stock returns are substantial.

The chart also demonstrates that earning below-market returns carries considerable risk. An investor whose stock returns fall only 1 percent below those of the S&P 500 index (9.2 percent compounded annually) limits his clients to initial withdrawals that are 8 percent less than those of the baseline portfolio, or 3.85 percent.

I won't contribute here to the debate on passive versus active investing, but given the risks and rewards of active investing, it behooves the adviser to take special care. A mistake in assumptions about achievable investment returns can obviously have draconian consequences for the client.

Bequests

The calculations of safemax so far have assumed that in the worst case, the client's portfolio could be completely exhausted at the end of 30 years. But what if the client wishes to leave a guaranteed bequest to his or her heirs? To explore this issue, we first ask the client to specify the minimum nominal value his or her portfolio should have at the end of 30 years, which will be the intended bequest. Then the safemax is recomputed using that nonzero value as a worst-case constraint.

The results are depicted in **FIGURE 13.13**, for a variety of terminal values of the portfolio, which is assumed to have an initial value of $100,000. We can see that if a client wishes to guarantee a bequest of $100,000, equal to the initial nominal value of his portfolio, he would have to accept a safemax of 3.92 percent, about 5 percent less than the safemax for the baseline portfolio. That does not seem a particularly onerous sacrifice, but as always, the client must determine that.

Naturally, as the desired bequest increases in size, the safemax must concurrently decline. For a $500,000 bequest, clients must shave withdrawals by more than 40 percent. This reduction may not be objectionable, however, if the client is not depending on his portfolio for the bulk of his income during retirement. In that case, the portfolio can be regarded primarily as a wealth-building instrument.

One word on the construction of Figure 13.13: the period of 1926–1932 in the Ibbotson database was excluded from the analysis. That's because the severe stock market decline of that time period introduced distortions in the results that I thought best to omit from serious consideration.

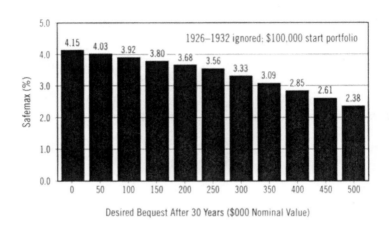

FIGURE **13.13** *Safemax for Planned Bequest*
*(63 Percent Stocks [Fixed], Intermediate Long-Term
Government Bonds, Tax-Deferred, 30-Year Longevity)*

Equity Allocations During Retirement

So far, we've assumed that the total equity allocation of the portfolio will remain fixed throughout retirement. However, it may seem intuitively advantageous to reduce clients' exposure to stocks as they age, so as to reduce portfolio volatility. **FIGURE 13.14** shows the effect on the safemax of reducing equity allocation (and increasing the bond allocation) by 1 percent each year during retirement, for a variety of initial equity allocations (in large-cap stocks only).

The maximum safemax for the 1 percent phasedown approach is 4.09 percent, which is marginally less than the 4.15 percent for the baseline scenario (also shown on the chart for comparison). Notice, though, that the "magic plateau" of maximum safemax is much narrower for the 1 percent phasedown curve than for the baseline curve. The conservative client may have to choose between adopting a more stock-heavy portfolio than preferred and accepting a significantly lower initial withdrawal rate.

What's more, not shown on the chart is the negative effect on accumulated wealth of reducing stock allocation over time. Space is too limited here to discuss the issue in full, but the effects are quite significant. This is another, larger trade-off that a client would have to countenance in adopting an equity phasedown plan.

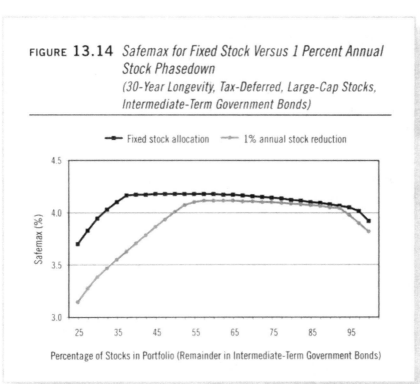

FIGURE 13.14 *Safemax for Fixed Stock Versus 1 Percent Annual Stock Phasedown*
(30-Year Longevity, Tax-Deferred, Large-Cap Stocks, Intermediate-Term Government Bonds)

Because of these limitations, unless the client is extremely conservative, I would not recommend reducing equity allocation during retirement if the client has significant long-term needs for withdrawals. If he does reduce equity, he may have to adopt a withdrawal rate lower than the optimum safemax.

Advising Clients on Sustainable Withdrawals

Over the years, I've used my research in my practice to guide the decisions of my clients on retirement withdrawals. Unless the client is unusually conservative, at age 65, I recommend an initial withdrawal rate of 4 percent to 5 percent for a tax-deferred account (somewhat less if the primary account is taxable). Although that is considerably higher than the safemax for the baseline portfolio, I justify it on three counts:

- ❑ I employ asset classes other than large-cap stocks and bonds in client portfolios, which should elevate the safemax.
- ❑ I counsel clients to reduce withdrawals temporarily during a bear market, which has an effect similar to the "floor-and-ceiling" withdrawal scheme examined earlier in the chapter.

❑ Most clients are satisfied with a 90 percent to 95 percent probability of success with their withdrawals and do not require the 100 percent assurance of the safemax.

Together, these three factors make a higher initial withdrawal rate seem comfortable. Naturally, if the client strongly desires to leave an inheritance, I recommend an appropriate adjustment to the initial withdrawal rate. When stock values seem fair, I recommend a withdrawal rate near the upper end of the range, or 5 percent. If stocks are considerably overvalued, I may recommend a lower initial withdrawal rate. However, these recommendations are never routine, because valuation is, to a certain extent, a matter of judgment.

During retirement, I monitor the client's withdrawal rate versus current portfolio value, making sure that reasonably safe levels are not exceeded. I advise the client to reduce withdrawals during periods of apparent danger. Although it depends on the client's sensitivity to portfolio volatility, I usually recommend a fixed equity allocation of 60 percent to 65 percent, lying on the magic plateau. This maximizes the withdrawal rate, while also providing significant opportunities for growth of wealth during retirement.

As always in giving financial advice, I present the options to clients and let them make the final decisions. Their psychological comfort is paramount.

References

Bengen, William P., series of four articles in *Journal of Financial Planning*. October 1994, August 1996, December 1997, and May 2001.

Ibbotson Associates, *Stocks, Bonds, Bills and Inflation 2004 Yearbook* (various years).

Stein, Michael K., *The Prosperous Retirement: Guide to the New Reality* (Emstco Press, 1998).

CHAPTER 14

Tools and Pools

Strategies for Increasing Retirement Cash Flow

ROBERT P. KREITLER

Before they retire, most clients concentrate on rates of return and on how much portfolio volatility they can live with. At and near retirement, however, their objectives change. They become concerned with how to maximize the size of the check in the mail each month and ensure that those checks will continue to arrive throughout their lifetime.

Advisers need to make the same philosophical and psychological shifts to meet the changing objectives of their retiring clients. To redesign their clients' portfolios, they need to understand the *tools* available that may increase retirement income in ways that will not prematurely exhaust capital. The next step is to help their clients manage their total assets in ways that meet multiple retirement objectives. They can accomplish that by assigning a separate *pool* of financial resources to support each objective and by using the tools to create a separate investment strategy and cash-distribution strategy for each pool.

This chapter reviews some of the traditional approaches to retirement-income distribution still used today, discusses their limitations, and offers methods that can make planning retirement income a far less risky business.

Conflicts and Hazards

As advisers consider how to help retiring clients restructure their portfolios, it's useful for them to understand that their clients may have two frequently competing objectives for using their assets: First, retirees want to live off income and leave principal for their heirs. At the same time, they want to create maximum lifetime income, and they're willing to consume principal to achieve this.

To achieve the first objective, retirees consume only the income from their portfolios, which can include dividends, interest, and portfolio appreciation. This is the total-return approach in which all categories of earnings are available for distribution. It's logical to adjust for inflation and calculate income and principal left to heirs in real terms.

With the second objective, retirees strive to maximize lifetime income and are willing to consume principal, leaving nothing for heirs. Logically, consuming capital maximizes cash flow. All other approaches provide less income. Many retirees will choose a combination of these two objectives.

Retirees and their advisers face three unknowns, or risks, as they plan lifetime income:

❑ The cost of future living expenses, including medical expenses
❑ Future portfolio returns
❑ Longevity risk, or how long each retiree will live

Clients face these risks at every stage in the life cycle, but they are particularly important for retirees, who have few options to restore capital once it's spent.

Living expenses. Future retirement costs are a function of future inflation, changes in lifestyle, and future medical advances and their costs, all of which are, of course, unknown. These costs can vary tremendously. The risk of cost increases is borne by the retiree, supporting family members, prior employers, and the government.

Employers and the government increasingly find that assuming the risk for these future costs is untenable and that doing so may even threaten the survival of the entities providing such benefits. Few employers index pensions for inflation, and most now cap medical insurance assistance. The government is also concluding that accepting unlimited risk for inflation and medical costs creates too large a burden for taxpayers. We are in the midst of a national debate about shifting some of these costs back to retirees through Social Security, Medicare, and Medicaid reforms. The net result is that retirees bear much of the risk for these future costs and their share of the risks will likely increase.

For those still saving for retirement, the solution for handling the risk of future increases in living expenses is to amass as large an asset base as possible before retiring. For retirees with a fixed asset base that isn't going to increase, the solution is to maintain flexibility. That means making as few irreversible decisions as possible. Fixed costs should be kept to a minimum. Expenses should be kept discretionary. Portfolios should be kept as large as possible. Once money is spent, it cannot be spent again at a later date to meet another need.

Portfolio returns. Future portfolio returns are unknown. The adviser and the retiree do not know how much future income can be drawn off a portfolio to live on. Long-term bonds or guarantees by insurance companies can provide some certainty, but their rates are well below what many retirees will wish or expect to receive from their entire portfolios. The rates are low, of course, because the entity issuing the bonds or the guarantees assumes the investment risk.

Like protecting against the risk of unknown future costs, the primary tools for protecting against unknown future portfolio returns are to maintain flexibility in making cash distributions and to keep surplus resources. Techniques that lock in portfolio management or distributions do not provide the flexibility retirees need to deal with unexpected events.

Longevity risk. Longevity risk arises because no one knows how long an individual will live. Retirees may live longer than they anticipate, and outliving their resources has severe consequences.

Longevity risk is one of the three risks that a third party is willing to assume. Insurance companies are uniquely capable of handling these risks by spreading the risk over a large number of individuals.

Advisers must deal with these three risks when designing strategies for retirees. Ironically, the first two risks discussed require maintaining flexibility, whereas protecting oneself against longevity risk can be handled by purchasing an immediate annuity from an insurance company, an irrevocable decision. Whether or not to make an irrevocable decision such as this is one of the many trade-offs a retiree will have to make. Advisers need to understand how to help their clients weigh the consequences of these trade-offs.

Tools

Financial advisers use two basic techniques to help create retirement cash flow:

❑ Withdraw only income from the portfolio.
❑ Withdraw both income and a portion of principal, doing so in a way that will not put the retiree in danger of outliving the principal.

Advisers and retirees need to fully understand all the tools available to implement one or more cash flow strategies. Some tools increase distributions more than others. Some are more complex than others. Financial advisers need to help retirees choose the specific implementation tools that best meet the retirees' objectives.

Taking Income From the Portfolio

1 *The unplanned approach: Taking withdrawals as needed.* Using this tool, retirees take what they need without regard to the ability of the portfolio to generate cash flow. This approach is entirely without a plan. Some retirees will spend too little, penalizing themselves with too little income and leaving too much for heirs. Others, in their early retirement years, are likely to spend at levels that the portfolio cannot sustain, leaving themselves impoverished in their later years. The unplanned approach, however, may work for very wealthy retirees whose portfolios' income-generating capability exceeds their income needs.

2 *Living off dividends and interest.* This is the approach followed by many of our parents and grandparents, who believed they should "never use capital." If the retiree never uses capital, he or she will most likely never run out of capital. If interest rates are about 5 percent and dividends are 2 percent, a portfolio's distribution will be between the two amounts, depending on the portfolio's mix of stocks and bonds. Annual distributions will vary based on many factors, but they're likely to be relatively stable and predictable. Over time, if stock appreciation adds to the portfolio's value, the retiree receives an increasing cash flow as dividends grow and through increased interest after rebalancing to buy more bonds. Other benefits of the approach include the built-in bias for long-term appreciation and the ease of understanding and implementation.

The primary disadvantage of this approach is that annual cash distributions are likely to be significantly lower than other options provide and lower than what the portfolio is capable of distributing. Greater cash flow is very important to many retirees, so this disadvantage can be significant. To generate more current cash flow from their portfolio, retirees may overweight bonds, which, over longer periods, historically have provided lower rates of long-term return than stocks, and thus reduce the total return of the portfolio, a second disadvantage.

3 *Taking a fixed dollar amount.* A retiree using this tool regularly withdraws a fixed amount from the portfolio. For example, a retiree might withdraw $50,000 annually from a $1 million portfolio. Once set, this amount may remain unchanged for many years. Because individuals frequently have greater trouble making decisions as they grow older, adjusting this number up or down may be difficult to do later in life even if such a change will better a client's situation.

The approach does have advantages, however: it's easy to administer and it makes it easy for the retiree to budget expenses. Because future returns are unknown, however, retirees either will take out less than the portfolio can sustain and thereby increase the amount they leave to heirs, or they will take too much from the portfolio in their early retirement years and face reduced income in their later years.

4 *Taking a fixed amount and adjusting withdrawals for inflation.* This tool takes the fixed dollar amount in tool 3 and increases it each year by the amount of inflation. In doing so, the retiree retains the benefits of the fixed-dollar approach but also receives increased income to offset inflation.

This option receives wide recognition in the literature. There are many articles discussing how an individual with a $1 million portfolio invested approximately 60 percent in stocks and 40 percent in bonds can withdraw $40,000 to $50,000 per year plus inflation and have a 90 percent chance of not exhausting principal. Monte Carlo simulations are used to support this conclusion. The analysis has a bearing on determining appropriate stock/bond allocations for retirement portfolios and helps one calculate how much should be saved before retirement begins. The distinction, however—and it's critical—is that this analysis is not useful for determining how much cash should be withdrawn from a portfolio each year once retirement has begun. The approach is rigid and inflexible.

Because of the frequency with which this tool is discussed in professional magazines, let's look at a similar problem to show why the approach may not be practical. When NASA prepares to launch a rocket, it runs massive computer models to determine the parameters such as direction and thrust needed to make the launch. This preparation is similar to using Monte Carlo simulations in determining the amount of assets needed before retirement and in establishing the initial portfolio composition and withdrawal rates.

Once the rocket is launched, NASA monitors its progress and periodically adjusts its course. NASA does not launch the rocket and consider its work done. Without ongoing adjustments, the rocket has little chance of reaching its destination. Monitoring and adjusting are necessary for managing retirement portfolios, just as they are for sending rockets into space. In an ever-changing world, periodic adjustments must be made so that retirees can stay on track for meeting their objectives.

The problem with inflexible tools is that they do not allow for those periodic changes needed to meet real-life dynamics. Because future events such as annual returns are unknown, sticking to a rigid, predetermined formula virtually assures retirees will either withdraw too little or too much, either of which means less-than-optimal use of their retirement resources.

Maintaining flexible withdrawals, as do the tools described below, makes it likely that retirees over time will be able to exceed the withdrawal rates projected by the Monte Carlo simulations. Flexibility, meaning the retiree's ability and willingness to cut back on spending in poor markets, helps assure that excessive withdrawals will not prematurely deplete the portfolio. The 90 percent odds of success—or 10 percent odds of failure—projected by Monte Carlo simulations are not good enough. Financial advisers must do better.

5 *Withdrawing a constant percentage of the portfolio.* Using this tool, a predetermined percentage of the portfolio value—6 percent, for example—is withdrawn each year. Because the withdrawal rate is fixed, the amount withdrawn changes as the portfolio value changes. After a series of bad years, the withdrawal amount will have dropped. Similarly, retirees will benefit from increased distributions after a series of good years. Although the income reductions may cause discomfort, the retirees should never exhaust their principal. The challenge is to determine an appropriate withdrawal rate. Choosing a low rate is likely to lead to increasing portfolio value over time, with commensurate increases in annual distributions. Choosing a high rate runs the risk that the portfolio will drop in value, with a commensurate reduction in annual distributions.

6 *Following the IRS minimum-distribution rules.* This tool applies only to an individual retirement account and begs the question of what to do with a taxable account. On the positive side, retirees who have all of their assets in IRAs and follow the new minimum-distribution rules to help determine their retirement cash flow are not likely to exhaust the principal in their IRAs. For example, assume that a husband and wife with a $1 million IRA take $37,736 at age 70½ as their first-year distribution. If their portfolio returns 7 percent per year, by the time they are 80, the withdrawal amount increases to $65,358, and when they're 90, it will be $90,914. Because of the low distribution rate in early years, the value of the IRA is likely to grow to a maximum of $1,335,000 by age 85 before beginning to drop.

For most retirees, there is a difference between the withdrawal amount the IRS requires and the optimal withdrawal needed for living expenses. Some may want to consume their IRA capital at a higher rate to meet their needs. Others could reinvest the excess withdrawals not needed to meet expenses in a taxable account and save the money for future expenses. The minimum distribution required by the IRS is not usually equal to the retiree's needs.

7 *Varying the annual distribution, based on portfolio performance.* Retirees willing and able to periodically adjust cash distributions to reflect portfolio performance can make higher withdrawals over time while still avoiding most of the risk of prematurely exhausting their capital.

One way of doing this is to set up two separate distributions. The first, a base payment, is an amount that the portfolio can sustain even in bad times. The second, a performance distribution, is based on how a portfolio performs. The performance distribution is higher in good years and cut

Developing a Flexible Formula for Determining Annual Withdrawals of Dividends and Interest

The client and adviser determine an annual withdrawal formula that includes:
- A percentage of the portfolio's value that will be taken as a base payment
- A percentage of portfolio returns in excess of the base payment to be taken as a performance payment

Returns in excess of this base payment are reinvested in the portfolio. For example, if a client decides to withdraw:
- A base payment of 4 percent and
- A performance payment of 40 percent of the returns in excess of the base, then

Portfolio value × 0.04 = Base annual payment

(Portfolio value increase in excess of 4 percent) × 0.40 = performance payment

(Portfolio value increase in excess of 4 percent) × 0.60 = increase in portfolio value

If the retiree's portfolio value for the year is $1 million, then:

Retiree's base annual payment	$1,000,000 × 0.04 =	$ 40,000
Portfolio annual return	$1,000.000 × 0.12 =	$120,000
Increase in excess of		
4 percent annual base	$120,000 – $40,000 =	$ 80,000
Performance returns		
distributed to retiree	$80,000 × 0.40 =	$ 32,000
Increase in portfolio value	$80,000 × 0.60 =	$ 48,000

Retiree's cash withdrawals for this year
      $40,000 base + $32,000 performance bonus = $ 72,000

back or even eliminated in bad years. To simplify administration, the performance distribution can be based on the prior year's performance and, therefore, always would lag portfolio performance by a year.

For example, a retiree with a $1 million portfolio sets a base withdrawal of $40,000 per year, or 4 percent of the portfolio's value. The retiree budgets his or her fixed expenses based on this amount. In bad markets, he lives on only this amount. There are many ways of setting a formula for the additional performance distribution. The retiree could distribute 40 percent of the annual return that exceeds the 4 percent base amount. The retiree could use this performance distribution for discretionary expenses, such as a new car, travel, or gifts to children and charity. The remaining 60 percent is left in the portfolio to add to capital to offset losses in bad years or to build the portfolio so as to provide higher base distributions in years to come.

If the total portfolio return in the example in the sidebar was 12 percent, the performance distribution would be $32,000, providing a total distribution including the base of $72,000. Total return is 7.2 percent— higher than what most advisers would typically consider a prudent withdrawal when using a rigid system.

A flexible distribution system can be structured in many ways. The retiree's flexibility and willingness to cut back in bad years protect the portfolio against the damage that occurs when large withdrawals are made from a portfolio after it has dropped in value.

The primary disadvantage with this option is that it requires the retiree to be willing and able to cut back in bad years. Many may not be in a position to do that. Flexibility permits one to take out larger amounts, with the understanding that cutbacks must be made when bad markets occur.

Consuming Capital

The way to maximize retirement cash flow is to consume capital. Most of the tools discussed below assume the retiree desires a cash flow that's guaranteed for a lifetime. There may be situations, however, in which retirees plan to consume a particular sum for a specific number of years and not for their entire lives. If retirees are assured lifetime income, they may see depleting a portion of their surplus capital as a logical choice for generating additional retirement cash flow.

Many retirees who want to consume capital want assurance that they won't outlive their capital. Providing guaranteed lifetime income requires finding ways to manage longevity risk—the risk of outliving one's financial resources. Insurance companies are prepared to assume that risk. By spreading out the risk over a large number of individuals, insurance companies can make a profit and still assume the risk that some people will live long lives. The product they offer to manage longevity risk is called an immediate annuity. It's the reverse of life insurance. People buy life insurance when they are concerned about dying early. They buy an immediate annuity when they are concerned about living too long.

Many people, including many financial advisers, view consuming capital as a financial sin. Therefore, they automatically reject the use of immediate annuities or any other retirement tool that calls for capital consumption. This attitude is by no means universal, however. At universities, where the employees are accustomed to 403(b) plans, annuities, and the concept of annuitization, potential retirees are far more receptive to using immediate annuities. As baby boomers with limited resources begin to face retirement, buying an immediate annuity or annuitizing a deferred annuity will become a much more interesting option for them to consider.

The increase in income from an immediate annuity can be significant. **FIGURE 14.1** compares the cash flow from an immediate fixed annuity with the cash flow from a 25-year government bond. Because underlying investments are similar (high quality with fixed payments guaranteed by the issuer), the example shows the increased income resulting from consuming capital with lifetime payment guaranteed by an insurance company. The immediate annuity for a couple, both age 65, provides 37 percent more income than the government bond.

If a 70-year-old couple purchases the annuity, the increase in income is 50 percent. The older the retirees are, the greater the increase in income they can realize. At age 80, the increase would be 101 percent.

With today's interest rates considerably lower than they were several years ago, annuity payments have dropped. However, the return on gov-

FIGURE **14.1** *$100,000 Investment:*
Joint Survivor With Husband and Wife, Life Only,
Current 25-Year Treasury Bond Is 4.85% *

| AGE | ANNUITY | | TREASURY ANNUAL | INCOME INCREASE |
	MONTHLY	ANNUAL		
65	$554.55	$6,654.60	$4,850	37%
70	607.78	7,293.36	4,850	50
75	688.78	8,265.36	4,850	70
80	811.21	9,734.52	4,850	101
85	992.37	11,908.44	4,850	146

*All data obtained January 12, 2005.

ernment bonds has also dropped and the relative advantage of the immediate annuity is still substantial.

Age 65 is probably the earliest a retiree should purchase an immediate annuity. The increased payment from capital consumption before this age is too small to offset the disadvantages of making the irreversible decision of consuming capital to buy the annuity. The increased cash flow from depleting capital is spread over so many years that it becomes questionable whether the small increase in payment is worth the loss in flexibility inherent in buying an immediate annuity. Two kinds of immediate annuities are available: fixed and variable.

Immediate fixed annuities. With an immediate fixed annuity, the insurance company sets and guarantees the amount of a retiree's monthly payment for life. The insurance company manages the funds and assumes both the investment risk and the longevity risk. Payment is an obligation of the insurance company and cannot change, no matter what happens to interest rates.

Immediate variable annuities. With an immediate variable annuity, the insurance company assumes the longevity risk, but the policyholder picks up the investment risk. The retiree chooses among investment options that the insurance company makes available in a way similar to the choices offered under deferred variable annuities. Monthly payouts vary according to how the selected investments perform.

The primary reason for choosing an immediate variable annuity rather than a fixed variable annuity is the expectation that the retiree, by picking up the investment risk, will be able to do better than the guarantee provided by the insurance company. The insurance company has higher internal costs, so the return must be high enough to cover these and still do better than the immediate fixed annuity.

Immediate variable annuities provide the benefits of allowing the investor to maximize cash flow and receive a lifetime guarantee while still managing a portfolio invested in stocks and bonds. Depending on how the investments perform, this can be good or bad.

Comparing the immediate variable products offered by the insurance companies can be difficult and complex. The offerings have many moving parts and the insurance companies add a lot of bells and whistles, making it difficult to understand what the contracts actually cost. The adviser may need to go beyond a simple reading of the prospectus and conduct independent analysis to fully understand how various products compare. (**FIGURE 14.2** provides one way to compare two policies.) Because of this, when structuring a portfolio that contains both traditional assets and immediate annuities, my preference is to use immediate fixed annuities to fill the retiree's needs for both fixed income and income that can't be outlived and use immediate variable annuities only if even more guaranteed lifetime income is desired. Shopping for immediate fixed annuities is relatively easy: find out the monthly payout that similarly rated insurance companies quote for the same investment and take the best deal, while retaining a preference for using only a quality insurance company.

FIGURE **14.2** *Immediate Variable Annuity Comparison*

$100,000 INVESTMENT MONTHLY DISTRIBUTION*

YEAR	COMPANY A	COMPANY B
1	$559	$568
2	$557	$566
3	$555	$563
4	$553	$561
5	$551	$558
6	$549	$556
7	$547	$553
8	$551	$558
9	$542	$549
10	$540	$546
11	$538	$544
12	$536	$541
13	$534	$539
14	$532	$537
15	$530	$534

ASSUMPTIONS USED

Husband and wife, both age 65, joint life only

Insurance charges	1.10%	1.25%
Portfolio admin. expense	1.00%	1.06%

Nonqualified money, assumed investment rate 5%, gross return 7%.

*All data obtained February 2005.

Figure 14.2 shows the projected 15-year payouts for immediate variable annuity illustrations provided by two popular insurance companies (A and B). Comparing immediate variable annuities is best done by looking at their performance over time, not just for one year. That's because salespeople have tricks for making the first-year numbers look good.

In buying an immediate variable annuity the client selects an assumed investment rate (AIR). The insurance company then quotes what the initial payout will be for that AIR. Future performance determines what the future payouts will be. If the actual performance over time (net after costs) is better than the AIR, the payouts will exceed the forecast. Similarly, if the performance is worse, the payouts will be less. Choosing a high AIR will make the product look good in the first year but will likely lead to disappointment in future years. For the illustration in Figure 14.2, the AIR is set at 5 percent for both Company A and B. In creating projections, the adviser also must select a predicted gross return of the underlying portfolio. In this example, the gross return is assumed to be 7 percent. Costs are 2.1 percent to 2.3 percent so net performance is a little below 5 percent. What can we learn from this chart?

First, because the monthly payouts projected over 15 years for the two companies are relatively close, we can conclude that these two products have a similar design. The selection of one company over the other would, then, depend on other factors such as the underlying investment choices, the credit rating of the insurance companies, and the quality of service the companies provide. Second, the payouts for both drop over time. This implies that the gross return on the funds will need to be higher than 7 percent to maintain the original payout. Costs are slightly higher than 2 percent, the difference between the 7 percent predicted gross return and the 5 percent AIR, and thus, with a net return below 5 percent, the payout drops over time.

Figure 14.2 shows the initial payout ($559 to $568 per month), a cash return of 6.7 percent, is considerably higher than could safely be withdrawn from a traditional portfolio. No surprise there; this is a characteristic of an immediate annuity. What's interesting is that the payouts from the immediate variable annuity are approximately the same as the $554 per month from the riskless immediate fixed annuity (Figure 14.1). A retiree should think pretty hard about whether he or she wants to take the additional risk inherent in these immediate variable annuities, because they require at least a 7 percent return to match the guarantee of the immediate fixed annuity.

This multiyear analysis technique also can be used to compare the performance of a base policy against a policy with enhanced provisions to show the cost of the enhancements. A client might question whether an enhancement with 3 percent in total costs requiring at least an 8 percent gross return to maintain a 5 percent AIR is worth purchasing.

Writing about immediate annuities in *The Investment Think Tank,* edited by Harold Evensky and Deena Katz (Bloomberg Press, 2004), Ibbotson, Henkel, and Chen used efficient-frontier software to integrate the asset-allocation question and the question of how much of a portfolio should be annuitized (both fixed and variable). They concluded that immediate annuities are an effective way to address longevity risk and that their use reduces the odds of prematurely exhausting principal. This should not come as a surprise, because managing longevity risk is the function of immediate annuities.

Managing Cash Flow

Using financial-management tools can make a dramatic difference in a retiree's life. Those entering retirement with portfolios that are smaller than they would like will find these tools particularly helpful, as they provide ways to maximize the retirement cash flow from their limited resources. Those with limited resources have little room for error and have the most to benefit from sound planning. Using the tools to increase a retiree's cash flow, however, doesn't complete the job of retirement planning. By dividing the retiree's cash flow into several pools—each managed to help the retiree meet a specific goal—an adviser can help that retiree successfully achieve multiple objectives.

Pools

The pools system is a method for using the tools described earlier to structure and manage a portfolio to meet a client's multiple retirement objectives. Creating an investment portfolio strategy when there are multiple and often conflicting objectives is challenging, and it's frequently impossible for an adviser to create an optimum strategy. Segregating a retiree's different objectives and dedicating a separate pool of assets to each objective make this problem manageable.

Clients like the pools system. Psychologists have found that people are comfortable segregating their assets based on the expected use, and using the term "buckets" or "pools" to describe the system has widespread appeal. Financial planners can use the pools concept to create financial plans that are not only more likely to meet multiple objectives but also easier for clients to understand.

Identifying the Pools

Creating a separate pool for each of the retiree's objectives is the start of the process. The investment strategy for each pool is then customized for its objective. No longer does an adviser have to struggle to make a single portfolio strategy meet multiple objectives.

Creating pools is a very flexible technique. To develop the optimal mix of pools for the individual, advisers need to help each client articulate his or her goals and concerns. Each individual will be different, but there are five pools that I find cover most retirees' basic objectives.

Pool 1: Lifetime income. This pool is designed to provide guaranteed income for life, with the capital depleted at death. Maximizing income with the guarantee that the retirees can't outlive their capital is the primary objective. Nothing is left for heirs. Social Security, pensions, and immediate annuities are in this pool. Any guarantees are by the issuing entity.

Pool 2: Preserved capital. Pool 2 is a traditional investment portfolio, typically holding stocks and bonds, which is designed to provide income for life. Retirees usually do not intend to exhaust the capital in this pool and desire to leave it to heirs.

Pool 3: Medical reserve. This pool contains the asset reserve designed to meet medical expenses that may be incurred late in life. The funds may be in a portfolio, or the retiree may have purchased long-term care insurance.

Pools 4 and 5: Capital consumption. These pools provide ways to increase cash flow by consuming capital. Because distributions include not only income but capital being depleted, pools 4 and 5 increase cash flow considerably (typically by 30 to 50 percent or more) compared with the amount the assets would generate in a traditional portfolio.

Pool 4 provides additional guaranteed lifetime income typically by taking capital from pool 2 to purchase immediate annuities. The benefits are increased cash flow and income for life guaranteed by an insurance company.

Pool 5 contains surplus capital that remains after all other financial needs have been covered using pools 1 through 4. These surplus funds can be spent for such things as travel, home improvements, or gifts to family and charity. Creating a surplus pool that generates increased distributions is the retiree's reward for successfully accumulating assets over his or her lifetime.

Using pools increases the importance of life planning and helps reduce the need for estate planning, a change that most clients welcome.

Creating an Investment Strategy

An investment strategy must be created that will dictate how each pool will be invested and how the pool will generate cash flow. Although specific for each pool, the strategies for each pool must also work together as a whole. I prepare an overall strategy for each client that contains separate sections for each pool. The strategy for each pool must cover:

❑ Cash distributions
❑ Asset allocation
❑ Use of qualified versus nonqualified money
❑ The amount to be invested in immediate annuities (and thus consumed)
❑ Use of fixed versus variable immediate annuities

Creating this strategy is the work financial advisers are paid to do. Much of it is art, and there is no simple formula.

Pool 1: Lifetime income. This is the easiest pool to manage. Typically, there are no investment decisions to make because Social Security, company pensions, and annuities have already been put in place. The retirement decisions required include questions such as when to start receiving payments, how to treat a surviving spouse, and whether the retiree wishes a time-certain option (guaranteeing payment for a certain number of years) should the retiree or spouse die prematurely.

Pool 2: Preserved capital. Pool 2 is the traditional portfolio with stocks and bonds and holds the assets that the retiree intends eventually to leave to heirs. These also are the assets the retiree can turn to if the assets in the other pools do not provide sufficient cash flow. Because pool 2 is not the primary source of income (pools 1 and 4 are the retiree's primary sources of income) and the time horizon is long, with the assets eventually expected to pass to heirs, its investment strategy may be more aggressive than is usually considered prudent for a retiree. The strategy may use a higher allocation to stocks and seek a higher long-term rate of return. There is no reason to be aggressive in setting the cash-distribution rate. Distributions can be based on dividends and interest or be set at a conservative 2 percent to 3 percent of the portfolio's value. Because the assets in pool 2 will likely be passed on to heirs, it's the logical location for IRAs, which can be passed to another generation tax efficiently.

Pool 3: Medical reserve. This pool holds the asset reserve designed to meet medical expenses. If a long-term care insurance policy is the primary source of funds to meet these costs, no assets are held and no investment management is required. Medical costs in excess of what is covered by long-term care insurance would be covered from other pools. If medical expenses are to be funded from the pool, the number of years expected to elapse before the funds are needed will dictate the asset allocation. If pool 3 assets are never used, they can be merged with pool 2 and passed on to heirs using "stretch" IRAs.

Pools 4 and 5: Capital consumption. Pool 4 is used to increase monthly distributions to supplement distributions from pool 1. Clients who want additional guaranteed cash flow for life can take money from pool 2 to buy an immediate annuity, thereby increasing cash flow without the risk of exhausting principal prematurely. If they want to control the investment decisions, they can buy an immediate variable annuity. Otherwise they should purchase an immediate fixed annuity or some combination of fixed and variable. Buying annuities over time (for instance at ages 65, 70, and 75), like dollar-cost averaging, reduces the risk of locking in at the wrong time. Additionally by staging purchases at five-year increments, the retiree can buy immediate annuities at older ages and benefit from significantly higher payouts that come with shorter life expectancies. Using taxable money to buy an immediate annuity may be the preferred

FIGURE 14.3 *Sample Investment Strategy*

BALANCE SHEET

		65	66
Pool 1	Lifetime Income	—	—
Pool 2	Preserved Capital	$ 500,000	$527,500
Pool 3	Medical Reserve	250,000	270,000
Pool 4	Immediate Annuities		
	Fixed	125,000	—
	Variable	75,000	—
Pool 5	Surplus Account	50,000	45,000
	Total	$1,000,000	$842,500

CASH FLOW

		65	66
Pool 1	Lifetime Income	$22,000	$22,880
Pool 2	Preserved Capital	12,500	13,188
Pool 3	Medical Reserve	—	—
Pool 4	Immediate Annuities		
	Fixed	7,500	7,500
	Variable	3,000	3,165
Pool 5	Surplus Account	5,000	5,000
	Total	$50,000	$51,733

approach because a portion of the distribution is the nontaxed return of principal. Immediate annuities purchased with IRA funds retain their character as IRAs, and the distributions are fully taxed.

Pool 5 is for surplus assets that are to be spent down. Since this spending is probably going to be done in the next five to 15 years, the funds should be invested conservatively so that the money will be available when needed. A laddered bond portfolio might make sense, with maturation dates tied to periods when the retiree plans to spend the money. This pool is a logical place for taxable money, because accessing it will have fewer tax consequences than distributions from IRAs.

70	75	80	85	90
—	—	—	—	—
$ 653,480	$ 854,072	$1,116,238	$1,458,879	$1,906,696
367,332	539,731	793,042	1,165,239	1,712,119
—	—	—	—	—
—	—	—	—	—
25,000	—	—	—	—
$1,045,812	$1,393,803	$1,909,280	$2,624,118	$3,618,815

70	75	80	85	90
$26,766	$32,565	$39,621	$48,205	$ 58,648
16,337	21,352	27,906	36,472	47,667
—	—	—	—	—
7,500	7,500	7,500	7,500	7,500
3,921	5,124	6,697	8,753	11,440
5,000	—	—	—	—
$59,524	$66,542	$81,724	$100,930	$125,256

A Trial Portfolio

Once advisers have spent time listening to clients, helping them define their retirement objectives, and discussing the available tools for creating retirement cash flow, the next step is to put together a proposed investment strategy that includes a pool for each objective. They should review this with the retiree and present a table similar to the one in **FIGURE 14.3**, which shows how the retiree's assets are allocated to the various pools and how much income is projected from each pool. I find clients provide the best guidance when they have something concrete to respond to.

With a table like the one in Figure 14.3 at hand, an adviser can review questions similar to those suggested below to determine how well the draft investment strategy fits the client's objectives:

1 Are you comfortable with the guaranteed monthly income? Do you want more?

2 Are you comfortable with the asset allocation of each pool and its expected volatility or risk?

3 Have we adequately protected against inflation?

4 Are we making too many irreversible decisions?

5 Have we reserved adequate resources to cover long-term health care expenses?

6 Have we kept sufficient emergency reserves?

7 Do we have the right trade-off between consuming capital and leaving assets to heirs?

Based on the client's answers and reactions, the adviser can change or fine-tune the overall strategy or the strategy of an individual pool to meet the client's objectives more closely. Seeing the strategy on paper may also help indecisive clients become clearer about their objectives. Combining the available tools with the concept of pools gives advisers the means to dramatically improve the quality of their clients' lives in retirement.

CHAPTER 15

Creating Portfolios With Lower Volatility

LOUIS P. STANASOLOVICH

If you're not losing money somewhere in your portfolio, you're not diversified enough. This test of diversification may seem a little silly at first glance, but good diversification means having investments in a portfolio that have low correlation or negative correlation to every other investment in the portfolio. In a truly diversified portfolio, one where all the investments have low correlations to one another, some investments will rise, others will not rise as much, some will move sideways, and still others will lose money. If each investment in the portfolio is essentially equally weighted and periodically rebalanced, the portfolio should perform so that steep peaks and deep valleys are eliminated or at least substantially curtailed. In fact, designed correctly, such a portfolio should reduce yearly volatility to levels similar to that of—yet provide substantially higher returns than—an intermediate-term bond fund. In fact, returns should be akin to those of equities (8 percent to 12 percent) over a 10- to 15-year period. This structure is called a *lower-volatility portfolio*.

The Best of Both Worlds

Imagine portfolios that may go down only a few percent (a three standard-deviation event, by the way) when the stock market, as represented by the Standard & Poor's 500 index, decreases 20 percent. And when the S&P 500 rises substantially (20 percent or more), the same portfolio would not rise nearly as much. This would enable the portfolio to have a smoother long-term return. After all, virtually no investor likes a portfolio to plummet, regardless of what the stock market is doing. Most investors will accept significantly smaller losses for lower returns in any one year when the markets rise substantially. Every behavioral science study known to man supports this theory. However, investors still would like to have a chance at earning those double-digit long-term returns. Lower-volatility portfolios, if created correctly, allow investors a chance to have both.

Navigating the Pitfalls of Overvalued Markets

Before we discuss how lower-volatility portfolios are constructed and how they work, it's important to consider why we should use portfolios that have a nonvolatile pattern of return and why do so now, when, after all, the stock market crash has come and gone. Won't the market continue on its pattern of steady yearly returns above 10 percent, just as it did in the 1980s and 1990s? Doesn't the market always increase at slightly more than 10 percent over periods of 10 to 20 years? The answer to both questions is no.

Unfortunately, financial markets are at a point that hasn't been seen since the mid-1960s—very low interest rates (in fact, before the Federal Reserve Board began increasing interest rates in May of 2004, the Federal-funds rate was at a 46-year low) and sky-high price-to-earnings ratios as measured by a 10-year normalized P/E ratio on the S&P 500. That combination produced from 1966 to 1982 a 17-year secular bear market for the S&P 500. Historically, a secular bear market generally provides little, if any, return over inflation and generally lasts from 15 to 20 years. True to form, the 1966 to 1982 period produced a 6.73 percent pretax compound return while inflation compounded at a 7.24 percent rate. Imagine a period lasting 17 years during which an investor lost almost 0.5 percent per year to inflation pretax. Yet, according to investing legends such as Robert Arnott, Jeremy Grantham, Bill Gross, Cliff Asness, John Hussman, Steven Leuthold, Robert Schiller, and even Warren Buffett, that's exactly the type of real returns (after inflation) we may experience during the next 10 to 15 years.

The 1966–1982 period also brought five cyclical bull markets and five cyclical bear markets. Each cyclical market move upward or downward generally lasts anywhere from 1½ to 2½ years. When people talk about a full market cycle over a five-year period, they're talking about a cyclical bull and then a cyclical bear market. A full secular market cycle is probably a 35- to 40-year period that incorporates a secular bull and a secular bear. During these secular bear markets, there are usually more than a few steeply declining markets with losses of 30 percent or more (cyclical downturns) as well as corresponding upswings. In other words, we're likely to have a great deal of volatility during the next 10 to 15 years.

Interest Rate Direction and the Bond Market

In August 2005 the Federal Reserve Board increased the Fed-funds rate to 3.50 percent. The historical norm is 4.50 percent to 5.50 percent. However, long-term rates have yet to rise, and it appears the Fed will continue to raise the Fed Funds rate until long-term interest rates rise. To what degree and how fast is anyone's guess. However, with coupons on bonds as low as they are, they provide little protection for total return if interest rates rise another 2.0 percent. Hence PIMCO managing director Bill Gross's prediction of a 4.0 percent nominal return on bonds during the 10-year period ending 2015. Others second that prediction.

How dramatic an effect can such returns have on a portfolio? For an answer, we must look back. Long-term government bonds from 1937 to 1981 had negative total returns for 15 out of 45 years. For that entire period, long-term bonds underperformed inflation before taxes. What most people don't know, however, is that intermediate government bonds with five-year maturities did not perform well either (see **FIGURE 15.1**).

From 1937 to 1981, a period of 45 years, five-year-maturity government bonds produced a total pretax return of 3.60 percent while inflation was 4.30 percent. As a result, these bonds lost 0.70 percent per year to inflation pretax for 45 years. However, that includes the high-inflation years of the 1970s. From 1946 to 1965, a 20-year period, inflation was just 2.80 percent, which is very similar to inflation rates of recent years and the rate in 2005. However, during that time frame, the pretax compound total return for government bonds was 2.20 percent while inflation was 2.80

Source: Ibbotson Associates, Stocks, Bonds, Bills and Inflation 2004 Yearbook

FIGURE **15.1** *Intermediate* Bond Returns in Rising Interest Rate Markets*

	TOTAL RETURNS	INFLATION	LOSS TO INFLATION	BEGINNING YIELD	ENDING YIELD
1937–1981	+3.60%	+4.30%	+0.70%	+1.29%	+13.96%
1946–1965	+2.20	+2.80	+0.60	+1.03	+4.09
1955–1959	+1.00	+1.90	+0.90	+2.80	+4.98
1994	−5.10	+2.70	+7.80	+5.22	+7.80
1999	−1.80	+2.70	+4.50	+4.68	+6.45

*5-year government bonds.

percent, providing a negative real return (after inflation) per year for 20 years. In other words, five-year government bonds lost 0.60 percent to inflation before income taxes over 20 years during a low inflationary period. Yields during that time actually rose from 1.03 percent to 4.90 percent. From 1955 to 1959, inflation was just 1.90 percent. Normally, an investor would expect bonds to do relatively well in a period like that, except that intermediate government bonds with five-year maturities, pretax, lost not only to inflation but they also lost principal four out of five years. Yields rose from 2.80 percent to 4.98 percent. The compound total return during that five-year period was just 1.0 percent. Only one year with an exceptionally positive 15 percent–plus total return prevented a complete washout.

Current conditions are ripe for that kind of performance between 2005 and 2010. As a result, bonds are likely to be a mediocre investment in the years ahead. We were in a nirvana economy during the late 1940s, 1950s, and early 1960s. There was full employment, or at least as full as it gets, balanced federal budgets, trade surpluses, a rising dollar, and very low inflation. Interest rates, however, were rising during that time. That's because the Federal Reserve was trying to keep inflation in check. In short, even though the economic situation was much better than it is today, bonds still did not fare well.

An Overvalued Stock Market

Believe it or not, the stock market is still at one of its highest valuation points in history.

FIGURE 15.2 is called a five-year normalization. Those spikes up and down are not the stock market moving up and down; they are P/Es moving up and down as earnings and price levels move. Put simply, a normalized P/E in this example is the average of the last five years' worth of earnings before a particular point, divided into the current price of that investment at that same point. A normalized P/E allows earnings to be smoothed because earnings are cyclical and can swing widely in any one- or two-year period. Each five-year period calculated in Figure 15.2 comprises four and a half years of actual earnings and six months of forecasted earnings. **FIGURE 15.3** is a 10-year normalization. In Figure 15.2, the spike within the first gray circle to the left is the end of the third quarter of 1929, 12 days before the crash. The stock market essentially fell for the next 2¼ years. Figures 15.2 and 15.3 depict P/Es falling, not the stock market. However, stocks for the most part rose and fell with the P/E, especially when there was a sharp change in valuation. The market fell through the end of 1931 more than 60 percent, peak to trough. What happened when really low P/E ratios were reached? The market for three out of the next four years, 1932 through 1936, increased more than

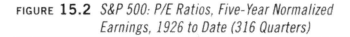

FIGURE **15.2** *S&P 500: P/E Ratios, Five-Year Normalized Earnings, 1926 to Date (316 Quarters)*

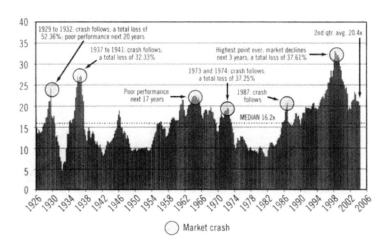

⭕ Market crash

CURRENT STATUS

Stocks are at the second-highest point in history.

Conclusion: Stocks are extremely overvalued.

METHODOLOGY

Normalizing: Earnings are far more cyclical than book value or dividends, so we think a smoothing technique is essential in making comparisons. The normalizing technique employed for the S&P 500 is to take the 10-year average, using the last 9 years of historical earnings and 1 year of future earnings.

Adjusted earnings: S&P 500 earnings have been adjusted in recent years to account for the big write-offs that companies have taken. Basically, adjusted earnings are the average of reported earnings and operating earnings. Adjustments go back to 1988.

Outliers: In early 1930 (P/E ratios <8) and in 1935–1937 (P/E ratios >24) normalized earnings were warped by the Depression's virtual earnings wipeout. These 12 quarterly outliers are excluded from decile distribution and median and average calculations on the previous histogram.

Earnings are very cyclical by nature, the ebb and flow can cause P/E ratios to move in erratic, less meaningful ways. Near the bottom of an economic contraction, with corporate earnings reduced dramatically, P/E ratios can look very high. However, it is at these types of economic nadirs (bottoms) when the best buying opportunities are often presented. This is why it is important to use normalized earnings. Normalizing earnings is simply a way to smooth out the distortions caused by economic expansions and contractions. Most normalized earnings are some sort of average. So it is true that in economic expansions, with rapidly rising earnings, the normalized earnings will lag current results. Conversely, in an economic contraction, with earnings falling, the normalized earnings will hold up better than current earnings. By employing a normalized earnings figure, it is much easier and more meaningful to make judgments regarding the valuations of the current market.

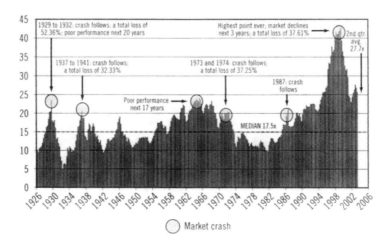

FIGURE **15.3** *Normalized P/E Ratios, Based on 10-Year Normalized Earnings, 1926 to Date*

○ Market crash

CURRENT STATUS

Stocks are at the second-highest point in history.

Conclusion: Stocks are extremely overvalued.

METHODOLOGY

Normalizing: Earnings are far more cyclical than book value or dividends, so we think a smoothing technique is essential in making comparisons. The normalizing technique employed for the S&P 500 is to take the 10-year average, using the last 9 years of historical earnings and 1 year of future earnings.

Adjusted earnings: S&P 500 earnings have been adjusted in recent years to account for the big write-offs that companies have taken. Basically, adjusted earnings are the average of reported earnings and operating earnings. Adjustments go back to 1988.

Outliers: In early 1930 (P/E ratios <8) and in 1935–1937 (P/E ratios >24) normalized earnings were warped by the Depression's virtual earnings wipeout. These 12 quarterly outliers are excluded from decile distribution and median and average calculations on the previous histogram.

Earnings are very cyclical by nature, the ebb and flow can cause P/E ratios to move in erratic, less meaningful ways. Near the bottom of an economic contraction, with corporate earnings reduced dramatically, P/E ratios can look very high. However, it is at these types of economic nadirs (bottoms) when the best buying opportunities are often presented. This is why it is important to use normalized earnings. Normalizing earnings is simply a way to smooth out the distortions caused by economic expansions and contractions. Most normalized earnings are some sort of average. So it is true that in economic expansions, with rapidly rising earnings, the normalized earnings will lag current results. Conversely, in an economic contraction, with earnings falling, the normalized earnings will hold up better than current earnings. By employing a normalized earnings figure, it is much easier and more meaningful to make judgments regarding the valuations of the current market.

30 percent each year; the one year it didn't, it was down only 0.20 percent. As a result, the stock market went from one giant bubble to a great buying opportunity in 1932, then back to the next bubble in 1935 and 1936. What happened in 1937? The market fell 35 percent.

From 1937 to 1941, the market was negative every year but one. The stock market bottomed out after the attack on Pearl Harbor, and then as the United States recovered economically and the Allies won World War II, P/Es peaked in 1946 (note that in 1945, inflation was 18 percent). What happened in 1946? The armed forces came home. The economy started to slow down because the federal government was not borrowing $500 billion for the war effort—an amount that was astronomical in comparison to the size of the economy at that time. P/Es slowly dropped down to the low point of 1949. The total return of the stock market from 1929 to 1948, a secular bear market, was 3.10 percent. That actually wasn't terrible in terms of real returns because inflation increased only 1.70 percent during that time because of the Depression. From 1901 to 1921, a secular bear market returned zero over inflation for that 20-year period. A phenomenal secular bull market followed from 1921 to 1929. The stock market compounded at 27 percent per year during that short period, which led to the infamous 1929 bubble. The secular bull market of 1949 to 1965 was a period of generally rising interest rates that started with very low P/Es—much different from today.

As the stock market peaked in 1966, interest rates were relatively low and P/E ratios were relatively high, although a bit lower than in 1929. From 1966 to 1982, as mentioned earlier, a secular bear market occurred, during which we had several cyclical bear and bull markets. In 1972, a cyclical bull bubble market (the era of the Nifty 50 stocks where P/Es ranged from 40 to 70) led to a 45 percent drop during 1973 and 1974. The stock market continued to move up and down during the late 1970s as interest rates skyrocketed, peaking in 1982. P/E ratios dropped to 10 on a five-year normalized basis. The period 1949 to 1965 brought a secular bull market. Although interest rates were generally rising, the market had low P/E ratios. From 2003 to 2005, interest rates continued to rise, but valuation points were the highest in history, as indicated in Figure 15.2. This double whammy of low interest rates and historically high P/Es did not give the stock market a very promising outlook.

At the secular bubble market peak in late 1999 to early 2000, the five-year normalized P/E was 38. From April 2000 to mid-October 2000, the S&P 500 fell 45 percent peak to trough. Then in October 2002, the market began to rise again. At that point, P/Es also rose to their 2005 level, on par roughly with 1966 and approximately equivalent to those of 1929 on a five-year normalized basis.

In Figure 15.3, a 10-year normalized P/E chart provided by the Leuthold Group, everything looks similar to the five-year normalization chart in Figure 15.2, with the exception of the 1935–1936 bubble, which doesn't look quite as expensive, and the 1999–2000 bubble, which is more expensive at a 43 P/E, the highest of all time. Here's what's most disturbing: the year 2005 marks the second-highest point in history on a 10-year normalized basis. We can also observe from the 10-year normalization chart in Figure 15.3 that soon after each one of the peaks, stock market value declined significantly.

The View From Here

FIGURE 15.4 shows how the stock market has historically performed in the ensuing 10-year period after inflation once the stock market attains a certain P/E level.

P/E levels are normalized on a 10-year basis and divided into quintiles. For a purchase of the S&P 500 at an inexpensive P/E—for example, in the bottom 40 percent—returns over the next 10 years exceeded approximately 11 percent per year on average, compounded after inflation. Obviously, these two least expensive P/E ratio quintiles provided the best-performing returns. The last quintile is the one with the most expensive P/Es and consequently the lowest returns. In fact, there is virtually no return after

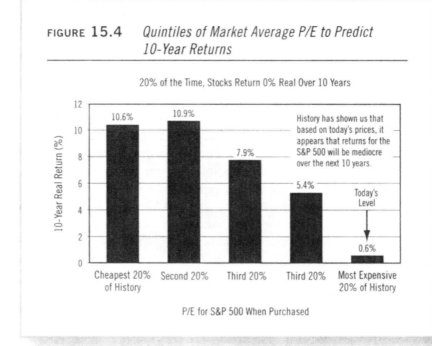

FIGURE **15.4** *Quintiles of Market Average P/E to Predict 10-Year Returns*

20% of the Time, Stocks Return 0% Real Over 10 Years

History has shown us that based on today's prices, it appears that returns for the S&P 500 will be mediocre over the next 10 years.

10.6%   10.9%   7.9%   5.4%   Today's Level   0.6%

Cheapest 20% of History   Second 20%   Third 20%   Third 20%   Most Expensive 20% of History

10-Year Real Return (%)

P/E for S&P 500 When Purchased

Source: GMO, Standard & Poor's data for 1926–2003

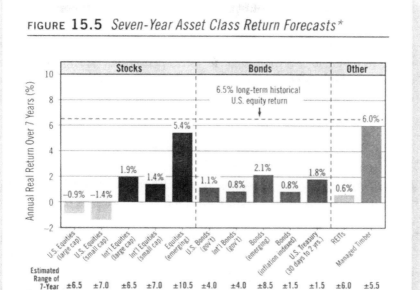

FIGURE **15.5** *Seven-Year Asset Class Return Forecasts**

*The chart represents real return forecasts (after inflation) for several asset classes as of August 31, 2005. These forecasts are forward-looking statements based on the reasonable beliefs of GMO and are not a guarantee of future performances.

Long-term inflation assumptions: 2.5% per year.
Return forecasts for international equities are ex-Japan.

Source: GMO

inflation. Based on the 10-year normalization chart in Figure 15.3, 2005 marks the most expensive quintile. And what could be worse? It is not merely in the top 20 percent of the most expensive P/E ratios in history; it's actually in the top 10 percent.

FIGURE 15.5 is an internal forecast of what you can expect for returns going beyond 2005 after a 2.5 percent inflation rate for the following seven years, according to Grantham, Mayo, Van Otterloo & Co. (GMO). In other words, the returns are net of inflation.

To obtain a nominal return, simply add 2.5 percent to each return on the chart. Expected returns for both large and small U.S. stocks are expected to be minuscule. Large and small international stocks are expected to perform somewhat better but are still nothing to write home about. Emerging-market stocks offer the best equity-return opportunities but are not considered a mainstream holding to replace the majority of traditional equities. The forecast for bonds is not a whole lot brighter. Every category, except for emerging-market bonds, is forecast to provide nominal returns of approximately 4 percent or less. In fact, short-term (30 days to two years) U.S. Treasury securities, essentially money market funds, look more attractive for the long term. This outlook echoes Gross's forecast for bonds.

What can we conclude from this information? Simply this: if one is going to invest in the traditional 60 percent domestic stock/40 percent domestic bond model, then in all probability the portfolio is not going to earn much more than 3 percent over the next seven years.

Viable Alternatives

Real estate investment trusts (REITs) have probably been the best-performing asset class since the beginning of 2000 (see Figure 15.5). Their forecasted return is approximately what will be delivered in the form of a dividend. Managed timber can be used as a forecast for what commodities will provide because managed timber and commodities are the most attractive asset classes in terms of potential return. Jeremy Grantham, portfolio manager at GMO, has stated that he likes hedge funds. He believes that they will earn their historical range of returns of 8 percent to 12 percent per year long term.

In considering how to invest in such a difficult period, it's prudent to look at how innovative investors are investing. Some of the most innovative investors are college endowments. One of the leading college endowment programs is run by Yale University. In 2004, *Pensions & Investments Age* reported on a study Harvard University performed on Yale's endowment that found that 77 percent of Yale's portfolio was not in U.S. stocks, U.S. bonds, or cash. Harvard itself now has more than 60 percent in investments other than U.S. stocks, U.S. bonds, and cash. In fact, Harvard has $2 billion of its $21 billion portfolio in timber. The *Wall Street Journal* reported in 2004 that Princeton had about 53 percent of its endowment directed to these alternative investments, with a goal of increasing that to 60 percent. The University of Chicago had approximately 40 percent in alternative investments two and a half years ago, and MIT directs more than 40 percent to alternative or nontraditional investments.

College endowments are purchasing alternatives or nontraditional investments such as private equity, real estate, commodity plays, managed futures funds, hedge funds, venture capital, managed timber, et cetera. They also use emerging-market equities and emerging-market bonds to drive some of their returns. Lower-volatility portfolios incorporate many of these same investments. Why? Because they have such a low correlation to one another. And low correlation—if the portfolio is constructed correctly—prevents major losses and provides a steadier return.

Uncovering Correlations

Earnings yield is a key component of determining returns on equities. If a stock has a P/E of 20, for example, that means the earnings yield (earnings divided by the price of the stock) is 5 percent. Investments, historically, have moved in lockstep as one investment adjusts to other investments over a few years. If the stock market is in equilibrium before interest rates actually rise, stocks then have to ratchet up their earnings yield. That means their P/Es have to come down. How do they come down? The stock price falls and/or the earnings grow. But earnings do not grow in the long run at spectacular rates. Since 1886, corporate earnings have never grown more than 7.5 percent nor less than 4.0 percent during any period of five consecutive years. It's also important to keep in mind that the pricing of every investment relates to where interest rates are, especially in the long run.

The strategic asset allocation of most portfolios is poorly constructed, at best. Many portfolios are constructed using the four-corners approach to equity investing by buying mutual funds that purchase equities in the small-value, small-growth, large-value, large-growth categories, as well as adding some bonds and maybe a dash of international equities. The problem is most domestic equity and international equity investing styles correlate highly with one another.

To prove this point, let's first examine the domestic equity correlation of several domestic equity indexes (see **FIGURE 15.6**).

FIGURE 15.6 *Domestic Style Correlation*

36-MONTH CORRELATION

	1	2	3	4	5	6	7	8
1 Standard & Poor's 500	—	0.92	0.97	0.98	0.88	0.91	0.82	0.82
2 Nasdaq Composite	0.92	—	0.91	0.89	0.89	0.87	0.85	0.79
3 Barra Large-Cap Growth	0.97	0.91	—	0.92	0.83	0.83	0.76	0.72
4 Barra Large-Cap Value	0.98	0.89	0.92	—	0.88	0.94	0.84	0.87
5 Barra Mid-Cap Growth	0.88	0.89	0.83	0.88	—	0.95	0.96	0.93
6 Barra Mid-Cap Value	0.91	0.87	0.83	0.94	0.95	—	0.92	0.95
7 Barra Small-Cap Growth	0.82	0.85	0.76	0.84	0.96	0.92	—	0.96
8 Barra Small-Cap Value	0.82	0.79	0.72	0.87	0.93	0.95	0.96	—

Source: Legend Financial Advisors, Inc. 2005

FIGURE **15.7** *International Mutual Funds Versus S&P 500 Index*

36-MONTH CORRELATION

	1	2	3	4	5	6	7	8
1 Standard & Poor's 500	—	0.83	0.89	0.93	0.93	0.84	0.94	0.82
2 Julius Baer International Equity I	0.83	—	0.91	0.93	0.92	0.96	0.94	0.82
3 Dodge & Cox International Stock Templeton	0.89	0.91	—	0.97	0.95	0.90	0.95	0.91
4 Institutional Foreign Equity	0.93	0.93	0.97	—	0.97	0.91	0.97	0.89
5 Harbor International Institutional	0.93	0.92	0.95	0.97	—	0.91	0.97	0.88
6 Janus Overseas	0.84	0.96	0.90	0.91	0.91	—	0.91	0.84
7 T. Rowe Price International Stock	0.94	0.94	0.95	0.97	0.97	0.91	—	0.88
8 Tweedy, Browne Global Value	0.82	0.82	0.91	0.89	0.88	0.84	0.88	—

Source: Legend Financial Advisors, Inc. 2005

We can readily see that the lowest correlations are in the 70 percent–plus range, which is considered by Morningstar to be highly correlated and, as a result, poorly diversified. International mutual funds versus the S&P 500 fare no better. **FIGURE 15.7** indicates that all correlations are in the 70 percent–plus range or higher even with the S&P 500.

FIGURE 15.8 indicates that investors do obtain a great deal of diversification by investing in fixed-income investments. In short, fixed-income investments are a great diversifier because they have no correlation with equities.

The problem with traditional bond funds is that they can lose money when interest rates rise. Bank loan funds, on the other hand, receive increased interest on the variable-rate loans that they make to corporations as rates rise. Therefore, unlike bonds, principal losses are likely to be very small unless there is a default on one of the underlying loans, which is possible since the loans are senior secured loans to companies with ratings below investment grade. The Eaton Vance Prime Rate Reserve Fund is a bank-loan fund. It also has a low correlation to the stock market as well as

FIGURE 15.8 *Fixed-Income Mutual Funds Versus S&P 500 Index*

36-MONTH CORRELATION

	1	2	3	4	5	6	7	8
1 Standard & Poor's 500	—	0.19	0.38	0.67	**0.23**	**0.15**	0.49	0.04
2 Eaton Vance Prime Rate Reserve	0.19	—	0.21	0.58	0.01	**0.13**	0.00	0.04
3 Loomis Sayles Bond Institutional	0.38	0.21	—	0.58	0.44	0.69	0.84	0.71
4 Northeast Investors	0.67	0.58	0.58	—	**0.02**	0.10	0.51	0.26
5 PIMCO Foreign Bond Institutional	**0.23**	0.01	0.44	**0.02**	—	0.64	0.27	0.57
6 PIMCO Total Return Institutional	**0.15**	**0.13**	0.69	0.10	0.64	—	0.61	0.64
7 T. Rowe Price Emerging Markets Bond	0.49	0.00	0.84	0.51	0.27	0.61	—	0.44
8 T. Rowe Price International Bond	0.04	0.04	0.71	0.26	0.57	0.64	0.44	—

Source: Legend Financial Advisors, Inc. 2005

to all types of bond funds. It's an excellent diversification investment that will make money when interest rates are rising.

Some advisers say REITs are not truly real estate investments. Our definition of an asset class is an asset that provides a dissimilar price movement to that of other asset classes. **FIGURE 15.9** lists a number of REIT mutual funds.

All of the funds in Figure 15.9 have a very low correlation to the S&P 500 and have a very high correlation to each other. There are several reasons for this. First of all, the universe of REIT funds to invest in is narrow. Fewer than 200 investable REIT securities are available. Many of the REIT mutual funds own 30 to 70 of them. The funds, therefore, echo each other quite a bit. Investors who own two or three REIT funds in their portfolio are not obtaining a great deal of diversification among them. An investor will obtain a great deal by buying the first REIT mutual fund, but no additional diversification is gained by adding more REIT funds. **FIGURE 15.10** shows true portfolio diversification.

FIGURE **15.9** *REIT Fund Comparison*

36-MONTH CORRELATION

	1	2	3	4	5	6	7	8
1 Standard & Poor's 500	—	0.54	0.37	0.37	0.37	0.38	0.33	0.48
2 CGM Realty	0.54	—	0.49	0.49	0.47	0.50	0.49	0.54
3 Cohen & Steers Realty Shares Fund	0.37	0.49	—	0.99	0.99	0.99	0.98	0.97
4 Fidelity Real Estate Investment	0.37	0.49	0.99	—	0.99	0.99	0.99	0.98
5 T. Rowe Price Real Estate	0.37	0.47	0.99	0.99	—	0.99	0.99	0.97
6 Heitman REIT PBHG	0.38	0.50	0.99	0.99	0.99	—	0.98	0.98
7 Undiscovered Managers REIT A	0.33	0.49	0.98	0.99	0.99	0.98	—	0.97
8 Columbia Real Estate Equity Z	0.48	0.54	0.97	0.98	0.97	0.98	0.97	—

Source: Legend Financial Advisors, Inc. 2005

Some of the investments in Figure 15.10 even have negative correlation, such as Caldwell and Orkin Market Opportunity Fund, which is a long-short fund. In fact, several of these funds short in some way, except for Cohen and Steers Realty Shares Fund and the commodity fund. As a result, fairly low correlations among most of these funds are evident. However, Leuthold, for example, had a higher correlation for a period of years because, within its Core Investment Fund, it increased the number of domestic equities for the period 2002–2005 (although the number has fluctuated during that time), causing the fund to perform a lot more like an S&P 500 fund. In 1998 or so, the fund might have had only 40 percent in equities and was actually shorting some equities. This fund shorts both equities and fixed income at times. It periodically owns REITs, commodities, high-yield bonds, emerging-market bonds, and equities, among many other investments. It invests in multiple asset classes. If this were a hedge fund, it would be considered a macro fund. The Merger Fund invests in announced merger arbitrage deals. It uses a hedge fund strategy, except it doesn't have the leverage. The Merger Fund has one of the lowest historical risk profiles of any mutual fund in the Morningstar universe since 1989.

FIGURE **15.10** *Truly Diversified Portfolio Correlation*

36-MONTH CORRELATION

	1	2	3	4	5	6	7	8
1 Standard & Poor's 500	—	0.19	**0.44**	0.79	0.60	0.27	0.37	**0.28**
2 Eaton Vance Prime Rate Reserve	0.19	—	**0.10**	0.34	0.35	0.28	0.24	0.13
3 Caldwell & Orkin Market Oppportunity Fund	**0.44**	**0.10**	—	0.44	**0.34**	**0.22**	**0.17**	0.06
4 Leuthold Core Investment	0.79	0.34	**0.44**	—	0.56	0.49	0.43	**0.04**
5 Merger Fund	0.60	0.35	**0.34**	0.56	—	0.10	0.41	**0.10**
6 Hussman Strategic Growth	0.27	0.28	**0.22**	0.49	0.10	—	0.23	0.23
7 Cohen & Steers Realty Shares Fund	0.37	0.24	**0.17**	0.43	0.41	0.23	—	**0.21**
8 Oppenheimer Real Asset A	**0.28**	0.13	0.06	**0.04**	**0.10**	0.23	0.21	—

It has had only a 6.2 standard deviation over time. These types of investments offer substantially more diversification than the run-of-the-mill equity mutual funds.

Exchange-Traded Funds

Can a lower-volatility portfolio be built with exchange-traded funds? The answer is generally no. When evaluating exchange-traded funds, it is important to note the bulk of them are based on U.S. indexes that correlate highly to one another and are capitalization weighted. In other words, the biggest stocks are worth the most. General Electric, at last count, was approximately 650 times the size of the smallest stock in the S&P 500. In other words, the top 50 stocks are driving the S&P 500, unless an equally weighted S&P 500 index is used. There is one exchange-traded fund that is constructed in this manner, the Rydex Fund. Since 1961, the equally weighted index has outperformed the S&P by 2 percent per year compounded. There were times throughout history it underperformed substantially, namely in the late 1990s. Since 2000, though, the equally weighted index has performed significantly better than the capitalization-weighted index. A capitalization-weighted index is flawed because an investor is investing a disproportionate amount of money in stocks that have already appreciated. Equal-weighted indexes prevent the investor from owning too much of a good thing, such as tech stocks in 2000 or oil in 1981. Therefore, when using a domestic large-cap index, to minimize risk and increase returns, it's best to use an equally weighted S&P 500 index.

Another new development in the world of exchange-traded funds is the commodity-based funds. We expect to see broadly diversified commodity-based index funds in the near future. Cohen and Steers run a REIT-based ETF. However, actively managed ETFs that use hedging strategies appear to be a long way off.

Designing a Lower-Volatility Portfolio

The goal of designing a lower-volatility portfolio is to attempt to earn "equity-like" returns with almost only "bond-like" risk. For the purposes of the illustrations that follow, portfolios are rebalanced annually back to targets at year-end. In real life, if a client adds or withdraws a substantial sum relative to the portfolio's size, the portfolio is rebalanced. All calculations in the following illustrations are performed in the same manner that Morningstar performs its calculations. All performance numbers are net of our fee schedule.

Lower-volatility investing is designed to minimize or even avoid loss. Although no investment periods are ever exactly alike, the years 2000 through 2002 illustrate how well lower-volatility portfolios protected capital during these three negative years. **FIGURES 15.11** through **15.14** illustrate four of Legend Financial Advisors' model portfolios. In each case, the portfolios had minimal losses or, in some cases, all gains in each of those three years.

During that three-year period, the stock market as represented by the S&P 500 dropped approximately 45 percent peak to trough. An index must appreciate 82 percent to get back to breakeven. If an investor has even a 10 percent loss during this time period, the gain needed to break even is 11 percent. In other words, if losses are minimized, huge wins are not needed to attain good long-term returns.

In Figures 15.11 through 15.14, each lower-volatility portfolio has a standard deviation roughly equivalent to that of bonds while producing returns that match or exceed those of equities. (Technically, standard deviations are not directly comparable to one another. Instead, they measure the volatility around the arithmetic mean return. The point, however, is that the volatility is low.) As Figures 15.11 and 15.14 show, for the period

1996 to 1999, the lower-volatility portfolios trailed far behind the S&P 500 especially in 1998 and 1999. Diversification will never work in a euphoric market where one asset class (the S&P 500 in this case) dominates all other asset classes. In the longer run, the more the period lengthens, the better diversification works.

The real measure of success is in the reward-to-risk ratio calculation shown in Figures 15.11 through 15.14. This calculation is derived by simply dividing the compound return by the standard deviation. This allows dissimilar portfolios to be compared on a risk-adjusted basis. In all cases, the lower-volatility portfolios' reward-to-risk ratios substantially exceed that of the S&P 500 (cap weighted). To provide the reader with a historical perspective, the S&P 500's reward-to-risk ratio since 1926 has been approximately 0.5. In fact, the only investments that have approached the reward-to-risk ratios of the lower-volatility portfolios have been investment-grade bonds (1.0), junk bonds (1.3), and convertible bonds (1.3).

The reduced volatility for these portfolios shows up clearly in the monthly returns shown in each figure when each portfolio is compared with the S&P 500. Casual observation reveals how much less volatile the returns are than the S&P 500's. Yet the long-term return of the lower-volatility portfolio (as illustrated by the growth of the $1 million section of each of the figures) is comparable to that of the S&P 500 for the portfolios in Figure 15.11 (Average Return, Minimal Risk) and Figure 15.14 (Ultra-Low Risk, Comparative Return). The lower-volatility portfolio substantially outperforms the S&P 500 in the portfolios in Figures 15.12 (Optimal Return, Below-Average Risk) and Figure 15.13 (High Return, Low Risk).

Lower volatility is what most investors want. Yet by properly constructing a lower-volatility portfolio, it is not necessary to give up equity-like long-term returns to maintain it.

FIGURE 15.11 *Average Return, Minimal Risk, Lower-Volatility Model Portfolio*

RETURNS (%)

	1996	1997	1998	1999	2000	2001	2002	2003	2004	2005
January	0.34	1.13	0.05	1.70	0.55	1.09	-0.06	0.79	0.71	-0.5
February	1.38	-0.54	1.10	-0.79	2.96	1.46	-0.74	-0.20	0.16	1.14
March	1.00	1.16	1.56	1.41	-0.18	-0.70	-0.17	-0.40	0.06	-0.34
April	1.12	0.47	0.38	0.84	1.35	-0.24	0.04	1.53	-0.90	-0.42
May	1.75	1.22	0.61	0.33	2.17	1.27	-0.02	2.85	0.03	0.19
June	0.41	1.42	2.86	0.65	0.12	-0.61	-2.29	1.10	0.83	0.57
July	-0.45	2.51	0.09	0.61	0.21	0.14	-2.33	1.15	-0.58	
August	1.07	0.63	0.03	0.05	1.31	0.02	0.61	1.19	0.38	
September	1.13	2.79	1.14	0.54	1.64	-3.19	-0.33	0.67	0.62	
October	1.63	1.52	-0.59	-1.33	0.64	0.34	0.29	1.89	-0.33	
November	1.57	0.80	0.84	0.60	2.65	0.20	2.21	1.33	1.99	
December	0.67	1.14	2.01	1.51	2.09	0.47	-0.93	1.13	0.19	
Annual Returns										
LVP*	12.24	15.18	10.52	6.25	16.59	-1.89	-3.75	13.81	3.19	0.56
S&P 500	22.93	33.34	28.66	21.08	-9.07	-11.86	-22.03	28.68	10.90	-0.81

*annually rebalanced.

	LVP	S&P 500		MODEL	S&P 500
Annualized standard deviation	3.940	17.541	Negative monthly returns	27.00	44.00
Annualized compound return	7.419	8.956	% of negative monthly returns	23.68%	38.60%
Correlation to S&P 500	0.361	1.000			
Reward-to-risk ratio	1.883	0.511			

REPRESENTATIVE HOLDINGS	SYMBOL	DESCRIPTION	WEIGHTING (%)
Eaton Vance Classic Senior Floating Rate†	EIFRX	Floating-rate senior secured bank loans	24.75
Caldwell & Orkin Market Opportunity	COAGX	Long/short growth & value	24.75
Leuthold Core	LCORX	Tactical asset allocation	24.75
Merger	MERFX	Announced mergers & acquisitions arbitrage–large-cap	24.75
Cash (non-interest-bearing account)		Cash	1.00

†Eaton Vance Prime Rate Reserve used until May 1999.

All returns are pretax and net of fees.

LOWER-VOLATILITY PORTFOLIO—GROWTH OF $1 MILLION

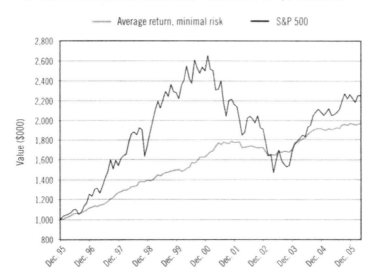

LOWER-VOLATILITY PORTFOLIO—MONTHLY RETURN

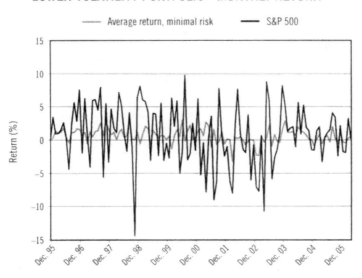

Source: © Legend Financial Advisors, 2005

FIGURE 15.12 *Optimal Return, Below-Average Risk, Lower-Volatility Model Portfolio*

RETURNS (%)

	1996	1997	1998	1999	2000	2001	2002	2003	2004	2005
January	—	—	—	—	—	-3.28	-0.37	0.86	0.51	-0.31
February	—	—	—	—	—	3.04	-1.68	-0.30	0.02	2.41
March	—	—	—	—	—	0.15	-0.04	-0.40	-0.24	-1.02
April	—	—	—	—	—	-0.71	-0.08	1.73	-1.76	-1.21
May	—	—	—	—	—	1.48	-0.27	3.83	-0.10	0.56
June	—	—	—	—	—	-0.85	-2.68	1.13	1.14	0.89
July	—	—	—	—	0.49	0.30	-3.74	1.57	-0.98	
August	—	—	—	—	2.91	0.05	0.39	1.79	0.05	
September	—	—	—	—	3.65	-3.96	-0.87	0.72	1.12	
October	—	—	—	—	0.91	-0.03	0.42	3.24	-0.76	
November	—	—	—	—	3.65	0.10	1.99	2.31	3.52	
December	—	—	—	—	3.27	0.74	-1.38	1.35	-0.04	
Annual Returns										
LVP*	—	—	—	—	15.77	-3.12	-8.10	19.26	2.42	1.27
S&P 500	—	—	—	—	-8.70	-11.86	-22.03	28.68	10.90	-0.81

*annually rebalanced.

	LVP	S&P 500		MODEL	S&P 500
Annualized standard deviation	6.347	15.503	Negative monthly returns	25.00	27.00
Annualized compound return	4.980	-2.345	% of negative monthly returns	41.67%	45.00%
Correlation to S&P 500	0.325	1.000			
Reward-to-risk ratio	0.785	-0.151			

REPRESENTATIVE HOLDINGS	SYMBOL	DESCRIPTION	WEIGHTING (%)
Leuthold Select	LSLTX	Sector rotation	17.33
Caldwell & Orkin Market Opportunity	COAGX	Long/short growth & value	24.75
Leuthold Core	LCORX	Tactical asset allocation	24.75
Leuthold Grizzly	GRZZX	100% Short	7.43
Merger	MERFX	Announced mergers & acquisitions arbitrage–large cap	24.75
Cash (non-interest-bearing account)		Cash	1.00

All returns are pretax and net of fees.

LOWER-VOLATILITY PORTFOLIO—GROWTH OF $1 MILLION

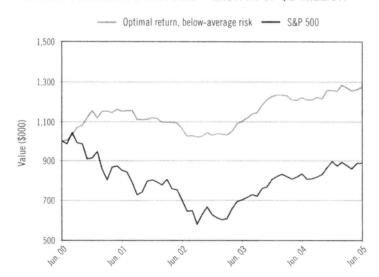

LOWER-VOLATILITY PORTFOLIO—MONTHLY RETURN

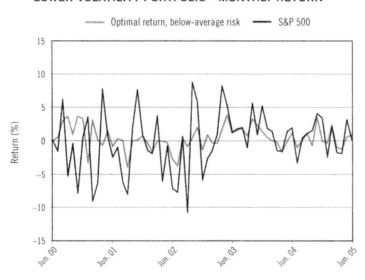

Source: © Legend Financial Advisors, 2005

FIGURE 15.13 *High Return, Low Risk, Lower-Volatility Model Portfolio*

RETURNS (%)

	1996	1997	1998	1999	2000	2001	2002	2003	2004	2005
January	—	—	—	—	—	2.98	1.06	0.54	1.26	−0.61
February	—	—	—	—	—	1.40	−0.05	0.14	1.10	1.32
March	—	—	—	—	—	−2.83	1.68	−0.10	0.35	−0.24
April	—	—	—	—	—	1.02	0.73	2.25	−2.13	−0.70
May	—	—	—	—	—	1.48	0.70	4.14	0.51	0.61
June	—	—	—	—	—	−1.52	−2.12	0.83	0.81	0.83
July	—	—	—	—	—	0.31	−2.00	0.67	−1.13	
August	—	—	—	—	—	0.59	1.07	1.71	0.17	
September	—	—	—	—	—	−3.15	−1.28	1.13	1.13	
October	—	—	—	—	−0.03	0.29	0.17	2.21	0.37	
November	—	—	—	—	2.12	1.47	2.17	1.69	2.15	
December	—	—	—	—	2.96	1.17	0.70	1.73	0.89	
Annual Returns										
LVP*	—	—	—	—	5.11	3.08	2.76	18.23	5.55	1.19
S&P 500	—	—	—	—	−7.81	−11.86	−22.03	28.68	10.90	−0.81

*annually rebalanced.

	LVP	S&P 500		MODEL	S&P 500
Annualized standard deviation	5.211	15.457	Negative monthly returns	14.00	25.00
Annualized compound return	7.433	−2.267	% of negative monthly returns	24.56%	43.86%
Correlation to S&P 500	0.584	1.000			
Reward-to-risk ratio	1.426	−0.147			

REPRESENTATIVE HOLDINGS	SYMBOL	DESCRIPTION	WEIGHTING (%)
Highland Floating Rate–Institutional	XLFZX	Floating-rate senior secured bank loans	22.00
First Eagle SoGen Global–Institutional	SGIIX	Global mid-cap value equities & fixed income	11.00
Caldwell & Orkin Market Opportunity	COAGX	Long/short growth & value	11.00
Leuthold Core	LCORX	Tactical asset allocation	11.00
Merger	MERFX	Announced mergers & acquisitions arbitrage–large cap	11.00
PIMCO All Asset–Institutional†	PAAIX	Tactical asset allocation	11.00
Arbitrage	ARBFX	Mergers & acquisitions arbitrage	11.00
Hussman Strategic Growth	HSGFX	All-cap hedged equity	11.00
Cash (non-interest bearing account)		Cash	1.00

†Performance calculated as of fund inception in August 2002.

All returns are pretax and net of fees.

LOWER-VOLATILITY PORTFOLIO—GROWTH OF $1 MILLION

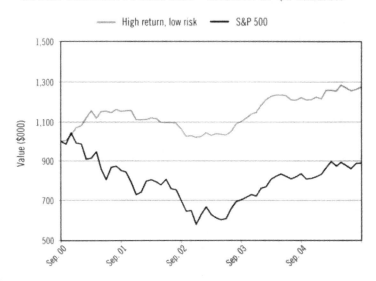

LOWER-VOLATILITY PORTFOLIO—MONTHLY RETURN

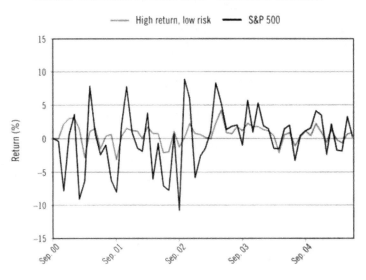

Source: © Legend Financial Advisors, 2005

FIGURE 15.14 *Comparative Return, Ultra-Low Risk, Lower-Volatility Model Portfolio*

RETURNS (%)

	1996	1997	1998	1999	2000	2001	2002	2003	2004	2005
January	0.89	0.97	0.40	0.88	0.14	2.20	1.16	0.69	1.50	-0.28
February	0.96	0.09	1.15	-0.46	1.88	1.06	-0.31	0.17	0.79	1.01
March	0.85	0.68	1.36	1.22	0.47	-2.04	1.53	0.36	0.38	0.01
April	0.85	0.39	0.40	1.38	0.63	0.39	0.81	2.15	-1.28	-0.47
May	1.22	1.31	0.45	0.21	1.41	1.32	0.60	3.52	0.40	0.42
June	0.39	1.30	1.41	0.91	0.76	-0.99	-1.85	1.07	0.70	0.81
July	-0.42	1.66	-0.06	0.51	0.30	0.53	-2.27	0.56	-0.67	
August	0.93	0.29	-0.91	0.30	1.11	0.71	0.37	1.28	0.16	
September	0.96	2.05	0.78	0.62	1.33	-2.43	-1.17	1.24	0.86	
October	1.01	0.31	0.00	-0.43	-0.12	-0.42	-0.17	1.83	0.35	
November	1.36	0.53	0.92	0.67	1.41	1.30	1.87	1.63	1.59	
December	0.43	0.68	1.19	1.62	2.14	1.02	0.93	1.41	0.70	
Annual Returns										
LVP*	9.83	10.73	7.29	7.66	12.09	2.57	1.42	17.07	5.59	1.50
S&P 500	22.93	33.34	28.66	21.08	-9.07	-11.86	-22.03	28.68	10.90	-0.81

*annually rebalanced.

	LVP	S&P 500		MODEL	S&P 500
Annualized standard deviation	3.413	17.541	Negative monthly returns	19.00	44.00
Annualized compound return	7.875	8.956	% of negative monthly returns	16.67%	38.60%
Correlation to S&P 500	0.524	1.000			
Reward-to-risk ratio	2.307	0.511			

REPRESENTATIVE HOLDINGS	SYMBOL	DESCRIPTION	WEIGHTING (%)
Highland Floating Rate–Institutional†	XLFZX	Floating-rate senior secured bank loans	49.50
First Eagle SoGen Global–Institutional	SGIIX	Global mid-cap value equities & fixed income	7.07
Caldwell & Orkin Market Opportunity	COAGX	Long/short growth & value	7.07
Leuthold Core	LCORX	Tactical asset allocation	7.07
Merger	MERFX	Announced mergers & acquisitions arbitrage–large cap	7.07
PIMCO All Asset–Institutional‡	PAAIX	Tactical asset allocation	7.07
Arbitrage**	ARBFX	Mergers & acquisitions arbitrage	7.07
Hussman Strategic Growth††	HSGFX	All-cap hedged equity	7.07
Cash (non-interest bearing account)		Cash	1.00

†Eaton Vance used until October 1999 for Highland.
‡Performance calculated as of fund inception in August 2002.
**Performance calculated as of fund inception in October 2000.
††Performance calculated as of fund inception in August 2000.

All returns are pretax and net of fees.

LOWER-VOLATILITY PORTFOLIO—GROWTH OF $1 MILLION

LOWER-VOLATILITY PORTFOLIO—MONTHLY RETURN

Source: © Legend Financial Advisors, 2005

CHAPTER 16

Reverse Mortgages in Distribution Planning

ROXANNE ALEXANDER AND
MICHAEL J. ANDERSON

Mark and Ann Davenport are one of the many baby boomer couples approaching retirement. He's 50, she's 53, and they have moderate savings. They're planning to retire soon and are visiting their financial planner for consultation on their retirement goals. They wish to determine whether their current assets can sustain them for their entire retirement. Jane Smith, their financial planner, reviews with the Davenports their current goals, assets, income, liabilities, and projected asset depletion and constructs a Monte Carlo analysis. Using moderate assumptions, she determines that their assets are likely to be able to sustain them throughout their retirement.

Smith does have some concerns, however, and she shares them with the Davenports: What if there are significant unforeseen expenditures that deplete the Davenports' funds? What if the market's doldrums extend even beyond the odds shown in the Monte Carlo analysis? What if ... ? What if ... ? Given these concerns, Smith wishes to model other options for the Davenports to consider.

The Davenports have mentioned to Smith that they want to live in their house throughout retirement. It is an asset of significant value. She wonders about the possibility of tapping into the equity in the house without taking out a home equity loan for which the Davenports would be required to make current payments. One way to do that, Smith realizes, is a reverse mortgage.

The Reverse Mortgage: A Viable Option?

Used properly, reverse mortgages may be a valuable retirement-planning tool, adding a significant income stream from most clients' biggest asset: their home. This chapter offers essential information about the issues—both basic and advanced—associated with reverse mortgages. It also presents a strategy analysis—designed to uncover both positive and negative consequences—for use in planning a reverse mortgage.

During the past few years, home equity has become a large part of the asset base of most home owners. In some areas of the country, housing prices have increased by as much as 126 percent since 2000 and are expected to increase in the future (see **FIGURE 16.1** for a table of major cities).[1]

With home prices experiencing such substantial growth since 2000, many home owners have secured home equity loans or lines of credit to finance large purchases. In several parts of the United States, housing returns exceeded the average stock or bond investment gains, especially during the tumultuous markets that marked the turn of the century.

FIGURE 16.1 *Housing Price Increases in Major Cities*

METRO AREA	MEDIAN PRICE	FIVE-YEAR PRICE CHANGE[a]	FORECASTED CHANGE[b]
Boston	$338,000	73.60%	8.00%
Chicago	254,000	49.60	8.30
Detroit	156,000	23.50	4.50
Los Angeles	418,000	125.70	5.80
Miami	246,000	106.00	16.40
New York	360,000	87.50	11.90
Philadelphia	199,000	71.00	11.40
San Francisco	576,000	82.00	14.40
Seattle	289,000	38.50	10.10
Washington, D.C.	335,000	99.00	14.90

[a] Q4 1999 through Q4 2004.
[b] Q1 2005 through Q1 2006.

Source: Fiserv CSW

FIGURE **16.2** *Major Market Indicies: Year-End 1999 to Year-End 2004*

INDEX	ANNUALIZED RETURN	FIVE-YEAR TOTAL RETURN
S&P 500	−2.30%	−10.98%
Nasdaq	−11.77	−46.53
Russell 3000	−1.60	−5.69
Dow Jones Industrial	0.65	3.32
Lehman Aggregate	7.71	44.97
Lehman Intermediate	7.21	41.65

Source: Morningstar Principia

FIGURE 16.2 offers a profile of the returns of the major market indexes from December 31, 1999, to December 31, 2004.

As the population ages, many retirees are finding that their homes may be the only hope of funding the cost of longevity. A reverse mortgage is a planning option available for people over age 62 who have limited cash (or who have used up their liquid assets) and have a large equity position in their home. Although this option has existed since the mid-1980s, less than 1 percent of qualified home owners actually had a reverse mortgage as of 2001.[2]

What Is a Reverse Mortgage?

Reverse mortgages allow home owners to borrow against the equity in their home while still maintaining home ownership. Unlike a conventional mortgage, no monthly payments are involved. Instead, the lender makes payments to the borrower. The borrower must completely own the home or be able to use the initial proceeds of the reverse mortgage to pay off any small existing debt on the property. The borrower does not have to sell his home, and he may use the proceeds for any purpose, including medical expenses or day-to-day living expenses. The Federal Housing Administration (FHA) sets a borrowing limit of approximately $312,000, which may be received as a lump sum, monthly payments, or a line of credit.[3] Lines of credit and monthly payments may be combined. Borrowers may obtain larger sums from private lenders, depending on the value of the home.

Types of Reverse Mortgages

Several types of reverse mortgages are available. They're offered by different organizations and may have different eligibility requirements. Essentially, there are three types of reverse mortgages:

- ❑ Federally insured home equity conversion mortgages (HECMs), administered by the Department of Housing and Urban Development (HUD)
- ❑ Single-purpose reverse mortgages, offered through state or local government
- ❑ Proprietary products, offered by banks, mortgage companies, or other private lending institutions.

HUD encouraged an expansion in the reverse mortgage market with the introduction of the HECM program, through which the agency insures reverse mortgage loans made under the terms of the program's rules.[4] The HECM resulted from the National Housing Act of 1987. The other proprietary reverse mortgage products are also commonly available through Fannie Mae (Home Keeper) and loan originator Financial Freedom Senior Funding Corporation.[5]

Home Equity Conversion Mortgages

The FHA home equity conversion mortgage (HECM) is the most common form of the reverse mortgage.[6] It's available through many different lenders, and it's the only one insured by the federal government. HECMs have no asset or income limitations to qualify.[7]

Section 203b (HUD). This section of the National Housing Act sets home value limits by county. For 2005, the HECM loan limits ranged from $172,632 to $312,895. If a home is worth more than these limits, the geographic county limit is used to determine the eligibility amount. For example, if a county limit is $172,632 and the house is worth $250,000, then the assumed value is $172,632.

Fannie Mae Reverse Mortgage Products

Fannie Mae developed its proprietary reverse mortgage products in the 1990s. One—Home Keeper—is used to provide an income stream based on equity in a current residence; the other—Home Keeper for Home Purchase—is used to provide an income stream to purchase a residence. Home Keeper for Home Purchase allows a homeowner to use the equity in the current home to directly purchase a new home, as well as to establish a line of credit to draw down the equity in the new home. This process can decrease costs because it's completed with one transaction.[8] The eligibility requirements for the Home Keeper reverse mortgages are almost identical to those for the HECM. The differences between the two lie more in the FHA insurance that backs the HECM and in the calculation of the loan cap amount.[9]

Financial Freedom Products

Financial Freedom Senior Funding Corporation is among the larger and most prominent reverse mortgage loan originators in the country. Its proprietary product, called the Financial Freedom Cash Account, has a variety of options that allow seniors to access equity in their homes.[10] Both Financial Freedom and Fannie Mae lenders may also originate HECMs, but each has its own proprietary products.

Eligibility Requirements

To be eligible for each of these products, the borrower must
- ❑ be at least 62 years old
- ❑ own the property being mortgaged
- ❑ occupy the property being mortgaged as his primary residence
- ❑ receive counseling regarding reverse mortgages from a counselor approved by the HECM program or by Fannie Mae (for the HECM or Fannie Mae products)

Financial Freedom allows counseling to be provided by an independent counselor.[11] **FIGURE 16.3** summarizes the eligibility requirements for all three product categories.

The property being mortgaged must also meet certain criteria:

FIGURE 16.3 *Borrower Eligibility Requirements*

REQUIREMENTS	HECM	FANNIE MAE HOME KEEPER	FINANCIAL FREEDOM CASH ACCOUNT
Age	62	62	62
Ownership	Yes	Yes	Yes
Property	Primary residence	Primary residence	Primary residence
Counseling	Approved counselor	Approved counselor	Independent counselor

❑ The mortgaged property must be a one-family residence, a detached home, or a structure with no more than four "home" units (for example, a conjoined townhouse).

❑ If the property is a cooperative or mobile home, it must meet HUD standards.

❑ Overall, the property must meet minimum local ordinances for repair/cleanliness standards. If it does not, the borrower may fund the repairs from the reverse mortgage payments.[12]

Key Product Differences

Although similar in most respects, the three product categories are different in certain key ways:

❑ The HECM is the only one that's government insured.

❑ All of the products offer a variety of ways for the borrower to receive the funds, including a lump sum, a credit line, monthly payments, or a combination of these. The major differences lie in the interest rates charged: the HECM uses a variable Treasury bill interest rate plus an added margin rate, the Fannie Mae products use variable certificate of deposit rates plus a margin rate, and the Financial Freedom products use a variable Libor (London interbank offered rate) plus margin.

❑ The maximum benefit a borrower can receive from HECM is $312,895, depending on the geographical area.[13] The Fannie Mae Home Keeper maximum benefit is $359,650,[14] and the Financial Freedom Cash Account loan amount maximum is approximately 30 percent of the home value. (For example, on a $3 million home, this amount can be significantly more than the maximums allowed with HECM or Fannie Mae products.)

❑ The HECM and Fannie Mae products do not affect Social Security or Medicare eligibility; nor do they generally affect Supplemental Security Income (SSI) or Medicaid benefits (payments must be spent within a reasonable time after receipt). (See "Tax Issues," page 293.) The effects of using the Financial Freedom products with respect to Social Security, Medicare, SSI, and Medicaid benefits are typically also negligible. To avoid compromising eligibility for Medicaid or SSI, borrowers should avoid accumulating the payments.

FIGURE 16.4 summarizes how the features of the three product categories compare. Note that the Financial Freedom products are not available in every state, but the HECM and the Fannie Mae products are.

Maximum Mortgage Amounts

The amount that may be borrowed through a reverse mortgage depends on a variety of factors across the different products. For HECM and Fannie

FIGURE **16.4** *Key Features*

	HECM	FANNIE MAE HOME KEEPER	FINANCIAL FREEDOM CASH ACCOUNT
Government insurance	Yes	Yes	Yes
Flexibility	Lump sum, credit line, or both	Lump sum, credit line, or both	Lump sum, credit line, or both
Interest rate	T-bill + margin	Variable CD + margin	Libor + margin
Maximum benefit	$312,895	$359,650	30% of property value (approx.)
Effects on SS/ Medicare benefits	None	None	None
Effects on Medicaid/SSI	None*	None*	None*
Available in all states	Typically	Typically	No

*Specific tax situations may be affected differently.

Mae—whose maximums are $312,895 and $359,650, respectively—the driving factors are the maximum claim amount (derived by the location and the value of the home), age of the borrower, and interest rate. The amount that may be borrowed on Fannie Mae products is derived by a formula that factors in age of the borrower, the value of the home, and the adjusted value of home. "Adjusted value of home" is a key difference between HECM and Fannie Mae, because Fannie Mae bases its lending limit on the average home price in the United States and not on regional prices. Financial Freedom product maximums have a much higher cap, but it works out to approximately 30 percent of the home value.

To illustrate the differences, let's consider an example. Suppose a client, age 75, has a $3 million home in Seattle (ZIP code 98122). Approximately, how much may he borrow with each of the three products? All of the different agencies and lenders have a variety of reverse mortgage

FIGURE **16.5** *Loan Maximums*

AGE
75

HOME
City and state: Seattle, WA
County: King
Home value: $3,000,000
Liens: $0

	REVERSE MORTGAGE PROGRAMS		
	FHA/HUD MONTHLY	FANNIE MAE HOME KEEPER	FINANCIAL FREEDOM CASH ACCOUNT
Cash available	$185,890	$136,994	$924,378
or Monthly income available	$1,215	$1,185	N/A
or Credit line available	$185,890	$136,994	$924,378
Annualized growth rate	5.48%	N/A	5.00%
Credit line value in 5 years	$242,756	$136,994	$1,179,767
Credit line value in 10 years	$317,020	$136,994	$1,505,715

Note: All maximums are estimates.

Source: Reverse Mortgage Calculator at www.financialfreedom.com

calculators. We found Financial Freedom's calculator to be the most user-friendly. **FIGURE 16.5** shows how much this client may borrow.

Reverse Mortgage Costs

The largest differences among the reverse mortgage products available are the costs of each product and the maximum benefit each provides.

The costs break down as follows:
- ❑ Interest rate applied to the loan
- ❑ Mortgage insurance (HECM)
- ❑ Origination fees and/or points
- ❑ Service fees (annually or monthly)
- ❑ Closing costs (inspections, appraisals, credit checks, et cetera)
- ❑ Restructuring fees

❑ Shared-appreciation fee
❑ Attorney and title fees
❑ Shared-equity ("maturity") fees

HECM reverse mortgages charge an up-front mortgage insurance premium equal to 2 percent of the loan amount and a 0.5 percent annual service fee. The lender also typically charges an origination fee (no more than $2,000, or 2 percent of the maximum loan amount). None of these includes the interest that is added to the loan balance, typically done monthly.

To get a better sense of these costs, let's consider an example. Assume a client with a $500,000 home decides to get a HECM. He can borrow $100,000 on the home. The up-front cost will be $2,000 plus an annual fee of $500 (2 percent up front, 0.5 percent annually). These costs do not include any interest accrued on the loan balance or any origination fee, which could come to an additional $2,000. Assume also that the current interest rate for a HECM is 5.3 percent: 2.3 percent (three-month T-bill rate) + 3 percent margin interest rate. In the first year, $5,300 will be added to the existing balance. This amount will increase with the value of the home; the amount that can be borrowed will likely increase as well. All reverse mortgage products have adjustable rates, but the rates are typically capped to limit how much they can be adjusted during the loan's lifetime. A restructuring fee of $20–$35 applies if the borrower decides he wants to change the amount borrowed or how he receives the funds. Unlike other products, a HECM offers the flexibility to make such changes frequently. The borrower would also have to pay for an appraisal. One big advantage of the HECM and part of the reason for its greater costs is that HUD will pay the lender the difference between the home value and the loan balance when the owner dies or if the owner sells the property (in cases where the loan exceeds the value of the property).[15]

Fannie Mae Home Keeper product costs are slightly different than those of HECM. Loan origination and closing costs may be financed by the loan. The products we researched require no mortgage insurance, and the origination fees are no more than $2,000 or 2 percent of the property's appraised value. In addition to obtaining an appraisal, the borrower must get the home inspected. The lender may also check the borrower's credit and charge other miscellaneous closing costs.

Financial Freedom offers the widest variety of cost options in its proprietary products. Its Cash Account product has three options: the Simply Zero option, the Zero Point option, and the Standard Option. Costs are as follows:

❑ Simply Zero has no origination fee and no closing costs (except

FIGURE 16.6 *Product Costs*

COSTS	HECM	FANNIE MAE HOME KEEPER	FINANCIAL FREEDOM CASH ACCOUNT SIMPLY ZERO	ZERO POINT	STANDARD
Mortgage insurance	Lesser of 2% of home value or maximum claim amount	No	No	No	No
Origination fees/points	Lesser of $2,000 or 2% of home value (may be financed)	Lesser of $2,000 or 2% of home value (may be financed)	None	None	Lesser of $2,000 or 2% of home value (may be financed)
Interest rate	T-bill + margin	Variable CD + margin	Libor + margin (adjusted semi-annually)	Libor + margin (adjusted semi-annually)	Libor + margin (adjusted semi-annually)
Annual fee	0.5%	None	Yes	Yes	Yes
Restructuring fees	$20–$35	None	Yes	Yes	Yes
Closing costs	Various	Various	None (except state and local taxes)	$3,500 (not including taxes)	None (except state and local taxes)
Miscellaneous	Gov't insured; unused credit line grows by 5%	No credit line growth	Any closing costs may be financed in loan	Unused line of credit growth rate of 5%; any costs may be financed in loan	Unused line of credit growth rate of 5%; any costs may be financed in loan

for local or state taxes), but it has a semiannual adjustable rate: Libor + 5 percent margin.

❑ The Zero Point option has no origination fee, with closing costs not to exceed $3,500 (excluding local or state taxes), and it has a rate of Libor + 5 percent adjustable semiannually. The difference here is that the Zero Point option includes an unused line of credit growth rate of 5 percent, and the borrower is required to draw only 75 percent of the amount available (versus 100 percent with the Simply Zero option).

❑ The Standard Option's origination fee is a scaled percentage of the home value (maximum 2 percent). This is an open-ended revolving line of credit—the unused portion grows by 5 percent. Again, it's an adjustable rate, for which the cap in 2005 was approximately 13 percent.

FIGURE 16.6 summarizes the costs of the different products.

Obtaining the Loan

If you've determined that your client actually needs a reverse mortgage, how does he go about getting one? The process is fairly similar to that of getting a home mortgage. The big difference is that reverse mortgage lenders require the borrower to attend a form of counseling before getting the loan. As part of the counseling, potential borrowers learn about other options and receive information to help them determine whether a reverse mortgage is right for them, although one would hope that the choice has already been discussed with a financial adviser. Once the borrower completes the counseling, a certificate is awarded to the prospective borrower. This certificate (issued by either HECM or Fannie Mae Home Keeper) will give the borrower access to a lender.

The next step is to select and contact a lender and set up a loan interview. Approved lenders are available on the agency websites or by phone for each of the major products (HECM, Fannie Mae, and Financial Freedom). The lender will provide the borrower with a loan application, a loan agreement, a good-faith estimate, and any other required documents. Once these documents have been filled out and submitted, the lender will typically set up an appraisal, followed by an inspection. The lender will also help the borrower research to see that the property has a clear title and check for any other encumbrances. Typically, once the loan process has been finalized, the borrower will have a set time period within which to close out the loan. The borrower should keep in mind that all rates on reverse mortgages are adjustable.

Cost-Benefit Analysis

Because of the high fees associated with the transaction, reverse mortgages should be used only as a last resort. These types of loans are costly because they're rising-debt loans, meaning interest is added to the principal balance each month. And lenders charge several fees, including origination fees, and closing costs can add more than $15,000 to the total costs. As a result of the capped loan amount, the fees in some cases can end up being a large percentage of the actual loan (ranging from 10 percent to 15 percent), depending on the loan amount and the fees required by the lender.[16]

The loan does not have to be paid back until the borrower moves out of the residence or dies. This payback clause extends to the living spouse of the original borrower. The provision may be a disadvantage to the borrower's family members, however, if they can no longer inherit the home or cannot afford to pay off the loan at the time of death and need to sell the home to do so. In some circumstances, the better option for the borrower may be to trade down into a lower-cost home and pocket the difference. The borrower should evaluate the possibility of selling the home and renting versus taking the reverse mortgage.

In many cases, while the reverse mortgage is in effect, the value of the home may increase over and above the principal borrowed plus added interest. The heirs may refinance the gains or sell the home to pay off the reverse mortgage. It's important to read the shared-appreciation provision in the contract. This provision gives the lender a share of the appreciation in the property between the date the loan is closed and the date it ends. In cases where the value remains the same or declines, the lender ends up owning most or all of the home equity, although the owner is still responsible for maintaining the property and for paying the taxes and insurance. If the borrower fails to pay these expenses, the reverse mortgage lender may require repayment. Contrary to popular belief, the lender does not want the actual home as repayment.[17]

The decision to leverage a home may have negative psychological effects on the borrower. Many elderly people have saved extensively to pay off their home, and they may have emotional attachment to the property. They may wish to pass on the home to heirs and prefer to maintain debt-free ownership. The thought of borrowing money early in their retirement and possibly needing extra cash flow for medical expenses later on is not very comforting.

Of course, reverse mortgages also bring benefits. For example, the debt may not be passed on to heirs, and none of the borrower's other assets are affected by the reverse mortgage loan. The amount the borrower owes may not exceed the value of the property at the time of repayment. If the borrower lives longer than the actuarial table predicts, he continues to receive payments.[18]

Reverse mortgages may be worth considering if the borrower does not wish to leave his current home or cannot find suitable alternative living quarters. Comparable properties are likely to have appreciated significantly over time. If the borrower does not plan to leave the residence to heirs, then a reverse mortgage may be an option. Reverse mortgages are relatively expensive for the first two to three years, so it's important to evaluate life expectancy and how long the borrower plans to keep the loan.

When it comes to interest rates, points, and payment terms, the yardsticks used to analyze reverse mortgages are similar to those used for traditional mortgages. However, reverse mortgages are more complex, and the eventualities are not always obvious.

Tax Issues

Proceeds of reverse mortgage loans are tax-free and do not affect Social Security or Medicare benefits because the proceeds are not considered income. However, the effect on need-based public assistance (Medicaid, SSI) has been debated. If the borrower retains or saves the proceeds beyond the month of receipt, a potential problem could arise if this money is counted as an asset for eligibility purposes.[19] Unlike the interest on conventional mortgages, interest on the reverse mortgage loan may be deducted only in the year the loan interest is paid, which is at the end of the loan. The borrower does not get a yearly interest deduction as do holders of conventional mortgages.[20]

Checking for Fit

Situations often arise when it may be quite appropriate for planners to consider the use of a reverse mortgage to address the cash flow needs of their clients. These mortgages are clearly a valuable solution for seniors whose only asset is their home and who have no other sources of income to draw on as their bills are rising. They're likewise a suitable choice when other sources of income are not keeping up with living expenses. But other circumstances aren't quite so clear-cut. The following examples offer ways of assessing whether a reverse mortgage is the right choice.

A Reverse Mortgage? Yes

Let's have a look into the future. The Davenports—the couple we met at the beginning of the chapter—are now ages 74 and 77 and retired. They have weathered the last 25 years modestly, but recent down markets have reduced their assets significantly. Adding to the unexpected depletion, Mark recently took $150,000 out of their accounts and bought a one-third interest in a penthouse condominium, but its value has dropped to $50,000 (the condo market finally went bust).

Jane Smith, the Davenports' financial planner, has since retired, and her protégé, John Doe, has taken over her practice. Servicing the Davenports as clients has become a very simple matter. They come in only once a year to review their overall investments. Since Doe took over the practice, it has become more investment oriented and he rarely reviews the Davenports' capital needs to see how they're doing. The Davenports have been reviewing their information and are starting to become concerned that they may not have sufficient assets to maintain their lifestyle of $100,000 per year after tax. This prompts a visit to John. After taking the Davenports' current information, John decides to give Jane a call out of retirement to help him, as capital needs are not his strongest area.

The Davenports' assets, income, and other assumptions are as follows:

- ❑ Mark's IRA: $320,000
- ❑ Ann's IRA: $65,000
- ❑ Joint investment assets: $230,000
- ❑ Checking/savings: $75,000
- ❑ Home value: $900,000
- ❑ Portfolio is currently 50 percent equity investments and 50 percent bonds
- ❑ Annual after-tax need in today's dollars: $100,000
- ❑ Total Social Security benefits approximately: $42,000
- ❑ Annual shortfall: $58,000 after taxes
- ❑ Live in Seattle (ZIP code 98122)

John and Jane analyze the Davenports' information and assume a 7 percent nominal rate of return (or 4 percent real) on the Davenports' portfolio. They plug the Davenports' data into their planning software and come up with a potential shortfall when Mark reaches age 87. Mark and Ann's families have a history of longevity, so John and Jane use a mortality estimate of 92 for Anne and 90 for Mark. **FIGURE 16.7** illustrates the results of Mark and Ann's simple straight-line estimate of expenditures.

Figure 16.7 shows that even if the Davenports earn the assumed rate of return, with no fluctuation, they will likely see a shortfall when Mark is age 87 and Ann is 90. If they have subpar returns over the next few years, the potential for problems will be even greater.

John and Jane consider the Davenports' options. They could recommend increasing the equity allocation for potentially higher long-term

FIGURE **16.7** *Estimate of Expenditures*

EVENT OR AGES	YEAR	BEGINNING PORTFOLIO VALUE PRIORITY	ADDITIONS TO ASSETS	POST-RETIREMENT INCOME	INVESTMENT EARNINGS	TAXES	GOALS/ FUNDS USED RETIREMENT	ENDING PORTFOLIO VALUE
75/78	2005	$690,000	$0	$42,000	$44,613	$6,931	$100,000	$669,682
76/79	2006	669,682	0	43,260	43,027	6,901	103,000	646,068
77/80	2007	646,068	0	44,558	41,203	6,846	106,090	618,893
78/81	2008	618,893	0	45,895	39,120	6,673	109,273	587,962
79/82	2009	587,962	0	47,271	36,773	6,697	112,551	552,758
80/83	2010	552,758	0	48,690	34,112	6,537	115,927	513,095
81/84	2011	513,095	0	50,150	31,056	7,378	119,405	467,517
82/85	2012	467,517	0	51,655	26,812	19,079	122,987	403,918
83/86	2013	403,918	0	53,204	22,017	20,783	126,677	331,679
84/87	2014	331,679	0	54,800	16,680	21,407	130,477	251,275
85/88	2015	251,275	0	56,444	10,756	22,049	134,392	162,034
86/89	2016	162,034	0	58,138	4,198	22,711	138,423	63,236
87/90	2017	63,236	0	59,882	0	12,679	x 110,438	0
88/91	2018	0	0	61,678	0	2,871	x 58,807	0
89/92	2019	0	0	63,529	0	2,957	x 60,572	0
90/93	2020	0	0	65,435	0	3,046	x 62,389	0
Ann's plan ends	2021	$0	$0	$67,398	$0	$3,137	x $64,260	$0
Mark's plan ends	2022	$0	$0	$34,710	$0	$1,554	x $33,156	$0

Source: MoneyGuidePro, Portfolio Value Chart

returns. Jane feels the Davenports will not like this option because the change will also increase the volatility of the portfolio and the potential investment losses could be greater. John convinces her to rerun the analysis,

FIGURE **16.8** *Estimate of Expenditures, With Higher Equity Allocation*

EVENT OR AGES	YEAR	BEGINNING PORTFOLIO VALUE PRIORITY	ADDITIONS TO ASSETS	POST-RETIREMENT INCOME	INVESTMENT EARNINGS	TAXES	GOALS/ FUNDS USED RETIREMENT	ENDING PORTFOLIO VALUE
75/78	2005	$690,000	$0	$42,000	$54,213	$7,448	$100,000	$678,766
76/79	2006	678,766	0	43,260	53,067	7,438	103,000	664,655
77/80	2007	664,655	0	44,558	51,668	7,404	106,090	647,387
78/81	2008	647,387	0	45,895	49,989	7,221	109,273	626,776
79/82	2009	626,776	0	47,271	48,023	7,338	112,551	602,181
80/83	2010	602,181	0	48,690	45,701	7,201	115,927	573,443
81/84	2011	573,443	0	50,150	43,014	7,044	119,405	540,157
82/85	2012	540,157	0	51,655	39,436	12,534	122,987	495,727
83/86	2013	495,727	0	53,204	34,708	20,537	126,677	436,425
84/87	2014	436,425	0	54,800	29,319	21,407	130,477	368,660
85/88	2015	368,660	0	56,444	23,213	22,049	134,392	291,877
86/89	2016	291,877	0	58,138	16,319	22,711	138,423	205,200
87/90	2017	205,200	0	59,882	8,563	23,392	142,576	107,677
88/91	2018	107,677	0	61,678	0	23,696	x 145,660	0
89/92	2019	0	0	63,529	0	2,957	x 60,572	0
90/93	2020	0	0	65,435	0	3,046	x 62,389	0
Ann's plan ends	2021	$0	$0	$67,398	$0	$3,137	x $64,260	$0
Mark's plan ends	2022	$0	$0	$34,710	$0	$1,554	x $33,156	$0

Source: MoneyGuidePro, Portfolio Value Chart

using a higher rate of return (8 percent) by increasing the equity portion to approximately 80 percent. **FIGURE 16.8** shows the results.

At best, the increased equity allocation gives the Davenports an extra year of required income. A basic Monte Carlo analysis on both scenarios sets up the probability of success at less than 40 percent, with a greater than 60 percent probability of failure for both the original investment mix and the increased equity allocation.[21] Even if the Davenports lower their income need to 90 percent of their current expenditures, the probability of success in both scenarios is less than 40 percent.

The Davenports have always wanted to stay in their home—their most valuable asset. Jane and John consider possible reverse mortgage options for the Davenports to increase their income stream enough to make a difference in the future. The Davenports will be able to borrow approximately $185,890, using a HECM mortgage through HUD, $114,904 through Fannie Mae, and $223,935 through a Financial Freedom Cash Account reverse mortgage.[22] Let's assume they choose the Financial Freedom product because of the amount available to borrow and the growing credit line. Jane and John also add back in the $50,000 condo investment since Mark is sure he can sell it. If the Davenports let the credit line grow for 10 years to $383,005 before drawing on it, the odds are much more favorable that they will not outlive their assets and still retain ownership of their home (see **FIGURE 16.9**, pages 298–299).

With the reverse mortgage as part of the plan, Jane feels more comfortable about the Davenports' long-term outlook than she does without it. Monte Carlo analysis provides a 60 percent probability of success once the buffer from the reverse mortgage is factored in. If the Davenports spend only 90 percent of the forecast—which is feasible because as they age more they will travel less—the probability that they will be able to accomplish their goals goes up to 90 percent. For the Davenports, a reverse mortgage is a viable solution.

A Reverse Mortgage? Maybe Not

Doris Green, married for more than 50 years, was recently widowed. She is 82. She has lived in her present Florida home for the last 15 years and is emotionally attached to the home because it's on the water and has appreciated significantly in value over the years. She remembers paying about $200,000 for it; it is now worth well over $1 million. She would like to leave the house to her 48-year-old daughter, Carole, who lives in New York. Doris is very proud of her daughter, who is her only child.

Doris believes that Carole will be ready to move to Florida shortly because she has been practicing law for more than 20 years, has accumulated a large amount of savings, and is ready to slow down. Doris thinks Carole will have about $2 million in assets once she sells her apartment in New York. Carole is divorced with no children.

FIGURE **16.9** *Estimate of Expenditures With Reverse Mortgage Loan*

EVENT OR AGES	YEAR	BEGINNING PORTFOLIO VALUE		ADDITIONS TO ASSETS
		ASSIGNED	PRIORITY	
75/78	2005	$0	$740,001	$0
76/79	2006	0	724,241	0
77/80	2007	0	705,436	0
78/81	2008	0	683,329	0
79/82	2009	0	657,782	0
80/83	2010	0	628,140	0
81/84	2011	0	594,318	0
82/85	2012	0	555,966	0
83/86	2013	0	512,713	0
84/87	2014	0	459,800	0
85/88	2015	0	389,785	0
86/89	2016	0	311,059	383,005
87/90	2017	0	648,951	0
88/91	2018	0	598,145	0
89/92	2019	0	541,195	0
90/93	2020	0	477,614	0
Ann's plan ends	2021	$0	$406,916	$0
Mark's plan ends	2022	$0	$328,569	$0

Doris has $250,000 in savings invested in a taxable money market account, but, of course, she is not sure how long she will live. Doris is not averse to investing in the stock market, but she doesn't know how. She has had minimal health problems and has a very old long-term care policy, which she doubts she will need to use. Her parents died at 85 and 73 of natural causes. Her father died of a heart attack, and Doris suspects

POST-RETIREMENT INCOME	INVESTMENT EARNINGS	TAXES	GOALS/FUNDS USED RETIREMENT	ENDING PORTFOLIO VALUE
$42,000	$49,726	$7,486	$100,000	$724,241
43,260	48,423	7,488	103,000	705,436
44,558	46,892	7,468	106,090	683,329
45,895	45,114	7,283	109,273	657,782
47,271	43,085	7,447	112,551	628,140
48,690	40,746	7,330	115,927	594,318
50,150	38,094	7,192	119,405	555,966
51,655	35,106	7,026	122,987	512,713
53,204	31,457	10,898	126,677	459,800
54,800	26,654	20,992	130,477	389,785
56,444	21,270	22,049	134,392	311,059
58,138	44,600	9,428	138,423	648,951
59,882	41,095	9,206	142,576	598,145
61,678	37,166	8,941	146,853	541,195
63,529	32,780	8,630	151,259	477,614
65,435	27,903	8,239	155,797	406,916
$67,398	$22,500	$7,774	$160,471	$328,569
$34,710	$12,705	$24,898	$165,285	$185,802

that she will pass on the same way. She is thinking of taking out a reverse mortgage just in case she runs out of money, but she spends only about $30,000 per year and most of this goes to maintenance and property taxes on the house. She receives $850 per month from Social Security.

Doris has several options available to her other than taking out a reverse mortgage. Because Doris may not need extra cash flow over and above her

FIGURE **16.10** *Current Versus 60/40 Allocation*

GOAL	PRIORITY AND ESTIMATE CURRENT PLAN	PERCENTAGE OF GOAL FUNDED SCENARIO 1
Retirement living expense	95%	100%
Safety margin	Current dollars: $0	$34,439
Value at end of plan	Future dollars: $0	$52,091

Source: MoneyGuidePro

money market fund (other than to provide a psychological cushion), the costs of obtaining a reverse mortgage outweigh the potential value. Because Carole has significant assets and will be inheriting the home, Doris could arrange for Carole to pay the property tax and maintenance on the home in the meantime and thereby free up extra cash for Doris.

If Doris lives another 13 years and her needs continue as they've been, one of her options could be to change her allocation from 100 percent money market to at least a 60/40 fixed/equity mix (let's assume an approximate total return of 7 percent) to have any reasonable cushion. She should avoid taking a reverse mortgage unless she has a large unforeseen medical problem or a large expense, because she will likely manage to live on what she has and be able to leave the home to her daughter free and clear. She can also take comfort in the fact that she has this large asset—her home—available if absolutely necessary, but she does not need to access equity at this time as long as she changes her investment allocation. **FIGURE 16.10** shows reasonable attainment of Doris's goals, given an increased equity allocation to her portfolio. The current plan shows Doris leaving her money in money market funds only. Scenario 1 results reflect the changes to a 40 percent stock allocation.

FIGURE 16.11 shows the flow of Doris's assets and goals, with her portfolio invested at 60 percent fixed income and 40 percent equity (7 percent total return).

For Doris to fund approximately 90 percent of her goals, a Monte Carlo analysis shows the probability of success at 95 percent if she changes her allocation to a 62 percent fixed, 38 percent equity allocation.[23] This mix would enable Doris to meet her goals without having to tap into home equity.

FIGURE **16.11** *Assets and Goals*

EVENT OR AGES	YEAR	BEGINNING PORTFOLIO VALUE PRIORITY	POST-RETIREMENT INCOME	INVESTMENT EARNINGS	TAXES	GOALS/ FUNDS USED RETIREMENT	ENDING PORTFOLIO VALUE
82	2005	$250,000	$10,200	$16,045	$1,649	$30,000	$244,596
83	2006	244,596	10,506	15,627	1,592	30,900	238,237
84	2007	238,237	10,821	15,141	1,527	31,827	230,845
85	2008	230,845	11,146	14,582	1,306	32,782	222,485
86	2009	222,485	11,480	13,954	1,462	33,765	212,692
87	2010	212,692	11,825	13,225	1,345	34,778	201,618
88	2011	201,618	12,179	12,405	1,215	35,822	189,166
89	2012	189,166	12,545	11,488	1,090	36,896	175,212
90	2013	175,212	12,921	10,464	986	38,003	159,609
91	2014	159,609	13,309	9,324	870	39,143	142,228
92	2015	142,228	13,708	8,059	741	40,317	122,936
93	2016	122,936	14,119	6,658	599	41,527	101,587
94	2017	101,587	14,543	5,113	443	42,773	78,027
Doris's plan ends	2018	$78,027	$14,979	$3,412	$271	$44,056	$52,091

Proceed With Care

Although the many reverse mortgage products on the market are very similar, there are numerous differences that borrowers and advisers should be aware of before going forward. Reverse mortgages can be a useful planning tool for clients who have limited or unviable alternatives, but given the high costs and lack of history on the outcomes of these loans, they should be used as a last resort.

There are several options available for advisers and their clients to consider before taking equity out of a home and having to incur the associated costs.

❑ Plan for other options, such as giving equities a greater weight in the investment allocation mix, if the client's risk tolerance permits.

❑ If the client plans to leave the home to heirs who have liquid assets, have the heirs lend the client money in return for the asset on death.

❑ Sell the home, downsize, and either invest the difference or use it for current needs.

❑ Consider suitable annuity products that may provide the income stream needed without the high costs.

In certain situations, however, there may be little choice. A reverse mortgage may be the best answer, for example, for clients who cannot manage to move because of disability. Or it may be impossible for them to find a comparable home for a lower price. If a reverse mortgage is selected, advisers and clients should be aware of all of the costs. Although some costs often can be "hidden" away within the loan, others are quite clearly spelled out and must be considered. Most important, advisers and clients must educate themselves about the risks and potential pitfalls before making the decision to use reverse mortgages.

Chapter Notes

1. Information pulled from Sarah Max, "This Year's Hottest Zip Codes," http://money.cnn.com/pf/features/lists/topzipcodes/index.html.

2. Andrew D. Eschtruth and Long C. Tran, "A Primer on Reverse Mortgages," *Just the Facts on Retirement Issues* no. 3 (October 2001): 1–2.

3. Joanna Sabatini, "Reverse Mortgages Surge Ahead," *Investment News* (May 3, 2004). Details are also available on the HUD website, http://www.hud.gov/offices/hsg/sfh/hecm/hecmabou.cfm, which explains that the borrowed amount is capped at approximately $312,000, depending on geographic area, and may be increased by 150 percent for traditionally high-priced areas like Alaska, Hawaii, and Guam.

4. Victoria Wong and Norma Paz Garcia, "There's No Place Like Home: The Implications of Reverse Mortgages on Seniors in California," *Consumer's Union of U.S., Inc.* West Coast Regional Office, 1999. p. 6.

5. Information pulled from AARP website: www.aarp.org/revmort.

6. Information pulled from Long Term Care Link website: http://www.longtermcarelink.net/files/reverse.html.

7. Information pulled from HUD website: http://www.hud.gov/offices/hsg/sfh/hecm/hecmabou.cfm. The HUD website on reverse mortgages is a valuable information source that can give a client a preliminary introduction to the HECM

reverse mortgage without committing to a counselor or private institution loan originator. There are also links to find counselors and lenders when the borrower is ready.

8. Wong and Garcia, "There's No Place Like Home," p. 9.

9. Material in this section is referenced from Fannie Mae's *A Guide to Understanding Reverse Mortgages,* available for download at www.fanniemae.com.

10. Information pulled from Financial Freedom website: http://www.finan cialfreedom.com, which has detailed materials about the government products available through HECM, Fannie Mae, and Financial Freedom's own proprietary products.

11. Referenced at multiple sites and materials: http://www.hud.gov/offices/hsg/ sfh/hecm/hecmhome.cfm, http://www.aarp.org/revmort/, and Fannie Mae's *A Guide to Understanding Reverse Mortgages,* available for download at www.fan niemae.com.

12. Referenced at multiple sites and materials: http://www.hud.gov/offices/hsg/ sfh/hecm/hecmhome.cfm, http://www.aarp.org/revmort/, and Fannie Mae's *A Guide to Understanding Reverse Mortgages,* available for download at www.fan niemae.com.

13. Information from HUD website: http://www.hud.gov/offices/hsg/sfh/hecm/ hecmabou.cfm.

14. Fannie Mae's *A Guide to Understanding Reverse Mortgages,* available for download at www.fanniemae.com.

15. Information from HUD website: http://www.hud.gov/offices/hsg/sfh/hecm/ hecmabou.cfm.

16. Federal Trade Commission, Facts for Consumers. "Reverse Mortgages: Pro- ceed with Care," Bureau of Consumer Protection, Office of Consumer and Business Education, November 2003.

17. Eschtruth and Tran, "A Primer on Reverse Mortgages," p.1.

18. Information pulled from HUD website: www.hud.gov/buying/rvrsmort .cfm.

19. Wong and Garcia, "There's No Place Like Home," p. 19.

20. Thornburg Mortgage, www.thornburgmortgage.com.

21. Results obtained from MoneyGuidePro's Monte Carlo analysis tool, www .moneyguidepro.com.

22. Reverse Mortgage Calculator available at www.financialfreedom.com.

23. Results obtained from MoneyGuidePro's Monte Carlo analysis tool.

CHAPTER **17**

Life Insurance Benefits— No Waiting

DOUGLAS HEAD

In the viatical and life-settlement industry, revolutions are not uncommon. There is little to indicate that the days ahead won't change this industry as radically as it has changed in the recent past. But this is a book meant to inspire thought. So here is the radical thought: life insurance has value like other assets and consumers ought to know what their policies are really worth.

When you talk to people about life insurance—in fact, even when you talk to a life insurance salesperson—the discussion generally revolves around the idea that the policy sold today will pay a claim when you die. When the producer of life insurance, the agent, discusses the value of insurance, he will emphasize that point. If you have a concern about the value of your life or the retention of your assets, you'll consider the purchase soberly and seriously.

In this discussion, the agent will tell you a few other things too. There are different kinds of life insurance. Some of them involve premiums for the loss of life only. Others can serve as investment vehicles, and still others have purposes associated with the need to pass assets on to the next generation. But the essential idea is that in purchasing a policy, the buyer is a good citizen, thinking about his future and his family's welfare.

Generally, the idea behind insurance, for many generations, has been to spread the risk. A few people will die early, in accidents or from disease. Most of us will survive and our premiums and the investments made by the insurers will allow for claims by those who do not make it to old age, along with some capital accumulation for those of us who do.

That is the theory. Here are a few facts.

- ❑ Large numbers of insurance policies lapse with no claim ever being filed.
- ❑ Many people acquire small policies at their place of work.
- ❑ Many others acquire policies designed to ensure that their children attend college.
- ❑ Some acquire policies for business when they're taking out large loans that must be repaid through business activity or from the policy.
- ❑ Some acquire policies to ensure that they'll have enough money to cover the taxes on their estates.
- ❑ A few acquire policies solely for emotional reasons, sales that are inappropriate or just plain wrong for the consumer.

Stuff Happens

Premiums go up on many policies over the years. What happens when the reasons for acquiring insurance or life circumstances change? That is clearly what happened for the many young Americans who died from AIDS in the early part of the 1990s. They were just beginning their lives and, in many cases, did not expect even to have an interest in life insurance. But often their employers offered a policy or their families made certain they had one. Confronted with desperate financial circumstances and a desire to see the benefit from the insurance, these policyholders had policies that were of no use to them. Despite their desperate circumstances, they could realize the value of the policy only by selling it for less than the face value.

That was the plain vanilla option for many victims of AIDS in the 1990s. Dying, without heirs, desperate for medication, and often too young to have accumulated many other assets, these victims sold their policies—and the viatical industry emerged. But changes occurred in the 1990s in the field of AIDS medication just as fast as in the life insurance industry, reshaping the industry yet again.

Here's what happened:

- ❑ In 1990, virtually no policies could be exchanged for value.
- ❑ In 1995, about $500 million in policies were sold by people with terminal illness, most of them with AIDS.
- ❑ By 1997 an odd assortment of people had taken out policies that were loosely underwritten on the lives of people with AIDS, while insurers struggled to revise applications and underwriting procedures.
- ❑ In 2000, the AIDS epidemic had lost its intensity and the viatical market for policies of both sellers and buyers shrunk to perhaps $100

million. Investors in AIDS policies were complaining to regulators at all levels because their investments were not maturing on schedule.

❑ By 2005, a thriving new industry called the life-settlement business had emerged.

Here's why.

In 2000, at a meeting of the National Association of Insurance Commissioners, the phenomenon of the new life-settlement industry was described. In testimony to the assembled insurance regulators, industry representatives from a large, institutionally funded company outlined its new business. They described to the regulators and other observers a market whose numbers did not appear to make sense. Policies of selected seniors whose life expectancies were impaired could be purchased for a percentage of the face value of the policy, and the purchasing company could profit from the fact that these policies were underpriced. At the same time, the policies were no longer needed, wanted, or of interest to the sellers.

Which policy owners were not interested? Who would sell? Thousands of policies were not wanted, not needed, not of interest. Lapse rates for insurance policies and cash redemption of the policies had always been factors in insurers' pricing policies. Actuaries for the insurers reported these lapse rates to regulators, and the regulators determined that the insurers' predicted lapse rates and policy pricing was appropriate.

Still, they were not lapsing. They were not being redeemed for cash value. They were simply sitting on the books with new owners paying the premiums. The problem of impaired life expectancies persisting on the books had begun to dawn on the insurers. Some of them faced it head on, but many avoided the discussion. One insurer told regulators there was a real need to get cash surrender values up so that the problem could be managed.

But thousands of Americans began to gradually become aware, however mysteriously, that their life insurance policy was an asset worth money *before* their lives ended. This being a factor, and a lucrative one to sellers and people who arranged the sale as well as to buyers interested in the new asset class, the sales occurred. Lots of them.

How the Market Works

In most situations, people with life policies rely on their professional advisers to help them review their assets. If they have a life insurance agent with whom they've worked for years, they will rely on that agent for advice in all sorts of matters. But they especially rely on the agent to "negotiate" for them the insurance contracts they carry.

For many insured individuals, their needs over a life of coverage change annually. Many insurers are developing new products to meet these needs. For example, right now, life insurers are seriously focused on new markets resulting from the rising concern of Americans about paying for their long-term care. Others are looking to develop alternative insurance instruments that meet the needs of clients with products geared to investment markets or related to annuities. Unpredictable events—including the horrific hurricanes of 2005, for example—cause major changes in the lives of many Americans daily. Given the tenuous strength of the government's ability to deal with the changes, more and more Americans want to be offered every possible opportunity to prepare for their own destiny with the advice of people they trust.

The growth of the life-settlement market has necessarily involved the ability of thousands of agents all over America to look out for the interests of their clients. The life-settlement business is driven by these professionals, who are in a position to evaluate and, most important, to negotiate the best insurance coverage for their clients. They have a huge range of options available to them from insurers. The insurers' new products are innovative and varied. But in a variety of circumstances, insured individuals just do not find that another insurance product meets their needs. And in a whole variety of other circumstances, the insurance industry does not have a product available that fits the needs of a seller. Remember that the insurance industry could not meet the needs of the AIDS-afflicted sellers of policies in the 1990s because the set of circumstances was unique. Despite the efforts of insurers, such as the emergence of advance death benefits, the products were insufficient to meet the needs.

Suitable for Sale

Which policies is an insured consumer actually able to sell?

Term Insurance

Term insurance does not have a lot of value in the life-settlement market. The policy has to be renewable if the insured is likely or potentially going to live beyond the current term, and the conditions under which it might be renewable must be consistent with the potential purchaser's underwriting policy. The circumstances under which these policies are sold are generally associated with the characteristics of the old viatical industry—short life expectancy and the inability of the seller to pay the premiums.

Whole Life

Whole life policies are not often sold in the life-settlement market. The cash value can be accessed and used for premium maintenance, or their benefits can be reduced and restructured. Generally, as some studies have shown, the premium structure and potential of a whole life policy may make the sale of the policy economically inadvisable for the insured, who can access the cash value of the policy to adjust its parameters.

Universal Life

Most policies sold in the life-settlement market are universal life policies. Their assumptions of interest rates, premium value, and financial plans of the insured allow for so many variations in circumstances that they are frequently used in financial plans that are designed to accommodate life changes. Such changes are exactly the circumstances that may lead a policyholder to encounter new needs that his policy does not meet. Regulators in Florida warn the public: "A combination of low interest rates and the rising cost of insurance could result in future elimination of your policy's death benefits and cash value. Make sure you ask your agent about this possibility. Also be sure you understand which cash values are guaranteed and which are not."[1] For an investor in a universal life policy, the attractive element is the fixed nature of the insurer-guaranteed death benefit.

Variable Life

Many policies sold in the market are variable life contracts. But the agents who deal in the sale of such policies must also be qualified as securities representatives. Complexity renders these policies more difficult to move in the settlement market.

Today, there are still many variable life policies that are just not a good fit for the owner. It is an ongoing concern for insurers. Reevaluate your needs, they advise consumers of insurance. For a whole variety of reasons, other options may be better. Tens of thousands of policies lapse each year, and tens of thousands of policies each year are surrendered to the insurer for cash value.

Preventing Lapses

The life-settlement industry's position is that no policy should lapse or be surrendered without a quick check of its value in the settlement market.

Regulation has radically altered this market. Some states have extensive regulation; others have none. Some regulations are hostile to the process; others are receptive and helpful. But there are costs associated with the transactions, and some of the regulations have costs. Some policies cannot be sold because the transactions would make no economic sense. Given the costs associated with the estimation of extended life expectancy and the costs associated with raising capital, buyers of policies are just not always able to buy a policy, and when they can, the policy will most likely have a face value in excess of $100,000.

Some people think that the life-settlement industry is simply wrong. After all, it involves investing in the life insurance of a stranger for eventual return. That objection was put to rest in the 1990s as the public considered the desperate circumstances of the policy seller with a predicted life expectancy of a year or two and no assets to pay premiums and immediate needs. But the argument resurfaces each time some observers claim that people should not invest in this market. They claim that the life-settlement industry is antithetical to the public interest in insurance and to the interests of sellers. But sellers and their financial advisers have found that there are a boatload of circumstances that are not and cannot be met by their policies, and so they sell.

Facing Controversy

In 2005, a new, problematic trend in the industry became apparent. Some policies are now obtained by entities or individuals who have little relationship to the insured. The policies are, in effect, issued for reasons that are not traditionally associated with the appropriate uses of insurance. This issue deserves serious public discussion, although it is not central to the life-settlement industry as it functions now. Nevertheless, insurers are deeply concerned about this trend and for good reason. Controversy has emerged as insurers' efforts to deal with this new challenge have led them to make dramatic statements about the "purpose of insurance" and the real needs of people who purchase it. They're scrutinizing charity-owned, company-owned, and investor-owned life insurance policies. The life-settlement industry shares their concern about sales in which the buyer has no insurable interest connection with the life of the insured. Regulators are struggling with this problem, and the life-settlement industry has distanced itself very strongly from these improper schemes. So in the revolutionary world of settlements, more changes are no doubt ahead.

This is not the first criticism the industry has faced. Opponents of the industry have argued for years—and argued for the insureds of the AIDS era—that the policies were worth more than the value for which they were sold. "Just hold the policy," they said. "Pay the premiums and your heirs will have a good deal." But the reality is that people sold because their current interests did not correspond to the long-term benefit represented in the policy.

That fact is just as true today in the settlement industry as it was in 1990: policies have value. If consumers need help figuring out the value of a policy, they can check with the life-settlement industry.

Chapter Notes

1. Tom Gallagher, "Life Insurance and Annuities: A Guide for Consumers," http://www.fldfs.com/consumers/literature/2003LIFEGUIDE.pdf.

CHAPTER 18

Longevity Risk Insurance

ROGER G. IBBOTSON, MICHAEL C. HENKEL, AND PENG CHEN

The standard of living of the elderly depends on total retirement income, which comes from three main sources: Social Security benefits, defined-benefit pensions, and personal savings. Although Social Security and pensions continue to provide a foundation for retirement income, retirement savings plans and other personal savings are expected to become the main sources of retirement income. This shift in retirement funding from professionally managed defined-benefit plans to personal savings vehicles means that investors need to make their own decisions about how to manage risks and generate income in retirement.

Our discussion of the three risk factors investors must confront when making saving and investment decisions for their retirement portfolios appears in chapter 15 of *The Investment Think Tank* (Bloomberg Press, 2004), edited by Harold Evensky and Deena Katz. They are: financial market risk, longevity risk, and the risk of not saving enough. In this chapter, we review the importance of taking longevity risk into consideration in planning retirement income and extend longevity-risk analysis to the various types of income sources and investment instruments to determine their effectiveness in alleviating that risk. Using Monte Carlo simulations, we illustrate the benefits of including lifetime-payout annuities—including immediate fixed- and variable-payout contracts—in retirement portfolios to help manage the risk of outliving one's assets. Also covered are the various types of insurance guarantees offered with payout annuities and how investors can differentiate them in terms of suitability and use.

Lasting a Lifetime

Longevity risk is the risk of outliving your assets. As life expectancies continue to increase, retirees must be aware of the possibility of a long lifetime and adjust their financial plans accordingly. This is especially important for those who retire early or have a family history of long lives.

Increasingly, today's retirees will need to balance income and expenditures over a longer period of time than did retirees in the past. This change results in part from the long-term trend toward earlier retirement. Nearly half of all men now leave the labor force by age 62, and almost half of all women are out of the workforce by age 60. Moreover, the decline in the average retirement age has occurred at a time of rising life expectancy for retirees. Since 1940, falling mortality rates have added almost four years to the expected life span of a 65-year-old male and more than five years to the life expectancy of a 65-year-old female. The probability that an individual retiring at age 65 will reach age 80 is greater than 70 percent for females and greater than 62 percent for males. Combined with the life expectancy of a spouse, the odds reach nearly 90 percent that at least one of the partners will live to age 80. For a broader sense of the potential longevity risk, **FIGURE 18.1** illustrates the survival probabilities of 65-year-olds. The first column shows the probability for married couples that at least one partner will survive to age 80, 85, 90, 95, and 100. The second column shows the probability that an individual (regardless of marital status) will survive to various ages. For married couples, in 78 percent of the cases, at least one spouse will still be alive at age 85.

Many investors use simple approaches to retirement planning that ignore longevity risk by assuming the investor needs to plan income only

FIGURE **18.1** *Chance of 65-Year-Olds' Living to Various Ages*

AGE	JOINT	INDIVIDUAL	MALE	FEMALE
80	90.6%	74.0%	68.0%	80.6%
85	78.4	56.8	49.3	65.3
90	57.0	36.3	29.5	44.5
95	30.9	17.6	13.4	23.0
100	11.5	6.0	4.2	8.6

Source: Society of Actuaries, 1996 U.S. Annuity 2000 Mortality Table

to age 85. Although 85 is the average life expectancy for a 65-year-old, we know that roughly half will live longer. For a married couple, the odds are almost 80 percent that one or both will live past 85. If advisers use an 85-year life expectancy to plan a client's retirement-income needs, many clients will use up their retirement resources (other than government and corporate pensions) long before they die.

This longevity risk—the risk of outliving one's resources—is substantial and is the reason why lifetime annuities (payout annuities) should be an integral part of many retirement plans.

Sources of Retirement Income

Social Security benefits, defined-benefit pension plans, and personal savings (including defined-contribution plan savings) are the main sources of retirement income. This section looks at their effectiveness in alleviating longevity risk.

Social Security and Defined-Benefit Pension Plans

Traditionally, Social Security and defined-benefit pension plans have provided the bulk of retirement income. For example, the Social Security Administration reports that 39 percent of income for persons 65 and older came from Social Security income in 2001 and 18 percent came from defined-benefit pensions. According to 2003 reports from the U.S. General Accounting Office, retirees received about 60 percent of their retirement income from Social Security and traditional company pension plans, whereas today's workers can expect to have only about one-third of their retirement income funded by these sources.[1]

Longevity insurance is embedded in Social Security and defined-benefit pension benefits. These benefits are paid out for as long as the investor (and typically the spouse) lives. The U.S. government is responsible for funding Social Security retirement benefits. In defined-benefit pension plans, the employer (as plan sponsor) agrees to make future payments during retirement and is responsible for investing and managing the pension-plan assets, thus bearing the investment and longevity risks. Because a defined-benefit pension plan typically covers a large number of employees, the overall longevity risk of the plan is significantly mitigated for the employer.

Retirees who rely on Social Security and defined-benefit pension plans for retirement income do not need to worry about longevity risk. The risk is effectively eliminated by the guarantee from the government and the employer. However, there has been a continuing shift from defined-benefit plans to defined-contribution plans since the early 1980s.[2] Along with this continuing trend, the percentage of private-sector workers who participate in a primary defined-benefit plan has decreased, whereas the percentage of such workers who participate in a primary defined-contribution plan has increased consistently since the early 1980s. Today, the majority of active retirement-plan participants are in defined-contribution plans, whereas most were in defined-benefit plans in 1980.

Defined-Contribution Plans and Personal Savings

Increasingly, workers are relying on their defined-contribution retirement portfolio and other personal savings as their primary sources of retirement income. With these changes, workers must now bear the longevity risk because there is no promise from their employer or the government that money will be available during retirement. Reliance on such sources of income also exposes workers to greater longevity risk than ever before. Moreover, they have to manage this risk themselves.

There are two ways to use personal savings to fund retirement income. A retiree may choose to receive a lump sum directly from the plan as a cash settlement and then invest and withdraw from the portfolio during retirement. This is typically referred to as a systematic withdrawal strategy. Alternatively, retirees who receive lump sums may purchase a lifetime-payout annuity with some or all of the proceeds, thereby preserving their assets and ensuring a stream of income throughout retirement. This approach is typically referred to as annuitization.

A Lifetime-Payout Annuity

Living a long life means more resources are needed to fund the longer-term income needs. Rational investors may decide to take on more financial risk, hoping to gain more return—if they can tolerate the risk. On the other hand, investors would also want to hedge against longevity risk because this type of risk exposure carries no potential financial reward.[3] In other words, investors should be willing to pay an insurance premium to hedge the longevity risk. The arrangement is very similar to the concept of homeowner insurance, which protects against hazard to one's home. Lifetime-payout annuities provide investors with the longevity insurance that so many retirees now require.

A lifetime-payout annuity is an insurance product that converts an accumulated investment into income that the insurance company pays out over the life of the investor. Payout annuities are the opposite of life insurance. Investors buy life insurance because they're afraid of dying too soon and leaving family and loved ones in financial need. They buy payout annuities because they're concerned about living a long time and running out of assets during their lifetime. Insurance companies can provide this lifelong benefit by spreading the longevity risk over a large group of annuitants and making careful and conservative assumptions about the rate of return earned on their assets.

Spreading or pooling the longevity risk means that individuals who do not reach their life expectancy, as calculated by actuarial mortality tables, will subsidize the payouts for those who exceed it. Investors who buy life-time-payout annuities pool their portfolios and collectively ensure that everybody will receive payments as long as they live. The unique longevity insurance features embedded in lifetime-payout annuities enable them to play a significant role in many investors' retirement portfolios.

Systematic Withdrawal Versus Annuitization

Payout annuities and systematic withdrawals present different advantages and risks to retirees. A life annuity, whether received from an employer-sponsored pension plan or purchased directly from an insurance company ensures that a retiree will have an income no matter how long he or she lives. However, if a retiree dies soon after purchasing an annuity, he or she would likely receive considerably less than what a lump sum and system-atic withdrawal strategy would have provided. Also, income from an an-nuity might be inadequate to pay for unexpected, large expenses, and the investor will also be unable to leave the annuity as a bequest.

Retirees who choose to systematically withdraw lump sums have the flexibility to preserve or draw down these assets as they wish, but they risk running out of assets if they live longer than expected, withdraw as-sets too rapidly, or suffer poor investment returns on their assets. Payout annuities offer a way to mitigate much of the financial uncertainty that accompanies living to a very old age, but they might not necessarily be the best approach for all retirees. An individual with a life-shortening ill-ness, for example, might be less concerned about the financial needs that accompany living a very long time.

Types of Payout Annuities

Two basic types of payout annuities are available: fixed and variable. A fixed-payout annuity pays a fixed nominal dollar amount each period. A variable annuity's payments fluctuate in value, depending on the per-formance of the underlying investments chosen by the annuity contract holder. Payments from both types of lifetime-payout annuities are con-tingent on the life of the investor. Other payout options are available with guaranteed payments for a specified period of time or with refund guarantees. Many retirement and insurance experts advocate the use of payout annuities indexed to inflation, which provide protection against cost-of-living increases.

The Fixed-Payout Annuity

FIGURE 18.2 illustrates the payment stream from an immediate fixed annuity. With an initial premium, or purchase amount, of $100,000, the annual income payments for a 65-year-old female would be $616 per month, or $7,392 per year.[4] The straight line represents the annual payments before inflation. People who enjoy the security of a steady and predictable stream of income may find a fixed annuity appealing. Despite the benefits of longevity insurance and fixed payout amounts, a retirement portfolio that consists only of fixed immediate-payout annuities has several drawbacks.

The first disadvantage is that the fixed annuity's payments are the same in nominal dollars year after year. That means real purchasing power is eroded by inflation as the annuitant gets older. The second, descending line in Figure 18.2 represents the same payment stream after a hypothetical 3 percent inflation rate is factored in. The annuitant receives the same nominal payment amount year after year, but adjusted for purchasing power, the value of that payment is much less over time. An investor contemplating a fixed-payout annuity needs to keep this in mind because the nominal value of the payment will remain fixed for the rest of the investor's life.

The second drawback of fixed annuities is that investors often cannot trade out of the fixed-payout annuity once it has been purchased.[5] Also, when an investor buys a fixed annuity, payments are locked in based on the interest rates current at the time of purchase. Payout rates from today's fixed-payout annuities are at historical lows consistent with current inter-

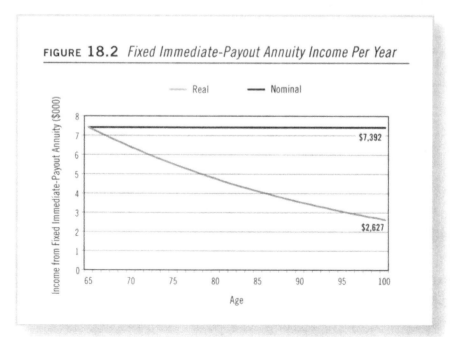

FIGURE **18.2** *Fixed Immediate-Payout Annuity Income Per Year*

est rates. A 65-year-old female might have received as much as $1,150 per month in the early 1980s in exchange for a $100,000 initial premium. In 2005, that same $100,000 buys only $600 per month.

The Variable-Payout Annuity

A variable-payout annuity is an insurance product that exchanges accumulated investment value into annuity units that the insurance company pays out over the lifetime of the investor. The annuity payments fluctuate in value depending on the investments held. To better understand variable-payout annuities, think of an equity-based mutual fund whose current net asset value (NAV) is exactly $1 per unit. The unit fluctuates every day. In any given day, week, month, or year, the price can increase or decrease relative to the previous period.

With a variable annuity, instead of getting fixed payments, investors get a fixed number of fund units. For example, each month, the insurance company promises to send 500 fund units, instead of 500 U.S. dollars. The insurance company converts these fund units into U.S. dollars at the going NAV value at the end of the month to determine how much to pay the investor. Therefore, the cash flow from the variable-payout annuity fluctuates with the performance of the funds chosen.

FIGURE 18.3 illustrates the annuity payment stream, in real terms, from a portfolio of 60 percent stocks/40 percent bonds, using a life-only payment

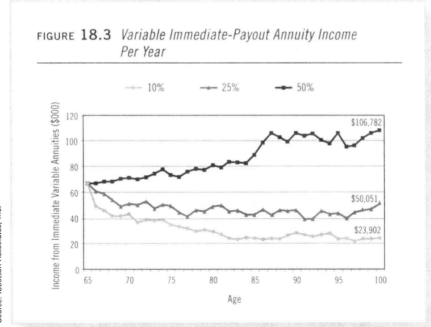

FIGURE **18.3** *Variable Immediate-Payout Annuity Income Per Year*

option in an immediate variable annuity. A Monte Carlo simulation was created to illustrate the various payment scenarios. The simulation is generated using historical return statistics of stocks, bonds, and inflation from 1926 to 2004; a $1 million initial portfolio; and a 3 percent assumed investment return (AIR).[6] The initial payment at age 65 is estimated to be $66,150.[7] The lines in the chart show the 10th, 25th, and 50th percentiles from the Monte Carlo simulations constructed. As Figure 18.3 indicates, there is a 10 percent chance that annual inflation-adjusted annuity payments might fall below $25,000 at age 100, a 25 percent chance that they might decrease to $50,000 or higher, and a 50 percent chance that they might grow to $106,000 or higher.

Single- and Joint-Life Payout Annuities

When considering retirement security, retirees need to consider the retirement income needs of their spouses. For example, if a married couple converted their savings into a single-life payout annuity for the husband, upon his death, payments would stop and his widow would experience a substantial decline in income. That problem can be solved by purchasing a joint-life annuity. Unlike a single-life annuity, which pays out only as long as the individual is alive, a joint-life annuity is structured to provide income for as long as either member of a couple is alive. Because a joint-life payout annuity on average makes payments for a much longer period than a single life-payout annuity, the joint option reduces the income payment each year. Depending on the couple's preferences, the annuity may be designed to provide the same income after the death of a spouse or a reduced income.

FIGURE 18.4 illustrates the different payments from a fixed-payout annuity for a single-life male, a single-life female, and a joint payout with 100 percent survivor benefit. The payment amount is calculated with an initial premium or purchase amount of $100,000. For a 65-year-old male, the payment would be $654 per month (or $7,848 per year). For a female, the payment would be $616 per month, or $7,392 per year. For a joint payout with 100 percent survivor benefit, the payment would be reduced to $6,492 per year.

FIGURE **18.4** *Fixed Immediate-Payout Annuities*

	SINGLE MALE	SINGLE FEMALE	JOINT
Immediate fixed annuity payment	$7,848	$7,392	$6,492

FIGURE **18.5** *Fixed Immediate-Payout Annuities with Period Guarantees*

	SINGLE MALE	SINGLE FEMALE	JOINT WITH 100% BENEFIT
Immediate fixed annuity payment	$7,848	$7,392	$6,492
Immediate fixed annuity payment with 10-year guarantee	7,584	7,236	6,492
Immediate fixed annuity payment with 20-year guarantee	6,960	6,828	6,360

Payment Period Guarantees

Annuities also vary in terms of the period for which payments are guaranteed. Some retirees who wish to purchase annuities may be concerned that early death could result in a short period of annuity payments; in that event, they would like a portion of their original premium payment made available to their heirs. They can arrange that by purchasing payout annuities with payment-period guarantee options. These guarantees ensure either a minimum number of monthly payments regardless of the age of death or a partial return of premium upon death. Choosing a guarantee period decreases the amount of income payout each period to the retiree. **FIGURE 18.5** presents the payment differences among fixed immediate life annuities with no guarantee, with a 10-year payment guarantee, and with a 20-year payment guarantee.

Guaranteed Payment Floors

Guaranteed payment floors may be added to immediate variable annuities. These floors guarantee that the monthly payment will not drop below a certain percentage of the first payment (for example, 80 percent). The goal is to ensure a minimum monthly payment without giving up the potential increase in payments provided by an immediate variable annuity. A guaranteed minimum income benefit (GMIB) is typically offered as an optional feature or as a rider to a variable annuity contract for an additional charge, generally ranging from 0.30 percent to 0.75 percent of the contract's account value.

Appropriate Level of Longevity Insurance

A life annuity can provide a higher level of income for a longer period than nonannuitized investments can because the assets of annuitants who die earlier than average are used to provide income to those who live longer than average. To make this possible, annuitants give up the right to include the annuitized money in their estates when they die. In other words, the annuitized resources cannot be bequeathed to the contract holder's heirs. Of course, individuals who wish to leave an inheritance can simply place the portion of their assets they would like to bequeath in some other investment vehicle and annuitize only the assets they expect to use for their own consumption.

Investors' Choices

An immediate life-payout annuity is clearly an effective way to manage longevity risk in retirement. However, life-payout annuitization is not an all-or-nothing decision; the choice is part of the broader question of how much to set aside for systematic withdrawal and how much to allocate for annuitization. Combining nonannuitized assets with annuitized assets can help investors manage financial market risk, longevity risk, and bequests for heirs. Chapter 15 of *The Investment Think Tank* illustrated that by annuitizing 50 percent of a retirement portfolio, investors can significantly reduce the probability of running out of money during their lifetime. Many other researchers have also analyzed the benefit of annuitizing a portion of a retiree's portfolio. For example, Ameriks, Veres, and Warshawsky (2001) found significant improvement in the likelihood that a retiree will maintain a target level of income with some annuitization. A retiree with a conservative asset allocation of, say, 20 percent stocks, 50 percent bonds, and 30 percent cash has a 33 percent chance of maintaining annual withdrawals of 4.5 percent of the initial account balance (adjusted each year for inflation) for 30 years. By annuitizing 25 percent of the portfolio, the probability of maintaining this level of annual income increases to 53 percent. Annuitizing 50 percent of the account balance increases the probability to 81 percent. A retired investor with a more balanced allocation—40 percent stocks, 40 percent bonds, and 20 percent cash—would see the likelihood of success increase from 76 percent with no annuitization to 85 percent with annuitization of 25 percent of assets. The likelihood climbs to 95 percent with annuitization of 50 percent of assets.

Investment strategies involving payout annuities to manage longevity risk during retirement—when most investors are spending rather than accumulating assets—need to be highly individualized. Many factors affect the amount of payout annuities an investor should buy to hedge against longevity risk. Obviously, the Social Security and defined-benefit pension benefits an investor expects to receive in retirement are key factors. The more an investor expects to receive from these sources, the less the need for longevity-risk management through payout annuities. The amount of retirement-portfolio assets relative to retirement needs is also important. Investors who accumulated more wealth have less need for longevity insurance because they have a lower probability of running out of money in retirement. Other factors include bequest preferences, age, financial-risk tolerance, and the investor's health and family health history. Investors with more modest bequest intentions might invest more in immediate life-payout annuities. Of course, investors who are not in good health have less need for annuities. Chen and Milevsky (2003) presented a model based on the classic utility-maximization framework. The optimal mix of annuitized and nonannuitized assets is determined by the investor's age and risk tolerance, the desire to leave an estate, and the fees and expenses of the products chosen.[8]

The percentage of retirees who purchase individual life-payout annuities is still small. There are several reasons for this: the availability of these annuities is limited, individual life annuities have associated administrative and other expenses, and immediate fixed annuities generally do not provide protection against inflation. The demand for payout annuities should grow as the market continues to develop innovative annuity products that appeal to consumer preferences. For example, demand for individual variable annuities that offer the potential for higher income payouts based on underlying portfolio returns is growing. Furthermore, as the baby boom generation approaches retirement in tandem with the trend toward individual responsibility for managing retirement assets, the demand for individual life annuities is likely to increase.

As RETIREES RELY more and more on personal savings to finance retirement, fewer of them will receive pension income guaranteed to last throughout retirement. The growth in the number of defined-contribution plans means that retirees will face greater responsibility and choices for managing their pension and other assets at and through retirement. Retirees will be at greater risk of outliving their assets and having insufficient income to maintain their standard of living through their retirement years. Such longevity risk suggests the need for additional longevity insurance through the purchase of immediate-payout annuities. We hope the information presented here will help investors who are looking to create a comprehensive investment strategy that ensures adequate income for a lifetime.

References

Ameriks, John, Robert Veres, and Mark J. Warshawsky (2001), "Making Retirement Income Last a Lifetime," *Journal of Financial Planning* (December 2001): 60–76.

Chen, Peng, and Moshe A. Milevsky (2003), "Merging Asset Allocation and Longevity Insurance: An Optimal Perspective on Payout Annuities," *Journal of Financial Planning* (June 2003): 64–72.

Ibbotson, Roger G., Michael C. Henkel, and Peng Chen (2004), "Controlling Longevity Risk in a Retirement Portfolio," chap. 15 in *The Investment Think Tank: Theory, Strategy, and Practice for Advisers*, edited by Harold Evensky and Deena B. Katz (Bloomberg Press).

Chapter Notes

1. U.S. General Accounting Office, *Report to Congressional Requesters: Private Pension* (June 2003); and Employee Benefit Research Institute, *2000 Retirement Confidence Survey.*

2. The Department of Labor reports that private-sector employers sponsored more than 56,000 tax-qualified defined-benefit plans in 1998, down from more than 139,000 in 1979, while the number of tax-qualified defined-contribution plans sponsored by private employers more than doubled from more than 331,000 to approximately 674,000 during the same period.

3. Living a long life is desirable in many respects; we are focusing only on the financial aspects of longevity in this study.

4. All quotes for immediate-payout annuities were obtained from www.immediateannuities.com on June 12, 2005, assuming a 65-year-old female living in Illinois and a $100,000 premium.

5. Payout annuities are available that allow the investor to withdraw money from them, but the investor typically has to pay a surrender or market-value-adjustment charge.

6. The AIR is an initial interest rate assumption that is used to compute the amount of an initial variable annuity payment. Subsequent payments will either increase or decrease depending on the relationship of the AIR to the actual investment return.

7. The initial payment is estimated by Ibbotson Associates.

8. Ibbotson Associates has a patent pending on the method of selecting optimal combinations of stocks, bonds, and other assets with annuity products while satisfying both retirement-income needs and bequest desires.

CHAPTER 19

Immediate Annuities
Structure, Mechanics, and Value

R. H. "RICK" CAREY AND JEFFREY K. DELLINGER

Having passed the hurdle of accumulating assets during working years, the next risk faced by retirees is living longer than their assets can sustain them and becoming financially dependent on others—children, relatives, friends, or the government. If we knew how long we would survive, we could invest our assets appropriately to support ourselves for this known period. In reality, length of life is a random variable, producing longevity risk.

Income annuities provide a sound solution to that risk. The annuity contract owner pays a premium and the annuitant receives regular, periodic annuity benefits regardless of how long he lives. Some annuitants may survive only a short time, whereas others will live well beyond age 100. Although the length of life for a single individual is unknown, the length of life for a large collection of annuitants is more predictable. For example, the survival curve for 1,000 females age 65 resembles the pattern in **FIGURE 19.1**.

The law of large numbers enhances predictability and permits individuals—who cannot safely absorb longevity risk—to transfer that risk to companies that can, by using a mortality pooling function. A state regulatory framework ensures that reserves held for annuity benefits not yet paid are sufficient to support these contractual obligations.

Working separately from Social Security and corporate defined-benefit pension plans, immediate annuities provide lifetime income that involves transferring all mortality risk away from the individual. In the United States, only insurance companies are authorized to write life-contingent immediate annuities.

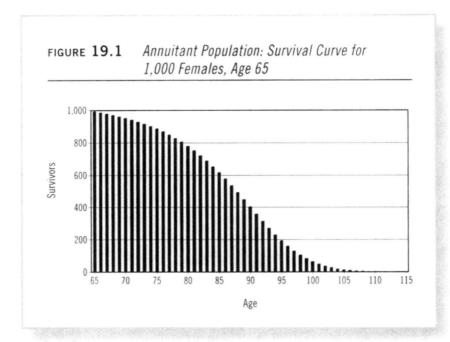

FIGURE **19.1** *Annuitant Population: Survival Curve for 1,000 Females, Age 65*

A distinguishing feature of immediate annuities is that the annuitant receives income for life from (a) his principal, (b) appreciation thereon, and (c) mortality credits that redirect value from individuals who no longer require longevity insurance to those who do. Because the third component is absent in self-managed and systematic withdrawal programs, immediate annuities have the capacity to provide a meaningfully higher level of income guaranteed to last for life than do any alternative instruments. That is, investments inside an immediate annuity produce income superior to identical investments outside an immediate annuity. Immediate annuities obviate the need to determine how to systematically spend down principal.

Structure

An *immediate annuity* is a contractual arrangement whereby a contract owner pays a premium to an insurance company in exchange for a series of regular, periodic annuity benefits. The *owner* is the person who has authority to exercise ownership rights within the immediate annuity contract, such as election of an annuity payout option and designation of beneficiary. The *annuitant* is the recipient of the annuity benefits and, for life-contingent annuity options, the person on whose life the annuity benefits are based. The *beneficiary* is a person designated to receive residual benefits, if any, following death of the annuitant. Immediate annuity contracts offer a variety of annuity payout options, whose terms define the duration, level, and frequency of income and the number of lives covered.

Types of Annuities

There are several types of immediate annuities. Immediate *fixed* annuities provide future benefits whose dollar amount per benefit is fully known at the time the contract is issued, although the duration of payments may depend on how long the annuitant lives. Single-premium immediate annuity (SPIA) is a generic name for this type of product offering.

Immediate *variable* annuities (IVAs) provide future benefits fully known in advance as to number of annuity units per benefit at the time the contract is issued. The amount of the benefit payments varies based on investment performance. Single-premium immediate variable annuity (SPIVA) is a generic name for this type of product offering.

Payout Options

Annuity payout options are categorized as non-life contingent, single-life contingent, and joint-life contingent. Non-life-contingent options include installments for a designated period of time and installments of a designated amount.

Single-life-contingent annuity option benefits are predicated on the continuing survival of a single annuitant. For the most basic *life-only* or *straight-life* annuities, benefits are payable for the lifetime of the annuitant and cease at death. This provides the maximum annuity benefit level among single-life options. Additional guarantees may be layered onto the life annuity, such as the option called *life with n years certain*, which provides that a fixed number of payments will be made regardless of how long the annuitant lives. A guarantee that promises that at least as much value will be paid out in benefits as was received in premium is called a *cash-refund* option when any residual upon the annuitant's death is paid to the beneficiary in a lump sum. It's called an *installment-refund* option when paid in continuing periodic installments. Such additional guarantees serve to lower the benefit amount.

Joint-life-contingent annuities have benefit payments predicated on the lives of two or more annuitants, often a married couple. Annuity options covering two lives provide benefit payments lower than for one life of comparable age because the benefit duration is potentially longer. A *joint and x percent to survivor* option provides annuity income while both annuitants are living and *x* percent of that level after the death of either the annuitant or joint annuitant. Common values of *x* percent are 66 percent and 75 percent, based on the thinking that living expenses reduce on the first death but by less than half. A *joint and x percent to survivor with n years certain* option provides the analogous additional guarantee. A *joint and x percent to secondary annuitant* option provides lifetime income for the named primary annuitant, which reduces to *x* percent for the lifetime of the secondary annuitant should the primary die first.

Numerous other common annuity options exist. Unique, customizable immediate annuity options may also be created for traditional retirement income, pension plans, state lotteries, magazine sweepstakes, and plaintiffs granted structured settlement damage awards.

A common objective of an immediate annuity is to provide maximum periodic income guaranteed to last a lifetime. Logically, inclusion of additional guarantees or refund features is hard to justify. If bequeathing assets to a beneficiary is also an objective, other ways are available to transfer wealth that are more efficient than an immediate annuity. Psychologically, the inclusion of additional guarantees that diminish income add comfort for prospective purchasers. Financial advisers play a role in preparing clients to use appropriate instruments to most efficiently achieve targeted objectives.

Immediate Fixed Annuity

Immediate fixed annuity benefits can be (a) level, (b) arithmetically increasing, (c) geometrically increasing, or (d) irregularly patterned. The same premium can fund the different annuity benefit patterns illustrated in **FIGURE 19.2**.

The graph in Figure 19.2 shows fixed annuity benefits payable at the beginning of the year for a designated period of 20 years, assuming a $500,000 premium and 8 percent interest. The benefit patterns are level, 4 percent arithmetic increase, and 4 percent geometric increase. As is true of all fixed annuities, the dollar amount of each payment is fully known at the time of purchase.

Since inflation compounds and its corrosive effect on purchasing power is magnified over a multidecade retirement horizon, a geometrically increasing annuity whose benefits similarly compound (for example, at 3 percent to 5 percent annually) may produce more constant real income than one with level or arithmetically increasing benefits.

To price immediate fixed annuities, insurers project the annuity benefits they expect to pay. For life-contingent annuities, the projected benefit stream reflects the probability an annuitant will survive to receive a payment. The insurer constructs a portfolio of fixed-income securities of suitable quality that replicate the payout pattern. Based on currently available yields at the time of purchase, the insurer uses this information to derive a present value, called the net premium. The net premium together with

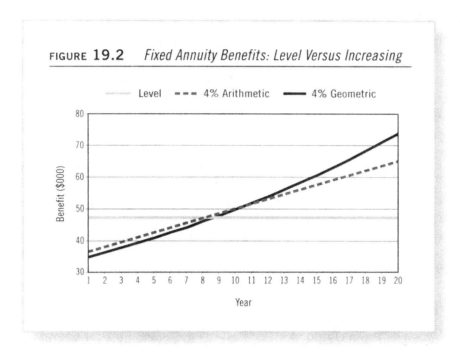

FIGURE **19.2** *Fixed Annuity Benefits: Level Versus Increasing*

the interest it earns is sufficient to provide annuity benefits and to cover administrative expenses, taxes, and profit. Loading to cover financial adviser and wholesaler compensation, contract issue, state premium tax, and other acquisition expenses is added to arrive at the gross premium.

Immediate fixed annuity prices—the premiums that convert to specific benefit amounts—change periodically, often monthly. Once an annuity contract is purchased, however, the benefit promised is guaranteed and is unaffected by any future changes in interest rates.

Immediate annuities with benefit levels that change annually in response to changes in a specific consumer price index (CPI) reflective of a market basket of goods and services purchased by retirees have been slow to become commercially available. This is because of the uncertainty inherent in projecting future benefit payments. Newer investment tools may foster such offerings.

Immediate Variable Annuity

What chiefly distinguishes immediate variable annuities from immediate fixed annuities is that with immediate variable annuities (a) the annuity owner determines how the premium is invested and (b) bears investment risks and rewards via changes in retirement-income benefits, which fluctuate with investment performance. The contract owner allocates the premium—both initially and subsequently—among investment subaccounts in the immediate variable annuity product. These, in turn, are invested in underlying funds analogous to but distinct from retail mutual funds. The underlying investment funds—domestic and international common stock, bond, money market, and specialty funds—may be managed by one investment manager (single-manager IVA) or by multiple investment managers (multi-manager IVA).

In contrast to immediate fixed annuities with level benefits, IVAs offer annuitants the prospect of retirement income that preserves purchasing power. For example, common stock subaccount performance—while not moving in lockstep with inflation—offers the potential over the course of one's retirement for an income stream that keeps pace with or outpaces inflation.

Another contrast to immediate fixed annuities, for which the rate of return on the underlying fixed-income securities portfolio that replicates the annuity payout stream is known, is that future rates of return on variable investment subaccounts are unknown. To address this, the contract owner selects a benchmark rate of return (often 3, 4, or 5 percent) known as the assumed investment rate (AIR). The initial annuity benefit afforded by the given premium is set so that the projected series of future income benefits at that level—based on the annuitant's age, sex, and the annuity option elected—when discounted at the AIR produce a present value equal to the net premium. If actual investment subaccount performance equals the AIR, annuity benefits will remain level because exactly the rate of return assumed in pricing the annuity is achieved. In this sense, the immediate variable annuity works exactly like an immediate fixed annuity.

The distinction of a variable annuity reveals itself when actual investment performance differs from that assumed. There must be some compensating mechanism, which is the benefit level. To the extent actual subaccount performance exceeds the benchmark rate of return (AIR) for the period between any two consecutive annuity benefit payments, greater value is achieved than was assumed, allowing the annuity benefit to rise. Similarly, if actual subaccount performance for the period is less than the benchmark return, the benefit falls. **FIGURE 19.3** summarizes this relationship.

One objective of an immediate variable annuity is to provide a rising level of income to offset the ravages of inflation. The lower the AIR elected, the more readily that objective is achieved. The lower the level of benchmark return chosen, the easier it is for actual subaccount performance to exceed it and drive annuity benefits higher.

The lower the benchmark return chosen, the lower the initial benefit but the steeper the rise of future benefits. Financial advisers are well positioned to educate their clients to think long term and to elect a lower

FIGURE **19.3** *Investment Performance Affects Benefit Level*

Investment performance > AIR	Benefit payments increase
Investment performance = AIR	Benefit payments are level
Investment performance < AIR	Benefit payments decrease

AIR that is more likely to generate an income stream that compensates for inflation. For example, 7 percent actual subaccount performance with a 3 percent AIR increases income roughly 4 percent in one year, enough to offset 4 percent inflation. Seven percent actual subaccount performance with a 7 percent AIR leaves income flat.

Although a higher AIR provides higher benefits early, an objective is to deliver an appropriate income stream well into the future, for the entirety of the annuitant's life. **FIGURE 19.4** compares annuity benefits using AIRs of 3 percent, 5 percent, and 7 percent.

Figure 19.4 shows variable annuity benefits payable at the beginning of the year for a designated period of 20 years, assuming a $500,000 premi-

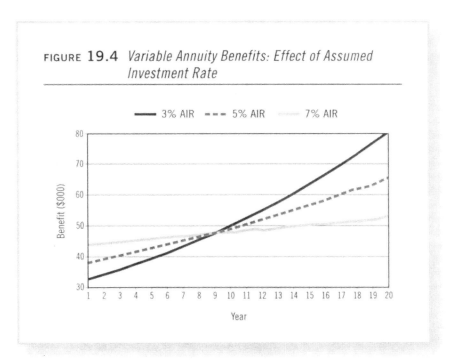

FIGURE **19.4** *Variable Annuity Benefits: Effect of Assumed Investment Rate*

FIGURE **19.5** *Annuity Benefit Equation*

Annuity benefit = Annuity units × Unit value

um and a constant 8 percent investment subaccount return. Although this graph is directly comparable to the earlier immediate fixed annuity graph, the fixed annuity benefits will progress as smoothly as illustrated whereas the variable annuity benefits will in fact fluctuate with actual subaccount performance.

Note that although the three income streams in Figure 19.4 are different, they share identical present value when discounted at the actual rate of return realized by the investment subaccount—that is, all annuity options share the same present value of benefits, with no annuity option more valuable than any other for a given amount of premium. Annuity option selection should therefore be predicated on the preferences of the annuitant.

Mechanically, the progression of IVA benefits is determined using *annuity units*. The same number of annuity units is paid on each benefit-payment date. The annuity unit value changes daily with subaccount performance. The dollar amount of annuity benefit payable equals the number of annuity units multiplied by the annuity unit value on the valuation date used to determine that payment (see **FIGURE 19.5**).

Annuity unit values increase by realized and unrealized capital gains, dividends, and interest income. They decrease by mortality and expense risk charges and asset-management fees. In contrast to *accumulation unit values*, which measure subaccount performance during the accumulation phase of a *deferred* annuity, *annuity unit values* used with an *immediate* annuity also

FIGURE **19.6** *Annuity Unit Value Equation*

$$\text{Annuity unit value}_{t+1} = \text{Annuity unit value}_t \times \frac{1 + \text{Subaccount performance}}{1 + \text{AIR}}$$

FIGURE **19.7** *Example: Subaccount Performs at 7 Percent During First Year*

$$\text{Annuity unit value}_1 = \text{Annuity unit value}_0 \times 1 + \frac{\text{Subaccount performance}}{1 + \text{AIR}}$$

$$= \$1.00 \times \frac{1.07}{1.03}$$

$$\approx \$1.04$$

1st Annuity payment $= 1,000 \text{ units} \times \$1.00/\text{unit} = \$1,000.00$

2nd Annuity payment $= 1,000 \text{ units} \times \$1.04/\text{unit} = \$1,040.00$

reflect the AIR. That's because the annuitant has already received investment credit to the extent of the AIR because it was assumed in determining the first annuity benefit that any premium not yet paid out in benefits would perpetually earn the AIR. As such, if the subaccount actually earns the AIR for a period, actual investment performance equals the assumption and no compensating benefit adjustment up or down is needed.

The formula in **FIGURE 19.6** shows how one annuity unit value is determined from another one year earlier.

For example, suppose the annuitant receives the value of 1,000 annuity units on each payment date. Further suppose that the initial annuity unit value is $1, the AIR is 3 percent, actual fund performance is 7 percent, and annuity benefits are paid annually. **FIGURE 19.7** shows how to determine the second annuity benefit.

When the contract owner invests in multiple subaccounts whose collective performance governs annuity benefit payments, the process is the same. The number of annuity units payable per subaccount is multiplied by the annuity unit value for that subaccount and the resultant dollar amounts are summed to determine the total annuity benefit for that period.

The contract owner may reallocate the percentages of each subaccount that govern annuity benefit payments. This may result in a different number of annuity units payable per subaccount, but again the number of annuity units payable per subaccount remains constant between such reallocations.

The mechanics of immediate variable annuities described here should not preclude financial advisers from recommending this longevity-risk-management instrument any more than from recommending mutual funds that use NAVs to determine value. In both instances, a number of units is multiplied by a unit value to arrive at a dollar amount.

The Right Fit

Investors accumulating assets generally diversify across asset classes. One rationale is that performance of the asset classes is less than perfectly correlated, resulting in the investor's aggregate portfolio experiencing lower volatility than the individual asset classes within it.

Another rationale is simply that investors have multiple objectives. They may desire capital appreciation, income, and safety of principal, with the relative balance among these three objectives varying based on the investor's psychological makeup and life stage. As a result, they may invest in common stocks, corporate and government bonds, and bank certificates of deposit, respectively.

In retirement, investor objectives may include (1) *inexhaustible* lifetime income, (2) income that keeps pace with inflation and allows the investor to maintain his standard of living, and (3) liquidity to meet emergency medical needs. Immediate annuities—whether fixed or variable—meet the first objective. Immediate variable annuities and geometrically increasing fixed annuities offer the potential to meet the second objective. Neither traditional variable nor fixed immediate annuities meet the third objective.

Like any financial instrument, degree of use depends on the objectives to be satisfied. To the extent the objectives include inexhaustible lifetime income and the potential to maintain standard of living, assets may be allocated to immediate annuities to the appropriate degree.

One should allocate sufficient assets to an immediate annuity instrument for it to make a meaningful contribution to the targeted objectives. Because investors have additional objectives, there exists some maximum percentage of assets that should be allocated to immediate annuities. As a general guideline—and not intended as investment advice, because each individual's needs and circumstances must be evaluated individually—allocating a range of 20–50 percent of investable retirement assets to fixed and variable immediate annuities is sometimes suggested.

There is a sweet spot of investable net worth that makes an individual a suitable candidate for an immediate annuity. With investable net worth that's too small, one is unlikely to be able to sustain oneself economically for the whole of life, and although an immediate annuity may stretch income to the maximum extent feasible, liquidity needs for day-to-day expenses may prevail. With sufficiently large investable net worth, one may be able to maintain a standard of living simply from dividend and interest income without ever having to systematically liquidate principal. In between these endpoints resides the population subset that represents suitable immediate annuity candidates.

Note, however, that high investable net worth correlates positively with above-average longevity because of access to quality health care, education about healthy lifestyle, and other factors. The result is that wealthy individuals who may not need immediate annuities for income generation may nevertheless find them attractive investments. Investments inside an immediate annuity produce income superior to identical investments outside an immediate annuity because the former consists of principal, appreciation, and mortality credits whereas the latter enjoys only the first two of these components; therefore, immediate annuities produce a superior rate of return for longer-lived annuitants than other investments.

Immediate annuity investors tend to reside in states with high concentrations of individuals age 60 and older. In 2003, top states for *annuity benefit payments* were New York, California, Connecticut, Florida, and Pennsylvania. Individuals between the ages of 55 and 71 are the primary target market for immediate annuities. Some individuals elect early retirement at age 55. In tax-qualified markets, mandatory distributions commence by age 70½. The most common issue age is 65.

Clients with assets in retirement savings programs like individual retirement accounts or 401(k) plans may have earmarked those assets from the start for the purpose of generating retirement income. As such, these may be the easiest assets to deploy in the form of immediate annuities. Nonetheless, a retirement-income financial plan—backed by the latest academic research on optimizing retirement income—should be created to determine which assets to deploy where. The factors investors consider when contemplating the purchase of an immediate annuity include the dollar amount of benefit payments, stability of the insurance company issuing the contract, product features, financial adviser recommendation, fees, and company brand name.

The Role of the Financial Adviser

The choice of an immediate annuity is not a simple one: the individual's standard of living during retirement years may be at stake; the purchase often involves large sums of money; and the election is irrevocable. For these reasons, even well-educated, financially sophisticated individuals may seek the counsel of a financial adviser knowledgeable about annuity options, AIRs, subaccounts, taxation, and contract structure.

Immediate annuity investors understand they've reached a point in their lives when they may not wish to return to work to produce new retirement assets or may be physically unable to do so. They cannot afford to make financial mistakes during the asset-liquidation phase of their lives. The gravity of decisions made to deploy an individual's lifetime retirement savings optimally is considerable.

Misconceptions about immediate annuities once retarded their sales. Some financial advisers mistakenly believed that annuitants who died early in the program forfeited the reserve held for that liability to the insurer, who reaped a windfall. Rather, the reserves released by deceased annuitants are a natural consequence of program construction and are redeployed to sustain longer-surviving annuitants.

Certain advisers believed that an immediate annuity sale represented the last commission they would ever earn on those assets because the premium could not be repositioned into other products later. In reality, the sale of a lifetime annuity to a client may now produce an annuity of trail commissions for the adviser equally as long as the lifetime annuity benefits for the client, effectively bonding the adviser-client relationship to an even stronger degree.

Some financial advisers believed that investors lost control of assets deployed into immediate annuities. What they actually lose is access to ad hoc lump-sum withdrawals beyond regularly scheduled annuity benefits. Contract owners still exercise elements of control, including the right to reallocate among investment subaccounts—whose performance governs annuity benefit payments—and to do so tax-free. They also have the right to name a new beneficiary and to vote on proxy matters associated with the investment funds underlying the subaccounts.

Interestingly, the pendulum is now swinging in the other direction. Financial advisers, upon further study, increasingly believe the highest and best use of annuities resides with immediate annuities.

Explaining the Advantages of Immediate Annuities

For the dual objectives of maximizing income and minimizing the probability of outliving it, an immediate annuity offers a compelling solution. Such a solution is easily amenable to visual comparison with alternatives, using charts and graphs to convey important information to clients clearly.

For example, consider a 65-year-old female contemplating application of $500,000 to the purchase of either a mutual fund or an immediate variable annuity. Assume both are invested identically. She wishes to achieve the maximum amount of income possible under the stipulation that she is willing to accept only a very low probability of outliving the income. Her financial adviser indicates that if she is willing to risk a 5 percent probability of outliving her income, she can initially receive $2,157 monthly from the mutual fund. With a 0 percent probability of outliving her income, she can initially receive $3,275 monthly from the IVA. Both benefits will increase annually by an equal percentage. She both increases income and eliminates any possibility of outliving it by selecting the IVA. If she elects the mutual fund, she gives up more than one-third of potential income and still risks running out of money.

FIGURE 19.8 shows the amount of monthly income from a mutual fund achievable for various probabilities of outliving the income that the $500,000 is capable of generating. It compares this income to the monthly income from an immediate variable annuity. Note that even if the client is willing to accept a 50 percent chance of running out of money by using a mutual fund for retirement income, she still receives less income than with the annuity.

Data from the shaded row in the chart in Figure 19.8—giving the client a 5 percent probability of outliving mutual fund income—appear in **FIGURE 19.9**.

FIGURE **19.8** *Pretax Monthly Income Funded by a $500,000 Initial Investment for a Female, Age 65*

MUTUAL FUND		IVA—LIFE ANNUITY	
Probability of Outliving Income	Initial Income	Probability of Outliving Income	Initial Income
1%	$2,050	0%	$3,275
5	2,157	0	3,275
10	2,237	0	3,275
25	2,417	0	3,275
50	2,739	0	3,275
71	3,275	0	3,275

Assumptions:
- Annuity 2000 Basic Mortality Table
- 8% investment performance
- 4% AIR
- Monthly annuity-due IVA benefits are projected, then mutual fund distributions are set equal to a percentage of IVA benefits so that the mutual fund balance is exhausted when 99%, 95%, 90%, 75%, 50%, and 29% of females originally age 65 have died

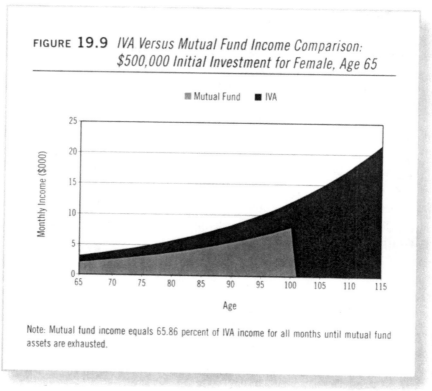

FIGURE **19.9** *IVA Versus Mutual Fund Income Comparison: $500,000 Initial Investment for Female, Age 65*

Note: Mutual fund income equals 65.86 percent of IVA income for all months until mutual fund assets are exhausted.

Source: Jeffrey K. Dellinger, *The Handbook of Variable Income Annuities* (John Wiley & Sons, 2006)

With rigorous mathematical analyses like that shown in Figure 19.9, financial advisers can demonstrate that immediate variable annuities provide real value to investors who want assurance of lifetime income.

Income Taxation

Internal Revenue Code Section 72(u)(4) defines an *immediate annuity* as an annuity purchased with a single premium or annuity consideration, with an annuity starting date no later than one year from the date of purchase and providing for a series of substantially equal periodic payments to be made no less than once a year during the annuity period. This code section and associated regulations govern personal federal income taxation of immediate annuities.

Non-tax-qualified immediate annuities—those for which the premium is paid with after-tax dollars forming a positive cost basis—contain a tax-excludable portion of each benefit equal to the investment in the contract divided by the number of years for which the annuity payments are expected to be made (see **FIGURE 19.10**). For life-contingent annuity options, the number of years annuity payments are expected to be made is determined

FIGURE **19.10** *Excludable Portion Equation*

$$\text{Excludable portion} = \frac{\text{Investment in contract}}{\text{Expected number of years of payments}}$$

by actuarial tables promulgated by the Internal Revenue Service. Once the cost basis is recovered, all future annuity benefits are fully taxable.

If a lifetime annuity contains a refund feature or a certain period, the value of this feature is subtracted from the investment in the contract for tax purposes. This adjusted investment in the contract is then used to determine the tax-excludable portion of each annuity benefit. For a life-only annuity, if there is unrecovered investment in the contract at the time of the annuitant's death, it is allowed as a deduction to the annuitant in his last taxable year.

Tax-qualified immediate annuities—generally those for which the premium is paid with pretax dollars and form a zero cost basis—have 100 percent of each annuity benefit taxable as ordinary income because neither the premium nor any appreciation thereon has ever been taxed.

Immediate annuity income is taxed at ordinary income rates, so retirees may consider applying traditional IRA or 401(k) tax-qualified account money to purchase their immediate annuities, because this money is already going to be taxed at ordinary income rates. Nonannuity investments held to provide liquidity during retirement may be better invested in taxable accounts, which enjoy lower tax rates on capital gains and dividends.

Comparing the Choices

Key to a client's decision-making process should be consideration of the question of how well an immediate annuity offering can achieve its basic mission. Satisfactory payout rates, prudent investment management, low cost, and financial strength of the insurer over many decades are important assessment factors.

Product features that are only peripheral to the core mission—those an insurer may use to differentiate its product from many comparable offerings in the marketplace—should be critically scrutinized because they may result in a lifetime of additional expense. Clients should evaluate whether additional benefits (for example, long-term care features) are worth the reduction in retirement income and consider whether the same need can be more efficiently satisfied through a separate product specifically designed to meet it.

The riskier the additional promises layered onto the basic immediate annuity product, the greater the need to consider whether the insurer is likely to be able to live up to these promises over many decades, including the periodic economic downturns that inevitably occur. Areas currently receiving attention in immediate annuity product design evolution include those shown in **FIGURE 19.11**.

Of the four product-development categories, one fundamentally changes the nature of the insurance company enterprise offering the annuity: payout floor guarantees effectively embed a series of put options into the product. Insurers must reserve appropriately and establish adequate risk-based capital to cover such a liability in the vast majority of future economic scenarios that may materialize.

Mortality is a *diversifiable* risk for insurers. It involves *independent* risk units, whereby pooling greater and greater numbers of annuitants leads to risk reduction as actual mortality experience moves closer and closer toward true underlying mortality rates.

In contrast, investment performance is a *nondiversifiable* risk for insurers. If a broad stock or bond market decline would otherwise cause variable annuity benefits to fall below the floor level but for the guarantee, then the insurer issuing the annuity is subject to a large quantity of additional claims simultaneously. Because the investment risks are not independent but rather highly correlated, pooling ever more annuitants will not reduce risk. To the contrary, if an annuity writer issues more such IVA contracts, its exposure to investment market risk stacks up.

Because an annuity writer offering such benefits effectively transforms itself to some degree from an insurance company (which assumes diversifiable risks) to a derivatives issuer (which assumes nondiversifiable risks), investors must analyze the offering and assess the financial strength of the issuer. Although prudent insurers will partially hedge risks of this nature in the derivatives markets, they are exposed to greater risk concentration and earnings volatility than they would be if such features were absent.

Assessing Value

Immediate variable annuities offer the following benefits:

- ❑ Lifetime income, with genuine transfer of longevity risk and freedom from anxiety about outliving assets
- ❑ Potential inflation hedge, with the opportunity for increasing income that keeps pace with or outpaces inflation

FIGURE **19.11** *Payout Floor Guarantees, Liquidity, Income Stabilization, and Underwriting*

Payout floor guarantees. These guarantees stipulate that no future immediate variable annuity benefit will be less than a certain percentage, say, 80 percent, of the initial benefit, regardless of investment subaccount performance—even in doomsday scenarios. Variations on the floor definition exist.

Liquidity. Contract owner access to ad hoc lump-sum withdrawals beyond periodic income benefits historically has been impermissible so as to keep annuitants who find themselves in ill health from withdrawing excess funds from the pool, leaving it inadequate to provide benefits to the longest-surviving members. This solvency practice safeguards the financial security system from "mortality anti-selection." Purchasers are made aware that the instrument is illiquid and that they should maintain separate, liquid funds to meet large expenses.

Some newer product designs permit a degree of liquidity in early years. Clearly, this comes with a cost, as life-contingent annuities are a long series of endowments where part of the premium is invested for a specific number of years and months and effectively shared among survivors at the point the annuity benefit for that period is due. To the extent liquidity infringes on this process, annuity benefits are reduced.

Income stabilization. Annuity benefits are payable monthly more often than any other frequency. Annuity benefit levels traditionally adjust each month in relation to subaccount performance. To assist with family budgeting and to avoid "mailbox shock," some immediate variable annuities offer benefits that are paid monthly but whose benefit level adjusts only semiannually or annually.

Underwriting. Individuals voluntarily purchasing life-contingent immediate annuities usually consider themselves in average to above-average health, resulting in individual annuitant mortality superior to (lower than) general population mortality. Although a host of factors affects annuitant mortality rates—smoking status, alcohol consumption, wealth, education, geographic location, and hobbies such as private piloting—age and gender tend to be the sole underwriting factors today in translating a premium into an annuity benefit level for a given annuity option.

Health underwriting could be performed to offer higher annuity benefits for the same premium to those with impaired health relative to those in excellent health, although data to appropriately rate medical impairments for annuitant populations are scant relative to data for life-insured populations. Medically underwritten annuities are termed *substandard annuities* or *impaired life annuities*. These are found today primarily in the structured settlement market.

❑ Asset diversification, professional money management, and freedom from serving as one's own chief investment officer at a time in life when one may not desire to perform or may be incapable of performing that function

❑ Ability to customize an investment mix that determines income level and to reallocate the investment mix periodically—on a tax-free basis

❑ Ability to customize longevity-risk protection via a multiplicity of annuity options that can cover one or more lives

❑ Tax deferral, with dividends, interest, and realized and unrealized appreciation taxed not as they occur but only when benefit payments are received

❑ Non-tax-qualified immediate annuities enjoy immediate-annuity income tax treatment, with part of each benefit being a tax-free return of principal—in contrast to alternative investment vehicles such as deferred annuities where taxable gains come out first

❑ Freedom from serving as one's own pension administrator at a time in life when one may not desire to perform or may be incapable of performing that function, because a properly established IVA meets tax-qualified minimum-distribution requirements

❑ Achievement of dual objectives of maximizing income and minimizing probability of outliving income

Immediate fixed annuities—with level or guaranteed increasing income—enjoy certain of the above benefits.

To illustrate the supremacy of immediate annuities in maximizing retirement income while minimizing the probability of outliving income, **FIGURE 19.12** compares IVA income to systematic withdrawals from an alternative investment vehicle (for example, a mutual fund, deferred annuity, or self-directed IRA).

Note how the annuity may provide a series of benefits that increase with advancing age, with no possibility of termination due to exhaustion of an individual's personal account. In contrast, note how alternative investment liquidation vehicles may provide a decreasing series of benefits at advanced ages under certain IRS required-minimum-distribution rules—even though investment performance is identical to that of the annuity.

The systematic withdrawal program provides a residual account balance to the beneficiary at the death of the owner, whereas the IVA does not.

Source: Jeffrey K. Dellinger, *The Handbook of Variable Income Annuities* (John Wiley & Sons, 2006)

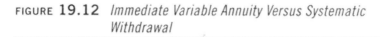

FIGURE **19.12** *Immediate Variable Annuity Versus Systematic Withdrawal*

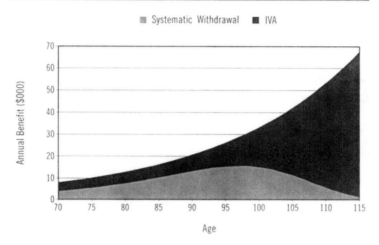

Assumptions:

- Same fund used for both cases, 8% assumed return each year
- IVA based on $100,000 premium, life annuity, male age 70, using Annuity 2000 Basic Mortality Table, 3% AIR
- Systematic withdrawals based on $100,000 starting value, withdrawals determined for tax-qualified plan participant, age 70, using IRS minimum-distribution requirements effective as of 2004
- Annual payments made at beginning of year

AN IMMEDIATE VARIABLE annuity is the optimal instrument for maximizing retirement income while minimizing—to zero—the probability of outliving that income. An IVA is superior to self-management, which fails to provide the mortality credits available through pooling and can result in an individual outliving his income. An IVA is superior to immediate fixed annuities—even geometrically increasing fixed annuities—because fixed annuities fail to invest to any degree in the asset class most likely to best inflation during a multidecade retirement horizon.

To the extent an investor's objective is to have the maximal inexhaustible lifetime income, that objective is optimally achieved on an expected-value basis by an immediate variable annuity. An investor should allocate a portion of his retirement assets commensurate with his desire to achieve this objective. Immediate annuities are inappropriate, however, for use in achieving the objectives of liquidity and bequeathing assets to heirs. An investor should allocate a portion of his retirement assets to nonannuity instruments commensurate with his desire to achieve those objectives.

Because investments inside an immediate annuity generate income superior to identical investments outside an immediate annuity, immediate annuities are particularly important for "stretching" inadequate retirement savings. Immediate annuities help individuals achieve greater retirement security than they can achieve on their own. Sales presentation tools unequivocally show the superiority of immediate annuities over alternative financial instruments for satisfying specific objectives.

CHAPTER 20

The Search for Software

JOEL P. BRUCKENSTEIN

Throughout the relatively short history of the financial-planning profession, the question clients most often ask their advisers undoubtedly has been "How much do I need to save for retirement?" That's about to change, if it hasn't already. It's a sure bet that the most common question clients ask financial planners is soon to be: "Which will expire first? Me or my portfolio?"

Advisers who can help clients successfully implement a distribution program during the golden years will be in great demand; those who can't will probably be looking for a new career. I believe it's fair to say that solving the retirement-distribution puzzle is the single greatest challenge facing our industry today, and the sheer complexity of the problem puts technology in a central role in arriving at the answers.

When Harold Evensky and Deena Katz invited me to write a chapter about the technology of retirement-distribution planning, I was both encouraged and perplexed. I welcomed the inclusion because technology is often underrepresented in industry literature and at conferences, but I was stumped because right now I cannot discuss a single excellent retirement-distribution software package; I've yet to see one.

Over the years, the profession and the software vendors who serve it have developed some reasonably good tools that can help address the retirement savings question; unfortunately, few if any software programs adequately addresses retirement distribution. This really should not surprise anyone. Aside from there being much greater need and demand for distribution tools today than there was in the past, it remains easier to solve the savings problem than the distribution problem. What's more, many would argue that it's easier to make adjustments to the savings plan over the course of the accumulation period than it is to change a distribution plan once it begins.

Thankfully, it appears that we are entering a new era of financial-planning software development, one in which considerable time and energy is devoted to helping clients enjoy a more financially sound retirement. A number of software developers are working on distribution-planning software, either as an addition to traditional comprehensive financial-planning packages or as a stand-alone application. Although it's too early to gauge how successful this first generation of distribution-planning tools will be, they are certainly a welcome step in the right direction. My guess is that none of the new programs under development will yield totally satisfactory results, but some early feedback I've received indicates that a number of these products are on the right track. They should be the beginning of a progression toward better tools for advisers and better advice for clients.

This chapter examines some of the factors that should be incorporated into any future distribution-planning software package and highlights both the challenges and opportunities developing such software presents. I hope it will spark further debate and accelerate development.

The Tech-Averse Adviser

Before we get into the nuts and bolts of retirement-distribution software, we'll need to address some broader issues regarding advisers and technology. The first has to do with applied technology—that is, a planner's use of technology to facilitate the work done for clients. In this regard, technology is seen as a tool, or a means to an end. Many advisers are either afraid of new technologies, confused by them, or just not interested in them. As a result, they tend to ignore such innovations until they become mainstream or until competitive forces force them to come up to speed. Such delays are a big mistake. I suspect that if advisers viewed these advances in terms of applied technology—that is, a means of improving their services to clients—they would make better decisions.

You don't need to understand the inner workings of a computer's central processing unit to benefit from a computer any more than you need to understand the workings of an internal combustion engine to drive an automobile, but for some reason many advisers are more cautious about technology than they are about driving. A rational examination of fatality statistics would suggest that advisers have more to fear from their automobiles than their computers.

The second issue has to do with *behavioral technology*. Behavioral technology is the practice-management art (and science) of creating an "innovation-friendly" environment—that is, one that welcomes new procedures and new software and hardware. I coined this phrase a while back to draw attention to how sorely lacking the profession and financial advisers are in this area.

Because advisers are a conservative bunch and tend to be cautious in their approach to new technologies, the profession bears an extraordinary opportunity cost, which is often ignored. This opportunity cost manifests itself in a number of ways. The following are just a few examples.

❑ A new firm builds a better portfolio-management program—one that compares favorably with today's market-leading program—and offers it at a lower price. Classic economic theory would suggest that this new company will enjoy immediate success, and that would be the case in many industries, but not necessarily in the financial-advisory business. Advisers will fret that the company is new and unproven. They will worry about its staying power. In the end, inertia on the part of potential customers may doom this promising new firm to oblivion, in spite of its superior product. And it doesn't end there. The next time an entrepreneur thinks about developing a new product for the industry, he may perform a little market research and come across the story of this predecessor firm. The history of that firm's failure may persuade the entrepreneur to take his money and skills elsewhere. So one opportunity cost we bear as a result of not supporting innovators is the likelihood of being doomed to less innovation in the future than would otherwise be the case.

❑ Firms that do not foster a technology-friendly workplace through investment, training, and incentives bear a much more direct opportunity cost. Imagine two financial-planning firms, firm A and firm B. Both opened up shop in 1995 with almost identical staffs, equipment, and client bases. Firm A invested very little in technology and training. As it grew, it added more staff, more space, and more paper files. The odds are that even if it hired quality staff and they all worked hard, the firm's margins shrank during the last 10 years. Firm B, on the other hand, grew by educating its staff and leveraging technology. As a result, it was able to grow its business by adding far fewer staff, far less space, and little additional paper. The firm's processes allow it to service a far larger client base at a lower cost. The owners of firm A may mistakenly think that they have saved money by minimizing the firm's technology outlays, but in fact they have incurred a huge opportunity cost.

The industry is approaching a major inflection point with regard to technology for advisers. In the past, we probably have not received the best software as fast as we could have, and this is largely due to our own choices. Planners should keep that thought in mind when making future purchasing decisions.

The Retirement-Distribution Challenge

Here is the problem in a nutshell: the baby boomers are about to retire, but retirement for boomers will not necessarily resemble that of their parents. Twenty or 30 years ago, the "mass affluent"—who now make up 25 percent of the U.S. population, earn a median income of $121,000 per year, and have investable assets of up to $1 million—were much more likely to be counting on a defined-benefit plan for most of their cash flow in retirement. In other words, the previous generation didn't have to worry about converting a pool of assets into an income stream; they were already assured of an income stream. They just had to make sure they didn't outspend it. What's more, some expenses, like medical costs, that might otherwise have upset their budgets were either partially or totally covered by their employers and/or the government.

Today, the picture is much different. During the past 20 years, much of the responsibility for generating retirement income has shifted to the individual. Defined-contribution plans have become commonplace, while as a percentage of the working population, the number of employees covered by defined-benefit plans has steadily decreased. Even those clients who are entitled to a pension, employer-subsidized medical benefits during retirement, and Social Security question the certainty of those benefits continuing throughout their retirement. In short, the number of boomers entering retirement who will be responsible in whole or in part for making their own retirement-distribution decisions is about to explode.

According to Purna Pareek, chief executive officer at AdviceAmerica, "77 million baby boomers will retire over the next two decades. It is estimated that retirees will control a significant asset base—in the neighborhood of $20 trillion." And in the more immediate future? "In 2006, $10.9 trillion in retirement assets will be held by 60+-year-olds," says David McClellan, vice president of adviser business development at Morningstar. That adds up to a lot of potential clients in need of retirement-distribution-planning help. Financial advisers must prepare themselves to deal with this deluge of advice seekers.

Advising Clients

Suppose a client nearing retirement comes to you with a portfolio of, say, $1.5 million and asks for your help in devising a withdrawal strategy. How would you respond? Not all that many years ago, financial advisers made some simple assumptions about rates of return, inflation rates, and income needs, and then projected them out for a period of time. For example, at "CFP school," they taught us to assume a constant level of income (adjusted for inflation), a constant rate of return, and a constant inflation rate.

The beauty of this model was that it allowed for simple calculations. You didn't even need a computer; a pocket calculator would do the trick, although a spreadsheet did speed up the process. The problem with this solution, we all recognize now, is that it has little if any basis in reality. The solution may be technically correct, but the scenario is artificial. It assumes that income need, inflation, and returns will remain constant throughout retirement. It also assumes that we know what inflation and rates of return will be throughout the period in question. Finally, it assumes that we know when the client will retire and when the client will die.

Clearly, none of these assumptions is realistic. Clients' income needs can vary during retirement; rates of return are not constant; and fluctuations in returns and the order in which those fluctuations occur make a critical difference to a client's retirement savings. And by the way, most people don't conveniently die when your projections say they will. Only about 4 percent of 65-year-old males die within a time period that coincides with their "average life expectancy." That means that if you rely on averages, you will be wrong 96 percent of the time. Imagine trying to justify those numbers to your clients, not to mention the regulators.

Perhaps the greatest fault with the earlier methodology was that it solved for a single "right" solution, implying a level of certainty that clearly did not exist. During the past five to 10 years, we've improved substantially on the earlier models. Most decent software today can account for uneven cash flows. We can use Monte Carlo simulations to illustrate for clients the impact of varying patterns of returns. We can even deal with issues that earlier models ignored, such as the variable impact of federal and state income taxes and the effect of required minimum distributions on the plan. But even with all of the improvements that have been made, most knowledgeable observers are convinced that the tools we currently use to advise clients about withdrawal rates are woefully inadequate.

So how should we go about helping the client solve the problem of planning income for retirement? For starters, I'm not sure that a single "right" solution exists. When we consider how we've "solved" the problem in the past, we see that there are only a limited number of variables, but some of those variables can have a huge impact on the plan. To do a better job, we must introduce additional variables. Doing so complicates the issue and introduces additional uncertainties. To provide meaningful advice to the client, part of the solution must include a method of framing the problem and the solution in a way that emphasizes factors we can't define as much as those we can. We must help clients embrace uncertainty and plan for it to the extent that they can.

Right now, there is no methodology for modeling the analysis—at least none that's accepted industrywide. So I'll offer some suggestions about how the modeling might be done and some factors that should be included in the analysis. These suggestions are by no means a comprehensive list but rather a starting point for further discussion.

The Risks of Retirement

Broadly speaking, there are five major areas of risk faced by retirees that any software solution must address:
- ❑ Funding risk
- ❑ Investment risk
- ❑ Longevity risk
- ❑ Catastrophic risk
- ❑ Lifestyle risk, or the risk of not spending enough

Funding risk. Funding risk is the risk of not having sufficient funds to retire. Clearly, this risk is better dealt with earlier than later, but even as clients approach retirement age, they can make some decisions to adjust for funding risk such as changing the investment mix and choosing to postpone retirement. In terms of software design, a program must be able to illustrate this potential problem to a client, as well as illustrate the impact of any suggested adjustments. Most good retirement-planning programs can already perform these tasks.

Investment risk. Investment risk, in this context, refers to the impact that negative investment returns or a disadvantageous series of returns can have on a plan. Today's tools, including Monte Carlo simulations, do a decent job of isolating and illustrating the risks of these factors, but they don't do a good job of illustrating alternatives, and they don't take a holistic approach to the entire distribution-planning problem.

Longevity risk. Longevity risk is simply the risk of outliving your retirement savings. I'm increasingly convinced that just arbitrarily setting a retirement period of, say, 30 years for the assets to last is insufficient. Assumptions about longevity, including the timing of deaths and the order of death, can affect the overall plan. We need to do a better job of illustrating these assumptions and incorporating them into the overall plan. Some software programs that are now available are capable of illustrating longevity risk, but they don't do it particularly well. Either the methodology is unclear or, more commonly, the output to the client (text, charts, or graphs) do not deliver the message in a way that makes the issues understandable to the typical client.

Catastrophic risk. Catastrophic risk can take a number of forms, but for retired folks, the most common catastrophes are health related. A serious physical condition not covered by health insurance, or a condition that requires long-term care (LTC), can easily destroy what are otherwise sound plans. Some financial-planning software programs—and some advisers—incorporate LTC decisions into their plans, but there is considerable room for technological improvement. For example, if some clients are not ideal candidates for LTC insurance, either because they have too few assets or too many, that should clearly be spelled out to them. For the folks in the middle—the ideal candidates for LTC—better tools to illustrate the risk/reward trade-off may be appropriate. In addition, there may be more than one method of acquiring the insurance (personal versus corporate purchase; annual payments versus single or 10 payments). The software should be able to clearly illustrate the pros and cons of the various approaches. Much of the current software cannot do this.

Lifestyle risk. A number of advisers and their clients are worried about lifestyle risk, or the risk of underspending and thus denying oneself the lifestyle one can afford. Risks are not always symmetrical. For example, behavioral finance teaches us that most clients aren't *risk* averse; they're *loss* averse. The typical client requires a $2 gain to balance out a $1 loss. The same can be said of distribution risk—that is, lifestyle risk as it applies to retirement-distribution planning.

In planning for retirement-income distribution, some practitioners try to solve for the highest sustainable withdrawal rate. They fear that if they fly too far under the radar, the client may experience a suboptimal lifestyle throughout retirement. Now, don't get me wrong: this is a real risk and something that certainly needs to be discussed with the client. Still, I suspect that in most cases clients would not assign the same weighting to the risk of underspending that they would to overspending. If they underspend, they may miss out on a few lobster dinners or a few trips they really wanted to take; if they overspend, they could find themselves destitute. To my mind, at least, that is not a symmetrical risk. The issue has relevance to software design: any comprehensive distribution model must weigh the various risk factors appropriately; a choice appropriate for one client may not be suitable for another. Advisers may also want to weigh the consequences—in terms of practice management and liability—of a client underspending versus a client overspending.

Methodology

The ideal software package, if it existed, would allow advisers to enter all relevant data, weigh it properly, and solve for the ultimate optimized solution. But as we illustrated earlier in the example of the client nearing retirement with a portfolio of $1.5 million, even small changes to the variables can cause large changes to the results, so a comprehensive software solution that incorporates all of the necessary variables and computes an optimal solution is beyond our current capabilities. Any dreams of optimization in the short term are just that—dreams.

The best we can do at the moment is to lay out a basic framework for clients and take them through a number of scenarios that illustrate the trade-offs inherent in their distribution decisions. We can start by dividing their needs or expenses into two baskets: essential (or nondiscretionary) and discretionary. The first responsibility of the planner is to make sure that the essential minimal threshold of spending is met. This can be done in one of two ways. Some have suggested gathering all of the assets and income streams together and, from that pool, allocating enough resources to make sure that the nondiscretionary needs will always be met.

Others have suggested that assets and cash flows, like expenses, should be divided into two groups: guaranteed income streams and other income sources. The first group would include things like Social Security income, pension income, annuity payments, and any other stable sources of income that the client will receive during retirement. The other group would include taxable investment accounts, individual retirement accounts, defined-contribution plans, any anticipated employment income during retirement, and other variable sources of income. Under this approach, one would first try to "match maturities." Essential needs, which may be subject to inflation, would be matched first against guaranteed income sources that are adjusted for inflation, like Social Security payments. Assuming that guaranteed income sources meet or exceed nondiscretionary expenses, the adviser will at least have carved out a minimally acceptable baseline for the client, and the discussion could then turn to how to best deploy the other income sources to generate a reasonable amount of discretionary income. If the essential income needs cannot be met through existing guaranteed income streams, then perhaps the discussion could turn to creating such a stream from a portion of the other income sources. One method of doing so would be to convert part of the investment portfolio into a stream of annuity payments.

Annuities. If the client is at least willing to consider annuitizing a portion of the investment portfolio, another series of decisions must be made. "Making Retirement Income Last a Lifetime," an excellent paper by Ameriks, Veres, and Warshawsky,[1] suggests that adding annuities to the portfolio mix can in many cases improve portfolio longevity.

Many questions remain, however, with regard to the deployment of annuities in the distribution-planning process. Is there an ideal time to annuitize? Should the annuitization take place at once or over a period of time? Is an immediate fixed annuity the only solution, or should a combination of fixed and variable immediate annuities be used? Of course, if you annuitize using only a fixed product, the payments will not adjust for inflation. How should advisers best adjust for this? I'm not smart enough to tell you how the model should be constructed, but I do know that the need for tools in this area is bound to grow significantly in the future. And it's worth mentioning—though beyond the scope of this chapter—that there is also a need for new financial products that can better meet the needs of clients. For example, might there not be a demand for an immediate fixed annuity with true inflation protection?

Social Security. A related issue, which is all too often overlooked in the financial planning process, is the decision about when to begin taking Social Security benefits. William Reichenstein, who holds the Pat and Thomas R. Powers Chair in Investment Management at Baylor University, has done some excellent work in this area, and some advisers model various scenarios for their clients, but generally speaking, in the world of financial-planning software, little if any attempt is made to help the adviser guide clients in this decision. Clearly, the tax situation plays a role in the decision, as does the couple's earnings history, their ages, and their health. In some instances, it's advantageous for one partner to begin taking benefits under one method, and then switch to a different method at a later date. Wouldn't it be great if our financial planning software at least alerted us to these opportunities?

Asset allocation. Once the discussion regarding nondiscretionary expenses is concluded, the conversation can turn to the trade-offs inherent in taking more investment risk to fund more lavish discretionary spending patterns. From a strictly empirical point of view, there wouldn't appear to be any advantage in dividing the income sources into two groups; in fact, one might argue that there are some disadvantages, since the division may result in some inefficiencies. From a behavioral-finance perspective, however, there could be some benefits in dividing the income sources. Numerous studies have shown that clients do actually practice this form of mental accounting, and anything that helps them frame the problem and arrive at appropriate choices should not be overlooked.

People suggest to me that advisers do not take a broad-enough view of asset allocation and that they make faulty decisions as a result. The argument goes that we should be including defined-benefit plans and Social Security in the asset allocation mix. Proponents of this methodology argue that failure to do so causes advisers to underweight equities in the portfolio. If a client has a 20-year life expectancy, we should view the Social Security payments as a 20-year government bond (using an appropriate discount rate) and value the pension as a 20-year corporate bond. The point of this exercise is not to come up with an exact bond-equivalent calculation for the payments but rather to illustrate the impact of this adjustment on the overall asset allocation. For clients who will receive a substantial portion of their retirement income from Social Security and/or defined-benefit plans, the impact on the overall allocation weightings will be substantial. Quite frankly, I'm not convinced that this methodology makes sense; however, if there are enough advisers out there who want it, software companies should probably include this sort of modeling capability as an option.

As for the actual design of the program, I'd suggest making the buckets of expenses and assets the central focus. Once those are laid out, a planner could employ drill-down menus or wizards to explore some of the individual options (to annuitize or not, how much to annuitize and when) and layer these strategies onto the basic model. There might also be drill downs, or wizards, to work through decisions on such things as choosing a pension lump sum versus an annuity, unlocking home equity through a sale or reverse mortgage, and making tax-optimizing withdrawals.

Where to Go From Here

By its very nature, distribution planning must be comprehensive. You cannot manage a portion of a client's distribution strategy the way you can a portion of one's portfolio. And such management has technological implications. If an adviser takes on the task of helping a client with distribution planning, the adviser will need to have a complete picture of the client's finances now and in the future, because the plan must be monitored on an ongoing basis. This indicates to me that, at the very least, software integration must improve, and it may be that additional tools, such as data-aggregation services, will be necessary to compile, manage, and update the data regularly.

It's an exciting time to be a financial planner, and it's an exciting time to be developing distribution-planning software. Distribution planning entails dealing with many variables and much uncertainty, but the industry must rise to the challenges. Failure to develop better tools is not an option; the current state of the art will not get the job done.

We need to develop software that's intuitive and scalable, yet sophisticated enough to incorporate all of the variables we've discussed here. By experimenting with various methodologies, we can all participate in the developmental process. And when a firm offers a new, promising product, we'd best jump at the chance to purchase it sooner rather than later. If we follow our usual pattern, and wait until a product is well established before making our purchase, both we and our clients will have missed the boat.

Chapter Notes

1. John Ameriks, Robert Veres, and Mark J. Warshawsky, "Making Retirement Income Last a Lifetime," *Journal of Financial Planning* (December 2001): 60–76.

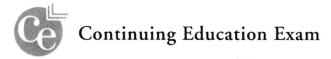

Continuing Education Exam

EARN 20 HOURS of continuing-education credit by passing the following exam on our website, http://www.bloomberg.com/ce, and entering code RIR897. The material covered has been previewed by the CFP Board of Standards.

ASSESSING THE RISKS

FIVE: Psychological Impediments to Retirement-Income Planning

1. Which of the following is not one of the misperceptions that contribute to poor retirement planning?
a. People tend to overestimate their life expectancy.
b. People expect their investment returns to average the same percentage each year.
c. People assume they can maintain their lifestyles by spending roughly the same amount of money each year.
d. People believe the need for money declines with age.

SIX: Lifelong Retirement Income: How to Quantify and Eliminate Luck

2. Stocks provide an adequate inflation hedge both for long-term accumulation portfolios and for distribution portfolios.
a. True
b. False

3. If a retiree is lucky, the start of his retirement will coincide with the start of a secular bull market.
a. True
b. False

4. Which of the following was not among the patterns observed in studying the success of a distribution portfolio for different withdrawal rates during a 25-year time horizon?
a. The contribution of luck is lowest near the sustainable withdrawal rate.
b. Once past the 6 percent withdrawal rate, the higher the withdrawal rate, the less significant the asset-selection factor is.
c. The longer the portfolio survives, the smaller the cumulative management costs over the life of the portfolio will be.
d. The contribution of asset allocation to the success of a portfolio peaks near the sustainable withdrawal rate. After that, the difference it makes declines sharply.

SEVEN: Balancing Mortality and Modeling Risk

5. Which of the following are ways to incorporate mortality probabilities into the distribution analysis?
a. Generate a random sequence of real returns and weight the withdrawal in each year by the probability that a person alive today will still be alive in the year the withdrawal is expected to take place.
b. Set up a distribution system whereby the withdrawal amount each year is a percentage of the nest egg balance. Mortality probabilities can be incorporated into the analysis by establishing a benchmark distribution amount, say $5,000, and calculating the probability that the actual distribution will be higher or lower.
c. Both of the above.

6. Life expectancies are rising for men and women who reach age 65 in 2005, although for men, these increases do not appear to have accelerated from previous rates.
a. True
b. False

7. HRS studies show that retired individuals are fairly accurate in predicting their life expectancies.
a. True
b. False

EIGHT: Monte Carlo Mania

8. Which of the following statements is true of Monte Carlo simulations?
a. Generally, reported results indicate that for nest eggs dominated by stocks, withdrawal rates of approximately 4.5 percent are sustainable for up to 30 years of retirement at least 90 percent of the time.
b. It tests enough of the possible sequences to generate a statistically meaningful result.
c. In the Monte Carlo calculations, both the sequence of returns and the average return of each iteration vary widely.
d. All of the above.

NINE: Understanding Required Minimum Distributions

9. Which of the following statements is false?
a. Although tax-sheltered annuities generally operate in the same manner as qualified plans, they are not subject to the "5 percent owner rule."

b. Although Roth IRAs are also subject to lifetime minimum-distribution requirements, the owner's required beginning is calculated differently.
c. For a qualified plan participant who does not own 5 percent or more of the company that is sponsoring the plan, the required beginning date is April 1 of the year after the individual retires if that year is later than the year he or she turns 70½.

10. Which of the following statements is false?

a. Although the regulations define "spouse" as an individual who is treated as such under applicable state law, for federal tax law purposes, only a member of the opposite sex may be considered a spouse.
b. The identity of the beneficiary has no effect on the amount or term of a lifetime RMD payout from an individual account.

11. Which of the following statements about annuity distributions is true?

a. The requirements for minimum distributions are no different when payouts are made from an annuity rather than from an individual account.
b. A distribution of the annuity contract will itself satisfy the minimum-distribution requirement.
c. Most of the rules that apply to annuities apply whether the annuity distributions are provided under a qualified plan, an individual retirement annuity, or a Section 403(b) tax-sheltered annuity.
d. The general rule for annuity payments is that distributions must be made as periodic payments, at least every six months.

SHAPING THE SOLUTIONS
TEN: Risk Management During Retirement

12. Recent actuarial studies indicate that the probability is that at least one member of a married couple (today each age 65 years old) will survive to

a. age 90
b. age 82
c. age 97
d. age 78

13. For most reasonable spending patterns, an aggressive asset allocation will only decrease the risk of running out of money too soon.

a. True
b. False

ELEVEN: Withdrawal Strategies: A Cash Flow Solution

14. According to Evensky and Katz, the paycheck syndrome has to do with clients' resistance to spending money from their nest egg.
a. True
b. False

15. Which of the following is not essential to an effective cash flow strategy?
a. Cash flow needs to remain consistent.
b. Market volatility must be tolerated.
c. The source of cash flow must be visible and reliable.
d. The strategy must accommodate the client's tendency to assign money to separate pockets.

16. Which of the following is not one of Evensky's concerns about the use of Monte Carlo simulations in projecting retirement income?
a. Most Monte Carlo simulations may assume that all ranges are normally distributed; in many cases, there is little justification for this assumption.
b. The introduction of probability via Monte Carlo analysis has resulted in unrealistic targets for a "comfort level" of success.
c. Monte Carlo simulations increase the accuracy of retirement projections.
d. Advising clients to radically reduce their standard of living in order to protect against the unlikely probability of three standard-deviation events is inappropriate.

TWELVE: Asset Allocation: The Long View

17. Which statement about the impact on investment returns of compounding over time is true?
a. After one year, the distribution is approximately normal, or bell shaped.
b. After 20 years, the distribution is decidedly nonnormal; it is most obviously not symmetric.
c. The distribution becomes more skewed as the underlying annual rates of return become more volatile, so that a 100 percent equity portfolio, for example, generates more skewed terminal wealth than does a balanced portfolio of equities and bonds.
d. All of the above.

18. The distinction between the median and the mean is merely a statistical one; it has no implications for money invested over long periods of time or the likelihood of achieving a retirement target.
a. True
b. False

THIRTEEN: Sustainable Withdrawals

19. The recurrence of major bear stock markets explains the failure of the "average rate of return" method of calculation. Such declines are powerful enough to overwhelm a portfolio already stressed by withdrawals.
a. True
b. False

20. Which of the following observations about asset allocation and its effect on the safe withdrawal rate is false?
a. An individual with 40 percent large-cap stocks in her portfolio cannot expect to safely withdraw more than an individual with 70 percent large-cap stocks in his portfolio.
b. Low returns from bonds seriously reduce the safe withdrawal rate for bond allocations greater than about 60 percent.
c. The higher returns of large-cap stocks are offset by their higher volatility when they're given allocations greater than about 70 percent.
d. None of the above.

FOURTEEN: Tools and Pools: Strategies for Increasing Retirement Cash Flow

21. Although investment returns and longevity are unknowns, living expenses, when planned carefully, are a predictable factor in planning withdrawal rates.
a. True
b. False

22. In planning retirement-income distributions, the principal drawback of taking a fixed amount and adjusting withdrawals for inflation is that
a. retirees will take out less than the portfolio can sustain
b. these distributions usually are not equal to the retiree's needs
c. the method requires the retiree to be willing and able to cut back in bad years
d. the approach is rigid and inflexible

SIXTEEN: Reverse Mortgages in Distribution Planning

23. Which of the following statements about reverse mortgages is false?

a. The borrower must completely own the home or be able to use the initial proceeds of the reverse mortgage to pay off any small existing debt on the property.

b. The borrower may not sell his home without written approval of the mortgagor.

c. The Federal Housing Administration sets a borrowing limit of approximately $312,000, which may be received as a lump sum, monthly payments, or a line of credit.

d. Borrowers may obtain larger sums from private lenders, depending on the value of the home.

24. Which of the following descriptions of the differences between reverse home equity conversion mortgages (HECMs) and reverse mortgages obtained through private lenders is inaccurate?

a. The HECM is the only one that's government insured.

b. The major differences lie in the interest rates charged.

c. The maximum benefit a borrower can receive from a private issuer is capped at 150 percent of the government benefit.

EIGHTEEN: Longevity Risk Insurance

25. The probability that an individual retiring at age 65 will reach age 80 is greater than 70 percent for females and greater than 62 percent for males.

a. True

b. False

26. Which of the following statements is false?

a. Current retirees receive about 60 percent of their retirement income from Social Security and traditional company pension plans, whereas today's workers can expect to have only 45 to 50 percent of their retirement income funded by these sources.

b. Guaranteed minimum income benefits are typically offered as an optional feature or rider to a variable annuity contract for a nominal additional charge, generally less than 20 basis points.

c. A client's desire to make significant bequests strongly suggests a significant allocation to immediate annuities.

d. None of the above.

NINETEEN: Immediate Annuities: Structure, Mechanics, and Value

27. Which of the following statements about immediate variable annuities is incorrect?

a. A low assumed investment rate (AIR) increases the probability of a gradually increasing payout.

b. Although the income streams will vary depending on the selected AIR, all annuity options share the same present value of benefits, with no annuity option more valuable than any other for a given amount of premium.

c. The annuity owner receives investment rewards via changes in retirement-income benefits, which fluctuate with investment performance. If actual performance for the period is less than the benchmark return, however, the insurer bears the loss rather than the annuitant.

d. None of the above.

28. Which of the following statements about immediate variable annuity payments is incorrect?

a. The progression of immediate variable annuity benefits is determined using annuity units. The same number of annuity units is paid on each benefit payment date.

b. The annuity unit value changes on key evaluation dates, in line with subaccount performance.

c. The dollar amount of annuity benefit payable equals the number of annuity units multiplied by the annuity unit value on the valuation date used to determine that payment.

d. None of the above.

INDEX

AARP (American Association of
Retired Persons), 9, 50
AARP, 6, 7
Abaimova, Anna, xi, 157–158,
163–183
Accredited Investors, 56
AdviceAmerica, 346
advisers
redefining retirement, need for,
55–57
working with boomers and
knowledge needed by, 13–16
*Against the Gods: The Remarkable
Story of Risk* (Bernstein), 65,
73
age-based asset allocation, 88–89
*Age Power: How the 21st Century
Will Be Ruled by the New Old*
(Dychtwald), 9
AIDS victims, insurance problems
for, 306–307
Alexander, Roxanne, xi, 160,
281–303
Alpha Group, 159
alternative minimum tax (AMT),
205
Ameriks, John, 320, 350
Anderson, Michael J., xi–xii, 160,

281–303
annuities
See also required minimum
distributions (RMDs)
life, 94–95
payments, 144–146
payout, 314–320
software tools, 350–351
substandard/impaired, 339
tax-sheltered, 142, 150–151
variable, 146
annuities, immediate
advantages of, 334–336, 338,
340–342
benefit equation, 330
choices for clients, 337–338
clients for, 332–333
defined, 324, 336
financial adviser, role of,
333–334
fixed, 246–249, 325, 326–327
income, 13
life, 100–101
liquidity, 339
payout options, 325–326, 339
systematic withdrawal versus,
340–341
taxes, 336–337

ABOUT BLOOMBERG

Bloomberg L.P., founded in 1981, is a global information services, news, and media company. Headquartered in New York, the company has sales and news operations worldwide.

Serving customers on six continents, Bloomberg, through its wholly-owned subsidiary Bloomberg Finance L.P., holds a unique position within the financial services industry by providing an unparalleled range of features in a single package known as the Bloomberg Professional® service. By addressing the demand for investment performance and efficiency through an exceptional combination of information, analytic, electronic trading, and straight-through-processing tools, Bloomberg has built a worldwide customer base of corporations, issuers, financial intermediaries, and institutional investors.

Bloomberg News®, founded in 1990, provides stories and columns on business, general news, politics, and sports to leading newspapers and magazines throughout the world. Bloomberg Television®, a 24-hour business and financial news network, is produced and distributed globally in seven languages. Bloomberg Radio℠ is an international radio network anchored by flagship station Bloomberg® 1130 (WBBR-AM) in New York.

In addition to the Bloomberg Press® line of books, Bloomberg publishes *Bloomberg Markets®* magazine. To learn more about Bloomberg, call a sales representative at:

London:	+44-20-7330-7500
New York:	+1-212-318-2000
Tokyo:	+81-3-3201-8900

CPSIA information can be obtained at www.ICGtesting.com
Printed in the USA
BVOW020028040112

279734BV00004B/10/P